«   «   WITH WOODEN SWORD   »   »

« « « « « « « « « «

WITH WOODEN SWORD

A Portrait of
Francis Sheehy-Skeffington,
Militant Pacifist

LEAH LEVENSON

Northeastern University Press   Boston
Gill and Macmillan   Dublin

1 9 8 3

» » » » » » » » » »

Editors, Robilee Smith and Penelope Rohrbach Stratton
Designer, Richard C. Bartlett

Copyright © 1983 Leah Levenson

First published in North America by Northeastern University Press, 1983

First published in Ireland in 1983 by Gill and Macmillan Ltd., Goldenbridge, Dublin 8, with associated companies in Auckland, Dallas, Delhi, Hong Kong, Johannesburg, Lagos, London, Manzini, Melbourne, Nairobi, New York, Singapore, Tokyo, and Washington

The photographs on the jacket, the frontispiece, and pages 6 and 30 are the property of Andrée Sheehy-Skeffington and are printed with her permission. The photographs on pages 136 and 141 are from the Sheehy-Skeffington Papers and printed with the permission of Andrée Sheehy-Skeffington. The photographs on pages 8 and 10 are by W. G. Colman, The Studio, Bailieborough, and were obtained through the cooperation of Tom Barron, Belmont, Bailieborough, County Cavan. The photographs on pages 16 and 17 are printed with the permission of the National Museum of Ireland. The photographs on pages 145 and 152 are printed with the cooperation of the Irish Transport and General Workers' Union, Dublin.

«   «   «   «   «   «   «   «   «

Library of Congress Cataloging in Publication Data
Levenson, Leah.
  With wooden sword
Includes bibliographical references and index.
1. Sheehy-Skeffington, Francis, 1878–1916.
2. Ireland—Politics and government—1901–1910.
3. Ireland—Politics and government—1910–1921.
4. Pacifists—Ireland—Biography.   5. Intellectuals
—Ireland—Biography.   I. Title
DA965.S53L48   1983   941.508'092'4   [B]   82-22560
ISBN 0-930350-42-1

»   »   »   »   »   »   »   »   »

Northeastern University Press ISBN 0-930350-42-1
Gill and Macmillan ISBN 0-7171-1325-6

Printed in the United States of America
88 87 86 85 84 83   5 4 3 2 1

For Sam
and
with gratitude to Andrée Sheehy-Skeffington

Contents

List of Illustrations

Of all people in modern Irish history, Francis Sheehy-Skeffington is the one closest to my heart. He was a rare bird — a journalist by profession but his real vocation was agitating on behalf of free thought, pacifism, feminism, socialism, and even vegetarianism. To many of his contemporaries he was an eccentric, a crank, a Dublin character. To me, he seems one of the few enlightened individuals Ireland ever produced who remained in Ireland — unlike Shaw, James Joyce, and O'Casey.

I think it is important for young Irish intellectuals to know that there was once an Irish writer — liberal, pacifist, socialist, pro-trade unions, anti-militarist — who never left home. They may discover from the story of his life that there is indeed a long-range answer to Ireland's problems: formation of a new I.R.A. — an Irish Rationalist Army.

— Samuel Levenson

Preface

My husband's desire to write a biography of Francis Sheehy-Skeffington arose while he was working on his *James Connolly* and *Maud Gonne*. Upon completion of the latter book, he began to collect material with that end in mind. This he did for several years and, during that time, both in the United States and in Ireland, we worked together. My respect and affection for Skeffington grew steadily: not only for him, but also for Hanna, his wife, and Owen, his son. Hanna was always by her husband's side, agitating for votes for women and for a free Ireland; Owen, an activist like his parents, became a senator in the Republic of Ireland.

In mid-1977, soon after our return from four months of research in Dublin, my husband died. He had collected what he considered to be as much material as he needed for a life of Skeffington and, as he wrote to a friend, was "looking forward with delight to the next two years of productive activity" (Samuel Levenson to Max Gartenberg, 30 March 1977). Upon my husband's death, I accepted the challenge of writing his book. I accept also full responsibility for this manuscript, based on his thorough research.

I am greatly indebted to Ken Hannigan of the Public Records Office, Dublin, whose University College, Dublin, undergraduate thesis on Francis Sheehy-Skeffington was used extensively in the preparation of this manuscript and who spent many hours sharing his considerable knowledge of the subject with us.

My appreciation goes also to the helpful staff of the National Library of Ireland, with special thanks to Fergus Gillespie of the Division of Manuscripts and Donal O'Luanaigh, Keeper. After my husband's death, much additional material was released to the National Library by Andrée Sheehy-Skeffington. Both she and the library staff were most cooperative in making this material available to me and in facilitating its use.

So many people have been of assistance that I cannot hope to thank them all properly. In Ireland, Andrée Sheehy-Skeffington, Father F. X. Martin, Roger McHugh, Monk Gibbon, Maurice Wilkins, Tom Barron (formerly principal of Bailieborough Model School, Bailieborough, County Cavan), Commander P. D. O'Donnell (Cathal Brugha — formerly Portobello — Barracks), Ulick O'Connor, Desmond Greaves, Edward Mac-Lysaght, Margaret Vanek, Basil Clancy, Charles McCarthy, Imogen Stuart, Liam O'Leary, Sheila O'Donoghue, Brian Bonner, Rosemary ffolliott, and John Jordan. In the United States, Helen Landreth (Boston College Library), Jacqueline Van Voris, Francesca Gobbi Stone, Morton Lebow, Jim Thomas, and Kenneth Higgins Porter.

Above all, I am grateful to Jerry Natterstad, the biographer of Francis Stuart, for reading and rereading this manuscript, for his superb literary criticism, for his encouragement, and for his friendship.

Leah Levenson
Worcester, Massachusetts
December 1982

« « WITH WOODEN SWORD » »

*Unwept, except by a few, unhonoured and unsung — for no
National Society or Club has gratefully deigned to be called
by his name — yet the ideals of Sheehy-Skeffington, like the
tiny mustard seed to-day, will possibly grow into a tree that
will afford shade and rest to many souls overheated with the
stress and toil of barren politics. He was the living antithesis of
the Easter Insurrection: a spirit of peace enveloped in the
flame and rage and hatred of the contending elements, absolutely free from all its terrifying madness; and yet he was the
purified soul of revolt against not only one nation's injustice
to another, but he was also the soul of revolt against man's
inhumanity to man.*

— Sean O'Casey (Feathers from the Green Crow)

1

Life's Patterns Formed

In the village of Bailieborough, County Cavan, stands a two-story
building, typical of those seen on the "High" streets of the little towns
throughout Ireland. Here, on 23 December 1878, Francis Sheehy-
Skeffington was born to Rose and Joseph Bartholomew ("J. B.") Skeffington
and christened Francis Joseph Christopher. During his lifetime, he was
destined to advance ideas for which Ireland — and, indeed, the rest of the
world — was not ready. But without compromise and without loss of faith in
his ideals, Francis Skeffington cheerfully endured ridicule, financial hardship, and frustration. The standard he set for those who followed him was a
high one, his life a brief one, his cruel death in 1916 a senseless one.

J. B., Francis Skeffington's father, was a teacher and scholar. At the
Royal University of Ireland, he won "Highest Place for Ireland in Experi-
mental Physics, and in English Language and Literature," earned the B.A.
"with First Class Honours and First Class Exhibition, value Forty Guineas,"
and received the LL.D. J.B.'s honors did not rest gracefully on his shoulders:
he was opinionated and he had complete confidence in his own judgment.

During his first teaching assignment, in the County Down village of
Ballykinlar, J. B. met and married Rose Magorian, the daughter of a local
farmer. Their marriage was solemnized in the Roman Catholic chapel in
Ballykinlar on 30 September 1869. Their marriage lines list J. B. as "22,
Bachelor," and Rose Magorian as "40, Spinster."[1] It is difficult to determine
what attracted J. B. to a woman eighteen years his senior but, given his tem-

perament, it is not surprising that he let nothing and no one stand in the way of his unconventional marriage. Parental objection on both sides must have been strong, for no member of either family acted as witness to the ceremony.

Little is known about Rose or, for that matter, about the Magorians. Judging by correspondence she carefully preserved, Rose was a member of a large, warm, and very religious Catholic family. Because of their extreme poverty, some of the family emigrated to the United States. Rose, too, spent many years in the States in an attempt to earn enough money, it is said, to save the family farm.[2] Presumably she did not return to Ireland until she had accomplished that goal.

Rose's siblings were semiliterate and always quite poor. She was the one who, through her marriage, attained a measure of financial security and higher social standing. This improvement in her status, however, did not cause a family rift; in fact, Rose wrote regularly to her relatives in the States until her death. Her son knew them only from that correspondence. At the time of his mother's death, he wrote his uncle in St. Louis: "It is a sad occasion which now makes it necessary for me to write. My poor mother is dead. . . . I hope you will write to me from time to time as you used to do to my poor mother; as, although I have never seen any of you, I should like to keep up communications with my American relatives.[3]

Little more is known about Rose's background or her ideas. Roger McHugh states in *The Shaping of Modern Ireland* that she had strong feminist leanings, and that she impressed them on her son.[4] If this is true, her ideas were undoubtedly formed while she was in the States — for it was there, in 1848, that the first organized freedom-for-women movement was founded. No concrete evidence proves Roger McHugh's point, however. Skeffington's sympathy for the women's movement more likely grew out of his awareness that his mother, who was undoubtedly intelligent, was forced into the background and never given a chance to develop her abilities.

A much clearer picture can be drawn of J. B. He was strong-minded, stubborn, and individualistic. He was also an excellent and dedicated teacher. In the nine years of his marriage preceding Francis's birth, he advanced steadily in his career. From his teaching position in Ballykinlar, he went on to become an inspector of primary education in Bailieborough. In the Civil Service Competitive Examination necessary for the position, J. B. won highest honors in every category and was the only candidate to pass in every subject. These facts he never hesitated to communicate to his son.

Francis Skeffington would have no recollection of his birthplace. Just a few years after he was born, J. B. was promoted again and the little family moved to Downpatrick, the scene of Francis's earliest memories. J. B. was now District Inspector (the only superior grade was that of Head Inspector) for the Downpatrick School District, County Down. He had come full circle, for his roots were in this part of Ireland.

The name Skeffington is derived from the village of Skeffington in

Leicestershire, England. Bearers of the name appear first in fourteenth-century records; by the middle of the seventeenth century dozens of Skeffing-tons, Skiffingtons, Skifentons, and Skivingtons had made their way to Ireland, where they pursued various humble occupations. Most of them settled in the province of Ulster on land which had been confiscated by the English and from which the natives had been forcibly evicted. Some of these immigrants were soldiers who settled on the soil to become farmers, garrison the area against the local clan leaders, and hold the territory for English nobles, in fealty to the English Crown. Some came to improve their economic conditions, some to escape religious persecution (these were dis-senters or secret Catholics in an England that enforced Anglicanism), some to avoid the wrath of creditors or the mothers of their illegitimate children.

By 1797 Francis Skeffington's direct forebears had become respectable small landowners and tradesmen, living in and around Dungannon, in County Tyrone, a relatively industrialized city where coal was mined and linen and pottery works flourished. Their freebooting days were long past, and they had all become, or remained, observing Catholics. During that period, some of the family left County Tyrone and settled in County Down — mainly in Downpatrick. It was an area where Francis Skeffing-ton's love for the mountains and for walking in the country developed; it was a love that never diminished. Located thirty-five miles south of Belfast, with a population in those days of approximately three thousand (presently some-what less), Downpatrick, then as now, offered limited attractions. What attraction it did offer was mainly historical — a cathedral restored to half the size of the original abbey, and the reputed burial places of Saints Patrick, Columba, and Brigid.[5]

One of those who left County Tyrone and settled in Downpatrick was George Lindsay Skeffington. There he and his wife, Mary Murphy, raised eight children. Those who visit the Downpatrick Cathedral will see a memo-rial tombstone, in a stone-and-rail enclosure, listing the date of his death as 24 May 1869, at the age of 75. Also listed on the tombstone are the death dates of his wife and of various children. J. B. Skeffington's death in Belfast, 19 August 1919, is also listed there — which implies that J. B. was George Lindsay Skeffington's son. J. B.'s marriage license, however, lists his father as Joseph Skeffington, dealer. [Records for the period are scarce and some-times faulty; consequently positive identification is impossible.] A genealog-ical opinion is that George Lindsay Skeffington seems to have been the right age to have been a brother of the elder Joseph Skeffington and thus J. B.'s uncle, but no further mention of the elder Joseph was found.[6]

This, then, was J. B.'s background. In his early thirties, a handsome, bearded man, he was back in Downpatrick with his wife, Rose, and his son, Francis, carrying out the onerous duties of District Supervisor with the devo-tion to education and the punctiliousness that would be reflected in the life of his son. He supervised the instruction given to ten thousand residents of an

Francis Sheehy-Skeffington's father, J. B. Skeffington. The exact date of the photo is not known, but, judging by the black armband and his approximate age, it may have been shortly after his wife's death in 1909.

area that included Downpatrick and fifteen other towns and villages. Most of the schools were small and located in outlying areas, so that J. B. traveled a great deal.

Even though J. B. was a high official in the National Education System, he insisted on keeping his son Francis's education in his own hands. In view of that fact, the system should be examined briefly. It had been developed early in the nineteenth century to ensure one standard of education for all pupils, free of sectarian bias. For the first time, Protestant and Catholic children would be educated together. With money provided by Parliament, the National Board built new schools and improved old ones; published textbooks; furnished paper, slates, and school supplies generally; and paid teachers' salaries.[7] The ideal of combined secular and separate religious instruction for all provoked violent reaction in many quarters. The Anglican opposition to the National Education System was great — a primary objection was that the government refused to allow Bible teaching except from a book of agreed-upon extracts. And, since the Anglicans opposed the system, the Catholic clergy was encouraged to view the whole concept with favor.

The plan to combine secular and religious instruction was commendable; unavoidably, however, it met with many difficulties in its implementation, a major one being the lack of trained teachers.[8] To cope with this problem, twelve "Model" National Schools were set up in 1846 to train teachers. Three such schools came under J. B.'s supervision. The precision with which he performed his duties is clear from his reports to the National Education Office in Dublin. One such report, submitted in February 1892, is typical. In nine and one-half pages, J. B. spelled out in minute detail his suggestions for improving instruction in reading, writing, arithmetic, spelling, grammar, geography, agriculture, science, needlework, and extras (under extras he listed "vocal music and drawing" as well as geometry, algebra, French, and Latin).

Not content with specifics, J. B. also advanced his ideas on the general picture of education. There were many reasons, he argued, why the national system should be improved as much as possible. It had now almost a monopoly on education in the country; education was usually an emigrant's only asset; and the knowledge students acquired was likely to become more valuable as electricity and chemistry became increasingly important as sources of power, light, and heat in an industrializing world. J. B. seemed to have a Victorian faith in the ability of natural science and the accumulation of facts to solve all of man's problems.

Health was always a major concern to J. B. — in fact, letters he wrote to Francis over the years often read like medical bulletins. Thus it is not surprising that his report urged that students march from class to class and sing while they marched. The marching, he pointed out, would be good exercise, and the singing would "cheer their spirits and rouse their energies."

High Street, Bailieborough, County Cavan. Over the chemist shop, in 1878, Francis Skeffington was born.

He concluded: "Since much of the habits and morals of children are formed or modified by their school life, how careful should teachers be to culti-vate . . . habits of order, virtue, morality, the feelings of kindliness for others, respect for authority, &c." The goal of the teacher, he wrote, should be to influence the children directly by precept and example; to affect and mold the children through their surroundings during their most impression-able years.[9] These, then, were the ideas to which Francis was subjected during his youth — for until he reached college age, his father was his only teacher.

   Not very much is known about Francis Skeffington's youth, but his childhood must have been a lonely one. Although he might not have learned as much academically in school as at home, at least he would have had an opportunity to make friends. He did receive a great deal of attention and affection from two Skeffington maiden aunts in Downpatrick, and he spent a great amount of time with Magorian cousins in the country. With them he went walking, cycling, and exploring in the Mourne mountains. Always very fond of his relatives, he did not lose touch with them over the years. (Many of them thought of him as "Joe," which must have pleased

J. B., whose full name was Joseph. From college days on, however, he was generally called "Frank," "Skeff," or "Skeffy.")

Following the guidelines that he set down for teachers serving under him, J. B. attempted to instill in Francis habits of "order, virtue, morality, and feelings of kindliness for others." In the opinion of St. John Ervine, Belfast-born dramatist and novelist, he succeeded. Many years later Ervine wrote to Francis's son: "Your father was a man of transparent honesty and uprightness. I do not believe he ever did a mean act in his life or that he was capable of thinking of one." [10]

J. B. also fostered in Francis a love of and respect for ideas. Thanks to his teachings, Francis believed that science, education, logic, discipline, scholarly effort, and independence of thought would inevitably bring order out of chaos, civilization out of barbarism, and reason out of emotion. He must have believed, also, that education was too important to be entrusted to professional educators. When Francis entered his own son in nursery school, he informed a startled headmistress that the boy was there simply to meet other children — and that if he ever found out that she was attempting to teach the child anything, he would remove him promptly. [11] Francis's feeling that his son needed to meet other children is surely a measure of his own boyhood loneliness.

Confident to the point of arrogance, J. B. was deeply in earnest about his beliefs. He never missed an occasion to express his opinions — called for or not — yet those opinions were intellectually honest. Accordingly, he always urged Francis to avoid writing a dishonest line.

Beyond question, J. B. was tyrannical. Department of Education records contain a report dated 1880 concerning a complaint launched by a teacher named Lynch from Kilmainham Wood School, County Meath, that District Inspector Skeffington had used his influence as a school inspector to compel Lynch to attend Roman Catholic services after school hours. By his own admission, J. B., a devout Catholic, considered his request right and proper. [12] It seems inevitable that Francis Skeffington should have turned to his mother for warmth, companionship, and affection. J. B. felt the lack of closeness keenly. After Rose's death, he wrote his son: "You were never able to appreciate my nature, and were unsympathetic. . . . I had no sympathy, while she had *you*." [13] Nor, all things considered, is it surprising that, as an adult, Francis placed a high premium on individual liberty. His father has been described as "a widely-read man of great intellectual curiosity, a hot temper, rigid principles, and a kind heart." [14] To this description should be added self-centered and egotistical. The belief that no one could educate his son as well as he could was perfectly in character.

His father's influence, although quite powerful, was only one of the many forces that shaped Francis's personality; the social composition of County Down also played an important role. Francis Skeffington was indeed fortunate to have been reared in County Down, if one believes — as some

In this building, J. B. Skeffington had his office. On the right can be seen a section of the model school that came under J. B.'s supervision.

do — that sociological alienation has its advantages. The dominant culture there, during his youth, was Protestant, pro-British, and anti-Catholic. The cleavage between the Catholic and non-Catholic communities was sharp, and Francis learned early about injustice and persecution. Catholics lived in all-Catholic ghettos of Downpatrick, working, marketing, and socializing only with other Catholics. The first time Rose Skeffington went marketing in Dublin, she asked to be told which were the "Catholic shops." [15]

There is much evidence to prove the thesis that being a member of a minority group, even an oppressed one, has its positive side. An outstanding case is that of Michael Davitt, known as the father of the Land League, whose ideas, ideals, and career were to influence Francis Skeffington greatly. Born in the Irish village of Straide in 1846, his family left Ireland in the early 1850s to settle in Lancashire. This was at the time of the "Great Clearances," shortly after the potato famine, when families were being turned out so that avaricious landlords could convert the rich land into huge grazing ranches. Davitt spent his youth in England — a member of a poverty-stricken minority — but in his home he learned love of Ireland and, all around him, he saw that the English worker was also oppressed. He came to hate the powers that held both the English worker and the Irish in subjugation. He always maintained that associating with children of different religious beliefs (the school he attended was Wesleyan) merely strengthened his own Catholic faith while teaching him tolerance and respect for the beliefs of others.[16]

James Connolly, whose life also would intertwine with Francis Skeffington's, is another example. He was born and reared as a Catholic in Presbyterian Scotland, but from the literary and radical element of Edinburgh he drew the intellectual weapons with which to combat the society that kept him and his fellows in dire poverty. He emerged an Irish patriot, feminist, labor leader, Marxist, and atheist. During the same era George Bernard Shaw, a Protestant, was being brought up in Catholic Dublin. Hesketh Pearson, in *G.B.S.: A Full-Length Portrait*, writes: "Both in church and at Sunday School he was taught to believe that God was a Protestant and a gentleman and that all Roman Catholics went to hell when they died, neither of which beliefs placed the Almighty in a very favourable light." This view was balanced by Shaw's religious instruction at home, which was in the hands of his Catholic nurse.[17] No doubt he would have become a socialist and reformer had he been raised in Protestant London — but being a member of a minority group must have facilitated the development of his critical range of observation.

In County Down, then, Francis Skeffington learned at first hand that Truth is not absolute and that people can live in a diversity of cultures. He was able to retain his own basic beliefs while absorbing, as his father had, those elements of another culture that were useful — a respect for hard work and for scientific thought, and even a certain sympathy for movements designed to better social conditions, which were a part, though not a major one, of Victorian civilization. He learned to reject the bigotry of the Protestant majority while viewing with some clarity and skepticism the errors of his own group.

J. B.'s influence and geography aside, events that occurred and the political climate that prevailed during Skeffington's youth inevitably played a major role in his development. The population of Ireland in 1841, preceding the Great Famine, was more than 8 million. Within ten years it had dropped to 6. 5 million as a result of death, emigration, and a sharp decline in the birth rate. Prior to 1845, early marriages were the rule, but after the famine marriage patterns changed radically and late marriages became the custom. This was partly because celibacy was an effective form of birth control and partly because of the mental and emotional strain that resulted from the calamity. With the declining birth rate and the continued emigration, by 1911 the population of all Ireland was less than 4. 5 million.[18] Reflecting his great love for Ireland, Francis Skeffington would wage a constant fight to upgrade living conditions there in an attempt to reverse this trend.

One of the effects of the Great Famine on Catholics who survived it and continued to live in Ireland was a religious revival. Prior to the famine, figures show that only 40 percent of the Catholic population attended Mass.

Over the years that followed, this figure increased to around 90 percent. Convinced that the horrors of the famine were the result of their sins, Catholics turned more strongly to the church than ever before; the Skeffingtons were no exception. Among their cherished possessions was a communion certificate headed "A Precious Remembrance to a Faithful Soul," portraying the wafer and the wine and showing that on 9 June 1887 Francis Skeffington had received the first Holy Communion and was confirmed 16 June 1889 — at age eleven. His strongly religious upbringing and its restrictions may have contributed toward his eventual decision to break with Catholicism — difficult though it was.

Another result of Ireland's tragedy was the launching of a secret Brotherhood in 1858 by James Stephens, a survivor of the Young Ireland Rebellion of 1848. Its aim was to fashion Ireland into a democratic republic — as such, it was the beginning of a movement that was to become known as Fenianism. The exceptionally talented men who were part of this new movement produced political writings that would have an influence far beyond the years of their lives. Although Francis Skeffington became disillusioned with the type of leaders who came to represent the Fenian movement — with what he considered their impracticality and their inordinate stressing of the revival of Gaelic — there can be no doubt of the influence on him of the thinking of those early Fenian leaders.

The man whom Francis Skeffington considered "the greatest Irishman of the nineteenth century" [19] was Michael Davitt, and Davitt's influence on him was immeasurable. In 1879, one year after Francis was born, Davitt founded the Irish National Land League, which brought together every shade of nationalist into one huge agrarian movement. Skeffington's earliest memories were of his father entertaining him with stories of the exciting days of Land League agitation and the government's response to the movement, which was both predictable and repressive — the Protection of Persons and Property Bill, known as the Coercion Bill of 1881, which gave the chief secretary special powers to deal with agrarian violences: powers that he did not hesitate to use. Whether J. B. also pointed out that at the same time a politically expedient Land Act — the Land Act of 1881, which gave the farmer a certain amount of protection in the form of rent control and tenure — was passed is a moot point.

Within a year of the introduction of these new repressive measures, approximately ten thousand Irish families were evicted from their farms and two thousand agrarian outrages, as they were called, took place. That same year the Invincibles, a group of Fenian extremists, murdered the new Chief Secretary of Ireland, Lord Frederick Cavendish, and his undersecretary, T. H. Burke, in Phoenix Park, Dublin. These were the surface manifestations of a subterranean movement toward a separate nation divested of English influence, toward an Ireland that was Irish, proud of its ancient culture and ancestral tongue. This movement began to affect the general public in 1884, when a prosperous civil servant, Michael Cusack, founded the Gaelic Athletic Association, designed to spark the revival of games such as Gaelic football and hurling. Because of the type of young athlete the association attracted, there was an almost immediate surge of the desired nationalistic pride. It is not without significance that of the seven founders of the Gaelic Athletic Association, four were Fenians. From its inception, it had more than its share of political activists. Francis was fifteen when Douglas Hyde and Eoin MacNeill founded the Gaelic League, whose aims were to preserve Irish as the national language and extend its spoken use. They also hoped to further the study and publication of existing Gaelic literature, and the cultivation of a modern Irish language literature.

J. B. saw the revival of Gaelic as a revival of national honor and self-respect. He was so moved by its desirability and importance that he wrote letters to a newspaper expressing his approval, with documentation. Each letter brought a vigorous, cogent response to his arguments by someone who signed himself "Shamrock." Young Francis, sitting quietly reading, listened with interest and enjoyment as J. B. and his friends discussed the replies, speculated about the identity of the writer, and denounced him for his cowardice in remaining anonymous. There is no indication that J. B. ever did learn that the view beautifully expressed, that Gaelic was irretrievably dead and that "the study of Esperanto would be more useful to the youth of Ireland" than instruction in the books of O'Growney[20] was that of his son, "Shamrock."[21]

NOTES TO CHAPTER 1

1. Catholic parish registers for Tyrella and Ballykinlar, obtained by Rosemary ffolliott, genealogist.

2. Owen Sheehy-Skeffington, "Francis Sheehy-Skeffington," in *1916: The Easter Rising*, ed. O. Dudley Edwards and Fergus Pyle (London: MacGibbon and Kee, 1968), p. 136n.

3. F. Sheehy-Skeffington to Patrick Magorian, 25 April 1909. Sheehy-Skeffington Papers, National Library of Ireland, Dublin. Correspondence was taken from family papers released to the National Library of Ireland by Andrée Sheehy-Skeffington and consulted by special permission before being catalogued. For this reason, catalogue reference numbers are not given. This applies throughout the manuscript. Unless noted otherwise, all letters cited in notes are from the Sheehy-Skeffington Papers.

4. Roger McHugh, "Thomas Kettle and Francis Sheehy-Skeffington," in *The Shaping of Modern Ireland*, ed. Conor Cruise O'Brien (London: Routledge & Kegan Paul, 1960), p. 126.

5. Although Saint Patrick, the great patron saint of Ireland, is only presumed to have been interred there, pilgrims have flocked to Downpatrick for centuries.

In fact, so much erosion was caused by the removal of holy soil as mementos that a huge slab of unhewn granite was brought down from Francis Sheehy-Skeffington's beloved Mourne mountains and placed over the grave.

6. Survey made for Samuel Levenson by Rosemary ffolliott, genealogist, Dublin.

7. Eustas O'Heideain, O.P., *National School Inspection in Ireland: The Beginnings* (Dublin: Scepter Books, 1967), *passim*.

8. Thomas Barron, Bailieborough, County Cavan, Ireland, unpublished paper. Mr. Barron was formerly principal of Bailieborough Model School. He tells us that in 1843 one of J. B. Skeffington's predecessors as inspector of the school system, John Fisher Murray, wrote: "The ignorance of the teachers generally speaking, is another barrier to improvement. To an arrogance and selfconceitedness peculiarly their own, many of the country schoolmasters and mistresses unite an ignorance of everything except reading and writing, with an occasional smattering of mathematics. I found few who knew anything of English Grammar, fewer still who were acquainted with Geography."

9. J. B. Skeffington, *Report to National Education Office* (Dublin, February 1892).

10. St. John Ervine to Owen Sheehy-Skeffington, 18 November 1955. Ervine wrote that he had talked with Francis Sheehy-Skeffington only an hour before his execution. Ervine was in the British army during World War I and must have been stationed at Portobello Barracks during the Rising. He states that Francis told him he was opposed to the Rising and added his own opinion that the Rising was "a damned silly and ignominious performance, and the wretched state of the backstreet republic it produced is positive proof of the fact."

11. O. Sheehy-Skeffington, "Francis Sheehy-Skeffington," p. 136n.

12. *Department of Education Records* (Dublin: Public Records Office), Ed 9 File No. 1002, 1880.

13. J. B. Skeffington to F. Sheehy-Skeffington, 16 October 1911.

14. O. Sheehy-Skeffington, "Francis Sheehy-Skeffington," p. 135.

15. Ibid., p. 136.

16. Francis Sheehy-Skeffington, *Michael Davitt* (London: MacGibbon and Kee, 1967), pp. 17–19.

17. Hesketh Pearson, *G.B.S.: A Full-Length Portrait* (New York: Harper & Brothers, 1950), pp. 9–10.

18. George Dangerfield, *The Damnable Question* (Boston: Little, Brown, 1976), pp. 11–12.

19. F. Sheehy-Skeffington, *Michael Davitt*, p. 215.

20. Father Eugene O'Growney was a professor of Irish at Maynooth and the author of a much-used textbook for the study of Irish.

21. Eugene Sheehy, *May It Please the Court* (Dublin: C. J. Fallon Limited, 1951), pp. 33–34.

2

Independence

In the summer of 1896, at seventeen, Francis Skeffington entered University College, Dublin, with strong opinions already formed and strength of character enough to resist the efforts of others to supplement them, to supplant them, or to change them. His ideas gained attention quickly; his appearance even more quickly. Short — not much over five feet five — deceptively frail-looking, and with a soft, fair, badly trimmed beard, he always dressed in a rough gray tweed suit with knickerbockers, long stockings, boots at least one size too large for his feet, and, as time went on, a large button in his lapel proclaiming "Votes for Women." Because of his solitary childhood and the need to be self-sufficient, Francis brought with him to college an imperviousness to public opinion — an indifference to the impression he might be making on others. Some maintained that he dressed as he did to call attention to himself. A letter from the Dean of Studies at the university, Father Joseph Darlington, written many years later, gives Skeffington's own view:

«   «   «   «   «   «   «   «   «

The Secretary of the Royal University wrote to me as a friend of Mr. Skeffington's to say that he had some lucrative work to assign and he would like to offer it to Mr. Skeffington if Mr. Skeffington would consent to wear a black Coat, during the few hours he would appear in public; he added that as *I knew* Mr. Skeffington so well would I sound him on the point. On doing so Mr. Skeffington replied: that the principles he saw to be the true ones he must be true to & any material advantages which conflicted must be sacrificed: one principle was against Convention in Dress: he had decided to be always free in that matter and though the money would have been a help just then he refused the work.[1]

»   »   »   »   »   »   »   »   »

It was during this period that Skeffington developed a lasting love for Dublin. When, in 1915, he was offered employment in the United States, he said, "I'd rather be in jail in Dublin than free in New York."[2] Walks in the city were visually exciting and the surrounding countryside was beautiful

Gardens to the rear of University College, Dublin, as they were when Francis Skeffington was a student there.

for cycling as well as for walking — Francis took full advantage of both. At the college he was busy and stimulated. University College, when he entered, had an enrollment of not much more than a hundred. Housed only half a mile from Trinity College, members of the University College's community were conscious of being overshadowed by Trinity and its distinguished faculty. Trinity's famed classics professor, J. F. Mahaffy, is reputed to have said that it was a mistake to establish a separate university "for the aborigines of this island — for the corner-boys who spit into the Liffey," and to have used James Joyce as a "living argument" for his contention.[3] For Skeffington, however, the caliber of some of his fellow students amply made up for the instructors' shortcomings.

Founded as Catholic University in 1854 by Cardinal John Henry Newman, the school's goal was to become the Catholic equivalent of Trinity. For the first twenty-five years, however, with neither private endowment nor government support, it barely survived. Help came for the virtually defunct university in 1879 in the form of the rather inadequate Universities Bill. The government, albeit willing to provide for higher education in Ireland, was at the same time eager to ensure that education be as secular as possible. Trinity College was too small and too Protestant to serve the many Catholic students. Consequently, the bill provided for support of University College —

The National Library of Ireland. The entrance is to the left of the main gate, where horse-drawn carriages are standing. To the left rear of the figure at the gate can be seen the steps upon which young Francis Skeffington spent many hours arguing with James Joyce and others.

the new name — but as a part of the Royal University, not as an autonomous unit. Royal University, with constituent colleges in Cork, Galway, and Belfast, had only examining and degree-granting powers — and examinations were given only in secular subjects. In 1883, thirteen years before Skeffington enrolled in University College, the Jesuits took over the institution. Father William Delany, one of Ireland's most effective educators, became president of the university. Despite pressure from many Catholic groups to increase the amount of religious instruction offered, Father Delany held fast and made no changes. His contention was that seeing part of the faculty in surplices was enough of a shove in the ecclesiastical direction.[4]

Class attendance was not compulsory and books were scarce, so the students depended on the nearby National Library of Ireland. Skeffington found the second-hand bookshops and the book-barrows invaluable as well. He would spend hours browsing in Webb's, Neale's, Massey's, and Clohessy's, all of them well stocked. He tried never to miss the monthly book sales at Bennett's, the auctioneer on Ormond Quay, and he made the profitable discovery that the overflow from Bennett's appeared on the book carts in Aston's Row.

Skeffington interspersed his work in the National Library Reading Room with periods of heated discussion on the library steps. Always a central

figure in these gatherings, he was never reluctant to air his views on literature, politics, and life in general. They were not conventional views by any
means. Skeffington was an ardent feminist and an equally ardent pacifist. All
political and economic reforms, he believed, could be effected without the
shedding of one drop of blood. In addition, he was a vegetarian and an anti-
vivisectionist. He neither drank nor smoked and denounced these habits in
others vociferously. (A member of the family says: "The only dissipations I
ever heard Frank guilty of were chess and argument."[5] A university contemporary, C. P. Curran, thought the controversies Skeffington stirred up
"lacked a sense of proportion and were, as often as not, trivial." He felt, too,
that "for all their modernity" Skeffington's ideas were "stereotyped."[6]

As Curran saw Skeffington, his behavior "seemed to be regulated in
accordance with long-settled opinions privately arrived at." Although
Curran admired Skeffington's persistence in following his health principles — forgoing tobacco, liquor, and meat — he found his friend's habit of
eating in the local vegetarian restaurant appalling. "These were days when in
London the Eustace Miles restaurants mixed moral principles with dietetic
statistics on their depressing menu cards and the same atmosphere pervaded
the old Vegetarian restaurant in College Street," he writes. He marveled also
at Skeffington's energy, his rapid movements, his seeming never to do
anything purposelessly. The only time Curran observed him sitting still was
over a chess board, where he "could play blindfold two or three simultaneous
games; any time I happened to be one of his adversaries he invariably won."[7]

Skeffington was reading for his degree in the modern language course,
and this puzzled Curran — political economy or history would have been
his guess. He saw Skeffington as a pragmatist who, though he professed a
love for the theater and attended all opening nights, really had little use for
anything but the social content of literature and no enthusiasm whatsoever
for poetry. Curran had in his library Skeffington's copy of George Meredith's
Diana of the Crossways, which he may have borrowed and neglected to
return. He writes that Skeffington "followed every word of it with his pencil,
underscoring each line with impulsive assiduity and with an overflow into
the margins of admiring or exclamatory markings."[8] Those markings, to
Curran, indicated that Skeffington admired Meredith less for his wit than for
his social criticism and his attitude toward women. Possibly a young,
idealistic Skeffington could have used both as a measuring rod for art. But a
letter from him to a cousin presents a somewhat different picture. Sending
her a birthday present of books, as he always did, he listed them: "Jane Eyre;
Wilkie Collins' Woman in White; Pride and Prejudice — the author, Jane
Austen, is a particular favorite of mine, so I am curious to know how it will
please you."[9]

Curran felt also that Skeffington was "as deaf to music as he was blind to
the visual arts." To prove his point, he tells a story, apocryphal in tone, that
Skeffington was seen in the Louvre, not looking at the pictures but "quick-

stepping" the galleries to see if Baedeker's guidebook was correct in stating that it would take two hours just to walk through the galleries.[10] Curran's estimate of Skeffington does have its measure of validity, for his pleasures did tend to be organized and purposeful. In August 1899, for example, he took a cycling trip through northern France into Germany. From Metz he wrote his mother: "I am now within the bounds of the German Empire, having passed through some of the famous scenes of the war of 1870. . . . I have now definitely planned the rest of my journey, and I shall return home at the end of next week, reaching Dublin (for breakfast) on the morning of Saturday, the 26th. I hope you will find it convenient to be there then."[11]

How did Skeffington, with his broad range of interests, view his classmates? He must have considered them shortsighted victims of the ivory-tower syndrome, for it seemed to him that throughout the country discontent was fomenting a genuine revolution. This period in Ireland's history is brilliantly described by F. S. L. Lyons in *Ireland Since the Famine*. When Charles Stewart Parnell, Ireland's uncrowned king, died in 1891 at the age of forty-five, his Irish Parliamentary Party was left weak and ineffective. Lyons states that, although the years immediately following found the party and Parnell's followers disastrously split, the electors disillusioned, and constitutional nationalists possibly permanently injured, the young people's interest in politics did not diminish — in fact, it increased. In their opinion, the parliamentary movement had come to grief because of excessive reliance on the English; now the time had come to rely on themselves. This meant, at the very least, a return to the concept of Ireland as an independent nation and to the ideals of the brilliant Protestant Wolfe Tone, whose attempt to urge the Irish to follow the principles of the French Revolution had aborted. It meant as well the expansion of the Irish language revival. Small groups began to form clubs and societies dedicated to finding ways and means of creating a sense of Irish nationality. The influence of these societies, which were based mainly in the big cities, belied their small size. The excitement attending the centenary of the Tone-led Rebellion of 1798 can explain some of their popularity. As Lyons observes, "Every kind of nationalist paid homage to the United Irishmen including, no doubt, many who would have recoiled in horror from any enactment of Tone's insurrection."[12] The outbreak of the Boer War also strengthened these societies, for the nationalists were united in their condemnation of the war. Skeffington, unlike most of his fellow students, was well aware that he, in conjunction with some of the best minds of the time, was part of a cultural and political renaissance. He was part of a small group, to be sure, but it was a highly articulate one.

Early in his first year at University College, Skeffington began to devote a great deal of time to reviving the defunct Literary and Historical Society, commonly referred to as the L. & H. He became its first auditor and its most energetic recruiter. With what today would be considered a fine public relations sense, he would intercept new students who happened to be passing by the society's meeting room, call them by name, mention an honor or two they might have won in their Senior Grade examinations, and follow this gambit up by pointing out that it was their plain duty to join the society. C. P. Curran recalls that he was one of those intercepted — and that he joined immediately. Writing of the society, he comments: "In that far from stagnant tank Frank Skeffington was the cat-fish. Already the restless propagandist that he ever was, at no later date in his career did he show any trait of character, or express any opinion, or act from any point of view, which he had not made us all familiar with as students." [13]

During his tenure as auditor of the Literary and Historical Society, Skeffington spoke at almost every meeting and was awarded the silver medal for oratory. When his term ended in 1898, he continued to be an active member of the society and contributed a paper embodying his feminist views, "The Progress of Women." He was succeeded as auditor by Thomas M. Kettle, who was to become a close and lifelong friend. Tom's father, Andrew Kettle, had served as one of the first secretaries of the Land League of Ireland, and had even suffered imprisonment for his Land League activities. He had also been a secretary of the Tenants Defence Association. A highly successful Leinster farmer whose family, of ancient Norse stock, had settled in Ireland long before the Normans, he was one of Parnell's most enthusiastic supporters. He had passed that enthusiasm on to his gifted son. Young Kettle was educated at a Christian Brothers' school where, unlike the National schools, stress was placed on Irish history and Irish music and poetry. He also attended the fashionable Clongowes Wood College, where his academic record was superb.

Tall, handsome, black-haired, and clean-shaven, with brooding eyes and a large, rather soft, genial mouth, Kettle was always well dressed. It is reported that he once asked a tailor to make him "a new suit that would not look new and that, when old, would not look, old." He had what Roger McHugh refers to as a Dublin manner — witty, ironic, casual, and sympathetic — as contrasted with what might be called Skeffington's Ulster earnestness, his brisk handshake, his complete concentration on a point made humorously or casually.

There is no indication whatsoever that Skeffington ever envied Kettle — he was always much too secure within himself — but certainly Kettle was more popular with his peers. The average student could easily identify with him. He played cricket and football, and entered cycling competitions. These same students respected and admired Skeffington — but they did not identify with him. Although he too was interested in physical fitness, he believed it could be achieved by walking and abstaining from tobacco and alcohol. "Life is stimulating enough in itself without the need for artificial stimulants," he would say. [14] Eugene Sheehy, in *May It Please the Court*, writes that once Skeffington walked to Glendalough, in the Wicklow hills, and back in one day, a distance of about sixty miles, over mountain roads. Five or six other students started out with him, but only three of them attempted the return journey and after a few miles they gave up. The next day Eugene Sheehy saw Skeffington, who said, with his staccato, Downpatrick inflection, "I did not walk the last five miles, I stumbled, I fell, I crawled — *but* I *did* it." [15]

In debate, Skeffington and Kettle were equally persuasive, although they were poles apart in appearance and style of oratory. One can picture Kettle, hands grasping his lapels, outlining his points like the lawyer he was to become, tossing off the witticisms, the flowery sentences, the vivid phrases, the alliteration, and often sacrificing accuracy for the dramatic touch — and Skeffington, oblivious to the audience's reaction, making point after dogged point with precision and accuracy. The two men's ideals, however, were not dissimilar. Both felt a deep sympathy for the underprivileged; both fought valiantly for every "good" cause; both believed strongly in political and economic freedom for women; both wanted liberty for Ireland. But they differed widely in their approach to the achievement of their ideals. Skeffington thrilled to the formation of William O'Brien's United Irish League. He saw that this fresh and vigorous land agitation was needed to rouse the people who, by 1898, were bitter and apathetic as a result of repressive government measures and the squabbling of at least three factions within the Irish parliamentary party ranks. At the same time, he did not think of it as the final answer, for he sought the establishment of a workers' republic and a close union among all democratic nations.

Skeffington's hero was Michael Davitt. What he admired in Davitt illuminates his own character: freedom from the spirit of hate; a nationalism that was uncompromisingly democratic, never parochial, and always anticlerical; democratic sentiments that were more than political, that sought the elimination of the very poor and the very rich but shied away from dogmatic socialism as a threat to human liberty and freedom of expression; and repugnance to political opportunism, that is, an inability to betray one principle in order to obtain the triumph of another. Tom Kettle's hero, like his father's, was Parnell; home rule was his dominating passion. Robert Lynd, in *If the Germans Conquered England*, says that one of Kettle's first public acts was to organize a body of students to capture the Royal University organ and so prevent the playing of "God Save the King" at the degree-granting ceremonies. [16] This Skeffington could approve, but his priorities were different. He was a socialist. Kettle, though not hostile to socialism, tolerated it mainly because he felt there was much in it that was in line with medieval Catholicism and common sense.

Students at the end of the nineteenth century, it seems, were not much different from those of today. They approached college with practicality; for them there was no yesterday, and ideas *per se* left them cold. Those who looked to history for insight into the present, who worried about the future of the world instead of their own, and who dwelt in the realm of ideas were, to

the average student, "characters." In 1897, then, both Tom Kettle and
Francis Skeffington, for all their differences, were so considered. And, in
1898, another "character" joined them at University College: James Joyce.

Joyce was not much more than sixteen years old when he entered the
university. In his biography of Joyce, Richard Ellmann describes him as
having brown hair, parted toward the middle (when combed at all), a thin
nose, pale blue eyes, a slightly pursed mouth, and a stubborn jaw. "His
nearsightedness was becoming part of his personality," Ellmann writes, "for
rather than stare myopically, or wear glasses, he assumed a look of indifference." His clothes were generally unpressed and once, when asked his pet
antipathy, he replied, "Soap and water."[17]

Contrast Ellmann's description of Joyce with that of C. P. Curran in
James Joyce Remembered (and apparently also glorified):

«   «   «   «   «   «   «   «   «

> Tall, slim, and elegant; an erect yet loose carriage; an uptilted, long
> narrow head, and a strong chin that jutted out arrogantly; firm, tight-
> shut mouth; light-blue eyes which I found could stare with indignant
> wonder. . . . They gave an air of inscrutability and sometimes of lack
> of interest in the surroundings of the moment. . . . My friend Walter
> Callan told me that his attention was first caught by Joyce's careful
> attire, more studied than the average.[18]

»   »   »   »   »   »   »   »   »

Born in Rathgar, a suburb of Dublin, James Joyce was the oldest of ten
children, only five of whom survived infancy. His father, John Joyce, was
brilliant and witty, the spoiled only child of an only child, who drifted from
one school to another and then from one job to another. Never having lived
up to his potential and convinced that he was the victim of circumstances, he
centered his ambitions and hopes in James.

Because of fluctuating family finances, James Joyce could never be
sure just where he would be attending school — but his academic record
was always outstanding. During one of his family's more prosperous periods,
from 1888 to 1891, Joyce, like Tom Kettle, was enrolled at the posh
Clongowes Wood College. There he distinguished himself not only in his
studies — he was head of his class — but also in sports and amateur theat-
ricals. His brother Stanislaus says that Joyce accumulated a considerable
number of trophies for both hurdling and walking events. He must have had
some interest in politics during that period for, shortly after Parnell's "betrayal" and death, Joyce, then nine, wrote a poem called "Et tu, Healy." His
father was so pleased by it that he had it printed and distributed to friends.
This, says Ellmann, was the beginning of James Joyce's career as a writer.[19]

Another turn in the family fortunes meant Joyce was removed from
Clongowes and sent to the Christian Brothers School in Dublin, which he
disliked so much that he later chose to ignore this interval completely. In
1893 his father managed to get him enrolled in Belvedere College — a

superior Jesuit day school — and to have the fees waived. There Joyce studied happily, piling up honors, until 1898 when he entered University College.

The Literary and Historical Society attracted Joyce at once. During his first six months at the university, he participated so fully in its activities that he was elected to the Executive Committee and nominated, though defeated, for treasurer. He, Kettle, and Skeffington soon became good friends. By that time Skeffington, three years older than Joyce, had been at the university for two years, the auditorship of the L. & H. Society was behind him, and his reputation as both brilliant and eccentric was well established. On the surface none of these factors seemed to daunt Joyce, but his interpretation of their relationship as portrayed in the friendship of McCann (Skeffington) and Dedalus (Joyce) in *Stephen Hero* and in *A Portrait of the Artist as a Young Man* indicates otherwise.

In many ways the Joyce–Skeffington friendship resembled Joyce's love–hate relationship with Ireland. Skeffington was important to him but troubled him. This seems obvious from the way he portrayed Skeffington in his writings and from the many references (generally derogatory) in his correspondence. His respect for Skeffington's intellectual ability is clear. Joyce told his brother Stanislaus (who worshipped him and followed his career closely) that, after himself, Frank Skeffington was the most intelligent man at the college. [20] The importance of Skeffington's opinion of him and his reluctance to admit it is clear as well. For example, in 1903, when Joyce was in Paris, he wrote Stanislaus that he was determined to write only those things that "approve themselves to me. . . . So damn Russell, damn Yeats, damn Skeffington, damn Darlington, [21] damn editors, damn free-thinkers, damn vegetable verse, and double damn vegetable philosophy!" [22]

Clearly, however, Joyce and Skeffington enjoyed each other's company. Eugene Sheehy felt that Skeffington was "one of the first persons to recognize and appreciate the genius of Joyce." [23] They had in common not only brilliance and originality but a clarity, rare in such young men, concerning their ambitions. Joyce knew that he wanted to become an artist — either a writer or a musician; Skeffington wanted to improve the world. He knew precisely the causes for which he intended to crusade: the emancipation of women, the abolition of wars between nations, freedom for Ireland from British rule, anti-vivisectionism, vegetarianism. Within ten years he added socialism, limitations on the control of organized churches over people's minds, and an increase in the number and power of trade unions — without losing interest in his other causes. His inflexibility of purpose generated both fury and amusement in Joyce.

Not at all uncommon in Skeffington's early diaries are references to meetings with Joyce at the National Library, walks after the library closed, and lengthy discussions after an evening at the Sheehys. Joyce's taunts during these meetings, vividly portrayed in *Stephen Hero*, were met for the most part with equanimity. There were, however, two topics about which

Joyce may have succeeded in making Skeffington uncomfortable — sex and religion. The diaries indicate that Skeffington was giving a great deal of thought to both. Joyce was right to see himself in some ways as far more sophisticated than his friend; despite his youth, he was no stranger to "Monto," the red-light district of Dublin which, in his writings, he referred to as "Nighttown." Skeffington's stress on the virtues of virtue amused Joyce, although he did worry a bit when sexual purity was linked with the avoidance of syphilis and when the possibility of producing syphilitic children was mentioned. But he was wrong in his conclusion that Skeffington thought of females not in terms of beauty of form but only in terms of eugenics. Skeffington did, according to a 1903 diary item, take note of a statement in the *Review of Reviews* that "conception does not necessarily follow union," and he speculated whether there might be a "lawful, natural right way of preventing conception after physical union." He intended to inquire into this, he wrote, and he wondered how it might affect women.[24] He had a much more open mind than Joyce may have suspected.

It was on the subject of religion that Joyce took the greatest delight in baiting Skeffington — but actually their positions were not too divergent. As late as 1901, according to Ellmann, Joyce was "still occupied in crossing off his Catholicism."[25] In their discussions, however, he assumed a clear-cut position and questioned how Skeffington could continue to believe in Catholicism and still consider himself such a rational human being. Scornfully, he told his brother Stanislaus that his friend "had not yet considered the religious question, but he intended to devote a year to its consideration as soon as his work and studies left him time to do so." He added that Skeffington "was going to give his serious consideration to the problem whether laymen were permitted to think."[26] It is true that Skeffington's 1901 diaries contain jottings such as "2nd Commandment broken" and that this seemed to worry him. By 1902, however, entries questioning Catholicism were beginning to appear, such as "Talk of . . . Catholic Doctrine of midwifery — to save child, murder of mother — horrible!"[27]

A dialogue between Stephen Hero and MacCann in Joyce's *Stephen Hero* may fairly accurately describe a Joyce–Skeffington conversation. In answer to MacCann's point that life should be lived without any stimulants, Stephen asked if mountain climbing and bathing in the ocean, both of which MacCann enjoyed, could not be considered stimulants. There were natural stimulants and artificial stimulants, MacCann explained. Hard liquor, for example, though made from natural vegetable substances, was subjected to an unnatural process simply to satisfy artificially induced appetites. Stephen then asked how MacCann felt he represented normal humanity and was told, "in my manner of life." The dialogue continued:

«   «   «   «   «   «   «   «   «

"Your wants and the manner in which you satisfy them, is it?"
"Exactly."

"And what are your wants?"

"Air and food."

"Have you any subsidiary ones?"

"The acquisition of knowledge."

"And you need also religious comforts?"

"Maybe so . . . at times."

"And women . . . at times?"

"Never!"

»   »   »   »   »   »   »   »   »

Amused by the "moral snap of the jaws" and "the business-like tone of voice" with which MacCann said this, Stephen Hero "burst into a loud fit of laughter." [28]

Obviously Joyce considered Skeffington doctrinaire and something of a fanatic, but it could not have escaped Skeffington's notice — and possibly Joyce's as well — that his ideas were shared and his causes advocated by an Irishman living in London named George Bernard Shaw. Shaw was twenty-two years older than Skeffington, but they were much alike, down to the knickerbockers and the beard. Skeffington knew, too, that there were others in many countries who shared with him an inordinate faith in the power of rationality, a faith in people's ability to recognize their own best interests. A list might begin with Wolfe Tone and include figures such as William Thompson, a precursor of Karl Marx; James Keir Hardie, British labor leader and socialist; and presently the author and diplomat, Conor Cruise O'Brien. In the United States, such a list would include Thomas Paine, abolitionists William Lloyd Garrison and Wendell Phillips, and socialists Norman Thomas and Eugene Debs.

During the spring of 1899 Skeffington and Joyce were caught up in one of the most important cultural events of that decade. The Irish Literary Theatre came into being in Dublin, launched by William Butler Yeats, Edward Martyn, and Lady Augustus Gregory. Martyn, a member of the upper-crust Catholic gentry, was profoundly religious and conservative, but nevertheless keenly interested in any changes that were taking place in music, art, and literature. At this time he was deeply involved in the Irish revival and, as early as 1894, had been dreaming of writing plays in Irish. Yeats and Lady Gregory were also eager to foster drama of a truly Irish stamp. As their idea of a theater took shape, the three decided that a symbolic play by Yeats, *The Countess Cathleen*, would be their first offering.

Opening night was 9 May 1899, and a group of University College students attended — Skeffington and Joyce among them. As the play unfolded, the cleavage between the two became apparent. While Skeffington and other students booed passages in the play that they considered anti-Irish, Joyce applauded. For him no restriction could be allowed to interfere with the free expression of the artist. He was bothered not at all by the portrayal of the peasants as ignorant and superstitious. Weren't they? Skeffington, however, was horrified. No sooner had the final curtain been lowered when he and a group of like-minded students composed a letter of protest to be sent to the *Freeman's Journal*.

The letter expressed dissatisfaction with the subject of the play — the readiness of a high-born woman to sell her soul to buy bread to save the lives of starving Irish peasants — and what they considered Yeats's slanderous caricature of the Irish Catholic peasant. It read, in part:

«   «   «   «   «   «   «   «   «

> Mr. Yeats promised, if sufficiently supported, to "put on the stage plays dealing with Irish subjects or reflecting Irish ideas and sentiments."
> . . . The subject is not Irish. It has been shown that the plot is founded on a German legend. The characters are ludicrous travesties of the Irish Catholic Celt. The purpose of Mr. Yeats's drama is apparently to show the sublimity of self-sacrifice. The questionable nature of that self-sacrifice forces Mr. Yeats to adopt still more questionable means to produce an occasion for it. He represents the Irish peasant as a crooning barbarian, crazed with morbid superstition, who, having added the Catholic faith to his store of superstition, sells that faith for gold or bread in the proving of famine. . . . We recognise him as a fine literary artist. We recognise him, further, as one endowed with the rare gift of extending an infinitesimal quantity of the gold of thought in a seemingly infinite area of the tinsel of melodiously meaningless verse. . . . We feel it our duty, in the name and for the honour of Dublin Catholic students of the Royal University to protest against an art, even a dispassionate art, which offers as a type of our people a loathsome brood of apostates.[29]

»   »   »   »   »   »   »   »   »

When, next morning, the letter was left on a table at the university for signatures, Kettle, Joyce's closest friend, J. F. Byrne, and Richard Sheehy were among those who signed. Joyce refused to sign the letter — not, it seems likely, because of any firm ideological conviction in this case, but because he always enjoyed swimming against the tide. Many other students did not sign but, significantly, Joyce made a great point of his refusal and publicized it well.

Later that year Joyce refused to sign another Skeffington-inspired document under circumstances he portrayed dramatically in both *Stephen Hero* and *Portrait*. Czar Nicholas II of Russia had called for a conference of nations to discuss extension of the Geneva Convention to naval warfare, limitations on the use of explosive bullets and poison gas, and the establishment of a permanent Court of Arbitration. In response, twenty-six nations met at The Hague during the summer of 1899. To many liberals like William T. Stead, editor of the *Review of Reviews* and another hero of Skeffington's, it appeared that the dream of ages, the end of armed conflict between nations, was in sight. Stead had issued a special supplement concerned with the

Rescript, giving particular points for those who wished to help. Point number five gave Skeffington his inspiration: "Endeavor to secure the passing of a resolution in its favour by any association with which you are connected . . . undertake to obtain signatures to the International Memorial."

Accordingly, Skeffington set up photographs of Stead and the czar on a table near the entrance to one of the university buildings and began soliciting signatures for a testimonial to the czar. When Joyce came along with Byrne, he found Skeffington buttonholing students and holding forth on general disarmament and other means of providing the greatest possible happiness for the greatest number of people. Skeffington approached Joyce, asking him to sign. As Joyce tells it in *Stephen Hero*, Skeffington (MacCann) says, "It's a testimonial of admiration for the courage displayed by the Tsar of Russia in issuing a rescript to the Powers, advocating arbitration instead of war as a means of settling national disputes."[30] When Stephen refuses to sign, Mac-Cann says, "You are a reactionary then?" To which Stephen replies, "Do you think you impress me when you flourish your wooden sword?" Then, pointing toward the picture of the czar, he adds, "If you must have a Jesus, let us have a legitimate Jesus." MacCann says as he prepares to walk away, "I believe you're a good fellow but you have yet to learn the dignity of altruism and the responsibility of the human individual."[31]

Time and time again, Skeffington proved that rebuffs bothered him very little, that he was eminently fair, and that he was seldom petty. In these respects, Tom Kettle was much like him. When, on 10 January 1900, Joyce read his paper "Drama and Life" before the Literary and Historical Society, it was Kettle who proposed and Skeffington who seconded the motion for a vote of thanks — a vote that was passed unanimously but without enthusiasm. It is significant that some of those who argued on the paper attacked it for not being Irish enough, or for not being Catholic enough, but both Kettle, an earnest Catholic, and Skeffington, a questioning Catholic, praised it.

It was soon after this that Skeffington nominated Joyce for the auditorship of the Society. Joyce was defeated, though, by the man who one day would serve as Chief Justice of the Irish Free State, Hugh Boyle Kennedy. This same Hugh Kennedy, early in June 1901, became the first editor of a new college magazine, *St. Stephen's*. For his purposes, the timing of its birth seemed perfect to Joyce. The Irish Literary Theatre had followed its production of *Countess Cathleen* with Edward Martyn's *The Heather Field*, a play whose hero was an idealistic Irishman. Joyce liked it as he did the one that followed — Moore and Martyn's *The Bending of the Bough*. But in 1901 he felt the tide was turning. Plans were to produce Douglas Hyde's Irish language play, *Casadh-an-tSugain*, and a play adapted by Yeats and George Moore from Irish heroic legend, *Diarmuid and Grania*. As Joyce saw it, the Irish Literary Theatre was about to become offensively Irish. He proceeded to write a scathing article condemning the theater group for its parochialism and confidently submitted it to Kennedy at *St. Stephen's*. When Kennedy, after consulting with the advisor, Father Henry Browne, turned down "The Day of the Rabblement," as it was called, Joyce was livid. Immediately he went to President Delany, who refused to intervene in the matter. According to John Marcus O'Sullivan, a member of the editorial staff at the time, the rejection rested solely on Joyce's reference to D'Annunzio's *Il Fuoco*. This novel, with much else of D'Annunzio, stood in the Roman *Index Librorum Prohibitorum* (index of forbidden books).[32] Be that as it may, Joyce was not content to let the matter drop.

Skeffington, too, was having his difficulties with Kennedy and *St. Stephen's*. A piece he had submitted, "A Forgotten Aspect of the University Question," was rejected. The article, basically a plea for equal status for women at the Royal University, made a strong case for coeducation. In the original charter of that institution, it was clearly stated that "all Exhibitions, Scholarships, Fellowships, and other emoluments are to be open to women equally with men."[33] Skeffington praised this position but felt it needed to be extended and developed. Both male and female students needed to have the full benefits of university life. The use of all buildings, equipment, and the services of the teaching staff should be available to women. Only then could they have the contact with teachers and fellow students that Skeffington considered the prime advantage of a university degree. "When a genuine teaching University is established," Skeffington wrote, "all its privileges must be bestowed without distinction of sex," including admission to university societies and "proportionate share in the government of the University." Calling on the critics of coeducation to cast aside their prejudices, he wrote, "The mischievous isolation of each sex throughout the long years of training for life, followed by the inevitable sudden plunge into each other's society, is obviously unnatural, hostile to the development of character, and fraught with grave danger to morality."[34]

So eager was Skeffington to have these ideas disseminated that when, in mid-October, Joyce approached him at the National Library and suggested that they arrange to publish their rejected papers together, he hesitated not a moment. He might be able to get the printing done free, Joyce said, but as so often with Joyce, this hope did not materialize.

Gerrard Brothers, a stationery store across St. Stephen's Green from University College, which was equipped to do small printing jobs, agreed to print the two articles in pamphlet form. The firm undertook a great deal of work for the Jesuits and had supplied Cardinal Newman with stationery at one time. Bernard Shaw had visiting cards printed there; George Moore ran in and out from Ely Place nearby; and the Yeats family were well known to the shopkeepers. Mr. R. J. Gerrard, son of the owner at the time, remembered Skeffington coming in to see about the job but did not recollect seeing Joyce. Hutchins, in *James Joyce's Dublin*, says that it is unlikely that Gerrard would have accepted the work if he had realized its nature.[35]

Since Skeffington did not agree with Joyce's position on the Irish Literary Theatre and Joyce did not agree with Skeffington's position on women, they added a preface — a disclaimer, as it were: "These two essays were commissioned by the Editor of *St. Stephen's* for that paper, but were subsequently refused by the Censor. The writers are now publishing them in their original form, and each writer is responsible only for what appears under his own name."[36]

Neither Skeffington nor Joyce was particularly bothered by the furor that resulted from the publication of their two essays. Students and faculty alike were embroiled in discussions about the pamphlet, and *St. Stephen's* printed a lead article attacking Joyce for taking the attitude that artists must stand apart from the multitude. Skeffington's prime concern was that his point of view influence as many people as possible. He and Joyce sold the pamphlet at a price of two pence at the college gates, in as many shops as possible, through friends, and, of course, through family. (Some months later a batch of unsold copies was returned to Skeffington from Downpatrick with sixpence and, after collecting a shilling from a shop in Harcourt Road, he noted: "I have now 6/10/½ to divide with Joyce."[37] This was his first recorded venture in the world of business.)

During those university days, a great deal of Skeffington's social life centered around the home of David Sheehy, a Nationalist member of Parliament. Joyce's and Kettle's lives did as well. Patricia Hutchins, in *James Joyce's Dublin*, writes of the Sheehy home at 2 Belvedere Place: "For a number of years this tall, comfortable-looking house with its high granite steps, pillared door, and balcony on the first floor, was the meeting place for much of that middle stratum of Irish society, which stood somewhere between the landed gentry, colonist and conqueror in outlook for the most part, and the growing body of extreme nationalists, some of whom were later to become revolutionaries."[38]

The Sheehys were a large family — two boys, Richard and Eugene, and four girls, Hanna, Margaret, Mary, and Kathleen. David Sheehy and his wife, Elizabeth ("Bessie"), were warm-hearted, friendly people. Both had grown up in County Limerick. Bessie, some five years younger than David, was the daughter of Richard McCoy of Loughhill. David, the son of a mill owner, had begun his education at the Jesuit Seminary in Limerick and continued it at the Irish College in Paris. Conor Cruise O'Brien, in *States of Ireland*, says that Bessie "eloped with him from the convent where she was at school."[39] (Since she was over twenty-five when she married, though, this is difficult to reconcile.) As a youth, David Sheehy had been active in the revolutionary Irish Republican Brotherhood movement (the Fenians) and had served several sentences of hard labor in Irish jails for political offenses. He spoke with pride of the fact that he, along with William O'Brien, M.P., and others, refused to wear the prison garb assigned to "common prisoners,"

The Sheehy family, date unknown. Standing, left to right: Hanna, Richard, David, Margaret, Eugene, and Mary; sitting, left to right: Father Eugene, Kathleen, and Bessie.

and that, as punishment, they were left for weeks in winter weather without clothing in a cold cell. Not surprisingly, Skeffington had no trouble identifying with him and his ideas.

The second Sunday evening of each month was open house at the Sheehys.[40] The brightest and wittiest young people from the university gathered for conversation, parlor games, dancing, and singing. Although Skeffington for the most part participated wholeheartedly, Eugene Sheehy does recall that he would often see him sitting off in the corner, writing busily and oblivious to what was going on around him; "his fountain pen seemed to be always at the alert position."[41] Often, however, Skeffington and Joyce were paired off in charades, a game very popular with the group. Skeffington's acting was uproarious, and Joyce's quiet and deliberative; consequently, they made a successful team.

The gaiety, the conversation, and the relaxed atmosphere of the Sheehy home, so different from his own home, were a source of delight to Skeffington. The main attraction, however, was the Sheehys' bright, witty, and charming oldest daughter, Hanna. Hanna was slightly older than Francis — she was born 24 May 1877 — and just as well educated. She made no effort to conceal her boundless admiration for him and for his ideas, sentiments that were obviously not without their gratification. The Sheehy girls were a remarkable lot, well versed in the affairs of the day and in matters literary and able to hold discussions as equals with the brightest lights from the college. Their mother, Bessie, must be given a great deal of the credit for this. The family income was limited, since they depended mainly on David's stipend as an M.P., but Bessie saw to it that her children attended excellent schools. The boys went to Belvedere College; the girls to the Dominican Convent, Eccles Street. Next to Clongowes Wood for boys and Mount Anville for girls, these schools offered the finest education available.

The Sheehys would not have been able to afford to send their children to first-rate schools if it had not been for the substantial financial assistance available to exceptional students through competition in "exhibitions." These were open to girls as well as boys and the Sheehy girls had little trouble winning them. Such victories, they soon learned, did not mean that they would thereafter enjoy equal opportunity with their male competitors. This lesson, together with their mother's rejection of the idea that a woman's place was in the home, resulted in the development of four ardent feminists.

Many years later, in a radio interview, Hanna drew a picture of her early years. Her background makes clear why, aside from her physical charms, Francis Skeffington would have been drawn to the woman she had become. She had gone to Germany as a student when she was eighteen, and then later to France. "I think it is a mighty good thing to travel when young — though it was incipient tuberculosis that set me roving to the Rhineland," she said. "Later I went to Paris many times during student days. France and Germany are the countries I know best in Europe — and I admire both peoples." Did she think she had grown up in a "political household"? she was asked. Very strongly so, she thought. Both her parents were Fenians. Her uncle, Father Eugene Sheehy, had been in Kilmainham jail with Parnell, John Dillon, M.P., and Davitt. Her grandfather Sheehy had been a native Irish speaker who was beaten at the National school for every Irish word he spoke. She felt that her own schooling — at the Dominican Convent and later their College in Merrion Square — had given her "great independence of thought and action."[42]

The Sheehys' devotion to Ireland and to Irish freedom was always a great source of pride to Hanna. Her father and his brother had both intended to be priests. In the 1860s, however, students in Maynooth Seminary had to take the oath of allegiance to the British Crown and, in order to avoid this, their father withdrew both boys from the institution and sent them abroad to study. Both Sheehy boys went to Paris, where they attended the Collège des Irlandais. Eugene, the older, remained there when a cholera epidemic broke out in Paris, but he sent his younger brother, David, home. Back in Ireland, David became involved in the Fenian movement and was so active that he was forced to flee to the United States. It was upon his return that he met and married Bessie McCoy. As Hanna often said, "I owe my existence to the Oath."[43]

One of Hanna's earliest memories was of going to see her father in Kilmainham jail when she was only four. She remembered thinking of the prison yard as a sort of playground. When she was about ten he was in Tullamore jail, where, as a result of harsh treatment, he almost lost his hearing while, to quote Bessie, "Parnell was in Brighton with 'that woman.' "[44] Hanna's uncle, Father Eugene, as she said in her radio interview, had been imprisoned in 1881 because of his Fenian sympathies. In fact, he had been so active in the Land League that he was often referred to as the "Land League priest." As the parish priest of Bruree, County Limerick, he had exercised a strong influence over his young parishioners — one of them Eamon de Valera. Conor Cruise O'Brien has a photograph of his great-uncle, Father Eugene, given to him by the then prime minister, de Valera, on which de Valera has written, in Gaelic, "He taught me patriotism."[45]

Hanna entered college at eighteen. Always an exceptional student, she won a scholarship in 1897, an Honours B.A. in 1899, and "First Class Honours and Special Prize" in 1902. Despite all these honors, Hanna always felt, and always told others, that the greatest education she received was from Francis Skeffington. It was he, she maintained, who had given her an enduring interest in the women's movement. But she should not have minimized the effect that her mother and father and her Uncle Eugene had had on her thinking. If she had not already been an ardent feminist when Francis Skeffington met her, it is doubtful that he would have been as attracted to her as he was. In any event, their influence on each other was great.

In his piece on women at the Royal University, Francis had written: "The Graduates' Central Association might . . . find it possible to add to its programme an assertion of women's right to the preservation and increase of their present opportunities for University Education. But if this should not be feasible, then a separate organisation should be started, having this for its chief object."[46] Early in 1902, after a struggle on the part of Hanna and others, such an organization — the Irish Association of Women Graduates and Candidate Graduates — was formed. There already existed a similar association in England, and the Irish counterpart was greeted with great enthusiasm by the women of the university. Almost immediately, two hundred members joined up, and soon there were branches in Belfast, Cork, Derry, and Galway. The objectives of the association were threefold: to provide means of communication and mutual action in matters concerning the interests of the university women of Ireland; to equalize educational opportunities for men and women; and to supply the members with a placement service — a clearinghouse for applicants and employers.

Each year there was a struggle over the playing of "God Save the King" at the university's degree-granting ceremonies. In this battle, also, Hanna and Skeffington fought side by side, both while they were students and afterward. In 1906 James Joyce wrote his brother, Stanislaus: "I suppose you read about Skeff and his papa-in-law? They harangued student Dublin from a car outside the University Buildings and U. Coll., because *God Save the King* was played on the organ. 'There was a lady in the vehicle,' the paper says. David [Sheehy] said he was proud that day of Nationalist Dublin." [47]

Skeffington's thinking and conclusions clearly influenced an article by Hanna that appeared in the *New Ireland Review* in 1902. This was a reply to an article on women and the university by a Miss Daly, who apparently believed that the ordinary woman would find attaining the masculine level of study physically impairing and be morally tainted by competition outside her "special domestic sphere." Paradoxically, it appeared to Hanna, Miss Daly maintained that men could not say what rights women should have but that only women could make these decisions. Could women make these momentous decisions, Hanna asked, unless they had the advantage of equal opportunity with men in the university, the opportunity to discuss with the best-equipped and the most cultivated minds, a chance to sharpen their faculties and to develop the best in themselves through a liberal education? Education, she wrote, should be "a moulding and a discipline of character and intellect, a cultivation of heart as well as brain, a widening of the individual outlook, a deepening of the individual sympathy." To deprive women of the opportunities and advantages they would get from full privileges of the university would be, she felt, to the detriment of education generally. [48]

Conversely, Hanna's reasoning can be detected in an article by Skeffington in *St. Stephen's*. "The Final Report — The Position of Women" was part of a symposium on the recently issued University Commission Report, to which Skeffington, among others, had contributed. His piece conceded that the Commission Report strengthened the position of university women by recommending that they be admitted to the general university lectures along with male students. The advocacy of coeducation was a decided advance, he realized, as well as a triumph for the Irish Association of Women Graduates. He insisted, however, that "from the beginning, too, each of the new colleges (supposing the Commission's scheme is adopted) should have a certain proportion of women on its governing body, to ensure justice for women students until such time as women representatives of the Professors and Graduates are elected in the ordinary course." [49] As the report stood, it distorted the program of the association and watered it down, he maintained. Not unmindful of the effect his essay "A Forgotten Aspect of the University Question" had had on the University Commission, Skeffington knew that the fight was not yet over. Never could he be accused of being easily satisfied.

NOTES TO CHAPTER 2

1. Joseph Darlington, S.J., to Hanna Sheehy-Skeffington, 19 June 1916, marked "Confidential."

2. Hanna Sheehy-Skeffington, "Biographical Notice," in *In Dark and Evil Days*, by Francis Sheehy-Skeffington (Dublin: James Duffy and Co., 1916), p. xi.

3. Richard Ellmann, *James Joyce* (New York: Oxford University Press, 1959), p. 59n.

4. Ibid., p. 59.

5. Andrée Sheehy-Skeffington to Samuel Levenson, 9 March 1977, letter in author's possession.

6. C. P. Curran, *Under the Receding Wave* (Dublin: Gill and Macmillan, 1970), p. 114.

7. Ibid., p. 112.

8. Ibid., p. 115.

9. F. Sheehy-Skeffington to his cousin Mary, 4 April 1908.

10. Curran, *Receding Wave*, pp. 114–115. So far as music was concerned Francis Sheehy-Skeffington wrote in his "Facts and Fancies" in 1904: "I feel deeply my own ignorance of music. Should I not try to remedy it, to open up this new world?"

11. F. Sheehy-Skeffington to Rose Skeffington, 14 August 1899.

12. F. S. L. Lyons, *Ireland Since the Famine* (London: Weidenfeld and Nicolson, 1971), p. 247.

13. Curran, *Receding Wave*, p. 112.

14. O. Sheehy-Skeffington, "Francis Sheehy-Skeffington," p. 137.

15. Sheehy, *Please the Court*, pp. 32–33.

16. Robert Lynd, *If the Germans Conquered England and Other Essays* (Dublin: Maunsell, 1917), p. 137.

17. Ellmann, *James Joyce*, p. 66.

18. C. P. Curran, *James Joyce Remembered* (London: Oxford University Press, 1968), p. 4.

19. Ellmann, *James Joyce*, 32–33.

20. Ibid., p. 63.

21. The Darlington referred to is Father Joseph Darlington, then Dean of Studies at the university, a kindly priest, always eager to be agreeable, who was to become Skeffington's friend. A story is told that, when told of the impending marriage of one of his students, he said, "Just the very thing, Mr. Coyne, just the very thing. I was about to do the same myself." (C. P. Curran, "A Broadcast Talk from Radio Eireann, May 2, 1954," in *Struggle with Fortune: A Miscellany for the Centenary of the Catholic University of Ireland 1854–1954* (Dublin: Browne & Nolan, 1954), p. 226.)

22. Ellmann, *James Joyce*, p. 125.

23. Sheehy, *Please the Court*, p. 35.

24. Francis Sheehy-Skeffington, "Facts and Fancies" (notebook), 15 March 1903, Sheehy-Skeffington Papers.

25. Ellmann, *James Joyce*, p. 67.

26. Stanislaus Joyce, *My Brother's Keeper* (New York: Viking Press, 1958), p. 145.

27. Diary of Francis Sheehy-Skeffington, 9 November 1902, Sheehy-Skeffington Papers.

28. James Joyce, *Stephen Hero* (New York: New Directions, 1963), pp. 50–52.

29. *Freeman's Journal*, 10 May 1899, p. 6.

30. Joyce, *Stephen Hero*, p. 114.

31. James Joyce, *A Portrait of the Artist as a Young Man* (New York: Modern Library, 1928), p. 232.

32. Curran, *James Joyce Remembered*, p. 20.

33. Fathers of the Society of Jesus, *A Page of Irish History: Story of University College, Dublin, 1883–1909* (Dublin: Talbot Press, 1930), p. 453.

34. Francis Sheehy-Skeffington, "A Forgotten Aspect of the University Question," in *Two Essays*, by Francis Sheehy-Skeffington and James A. Joyce (Dublin: Gerrard Bros., 1901), pamphlet.

35. Hutchins, *James Joyce's Dublin*, p. 61.

36. F. Sheehy-Skeffington, "A Forgotten Aspect." There does not seem to be any evidence that the articles were actually commissioned; Ellmann feels that perhaps Kennedy simply "suggested" that a contribution of some sort would be in order (Ellmann, *James Joyce*, p. 92n.).

37. Andrée Sheehy-Skeffington, "The Hatter and the Crank," *Irish Times*, 5 February 1982.

38. Patricia Hutchins, *James Joyce's Dublin* (London: Grey Walls Press, 1950), p. 71.

39. Conor Cruise O'Brien, *States of Ireland* (Great Britain: Panther Books, Ltd., 1974), p. 22.

40. Richard Ellmann, *James Joyce*, rev. ed. (New York: Oxford University Press, 1982), p. 51.

41. Sheehy, *Please the Court*, p. 34.

42. Incomplete and undated transcript of a radio interview with Hanna Sheehy-Skeffington, Sheehy-Skeffington Papers.

43. Andrée Sheehy-Skeffington, "The French Connection," *Irish Times*, 26 October 1981.

44. O'Brien, *States of Ireland*, p. 34.

45. Ibid., p. 22.

46. F. Sheehy-Skeffington, "A Forgotten Aspect," p. 12.

47. Richard Ellmann, ed., *Selected Joyce Letters* (New York: Viking Press, 1975), p. 124.

48. *New Ireland Review*, Mar.–August 1902, pp. 148–151.

49. Francis Sheehy-Skeffington, "The Final Report: The Position of Women," in "University Commission: A Symposium," *St. Stephen's*, June 1903, pp. 252–253.

3
The Pattern Emerges 1901–1906

Descriptions of Skeffington during his university days vary considerably. Some give the impression that he was humorless, obstinate, and persistent. The story is told that, when police broke up an outdoor meeting at which he was speaking, Skeffington could be seen clinging to a lamp-post while the police tried to drag him away, saying — in his rather high-pitched voice — "One further point before I go."[1] On the other hand, friends remembered him as fun-loving, the eternal optimist, and lovingly involved with family and friends. There was a great deal of truth on both sides. His methodical ways, so very much like his father's, amused some and infuriated others. Examples abound. Diary items during the period of his courtship record times of his meetings with Hanna to the minute; his letters were just as precise. For example, after a weekend at home during 1901 when he was teaching in Kilkenny, he wrote to his mother: "I was in excellent time for the train on Monday morning; I had allowed myself as much time to ride to the station as it took me to come from it on Friday; but of course I did it in less, the streets being clear."

Skeffington was well aware of how much he resembled his father; as far as he was able, he fought against the tendency. In this respect — and in many others that he clearly recognized — his relationship with Hanna was helpful. As he confided to his diary, after spending "two happy hours" with her, he had criticized her "vagueness in walking & losing her way." She responded by telling him that he "bored" her with his speeches. "I wish you'd stop talking about these eternal little things; leave them to settle themselves & if they don't it doesn't matter," she had said. One wonders whether he could see how ironic it was that he then promised her he would do so "for a month."[2] Skeffington worried a great deal about the fact that he might not be living up to her estimation and, taking note of that at one point, he resolved to be "brave, strong, firm, calm & tolerant, energetic, gentle, & pure."[3] Again like his father, there was very little doubt in his mind that he could be all those things if he really set his mind to it.

Like both his parents, Skeffington was very fond of his family; he wrote often to his cousins in the north, and he was always happy to receive news from Downpatrick. His father, writing regularly to him from his tour of duty, spared him no details. "Bella [J. B.'s sister] awfully thin and worn keeping both shops going — and they have no servant," one letter read. About the town itself, he said: "The Shops seem much improved here, plenty of electric light in them, & many are much more tasteful than formerly but still no public electric & only horse trams."[4] Francis's letters to his mother were frequent; they reflected great concern for her health, and the genuine closeness between them.

J. B. in all his letters discussed his health or his son's in one aspect or another. When Francis, who was given to respiratory problems, developed influenza in December 1902, J. B. wrote urging him to take better care of himself. "It was a very bad turn you had," he wrote. "It shows you will need to be far more prudent as to your clothing especially inside woollens, and also as to hours & weather. . . . It is time you had a due sense of physical effects & bodily weaknesses."[5] Apparently J. B.'s advice did not go unheeded, for early in January Francis sent an "application" to Eugene Sandow, a physical culture advocate much in vogue at the time. In reply Sandow sent his book, *Curative Physical Culture,* and a note assuring him that his letter would be "treated in confidence," and that "if your case is not suitable for treatment under my system, I will frankly tell you so."[6] Diary items indicate that Skeffington duly enrolled for the Sandow course and practiced the exercises faithfully. They also indicate that for young Skeffington the exercises were an attempt to control "men's impurity."[7]

It is difficult to pinpoint how early in their relationship Skeffington and Hanna Sheehy realized that they were in love — but even before 1900 they were spending a great deal of time together in addition to the "Sunday evenings" at Hanna's home. They met at Bewley's for coffee (still a tradition in Dublin), took long walks together, and saw each other regularly at the library. Skeffington depended on Hanna to read his work and to edit it as well. In the Sheehy-Skeffington Papers in the National Library of Ireland can be found a typescript of a play in five acts, "In Dark and Evil Days," written by Skeffington in 1901 and including several pages in Hanna's handwriting. Her assistance did not go unappreciated. An item in Francis's diary notes that he had finished his play and that Hanna had offered to copy it. "My sweet betrothed indispensable to me in every direction," he wrote.[8]

Their courtship by early 1903 had progressed to the stage where the couple was making wedding plans and searching for a house. Hanna was teaching both German and French at the Rathmines Vocational School. Skeffington was registrar of University College, Dublin, and, in addition, writing and doing some tutoring in French, English, and Italian. He had also applied for a superintendentship of examinations at the university. His application to the governing board of the university for the position of registrar had simply listed his age and academic history and concluded: "I will spare you the fatuity of testimonials." He had been hired at a salary of one hundred pounds per year, the first lay registrar in the history of the university.[9]

Skeffington's full-time position did not deter him from the pursuit of his writing career. He submitted "In Dark and Evil Days" to the Queen's Royal Theatre prize drama competition, but in March 1903 he was informed that "the Committee have adjudged your play one of the unsuccessful ones."[10] He was more successful, however, in his contact with a new publication called *New Ireland*, a "Weekly Journal Devoted to the Industries, Language, Literature, and Politics of Ireland." Skeffington and Hanna were ecstatic over a letter from P. J. Hooper, the editor, which read, in part:

«   «   «   «   «   «   «   «   «

Many thanks for the article which suited excellently. . . . It has occurred to me that perhaps we could come to an arrangement with you to contribute regularly to the paper — say a leading article and some five or six notes each week. If this suggestion recommends itself to you will you let me know. We should probably be able to pay about a guinea a week for this. . . . The subject I would suggest for the leading article is 'Is Ireland Progressing?' making special reference to the statistics on banking railways etc. recently published by the Agricultural Board or perhaps you may think of a more suitable subject yourself. The notes would of course be on current topics of which many will not fail to suggest themselves.[11]

»   »   »   »   »   »   »   »   »

Immediately upon receipt of Hooper's offer, Skeffington sent an acceptance letter. It was a start.

Skeffington had already done a considerable amount of thinking along the lines of the "notes" mentioned in Hooper's letter and had been sending samples to his father. A letter from J. B., sent from Wexford on 17 March 1903, indicated that he thought them good — "I see much less worthy press often." He enclosed clippings that he thought his son might want to use, and continued to do so from time to time. Skeffington's work was also appearing in the *Freeman's Journal* and, in London, an article on "The Irish University Question" was accepted by W. T. Stead for the *Westminster Review*. Payments for the former were never more than two pounds each and often less; for the piece in *Westminster Review* he received no money at all.

Except for the salary, however, there were definite signs that Skeffington was not happy with his position as university registrar. Letters to house agents and correspondence with *New Ireland* regarding a job offer on that publication indicate that the young couple was considering settling in London. "Consider well the future & the cost before taking an irrevocable step," J. B. cautioned.[12] The position on *New Ireland* had been offered to Tom Kettle first and, when he refused it, to Skeffington. After a few months of deliberation, however, Skeffington turned it down also. J. B. wrote him from Dungannon: "I daresay you were right — it would take double the salary to live in London though being a weekly, there should not be *much time* on it."[13]

Whatever spare moments Skeffington had were devoted to a novel he was writing, to his diary, and to a notebook — labeled "Facts and Fancies" — that clearly reflected his thoughts in 1903. Speculating on how rare it was to find "anyone who is a progressive *all* along the line," he cited examples: "Samuel Smith, M.P. is a pillar of the Vigilance movement, but a strong opponent of Women's Suffrage. Mrs. Fawcett, who demolished all Smith's arguments against women's suffrage, is herself a bitter Unionist & strongly anti-Irish; she lent her name to the whitewashing of the African concentration camps." [14]

Skeffington questioned his own attitudes as well. In "Facts and Fancies," he wrote, "How hard it is to root out the last vestiges of hereditary prejudice!" A female clerk in a department store had succeeded in taking the top off his fountain pen when he had been unable to do so, and "felt decidedly ashamed & crestfallen that a woman should have beaten me in strength of thumb!" He was able very soon to banish this feeling but thought it "a curious thing" that he should have it at all. "Had the shop-assistant been a man I should have experienced no such shame," he wrote. Another diary entry read, "How much more progress I might make, in journalism, in academics, in anything, if I were in a sympathetic circle to whom I could speak out my mind and show all that is in me!" It was the "ceaseless hypocrisy" he had to bring to his work situations that worried him. "I must teach my children always to be frank; and must at the same time try to provide congenial environment for them." [15]

On quite another topic, he wrote that he had been reading "Wild Traits in Tame Animals," and found himself enjoying a passage

«   «   «   «   «   «   «   «   «

appealing to the appetite of man for slaughter & for animal food. Had to pull myself up sharp. This is identical in essence with taking pleasure in voluptuous books or pictures, & should be checked just as much as the latter; yet how regularly & recklessly this taste — for bloodthirsty stories, &c — is encouraged in boys! Of course there are degrees; to me, for instance, such a passage, or even a momentary delight in it, would not be nearly as dangerous as in case of a voluptuous passage. Yet all enjoyment of this kind of reading, yielding to the atavistic animal instinct, verges on sin.

»   »   »   »   »   »   »   »   »

After writing that last word, he thought — and noted — "What a handy word *sin* is! altogether apart from obsolete theology, it is almost indispensable." [16]

Some of Skeffington's other diary entries point to another possible prejudice: "Professor J. J. Thomson, of Cambridge, is going to Columbia University; doubtless at very large salary. Americans have apparently started to buy up the brains of Europe!" [17] And further: "There is to be an International Chess Tournament in St. Louis in 1904; Lasker, in order to play, has got himself appointed Professor of Mathematics in the University of St.

Louis." [18] Commenting on an item in a London paper, he wrote, "Mrs.
Molineux, wife of the man recently acquitted in the 'Poison by Post' trial, is
seeking a divorce & has gone, with that object, to South Dakota, where the
marriage laws are lax. The despatch adds that public feeling is very strongly
against Mrs. Molineux, & that steps are being taken to *change the law* at
once, in order to prevent her from obtaining a divorce!!! Hail Columbia!" [19]

On 27 June 1903, the marriage of "Francis J. C. Skeffington, bachelor,
and Hanna M. Sheehy, spinster," took place in the Roman Catholic Chapel
of University College, at St. Stephen's Green. Their ages were recorded as
"full," his occupation as "Registrar and Journalist," hers as "Teacher," and
her father's as "Gentleman." [20] In a gesture rare for 1903 and for their
milieu, Skeffington gave ample proof of the strength of his feminist beliefs by
joining Hanna's surname to his — he was now Francis Sheehy-Skeffington.
It was an act that infuriated J. B. and one for which he never completely
forgave his son.

For their honeymoon, the young couple chose a cycling trip. Skeffington, writing to his mother late in August, described their itinerary: "We had a
week in Killarney after leaving Cork; then we went all round South Kerry,
round the coast & afterward through the mountains; & then went back to
Killarney for a few days, winding up with a climb up Carrantual, the highest
mountain in Ireland." [21] Returning to Dublin, the Sheehy-Skeffingtons
began their busy married life at 8 Airfield Road, Rathgar. The street was a cul
de sac and the house was small but charming.

A few months later, Skeffington, in his capacity as registrar, wrote to
James Joyce asking him to teach some evening classes in French at University College. [22] Late in 1902 Joyce had gone to France to study medicine at
the University of Paris, but he had returned to Dublin in April 1903 because
his mother was ill; Skeffington knew that Joyce was home and unemployed.
Joyce declined the offer, saying that he didn't think his French was good
enough. Ellmann says, however, that Joyce had chosen to interpret the offer
as a plot on the part of the university authorities to put him in their debt. [23]

Joyce had reached the conclusion that the trouble with Dublin was that
its newspapers were corrupt. He longed to start a paper, modeled on conti-
nental newspapers, and once more turned to Skeffington. He found a receptive ear. Joyce insisted that the paper must be literary rather than political, as
Skeffington would have liked. Finally they reached a compromise: Skeffington would be allowed space for general topics such as the emancipation of
women, pacifism, and socialism. That settled, they turned to the problem of
money. They had decided that two thousand pounds would be needed to get
started, but they did not know where to find the necessary capital. Padraic
Colum, one of the first Abbey Theatre playwrights and a friend of both,
reports in *Our Friend James Joyce* that Joyce came to him, "who was as far
removed from moneyed people as he himself was," to ask for help. [24] Colum
did have an American friend, Thomas J. Kelly, a millionaire of Irish descent

who lived near Dublin. Joyce thought him a likely prospect. So eager and enthusiastic was he to get the project underway that he walked fourteen miles to Kelly's home in Celbridge. Turned away by the gatekeeper, he wearily covered the fourteen miles back to Dublin. In reply to an indignant letter that he wrote Kelly after this episode, Joyce received two telegrams of apology and a letter indicating lack of interest in the opportunity offered him. With no other prospects to raise the money, the second Skeffington–Joyce publishing venture aborted.

Both Joyce and Skeffington were constantly in need of money. Entries in Skeffington's diary suggest that Joyce introduced Skeffington to pawn shops and indicate later that Skeffington pawned a ring (possibly Hanna's).[25] In 1903, however, Skeffington's salary as registrar enabled him to lend Joyce a little money from time to time. When Joyce was planning to leave Dublin with his woman friend Nora Barnacle in 1904, he again asked Skeffington for a loan. Skeffington's reply is so revealing that it is given here in its entirety:

« « « « « « « « «

I regret that I cannot give you the small pecuniary assistance you request, — for two reasons, either of which would be sufficient in itself. In the first place, I haven't got any money to spare just at present, — and perhaps I shouldn't add anything to that. But, in the second place, I am influenced by the fact that you were not straight with me on the last occasion when you asked for money. You spoke confidently of speedy repayment, which I am forced to believe you knew to be impossible. Had you straightforwardly asked me for the money as a *gift*, I should be more inclined to assist you *now*.

What you tell me as to your *arrangements* has *no* influence on my decision. I should be glad to know your address in Zurich, & to hear from you occasionally. You have my best wishes for your welfare, — and for that of your companion, which is probably much more doubtful than your own.[26]

» » » » » » » » »

The sanctimonious tone of the first paragraph resembles that in J. B.'s letters to his son. The second paragraph is equally revealing. Given the times and a strong puritanical attitude toward sexual matters, Skeffington was probably shocked that Joyce's traveling "companion" was a woman to whom he was not married. If so, he apparently was doing his best not to sit in judgment.

Joyce's correspondence indicates that he was unable to forget the letter or, for that matter, Skeffington or his ideas. In a letter to Stanislaus some six months later, he attacked Skeffington's defense of the position that the individual should sacrifice himself for the sake of the group:[27]

« « « « « « « « «

I am sure however that the whole structure of heroism is, and always was, a damned lie and that there cannot be any substitute for the individual passion as the motive power of everything — art and philosophy included. For this reason Hairy Jaysus [Joyce's name for Skeffington] seems to be the bloodiest imposter of all I have met. Tell him, if you meet him, that I am about to produce a baboon baby by sitting for six hours on a jug full of soda water and ask him will he be godfather.[28]

»   »   »   »   »   »   »   »   »

A month later (15 March 1905):

«   «   «   «   «   «   «   «   «

Bye the bye — in case I forget it — do not omit to slap Skeffington three times smartly on the bottom when you meet him next and say you "My brother that was in Po-lá [Pola[29]] is going to send you your two guineas, he says."[30]

»   »   »   »   »   »   »   »   »

Shorty thereafter, he again vented his spleen to his brother:

«   «   «   «   «   «   «   «   «

After all, it is only Skeffington, and fellows like him, who think that woman is man's equal. . . . By the way, is there no method you can suggest of annihilating Hairy Jaysus? Isn't he an insufferable object![31]

»   »   »   »   »   »   »   »   »

Some months before Joyce quit Ireland, Constantine (C. P.) Curran, then editor of St. Stephen's, had asked him to submit "something he could not market elsewhere," and he had obliged with "The Holy Office," which Ellmann calls Joyce's "first overt, angry declaration that he would pursue candor while his contemporaries pursued beauty."[32] Curran read part of it to Skeffington and ultimately turned it down. In June 1905, however, Joyce had fifty copies printed at his own expense and sent them to Stanislaus, instructing him to distribute them to all those interested. He cautioned him not to omit Skeffington, who noted receiving it in his diary: "N.L. [National Library] as usual. . . . Stan Joyce gave me 'The Holy Office.' I notice one change in part Jim recited to me last year — more than Spanish has become high 'Castilian.' Obscene!"[33] In the same diary entry, Skeffington noted that Joyce was purportedly at work on a novel.

By early June, Joyce had sent twenty-four chapters of that novel, Stephen Hero, to Stanislaus, saying they were to be shown only to Curran and to Vincent Cosgrave (a friend at the university and his model for Lynch in Ulysses). Curran, however, lent them to Tom Kettle, who must either have shown them to Joyce's friend J. F. Byrne or talked them over with him, for Skeffington recorded in his diary that "Byrne told me of Joyce's novel — Chapters up to 25 or 30 have recently been in Dublin with Stan. Curran & Cosgrave saw them; Byrne has appeared in it! though Joyce always denied having Epiphanized him; [Michael] Lennon also; row with [Father] Delany over paper. The child is a boy! Gogarty, says B., might easily go over to Trieste to horsewhip J. if he attacks G's mother."[34] In February Joyce wrote his brother that he had finished chapters twenty-five and twenty-six of Stephen

Hero and added, "I am working in Hairy Jaysus at present." But Skeffington's diary indicates he had no suspicion that he also was to be immortalized in the novel. Certainly he must have known it before his death in 1916, for it was serialized in *The Egoist* from February 1914 through September 1915. And it is difficult to believe that he would not have recognized himself in the character of MacCann.

Skeffington completed his own novel shortly after his marriage. It was actually his unsuccessful play redone, and it bore the same title, *In Dark and Evil Days*. He could find no publisher for it as a book, but it did appear serially in *St. Patrick's Magazine* under the pseudonym "Christopher Francis."[35] It is a poor novel, melodramatic, the dialogue stilted and filled with patriotic rhetoric. Throughout the book, however, Skeffington's compassion for the papists and his love of Irish freedom becomes vivid. But it is clear that his metier was not fiction, for there is a sharp contrast between the quality of the writing in the novel and that displayed in his articles and even in his registrar's reports. His style was florid at least:

«   «   «   «   «   «   «   «   «

It was a bright spring day in 1798, and the plains of Wexford, as yet unstained by military massacre, breathed out all the fragrance of the youthful year in response to the caressing rays of the sun. Sweetly sang the mating songsters on every tree and hedge, but nowhere, surely, more sweetly and contentedly than in the pleasant grove that stood close by Kyan's farm.[36]

»   »   »   »   »   »   »   »   »

Skeffington was also trying to publish an essay on Henry Grattan, the Irish patriot and statesman. For this piece he had been awarded, by the Royal University, the Chancellor's Gold Medal — but not without controversy. A letter from "The Secretaries" at Royal University brings the matter into focus. It reads, in part:

«   «   «   «   «   «   «   «   «

In reference to your English Prose Essay, for which you have been awarded the Chancellor's Gold Medal, we are directed by the Senate to state that the award has been made on the literary merits of the Essay alone, that the Senate does not hold itself in any way responsible for the opinions expressed in the Essay and that, if you decide on publishing it, you will insert a statement to this effect in the preface.

We wish to add that the Essay will not be printed by the University; it has not been customary to print the Essays to which the Chancellor's Gold Medal has been awarded.[37]

»   »   »   »   »   »   »»   »   »

Skeffington's friends were jubilant about his award. A letter from one applauded the selection of his subject, the success of the essay, and "above all" Skeffington's loyalty to his political beliefs.

«   «   «   «   «   «   «   «   «

You must have felt . . . that the expression of Irish national sentiments
in an essay which had to go before the examiners of a university
endowed by the English government, was not the best guarantee of
success; and while you are to be complimented upon the literary
standard to which your paper must have attained you are to be still more
congratulated upon having succeeded in gratifying a laudable ambition
without compromising your principles on an occasion when such
compromise seemed almost to be necessary for success.[38]

»   »   »   »   »   »   »   »   »

Other friends echoed these sentiments. The essay went unpublished, but not
for lack of trying. Skeffington approached such diverse outlets as Macmillan,
Longman's Green, the *Cornhill Magazine*, and *Donahoe's Magazine* of
Boston, Massachusetts.

The facts that Skeffington was now married and that he held a responsible position at the university deterred him not at all from endangering that
position by continuing his fight against the university's attitude toward
women. A document had been circulated by the Women Graduates Association asking that women be admitted on an equal basis with men.
Skeffington not only drafted the document but worked diligently to procure
signatures for it both within and outside the college. When his involvement
came to the attention of Father William Delany, the president, he sent
Skeffington a note pointing out that, as an officer of the college, Skeffington
really did not have the right to advocate opposition policy. In reply, Skeffington said that he knew of no official policy that he had violated, and that
he believed that the earlier admission of women to Trinity College had
increased the need for University College to follow suit, as proof of being no
less progressive. He added that he wished to submit his resignation with
six months' notice so that he might be free to express his opinions in the
future. Characteristically, Skeffington stated later that Father Delany's
action was not unfair and that, as president, he could not have acted in any
other way.

The decision to resign may have seemed hasty and rash (the family
income would now be cut by one hundred pounds); it was, however, neither.
Not too long before, he had written a letter to *New Ireland* protesting the
warm reception given by the bishops at Maynooth to Edward VII. He had
attributed their subservience to their desire to secure for Maynooth a share in
the grant that was expected to be forthcoming to a Catholic university.
Because of his position at the college, Skeffington had not dared to sign his
name to the letter. To him this was too high a price to pay for security.
Hanna agreed. Furthermore, she was teaching, neither of them was particularly interested in the pursuit of wealth, and both hoped that Skeffington
could meet their scanty requirements as a freelance journalist. He was not
unaware that his plans were grandiose. A 7 March 1904 item in "Facts and

Fancies" reads: "Three little (!) projects of the week; (1) to learn Irish, for historical & literary purposes; (2) to learn Russian, for modern literature; (3) to brush up Greek, & study the dramatists especially Sophocles, and (4) to make a systematic study of Botany with Hanna — an introduction to definite science for both of us." For years he had been dreaming also of starting a publication which he planned to call *The Dawn*; all his ideas would find a home there. He thought of it as, among other things, "a comic journal, sort of Irish Punch — a literary journal pure & simple &c."

During the next few years, Skeffington wrote for most of the short-lived publications of the day — the *Review of Reviews, New Ireland, The Nationist*, the *National Democrat*, the *Irish Peasant, Young Ireland*, and the American Socialist publication, the *Call*. At one time or another, he was the Irish correspondent for the French Socialist paper *L'Humanité* and for the *Manchester Guardian*. He wrote also for the London *Daily Herald* and continued to write for the *Freeman's Journal*. W. H. Brayden, editor of the last publication, absolutely refused to allow him to do any political articles. He would, he said, use only material on noncontroversial subjects from Skeffington's pen. Once, after reading an article that he had suggested Skeffington write on rats, he sent for its author. "Mr. Skeffington," he said, "I really do not know what I can do with you. You have written about rats as if they were an oppressed nationality."[39] In those publications in which he was allowed to express himself, Skeffington's favorite targets were Gaelic Leaguers, bishops, and conservatives; as time went on he concentrated more heavily on the need for women's suffrage and improved labor conditions.

Because the Skeffingtons' interests were so similar, because they worked so well together, and because they enjoyed being together, organizational activities became very much a part of their social life. Both were members of the Dublin Parliamentary Debating Society and the Catholic Graduates Association — indeed, Skeffington had been helpful in supplying names for a membership list when the latter organization was being launched in 1903. In what was to become a pattern, both resigned in 1904 "over a matter of principle." The "matter of principle," according to a letter from C. J. Murphy, the organization's secretary, seemed to be the right of nonmatriculated students at the Cecilia Street Medical School to belong to the association. "I must admire the courageous way in which you acted upon your convictions," Murphy wrote.[40] Francis was also a member of the Rationalist Press Association, based in London. Apparently he was not yet ready to have his stand on the issue of rationalism known, however. When he sent that association his membership dues, he asked — uncharacteristically — "to be entered on list of members under initials only: F. S. S."[41]

The social life of the Skeffingtons included long evenings of talk at the Sheehy home. The erudite and witty Tom Kettle would be there courting Mary, and Cruise O'Brien, who was to marry Kathleen, the youngest, would often be present as well. Much of the talk centered around their dissatisfaction with the Irish Party and with the United Irish League. They were critical of what they considered the hide-bound and antifeminist attitudes of both.

The Convention of June 1900 had found the Parliamentary Party forces reunited, with the U.I.L. as the official organization. At that time the membership had risen from thirty-three thousand to sixty-three thousand; by August 1901 it could boast of one hundred thousand members in one thousand branches. Although the U.I.L. was not as militant as the Land League had been, it did employ the boycott and various forms of intimidation. Fearing the League's strength, George Wyndham, the Chief Secretary — a minor poet and partly Irish — had reluctantly resorted to coercion. By the autumn of 1902 more than half the country had been "proclaimed" because of the League's illegal activities, and a number of M.P.'s had served terms in prison. Since these tactics did not come easily to Wyndham, he promoted a conference between landlords and tenants, thus laying the groundwork for his Land Act of 1903 — known as the Wyndham Act. Its main provision was that, subject to the approval of three-quarters of the tenants and, of course, the landlords, on any given estate, the government could purchase the land and resell it to the tenants at a rate below the existing rates.

The fact that William O'Brien, founder of the United Irish League, went along with the Wyndham Act — seeing it as a fine combination of "conference plus business" — was a source of disillusionment to Francis and Hanna and their circle.[42] They felt strongly that the tenants were being duped and that, furthermore, attempts to eliminate specific grievances would simply weaken the Home Rule movement. A new national consciousness was developing in these young people — partly as a result of the efforts of the Gaelic League, it must be said. In 1903 they felt that, with the Tory Party in control in England, there was little hope at the moment. Nevertheless, they also felt that self-respect, self-reliance, and a determination to be true to their ideals would go far to assure the survival and prosperity of Ireland, and in time bring about its freedom. A wave of optimism was engulfing them. Perhaps if the Liberal Party came into power in England, pledged as it was to Home Rule for Ireland, the Irish Party might have its opportunity.

This hopefulness of the younger generation, combined with their discontent, led, late in 1904, to the formation of the Young Ireland Branch of the United Irish League. Skeffington and Kettle were both instrumental in its formation, and Kettle was its first chairman. Immediately it attracted a varied group of gifted and dedicated men, such as P. J. Little, Richard and Eugene Sheehy, Cruise O'Brien, Richard Hazleton, William Fallon, Tom Madden, and James Creed Meredith. John Redmond and other party chiefs were delighted. They had been feeling out of touch with the younger generation because of the number of societies, groups, movements, and publications that had been springing up critical of the party and of its organizational arm, the United Irish League. Now there was a brilliant group of men —

many of them destined to wield great influence in the future, they felt sure — offering to cooperate with the U.I.L. As a consequence, the new organization was given the keys to the League's spacious rooms in O'Connell Street and some extremely favorable publicity. *The Leader*, edited by the irascible D. P. Moran,[43] greeted the formation of the young Ireland Branch enthusiastically in its issue of 10 December 1904. It had been hoped, said *The Leader*, that a few young, sensible men would step into the political arena. They were happy to see that young men like T. M. Kettle and other distinguished university men were doing just that.

Tom Kettle, out of the university since 1902, had been concentrating on his duties as editor of *St. Stephen's* and writing regularly for the *Freeman's Journal*. It seemed to him that at this point the college publication could safely be left to the young students, among whom there was considerable talent. It was time for him to make a change. A legal career did not appeal to him, although he was called to the Bar in 1905. He was, however, becoming interested in a career in politics. To further that ambition, he knew, it would be necessary to reach a broad audience. A new publication seemed to be the answer. In September 1905, then, Kettle's new weekly, *The Nationist*, came into being. He had a fine collaborator in his friend Francis Skeffington.

Knowing that there was always the possibility of ideological disagreement, Skeffington cautioned himself in his diary: "I must watch Kettle —not hamper him, or have friction — but be an adviser, &c. so that when crisis comes I may be able to pull him my own way."[44] When, finally, the first issue appeared, he wrote, "Nationist out; cultured, academic looking . . . past the Leader at first stride; more culture & variety than U.I. [*United Irishman*] but less force. Political note gd.; cloven hoof of Jesuits only visible in Clery's article on Scholarships."[45] Within weeks it became obvious to Kettle that he would not be able to handle *The Nationist* as a weekly without an assistant editor. Saying to Skeffington, "[I] don't agree with you in everything but you're a strong man & believe in ideals,"[46] he offered him the position. Skeffington accepted.

For the newly formed Young Ireland Branch of the United Irish League, *The Nationist* became a genuine source of encouragement and inspiration. It supported the Home Rule movement but attacked the complacency of its leaders, endorsed women's suffrage, and deplored the conditions under which Dublin workers lived. Although friendly to the aims of Sinn Fein — the Sinn Fein movement had started that year — it disapproved of its methods. As for the Gaelic League, the paper was extremely critical of its stands, with Skeffington writing that it "appears to be fostering all the predominant mental vices of the average Irishman — fluent, meaningless rhetoric, extravagance of thought and language, wild disregard for self-control."[47] At the same time, the paper heartily supported the development of Irish industries and the revival of national games, music, song, and other amusements. Naturally, *The Nationist* attacked the Unionists and was attacked by them — as well as by the Gaelic League, Sinn Feiners, and the clergy. "From this we may conclude that it was a reasonably fair and impartial little paper," Roger McHugh says in his profile of Kettle and Skeffington in *The Shaping of Modern Ireland*.[48] The great pity was that it was to have a very short life; the last issue was published on 5 April 1906, a mere half-year after its inception.

It was in *The Nationist* that Skeffington's "Dialogues of the Day," which added considerably to his reputation, first appeared.[49] The "Dialogues" gave him an opportunity to present controversial views in the form of conversations between characters labeled Baronet, Engineer, Curate, Barrister, and Bookman, to name a few. On the subject of Russia, for instance:

«   «   «   «   «   «   «   «   «

"These commotions in Russia," said the Baronet, comfortably, "make a man feel thankful he's living under the protection of the British Constitution."

"They make one feel thankful to be alive anywhere," said the Engineer in his sharp, staccato tones. "Organised Democracy is learning its power, thank God!"

"I thought," said the Curate with a slight sneer, "you didn't believe in God."

"I never said . . . ," began the Engineer, hotly; but the Barrister's smooth, even voice struck in: "No personal imputations, please! It isn't fair to brand a man as an Atheist because he doesn't agree with your theories on politics or education. But about Russia. Do you know what I consider the most striking feature of the Revolution?"

"The prominent part taken by the intellectuals," said the Bookman. "Not that there's anything new in that; it's a constantly recurring feature of revolution."

"More remarkable than that," said the Barrister, "is the solidarity of the Russian workmen with their Polish brothers. Witte thought he could treat Poland as he liked — counted on Russian race-prejudice to back him up. And behold he provokes a fresh general strike among these very Russians!"

"Organised labour knows no country," said the Engineer.

"Oh, doesn't it?" said the Curate. "How many English workingmen would you get to go on strike to secure freedom for Ireland?"[50]

»   »   »   »   »   »   »   »   »

Thus did Skeffington advance his ideas on the church, women's suffrage, and any other issue he considered vital.

With the expiration of *The Nationist*, Skeffington decided to publish the "Dialogues" weekly in pamphlet form and distribute them from door to door. For the first few weeks, several thousand copies were distributed free, with the hope that the recipients would be interested enough to subscribe. A self-addressed postcard accompanied the little paper instructing the reader to report "any irregularity in the delivery" and pointing out that "distributors have instructions not to place subscribers' copies in the letter-box, but to hand them in, stating for whom they are intended. As the paper will, however, be handed in without a wrapper, subscribers are requested to take their own precautions to ensure that it is not mislaid within the house — which might cause undeserved blame to fall upon the distributors."[51] Skeffington's attention to detail and his insistence on leaving nothing to chance are clearly reminiscent of his father.

The first issue of the "Dialogues" promised to give "concentrated expression" to all sides of a controversy and to take a stand for "freedom of opinion and business enterprise — the two things most needed in Ireland."[52] Readers were invited to use the paper as a forum. They were also urged to write giving their frank opinion of it, and many did. Letters arrived from Stephen Gwynn, Edward Martyn, Padraic Colum, and H. G. Wells — and one from Tom Kettle, which resulted in an amusing interchange. "Your first issue," Kettle wrote, "displays a liberality of mind and a power of imagining yourself into the skins and souls of other people that seems to be absolutely morbid. . . . A little more of the music of insoluble antithesis in your ears and you will be a cynic or a Hegelian. You once professed to be a social reformer! Do you not know that for a social reformer, narrow mindedness is the beginning of wisdom?" Skeffington retorted, "In this interesting comment I perceive the cautious flight of the eagle who is about to adapt himself to the role of the trained falcon."[53]

John M. Robertson — politician, rationalist, literary critic, liberal, and soon-to-become member of Parliament — offered a suggestion. Perhaps a single subject should be developed more thoroughly in subsequent numbers, he said, "but no doubt your first number is meant to be a sample of your range. . . . Dialogues . . . seems to me excellent & I hope you will carry it out."[54] Another subscriber wrote, "I am glad to find anyone standing up for Freedom of Speech not merely for freedom to say what he likes himself. . . . I am not a Nationalist, but I think the Nationalists, Gaelic Leaguers, etc. have just as much right to express their opinions as any Unionist, but no more . . . none of them have any right to prevent others saying their say."[55] James Joyce commented that "It is very 'brilliant'. Three pages of puff by F. S. S. at the end: full of thick typed catch phrases such as 'this novelty in Irish journalism' 'order at once' 'absolutely unique'. An advt appears for some booklet by (very big letters) THOMAS KETTLE, M.P."[56]

All the attention was very gratifying for Skeffington, but perhaps his most provocative correspondent was James Owen Hannay. Hannay was a Church of Ireland clergyman and an Anglo-Irish novelist, who published his theological writings under his own name but his humorous novels of Irish life under his pseudonym, George A. Birmingham. Skeffington and Hannay had met early in June[57] and had found conversation with each other

extremely stimulating. Hannay had taken to Hanna as well. He told Skeffington, after his first meeting with her, that he was sorry not to have had an
opportunity to talk with her at greater length. "True wisdom," he said, "has a
gentle voice & is drownded by brazen throated emptiness."[58]

After seeing the first issue of "Dialogues," Hannay sent in his subscrip-
tion and indicated that he thought the idea brilliant. If Skeffington could
keep up the standard of the first issue, he might succeed in making his
readers "*think*, a thing which most of our publications studiously refrain
from doing & which is yet, next to honesty, the thing most wanted in Irish
life." To him the dialogue was one of the most thought-provoking forms of
writing, for "the irritation occasioned in most of our minds by seeing other
people's opinions stated plainly & fairly, as it were by one of themselves, is
most excellent as a mental tonic."[59]

Other letters from Hannay followed and, in every case, Skeffington
found them enlightening. Since his early college days — as his conversations with Joyce indicate — he had given much thought to religion; consequently, one particular letter from Hannay intrigued him. Hannay had been
reading *Disestablishment in France* by Paul Sabatier, a French Protestant
theologian. The author, he wrote Skeffington, "regards 'clericalism' which
he very carefully distinguishes from Catholicism as the great enemy of
democracy & therefore of human progress." Hannay found the book particularly interesting "as an Irishman" and urged Skeffington to read it. He
hoped, he said, that "we as a people will have the wisdom not to confuse
clericalism, which is subversive of all human progress, with religion which is
essential to man's true well being; or even with Catholicism, which is
perhaps the noblest expression the world has ever found of the religious
spirit."[60] Subsequent events showed that Skeffington did not entirely agree.

By September 1906 it became obvious that the burden of turning out
even a small publication singlehandedly was too great; consequently, the 22
September issue was its last. But "Dialogues" had made its mark. Interviews
with such figures as Annie Kenney, the suffragist, and R. Lindsay Crawford,
the editor of the *Irish Protestant*, had not gone unnoticed. As a result,
Skeffington was promised that "Dialogues of the Day" would appear in the
Irish Peasant. That paper, under the editorship of W. P. Ryan, an ardent
Irish Irelander, had started as a small publication in Navan, but it now had
offices in Dublin and was being widely read. It seemed a suitable outlet for
Skeffington's writings, but just two months later that publication closed its
doors as well — a cardinal had lodged a complaint with the paper's owner,
Mrs. McCann, that the *Irish Peasant* was anti-Catholic. More fuel had now
been added to the fire of Skeffington's discontent with the clergy.

Years later, Skeffington reviewed a book by W. P. Ryan, *The Pope's
Green Island*, in which the author told of his "five years' battle against
clericalism." Skeffington gave him full marks for recording without bitterness his opinion that there was in Ireland a clerical group, "comprising

nearly all the older ecclesiastics and bishops, who entertain the most outrageously arrogant views of their mission and authority," but that, on the other hand, a great many laymen, mostly Catholic, were determined to stand up against these "clerical encroachments" on their rights. It was Skeffington's firm belief, however, that the fight against clericalism would not be successfully fought "in Mr. Ryan's genial, tolerant, serene spirit," but would "meet its Nemesis at the hands of the Irish Labour movement, which, by simply going about its own business and ignoring the fury which the clergy must continue to lavish upon it, will prove an effectively shattering force."[61]

NOTES TO CHAPTER 3

    1. McHugh, "Thomas Kettle and Francis Sheehy-Skeffington," p. 133.
    2. Diary of Francis Sheehy-Skeffington, 14 February 1902.
    3. Ibid., 3 September 1902.
    4. J. B. Skeffington to F. Sheehy-Skeffington, 19 February 1903.
    5. J. B. Skeffington to F. Sheehy-Skeffington, 19 December 1902.
    6. Eugene Sandow to F. Sheehy-Skeffington, 9 January 1903.
    7. Diary of Francis Sheehy-Skeffington, 9 January 1902.
    8. Ibid., 21 November 1902. The manuscript referred to here was seized by the British military when they raided the Sheehy-Skeffington home on 28 April 1916, three days after Skeffington's murder. It was later returned in battered condition with some pages missing.
    9. O. Sheehy-Skeffington, "Francis Sheehy-Skeffington," p. 137, and Hanna Sheehy-Skeffington's "Biographical Notice," in *In Dark and Evil Days*, by Francis Sheehy-Skeffington, p. xii. Hanna Sheehy-Skeffington gives 1902 as the year of her husband's appointment as registrar. Owen Sheehy-Skeffington records it as 1903. An undated bulletin issued by University College, Dublin, lists "Skeffington, Francis J. C." as "Registrar, University College, Dublin, 1901."
    10. Kennedy Miller to F. Sheehy-Skeffington, 17 March 1903.
    11. P. J. Hopper to F. Sheehy-Skeffington, 4 May 1903.
    12. J. B. Skeffington to F. Sheehy-Skeffington, 17 March 1903.
    13. J. B. Skeffington to F. Sheehy-Skeffington, 18 May 1903.
    14. "Facts and Fancies," 13 January 1903. As further examples, he cited Henry Grattan, an eighteenth-century Irish statesman, and Grattan's contemporary, M.P. Henry Flood, and their divergent attitudes in the face of parliamentary reform and Catholic emancipation. "Flood," he wrote," supported the first & opposed the second; Grattan's position was just the reverse. Yet both were men of great ability & noble ideals; & both these reforms are now acknowledged to have been necessary & salutary. So infinite as T. P. says are the amalgams of personality." (The T. P. referred to may have been T. P. O'Connor, contemporary editor and nationalist M.P., known universally as "T. P." or, on occasion, "Taypay.")

15. Ibid., 25 March 1903.

16. Ibid., 13 January 1903.

17. Ibid.

18. Ibid., 9 February 1903.

19. Ibid., 22 January 1903.

20. Marriage license of Hanna Sheehy and Francis Skeffington, Sheehy-Skeffington Papers.

21. F. Sheehy-Skeffington to Rose Skeffington, 28 July 1903.

22. F. Sheehy-Skeffington to James Joyce, 29 September 1903.

23. Ellmann, *James Joyce*, p. 145.

24. Mary Colum and Padraic Colum, *Our Friend James Joyce* (London: Gollancz, 1959), pp. 55–57.

25. Diary of F. Sheehy-Skeffington, 2 August 1902.

26. F. Sheehy-Skeffington to James Joyce, 6 October 1904, Joyce Collection, Department of Rare Books, Cornell University Library, Ithaca, N.Y.

27. Ellmann, *Selected Joyce Letters*, p. 54n.

28. Ibid., pp. 53–54.

29. Pola is a small town 150 miles south of Trieste, where Joyce resided for a time.

30. Ellmann, *Selected Joyce Letters*, p. 58.

31. Ibid., pp. 67–68.

32. Ibid., p. 171.

33. Diary of F. Sheehy-Skeffington, 23 August 1905.

34. Ibid., 12 September 1905. The Gogarty referred to is Oliver St. John Gogarty, with whom Joyce for a time shared quarters in Martello Tower, the setting for the first section of *Ulysses*.

35. Skeffington's novel, *In Dark and Evil Days*, was finally published after his death by James Duffy and Co., 1916, and reissued by that publisher in 1936.

36. Francis Sheehy-Skeffington, *In Dark and Evil Days* (Dublin: James Duffy and Co., 1916), p. 1.

37. Royal University of Ireland to F. J. C. Skeffington, Esq., 9 March 1903.

38. W. O'Brien to F. Sheehy-Skeffington, 5 November 1903. It is not clear which O'Brien this is.

39. Sheehy, *Please the Court*, p. 34.

40. C. J. Murphy to F. Sheehy-Skeffington, 12 January 1904.

41. F. Sheehy-Skeffington to Rationalist Press Association, 11 January 1904.

42. This attitude was shared by Michael Davitt, John Dillon, and the *Freeman's Journal*.

43. D. P. Moran formed the weekly *Leader* in September 1900 and was its editor for thirty-six years. he opposed interdenominational education, and believed that pushed to its logical conclusion "anti-clericalism" meant "anti-Church," (see 28 April 1906 *Leader*). He also disapproved of James Connolly and of socialism, protested the production of *Playboy of the Western World*, and advocated the revival of the Gaelic language. Over the years, he delighted in baiting Skeffington.

44. Diary of F. Sheehy-Skeffington, 15 September 1905.

45. Ibid., 21 September 1905.

46. Ibid., 28 September 1905.

47. McHugh, "Thomas Kettle and Francis Sheehy-Skeffington," p. 129.

48. Ibid.

49. *The Nationist*, 23 November 1905.

50. Ibid.

51. "Dialogues," July 1906.

52. Ibid.

53. Ken Hannigan, "The Evolution of Skeffy: Francis Sheehy-Skeffington and Irish Social Democracy 1906–1916," undergraduate dissertation, (University College, Dublin, 1973), p. 6.

54. John M. Robertson to F. Sheehy-Skeffington, 9 July 1906.

55. A. Purser to F. Sheehy-Skeffington, 24 August 1906.

56. Ellmann, *Selected Joyce Letters*, p. 99.

57. James Owen Hannay and Skeffington were introduced by R. Lindsay Crawford, of whom much more will be said later.

58. Hannay to F. Sheehy-Skeffington, 20 June 1906.

59. Hannay to F. Sheehy-Skeffington, 7 July 1906.

60. Hannay to F. Sheehy-Skeffington, 20 June 1906.

61. *Irish Review*, Vol. II (June 1912), pp. 222–224.

4
Davitt Immortalized 1906

Late in May 1906 Skeffington received a note from his friend Frederick Ryan, a socialist and journalist who, because he had never been able to earn a living writing, worked as an accountant. Although he was young, he had for years been connected with unpopular movements and little-known newspapers. He had been a member of the old Celtic Literary Society, had acted in the Irish National Theatre, and had even written a play — a crude production, by his own admission — called *The Laying of the Foundations*. He had contributed some excellent articles to *The Nationist*; one in particular was a crushing indictment of the entire legal system, which he viewed as utterly useless for the prevention of crime — indeed, even dangerous. Skeffington had been intrigued by and respectful of Ryan's ideas and abilities and, until Ryan's death in 1913, the two men maintained a close political, intellectual, and personal relationship. His May 1906 letter to Skeffington suggested that they meet with Kettle, William Maloney, and Maurice Joy (the latter two were friends of both Kettle and Skeffington). "If nothing better, we can at least talk things over," he wrote.

Ryan's request for a meeting was inspired by a landslide victory for the Liberals in the British elections of January 1906, a victory that had ended the lengthy Unionist rule. There seemed also to be a healthy shift toward more liberal thinking in Protestant groups such as the Independent Orange Order, which presaged a less sectarian approach to politics.[1] Ryan's thought was that the five men might form a nucleus for a National Democratic Committee. A meeting was duly arranged and held; Kettle suggested that they prepare a handbook that would present a program of democratic nationalism, each agreed to prepare an outline for such a handbook before their next meeting, and a committee was formed. It was their hope that Michael Davitt might be persuaded to become the committee's chairman. They even talked of starting a new weekly paper as the organ of their movement. Under Davitt's imprimatur, they felt, such a paper would be guaranteed a substantial circulation.

That evening they all read newspaper reports of Davitt's illness — he had undergone an operation on his jaw some weeks earlier and was still in the Mount Street Hospital. Stimulated by their discussion, reluctant to take leave of each other, and sure he would be eager to learn of their plans, they decided to visit him. They found Davitt gravely ill, however, and not allowed to have visitors. Skeffington recorded the events in his diary: "As the great democratic leader lies dying, we form a Committee to carry on his work. Strange!" And, two days later, " 'He's dying — can't live till morning'. . . . In night [Hanna] started up and hastily got out of bed in her sleep, frightened by a dream. Didn't look at time, but, as near as I can guess, it must have been just about midnight — the time Davitt died."[2]

Immediately after Davitt's death, a grief-stricken nation began to make plans for a public funeral. Davitt's will, however, strictly forbade it. If he died in Ireland, it stated, he wished to be buried at Straide, County Mayo, "without any funeral demonstration." If he should die while in America, he wished to be buried in his mother's grave near Philadelphia. If death occurred anywhere else except in Great Britain, he asked to be buried in the nearest graveyard with the simplest of ceremonies. Only if he died in Great Britain should his body be sent back to be buried at Straide, County Mayo. The will continued, "My diaries are not to be published as such, and in no instance without my wife's permission; but on no account must anything harsh or censorious written in said diaries by me about any person, dead or alive, who has ever worked for Ireland, be printed, published, or used so as to give pain to any friend or relative." If ever a will expressed the man, it was this one. His concluding sentence read, "To all my friends I leave kind thoughts; to my enemies the fullest possible forgiveness; and to Ireland the undying prayer for the absolute freedom and independence which it was my life's ambition to try and obtain for her."[3]

Although plans for a public funeral had to be abandoned, Davitt's followers refused to be cheated of this opportunity to honor a man who had done so much for Ireland. When his body was taken from the hospital to Clarendon Street Church, an enormous crowd followed and filled the church in relays even though the funeral arrangements had been given no publicity. Another crowd gathered at the graveside at Straide.

Davitt's death affected Skeffington profoundly. Now twenty-seven, this was actually his first brush with fatal illness. Somehow the sixty-year-old Davitt had seemed indestructible. As recently as two months earlier Skeffington had heard him speak at the Mansion House; it was all too sudden to comprehend. Just a few days after the funeral, Skeffington spent the whole day in the National Library reading some of Davitt's writings and the newspaper files concerning him. That night he wrote in his diary, "What a pity he did not live to write the history of Fenianism as he proposed! What a pity I never knew him!" He had thought of speaking to Davitt at the Mansion House meeting about the introduction of an anti-enlistment resolution and now regretted keenly that he had not done so. At home that night, before going out to visit Fred Ryan, he reread the letters Davitt had written to him and was struck by Davitt's "pathetic isolation." Later that night he confided to his diary that "the pain of his loss goes ever deeper." He added that though he felt that Ryan was the soul of the National Democratic Committee, he thought that he, Skeffington, was "nearest in temperament to Davitt."[4]

It seemed obvious to Skeffington that, because of Davitt's death, it would be necessary to postpone National Democratic Committee plans. It was, however, not in his nature to do nothing. His first move to advance Davitt's ideas and to keep them fresh in the public mind was to prepare a lengthy article about the activities of Davitt's last years. He called it "Clericalism and Democracy in Ireland" and considered the *Independent Review*, a British radical monthly, the right outlet for it. It was accepted for publication subject to two conditions: Skeffington must tone down or omit completely his sentence criticizing T. M. (Tim) Healy, M.P., and he must not give the impression that the *Review* endorsed the views expressed in the article. The editor suggested that the title be altered to indicate that the views expressed were those of Davitt and those who agreed with him. It might be called "Michael Davitt's Unfinished Campaign." Skeffington agreed.

His article used as its base Davitt's 1905 visionary article, "The Irish National Assembly (Session of 1910)." In it, Davitt had speculated on what the composition of an Irish National Assembly might be after the first Home Rule elections. He proposed that a liberal coalition would take control of the assembly away from the clerical and conservative party of John Redmond. Potent influences might bring this about, such as general enthusiasm for national and practical education aroused by the Gaelic League, and the boom in Irish manufacturing following a large investment of American money. In addition, he postulated that Irish bishops would consent to stop agitating for an Irish Catholic University in return for an annual grant of fifteen thousand pounds for University College in Dublin. An amusing and thought-provoking article, it had charmed Skeffington at the time of its appearance and he now made full use of it, particularly the section that foreshadowed the overthrow of the Irish Clerical Party.[5]

Davitt had written to Skeffington that he had "frequently had to 'bell the cat' in popular politics, only to be deserted by those who advised me most warmly to the adoption of such a course." He had also said, in a speech made at the Irish Party Convention of 1903, "I have been in a minority all my life." Skeffington used these lines as illustrative in his assessment of Davitt's character. He maintained that Davitt was partly responsible for this isolation. "He carried self-abnegation too far," Skeffington wrote. Simply because Davitt saw how dissension throughout Ireland's history had torn the country apart, he was too willing to sacrifice himself for the benefit of his country and too ready to stand aside for those who, because of their mediocrity, were able to influence the crowd more easily. Had he acted otherwise and used his prestige to gather all the democratic elements into some kind of organization, he might have left an established National Democratic Party to carry on his work.[6] It seems clear that Skeffington planned never to repeat Davitt's mistakes.

Skeffington saw very little hope that Davitt's prophecies would be fulfilled in the near future. "The United Irish League, for the most part, is in the hands of the bourgeoisie," he stated in the article's conclusion. "The Gaelic League, for the most part, is in the hands of the Catholic Clergy." He continued:

«   «   «   «   «   «   «   «   «

> The Castle and the clergy, enemies of old, but now steadily drawing closer together, in union against the democratic ideals which both dread — between them control virtually the whole field of life and endeavour in Ireland. The few, here and there, who see clearly and think honestly, are silent perforce. That they will become many, will draw together in a conscious, active organisation, I regard as certain; that they must ultimately bring about that triumph of Democracy in Ireland cannot be doubted by any one with faith in human progress. But not so soon as 1910, — unless miracles happen.[7]

»   »   »   »   »   »   »   »   »

In all fairness, it must be said that Skeffington's article was not a model of objectivity. To call it a strong attack on the power of the clergy and their lack of principle in obtaining their ends would probably be stating it mildly.

When the article appeared in the *Independent Review*, *The Leader*, with obvious enjoyment, attacked it in a full-page review that dripped sarcasm: "The writer [Skeffington] says that the U.I.L. is in the hands of farmers and shopkeepers who have profited by the land legislation in the past, and who are now anxious to prevent its benefits from extending to the labouring classes." "Apparently," the review continued, "the coming Democracy is to consist exclusively of labourers, workmen and students. The chief qualification evidently is the non-possession of property, or, we are reluctant to add, religion." Reluctantly or not, *The Leader* underlined the point:

«   «   «   «   «   «   «   «   «

> But the main theme of the article is that clericalism is the enemy. The priests evidently are regarded as wanting to "capture" everything. Moreover, anything Catholic is evidently regarded as the enemy of anything National. Our author has the complete lingo of the secularists. He writes of Davitt as "boldly championing secular education as against the denominationalists." He speaks of "the twin tyrannies of the country — that of the British Government and that of the Catholic episcopacy," and of "the arrogant spirit of clericalism and the independent spirit of democracy."

»   »   »   »   »   »   »   »   »

From a literary point of view, the attack concluded, the article was not worth reading, but "as a revelation of the mind of (alleged) coming 'Democracy' it deserves a look — and a laugh."[8]

The Leader's editor, D. P. Moran, possessed one of the most astringent new voices of the Irish-Ireland movement. For many years Skeffington was one of his favorite targets. Actually, Moran's biting, mocking comments and the occasional jeering ballad and cartoon contributed greatly to Skeffington's reputation as a Dublin character. He took the paper's attacks upon him lightly and Moran contended that Skeffington rather enjoyed the publicity. There were few people who greeted Moran as cordially when they met on the street as Skeffington, he said.[9]

The Leader was not alone in its denunciation of the Davitt piece. In the next issue of the *Independent Review* there appeared a brilliant reply to Skeffington's article by Tom Kettle called "Religion and Politics in Ireland." Kettle's thesis was that the Skeffington picture of clerical domination was too gloomy and, furthermore, shortsighted: it did not take into consideration that "there was no such thing in Ireland as Clericalism — only individual priests."

Although Skeffington was not swayed by Kettle's points, he did appreciate the brilliance of their presentation. Adverse criticism never seemed to bother him too much, but he was pleased when James O. Hannay wrote congratulating him on the article and on his "clearness of vision, a quality comparatively rare but not quite unknown among us, & your courage, a much rarer thing in Ireland. So rare that it may be reckoned for practical purposes an unknown thing."[10]

An indirect result of the publication of the Davitt article was an offer from T. Fisher Unwin, Publishers, to "prepare and edit" some of his own articles for publication as a book. "Indeed, perhaps, you may even now have ready a book which you desire to see published," the letter stated. Unwin indicated that he hoped to hear from or meet with Skeffington, saying that, since they had been the publishers of the *Independent Review* since its inception, they were always interested in the work produced by the paper's contributors.[11]

Not satisfied with simply doing an article on Davitt, Skeffington began to give a great deal of thought to undertaking a full-length biography. Barely six months later he was ready to take the first steps. Accordingly, he wrote to John Dillon, M.P., a close friend of Davitt's, to determine if an *"authorized"* biography was contemplated. "If the work has not already been assigned to some better-known writer," he wrote, "I beg respectfully to submit my name as one capable & eager to perform this task." He said nothing about his qualifications "from a literary point of view," but stressed that he had made a thorough study of Davitt's policies and methods and was completely convinced that they were more precise than those of his contemporaries. "Such a sympathy with one's subject is, I submit, an important asset in a biographer — I will even say, an indispensable asset. The biography of a great man, like the history of a nation, cannot be adequately written without a spirit of profound sympathy," he concluded.[12]

Skeffington corresponded with Mary Davitt, Davitt's widow, as well. Some months later, a diary item read: Visited Mrs. Davitt; rather severe; opposed to my project, not fair to the children; D. so much misunderstood, much affected by tenants' disregard of his advice in 1903, etc." [13] To publisher T. Fisher Unwin, he wrote that there were a great many applicants for the role of official biographer but that no decision had been made about who the writer would be or even whether it was the right time for an authorized biography to appear. "It has been urged upon Mrs. Davitt (with whom the final decision rests), on the one hand, that to postpone the issue of the biography for years would inevitably lessen the interest attaching to it; and, on the other hand, that the biography of such a combative man could not be written for many years without such reticences & restrictions as would deprive it of much of its value," he said. She was, he felt, leaning toward the latter view, and it seemed that no authoritative biography of Davitt, based on his private papers, would be prepared for at least ten years. This being the case, he wrote Unwin, he wondered if the publisher would consider what might be called an *ad interim* life of Davitt. A definitive work, of course, would require Davitt's papers, but the unauthorized book "might fill the field & achieve a considerable sale pending the production of the official biography." [14]

By 20 July 1907 Skeffington had a contract with T. Fisher Unwin for a work to be entitled *The Life of Michael Davitt*. He described the work in a letter to his friend R. Lindsay Crawford: "It's not 'official,' and will be compiled mainly from public sources; besides, Unwin limits me to 100,000 words, — little more than a monography." But, he added, the country needed to be reminded of Davitt's ideals "at the present juncture — especially in view of the Education Bill again next year, — and though my book will be inadequate, it may be useful as far as it goes." [15]

In 1908 Skeffington's *Michael Davitt* appeared. Reviews of the book were typical of the response to most of Skeffington's efforts — either strongly supportive or loudly disapproving. Skeffington's activities, needless to say, did not evoke mild reactions. The book received immediate attention in the Irish press, much of it far from favorable. In an unsigned *Sinn Fein* review headed "The Davitt Legend," the work was treated at length — and with great disdain. Skeffington was accused of forming Davitt out of his imagination and out of ignorance. After all, Mr. Skeffington was "in petticoats" when most of the events took place. The bulk of the review was a glorification of Parnell and a condemnation of Michael Davitt for deserting him. "As we leave down the book," the unsigned review concluded, "we hear again the voice of Mr. Davitt telling the voters of Ireland to strike down Parnell and Home Rule is theirs. . . . Surging in our ears are the raucous voices of the little men who slew the giant. . . . Parnell will be remembered in his haughty manhood, and Mr. Skeffington's type of heroes in a spirit of charitable allowance." The reviewer seemed to have been upset by the fact that Davitt had expected Parnell to tell him the truth about his relationship with Kitty O'Shea — and disturbed that Skeffington approved. "Parnell was a sinner," the reviewer said, "but he was not a cur." [16]

Other voices were raised against the book; *The Peasant*, in a strong editorial on 27 June, was one of them. The *New Ireland Review* for July carried a lengthy review, which did praise "Skeffington's considerable literary gifts" but deplored the fact that he had made his book a platform for his animus against the Catholic clergy. The book is called a "textbook of anticlericalism," and, according to the reviewer, "thus written, it does injustice to the memory of a great man, throws a cloud over a name which all who knew Davitt would wish to see enshrined in the whole-hearted veneration of his countrymen."[17]

Lindsay Crawford thought otherwise. Speaking on Davitt at a Sinn Fein meeting in West Belfast, he said that Davitt's life could be studied in the Sheehy-Skeffington book, which he would like to see in the hands of every Irishman.[18] In a letter to Skeffington, he said that the book was attracting much attention in Ulster. "It is a very instructive book, & as an analysis of the movement identified with Davitt hits off very accurately the whole situation . . . there is no figure in modern times that could appeal so strongly to the democratic instinct in Ulster as Davitt." Voicing a common complaint, he said that he would like to see it issued in a cheaper edition.[19] John M. Robertson, in a letter written on House of Commons stationery, said he was particularly struck by the closing pages and wondered how "your outspoken deliverance" would be regarded by the Irish press. He concluded, "In any case the book is sure to be widely read, being so vividly and ably written. I suppose Mrs. Davitt's objections were clerically inspired. She is not likely to get another life of her husband so sympathetically and effectively written."[20]

Outside Ireland, the book was, on the whole, very well received. Reviews appeared in the *Manchester Guardian*, the *Standard*, the *Daily News*, the *Daily Chronicle*, the *Morning Post*, and the socialist publication, the *New Age*, to name only a few. In the United States, the labor leader James Connolly reviewed it quite favorably in *The Harp*. He did, however, question Skeffington's assessment of Davitt's "knowledge of men." According to Connolly's thinking, "He gave his name and his services freely at the beck and call of men who despised his ideals and would willingly, but for their need of him, have hung himself as high as Haman." He was so honest, Connolly wrote, that he believed implicitly in the honesty of others, thus becoming "the tool of political crooks and social reactionaries."

On the whole, the Connolly review dealt not so much with Skeffington's life of Davitt, as with Davitt's life — his role in the history of Ireland. Connolly considered Davitt an unselfish but naive idealist who made two fatal errors. He abhorred clerical interference in politics, but when the chance came to rally all democrats against such interference by supporting Parnell, Davitt joined the attack and thus helped maintain the priesthood's full control of secular affairs in Ireland. He was just as sympathetic to the cause of labor in Ireland as in England, Connolly's review pointed out, but he surrendered himself into the control of men who were quite willing to play upon labor sentiments in England — where such sentiments might be made a menace to British aristocracy — but "were determined to scotch and oppose such sentiments in Ireland where they might become a menace to themselves."[21]

Skeffington was intrigued by Connolly's review. He had heard much about Connolly, but this was the first time their paths had crossed, so to speak. It was interesting that this contact should be through Davitt, for Connolly was much like Davitt — and very much like Skeffington. Both were deeply committed to the emancipation of women; indefatigable agitators and propagandists, both in the spoken and written word; immune to ridicule or pressure from any source; and convinced that their purposes could be accomplished through reason and education, combined with organization and militancy. They neither smoked nor drank and, as far as can be determined, they were faithful husbands. It seems natural that they should have been active in the same organizations — Socialist, feminist, patriotic — that took unsteady root in Dublin during the decade prior to the Easter Rising of 1916. Inevitably, Connolly was to reappear many times in Skeffington's life.

Neither words of praise for his book from sources outside Ireland nor the storm of abuse from within had very much effect on Skeffington. He considered the work merely a "primer" of Davitt and not an exhaustive study. It had been written to "revivify" the ideas of Davitt in Ireland (he knew full well that these ideas were not popular) and to "spread an appreciation of them" in Great Britain. This he was satisfied he had done.

Mrs. Davitt had hastened to inform the public that Skeffington's book was not an official biography of her husband. According to Edwards and Ransom in *James Connolly: Selected Political Writings*, her "Catholic piety was repelled by Sheehy-Skeffington's public profession of his abandonment of Catholicism and status as a freethinker,"[22] and that may be true. Skeffington's *Preface* ended the matter as far as he was concerned: "She [Mrs. Davitt] cannot be more anxious than I am to have it known that it has been written entirely on my own responsibility, and free from the restrictions in handling his material which are apt to hamper the endeavours of the most zealous official biographer." Her objections to any life of her husband other than an authorized one occasioned in him "neither astonishment nor resentment," for her position was "as intelligible as it is indefensible." As he saw it, "The giants of reform, of whom Michael Davitt was one, belong not to any single family, but to the world; to discuss the lesson of their lives is a right that cannot be denied to the humblest of their disciples."[23]

NOTES TO CHAPTER 4

1. This change in attitude came about to a great extent through the efforts of the liberal editor of the Dublin *Irish Protestant*, Robert Lindsay Crawford. A

statement of policy known as the Magheramorne Manifesto, which he drew up for the Independent Orange Order, was a direct appeal to Protestants for, among other forward-looking measures, greater religious tolerance (see F. S. L. Lyons, *Ireland Since The Famine*, p. 296).

2. Diary of F. Sheehy-Skeffington, 28 and 30 May, 1906.
3. F. Sheehy-Skeffington, *Michael Davitt*, p. 212.
4. Diary of F. Sheehy-Skeffington, 6 June 1906.
5. Michael Davitt, "The Irish National Assembly (Session of 1910)," *Independent Review*, April 1905.
6. F. Sheehy-Skeffington, "Michael Davitt's Unfinished Campaign," *Independent Review*, September 1906.
7. Ibid.
8. *The Leader*, 29 September 1906.
9. Ibid., 3 January 1914.
10. J. O. Hannay to F. Sheehy-Skeffington, 6 September 1906.
11. T. Fisher Unwin to F. Sheehy-Skeffington, 14 November 1906.
12. F. Sheehy-Skeffington to John Dillon, 28 February 1907.
13. Diary of F. Sheehy-Skeffington, 24 August 1907.
14. F. Sheehy-Skeffington to T. Fisher Unwin, 5 April 1907.
15. F. Sheehy-Skeffington to R. Lindsay Crawford, 24 August 1907.
16. *Sinn Fein*, 20 June 1908.
17. *New Ireland Review*, Vol. XXIX (July 1908), pp. 312–314.
18. *The Peasant*, 11 November 1908.
19. R. Lindsay Crawford to F. Sheehy-Skeffington, 18 July 1908.
20. John M. Robertson to F. Sheehy-Skeffington, 14 July 1908.
21. *The Harp*, editorial, August 1908. James Connolly's review appears in full also in *James Connolly: Selected Political Writings*, ed. Owen Dudley Edwards and Bernard Ransom (London: Jonathan Cape, 1973), pp. 210–214.
22. Edwards and Ransom, *James Connolly*, p. 209.
23. F. Sheehy-Skeffington, *Michael Davitt*, "Preface," p. 15.

5

A Gadfly's Progress   1906–1908

L ong before Skeffington wrote the Davitt biography, he was trying in every conceivable way to make his reputation as a writer. Of first importance was the establishment of a market for the dissemination of his ideas but, no doubt, he had no aversion to recognition as well. He was well aware also, though his father did not seem to believe it, that he needed to make money. Consequently, in 1905 he sought to be placed on the list of the Intermediate Education Board for Ireland from which "Examiners in English Lit. & Composition, or History & Geography" would be chosen for the year 1906. There is no indication that he met with success. He also attempted unsuccessfully to persuade A. P. Watt, a literary agent in London, to accept him as a client. And he continued to try to find publishers for his work on Grattan and his novel, *In Dark and Evil Days.*

Another venture — this one initiated jointly with Hanna — was the formation of the Irish Literary Supply Syndicate. A circular on the letterhead of the syndicate, signed by Skeffington as "General Secretary and Manager," offered to supply syndicated articles "*on Irish subjects* and *by Irish writers*, to the Irish Provincial Press." The claim was made that "a large staff of the ablest Irish writers, men and women differing in their political and other opinions, but all possessing an intimate acquaintance with Irish life and conditions" had been engaged. "Do you want to have the latest facts and prevailing views in the political world furnished to your readers by writers thoroughly conversant with political movements, and fully in sympathy with the editorial views of your paper?" the circular enquired. "Do you want to steer clear of politics altogether and to publish a series of articles on Social questions, Industries, Commerce, Science, Art, Literature or Sport?" Although the circular was sent to approximately 120 provincial newspapers, the syndicate seems to have suffered a speedy death.

Skeffington was also doing book reviews regularly for the *New Ireland Review.* One review in particular, of Stephen Gwynn's *Thomas Moore,* revealed clearly his profeminist bias. In discussing Gwynn's interpretation of Moore's family life, Skeffington objected to Gwynn's "un-modern treatment." Mrs. Moore was, he agreed, a quiet stay-at-home person, abjectly devoted to her famous husband; she rarely shared his social pleasures while

he sparkled and shone in salons. She was quite content with this arrange-
mcnt, "not having soul enough to expect better treatment; and that inasmuch
as [Moore's] genial and kindly nature made him a charming companion
when he *was* at home, their mutual relations were uniformly affectionate,"
Skeffington commented ironically. The review continued:

«   «   «   «   «   «   «   «   «

Masculine complacency loves to dilate upon the ideal nature of such a
situation, to extol the submissive wife for her patience and self-sacrifice,
while apparently struck with equal admiration at the man's condescen-
sion in occasionally returning home to light up his wife's solitude with
his presence. And Mr. Gwynn, from whom better things might have
been expected, falls into the old rut.

»   »   »   »   »   »   »   »   »

Gwynn's statement that Mrs. Moore "had her reward" infuriated
Skeffington. What was this reward? he asked. "He condescended to be
attached to her. That is all." Skeffington felt that Moore undoubtedly had
been no worse than other husbands of that period — and possibly better
than most. This did not excuse Gwynn, however:

«   «   «   «   «   «   «   «   «

It is astonishing and regrettable that, a spacious half century after
Moore's death, a man of Mr. Gwynn's acknowledged literary standing
should quote and endorse the early-Victorian exculpations of Moore as
all-sufficient, and should display no iota of consciousness that enlightened thought now regards the position of a wife from a standpoint
entirely different from that common fifty years ago.

»   »   »   »   »   »   »   »   »

The review made Skeffington's anti-Gaelic sentiments equally clear.
"Moore must be ranked among the most truly National of Irish writers," he
wrote. "No doubt such sentiments will seem rank heresy to the extremists of
the Gaelic League, by whom nothing that is not written in Irish is regarded as
Irish national literature. But signs are not wanting that the flood-tide of
Keltomania has exhausted itself, and that a saner spirit is penetrating the
ranks of the language enthusiasts."[1]

As a result of all his ventures, Skeffington's reputation was growing.
Joyce, now in Rome, took note of his activities as well as Kettle's election to
Parliament in August. "They are all in the public eye and favour: even Dr.
O. S. Jesus Gogarty," he wrote Stanislaus.[2] Skeffington was indeed in the
public eye — "favour," however, was another matter, for he never hesitated
to express unpopular opinions.

Early in 1907 he helped create another outlet for these opinions.
Skeffington's friendship with Frederick Ryan had ripened since their formation of the National Democratic Committee just before Michael Davitt's
death. Both were vitally concerned with furthering the cause of nationalism,
and neither had given up the idea of a newspaper as the instrument to do so.

They would call it the *National Democrat*, as they had planned to do when Davitt was alive. With difficulty, enough money was obtained and the first issue of the new monthly appeared in February 1907. An attempt was made to find advertisers but they were able to entice very few. The first issue carried ads for publications of the Humanitarian League (which opposed flogging, capital punishment, and prisoner abuse); for the *Reformers' Year Book, 1907*, edited by F. W. Pethick-Lawrence and Joseph Edwards; and for Maunsel and Co., publishers of Synge, Padraic Colum, Eva Gore-Booth, George Moore, and others. Paid assistance was out of the question but, eager to conceal the fact that it was purely a Ryan-Skeffington publication, they did not list their names on the masthead. Nevertheless, *The Leader* was not taken in. An editorial greeted the new *National Democrat*: "We have received yet another No. 1, Vol. 1. Knickerbockers are associated with extreme youth, and the latest 'long-felt want' to make its bow to the Anglo-Irish public, though it is called the 'National Democrat,' conjures up before us the vision of a paper in knickerbockers. . . . Though 'Democratic,' there is evidence of plenty of intellectual snobbery in it, and though 'national' we fail to find even one word of Irish in its pages."[3]

The paper's objectives were clearly enunciated. Skeffington and Ryan planned to furnish a platform for the dissemination of ideas that were "fermenting in other countries," as well as for the expression of every shade of opinion. The columns of the paper would be open to all those who wished to advance the democratic cause. Topics covered in the first issue were typical of those that would follow: a study of municipal elections in Dublin and Belfast; an item called "The Soap Bubble," which took up the question of foreign investments in Irish industry (Lever Bros., an American firm, was attempting to set up a "Soap Trust") and warned of the danger of building up a new oligarchy; an article about recruiting for the British army that showed plainly the editors' anti-war stance; and one called "Reactionary Protestantism," which needs no explanation.

An article by Skeffington called "Michael Davitt's Ideals" so incensed *The Leader* that its editors became sarcastic to the point of being vicious. It was a "cheap trick" to "clutch hold of a dead man," they stated, and went on:

«   «   «   «   «   «   «   «   «

Mr. Skeffington who, in true "democratic" spirit, has assumed a double-barrelled name, with a would-be aristocratic hyphen, proprietor and editor of the late lamented "long-felt want," called "Dialogues of the Day," clutches wildly at the late Mr. Davitt. We would say that Skeffy thinks that the mantle of Mr. Davitt has fallen upon him only that Skeffy, in a mantle, suggests so grotesque a picture that the suggestion might border on the personal. . . . Skeffy is of the opinion that Davitt would have been driven to found a party and a newspaper "to fight the twin tyrannies which oppress Ireland — the British Government and the Catholic Hierarchy." . . . Skeffy goes on: "With Davitt

gone, such a party is no longer a practicable entity — merely an aspiration. There is no one left with Davitt's unique, stainless record of unselfish service in the cause of Ireland." Of course, that is only the hyphened
democrats' banter; for no sooner has the reader finished the sentence
than the echo is expected to answer — Skeffy! This latest journalistic
spec., having the advantage of being dressed in knickerbockers, may
succeed in making the pace for others who have half a mind for the
priest-hunting job. Skeffy's "mates" — we think that it is the "democratic" term — had better hurry up if they are not to be altogether out-
distanced in the race. We wish the "National Hierarchy Hunter" all the
success he deserves.[4]

»   »   »   »   »   »   »   »   »

Such rhetoric indicated to Francis Sheehy-Skeffington that his voice was
being heard, and he was delighted. "Name known. That is 1906's chief
achievement. 1907 must make that pay," he wrote on Christmas day.[5]

Skeffington used his "Michael Davitt's Ideals" article to air his disagreement with Tom Kettle on the subject of clericalism. He called Kettle
"one of the most brilliant of the younger generation of Irish politicians," and
said that both he and Kettle stood for democratic advance and for the
"reconstruction" of the "whole fabric of Irish opinion." Unlike Kettle,
though, Skeffington believed that the enemy must be first recognized and
then assaulted. He saw that enemy as "twin tyrannies which oppress Ireland — the British Government and the Catholic Hierarchy." Kettle,
he said, used the Christian Science approach, that is, clericalism will
go away if you say it doesn't exist. He wished Kettle every success, he added,
but he himself had too little of the mystic in him to adopt Kettle's methods —
he preferred the "straightforward and courageous methods" of Michael
Davitt.[6]

Fred Ryan and Skeffington took identical stands on militarism as they
did on all issues. In a *National Democrat* editorial, they urged young Irishmen to see the logic in the stand of the Scottish-American capitalist, Andrew
Carnegie, who stated that Scotland was no longer fertile ground for recruiting for the British army and that young Scotsmen were beginning to realize
that "they were fitted for something better than to be food for powder." There
was an anti-militarist spirit at work in all the democracies, the editorial
stated, which offered the greatest hope for world peace. It was important to
have treaties between nations and to reduce and limit "the monstrous
armaments which make peace as expensive as war," but in the long run the
"simple determination" of peoples in all countries not to serve in the armed
forces, not to be "pawns in the selfish strife of dynasties," would prove the
most powerful weapon against war. Ryan and Skeffington thought it should
be obvious how important it was for men to refuse to enlist in the military in
countries where the armed forces might be used against their own kin. The
editorial concluded, "Ireland has special reasons for desiring to weaken, not

to strengthen, the British army; and this country should soon cease to provide human material to be expended in the subjection of Boers, Indians, Egyptians — or Irishmen."[7] It is ironic that Skeffington would meet his own death at the hands of an Irish recruit to the British army.

The *National Democrat* was also providing an excellent platform for Skeffington in furthering the cause of women's suffrage. He took advantage of it in "Votes for Women," an article pointing out that the climate for voting rights had changed dramatically. It was, it seemed to him, now recognized as one of the burning issues of the day; the efforts of the British Women's Social and Political Union, otherwise known as the Suffragettes — were "entirely" responsible for the change. He dated the breakthrough from 13 October 1905. On that day, Emmeline Pankhurst's daughter, Christabel, and Annie Kenney, her close associate in the suffragist movement, attended a meeting at Free Trade Hall, Manchester, at which the Foreign Secretary, Sir Edward Grey, was the principal speaker. After several of the speeches were concluded, Annie rose and shouted, "Will the Liberal Government give votes to women?" She then unfurled a banner that asked the same question. The women were evicted but not arrested — Christabel knew the law and knew that they would not be tried merely for disturbing the peace. But because she wanted to bring the matter into court — and even be taken to prison — she spit in the face of one of the policemen who had evicted them. That did it. She and Annie were taken to the police station, released without bail, and told to appear in police court the following morning. Christabel was sentenced to one week in jail and Annie Kenney to three days.[8]

"The right note had been struck at last," Skeffington wrote. The earlier years of peaceful effort by suffragists had not been fruitful, although they did lay the groundwork. But the "solid wall of prejudice, convention, and conservatism against which no logic was of any avail" had to be stormed. Skeffington deplored the fact that the Irish Nationalists, who themselves had faced police violence, were unsympathetic with "the brave women who were fearlessly facing prison and calumny to free their sex, just as Irishmen have so often done to free their country." To him, this attitude indicated clearly that it was impossible for men to imagine the position of a disenfranchised sex and that thus *only* women could successfully wage this struggle. "I hope the devoted members of the Women's Social and Political Union, undaunted by the abuse which is hurled at them, will proceed from violence to violence until their end is attained. And I have no doubt they will. These women are of the stuff of which martyrs are made," Skeffington concluded.[9]

Both Skeffington and Ryan were convinced that their paper's primary function was to criticize and thus clarify the issues of the day. They were strengthened in their conviction by many laudatory letters. Despite their readers' support, however, getting out the paper was becoming onerous. It was not simply that raising money was difficult — Skeffington was convinced they could manage that somehow — but both he and Ryan were involved in so many other things that the strain was proving too great. Furthermore, Ryan was not in good health and needed a complete rest. Thus the *National Democrat*, like so many publications of its type, was destined to have a short life.

The paper alone would not have been too burdensome for Skeffington. He was, however, working on the Davitt biography, fulfilling speaking engagements, and conducting a series of interviews in an attempt to gather material for articles. His request to Augustine Birrell, Chief Secretary for Ireland, for an interview is vintage Skeffington. He sent Birrell samples of recent writings in various British papers and claimed that he was not thinking of publishing the interview but merely wanted to satisfy himself "as to what is your outlook upon Ireland and her problems; so that, in anything I may subsequently write about you, I may feel that I understand your attitude & may be secure against even accidental misrepresentation. In return for this favour, I may perhaps be able to help you to understand certain phases of the Irish question which circumstances usually conspire to conceal from a Chief Secretary." [10]

He was also writing new "Dialogues of the Day," which made their reappearance in the May issue of the *National Democrat*. Now the characters included the Barrister, the Baronet, the Curate, the Colonel, the Engineer, the Mere Woman, and the Bookman. Once again the "Dialogues" served as an excellent platform for the airing of Skeffington's views on vaccination and vivisection (he was against both); women's rights and temperance (he was heartily in favor of both); the United Irish League, the clergy, devolutionists, and the Gaelic League (mixed feelings). A brief interchange between the Engineer and the Curate gives the flavor — and shows the bias — of the "Dialogues."

«   «   «   «   «   «   «   «   «

"That agitation about the fees for Irish," said the Engineer, "is a barefaced attempt to get an endowment for the Gaelic League out of the Taxes. I see it's now openly admitted to be such, and the League owns that it can't support its travelling teachers and organisers without this bribe."

"Why should not the Irish people," said the Curate, "do what they like with the taxes they pay?"

"Certainly," said the Engineer, "but that's different from an organisation appropriating the money in the name of the Irish people. I don't see that the Gaelic League has any more right to a bonus than the landlords."

"There aren't many like you in the country," said the Curate, "Anti-National Socialism is bound to collapse."

"By the way," said the Engineer, "what exactly *is* Anti-National Socialism?" [11]

»   »   »   »   »   »   »   »   »

One thing emerges clearly in the "Dialogues." "Mere Woman" is never given anything less than a high-minded line. The following interchange is typical. The Engineer speaks:

«   «   «   «   «   «   «   «   «

"Dublin is an old city. . . . There is no excuse for so modern a growth as Belfast. But that will only be remedied when the working men purify the Corporation, and insist upon the sanitary laws being strictly enforced."

   "And when women architects are employed," said the Mere Woman. "Men will never take sufficient thought for the hygienic requirements of a building — at least, not so long as women have to spend so much more time indoors than the superior male. That's one of the things women's suffrage will remedy."

   "The Suffragettes seem to be quieter at present," said the Colonel.

   "But none the less active," said the Mere Woman. "The exposure of that fraudulent anti-suffrage petition will open the eyes of some of our opponents."

»   »   »   »   »   »   »   »   »

Writing the "Dialogues" was for Skeffington an exciting intellectual exercise. He found equally stimulating all involvement with the theater. Both he and Hanna attended as often as possible and their diaries contain innumerable references to plays seen at the Abbey as well as plays that they reviewed. One such reference seems to indicate that Skeffington's first contact with William Butler Yeats was late in 1905. It was at a performance of Lady Gregory's *White Cockade*. "Yeats finally forces himself on me!" Skeffington wrote in his diary. He added that Yeats had been pleased that Skeffington liked Synge's plays. A somewhat later entry mentions that Skeffington attended a production of Synge's *Riders to the Sea*, and that he invited W. B. Yeats, Yeats Senior, Padraic Colum, and others for tea. "Pleasant," he recorded.[12]

   It was actually a Synge play that sparked a heated controversy at the Abbey in which Skeffington was deeply involved. A performance of *The Playboy of the Western World* had been interrupted by about forty dissidents, whose purpose was to keep the rest of the audience from hearing the play. Yeats called the police, an action that met with a great deal of criticism. Shortly thereafter a meeting was held at the Abbey Theatre at which Yeats attempted to defend himself — to the constant interruption of loud cheers, hisses, laughter, groans, and shouts of "Throw him out." His purpose in calling out the police, he said, had been to defend the playwright and the actors. A Mr. O'Donoghue rose to say that the forty demonstrators were merely performing a civic duty, since there was no government censor in Ireland. Another gentlemen, W. J. Lawrence, introduced himself as an "Irishman and an Irish play boy. (Laughter and applause)" He was not a member of any league or society, he said, but he had attended the performance at which the demonstration occurred. In twenty-five years of play-going, he had never seen a "more thoroughly intellectual, representative audience"; the play had had a fair hearing and because of "the indecent verbiage, blasphemy, and Billingsgate that was indulged in" should have been banned immediately. Skeffington's brother-in-law, Richard Sheehy, also spoke to condemn the play and to voice his approval of the demonstration. His future brother-in-law, Cruise O'Brien, did the same.[13]

Then Skeffington spoke. He was "both for and against," he said, and there was general laughter. "The play was bad [shouts of "hear, hear"], the organised disturbance was worse, the methods used to quell that disturbance were worst of all." It was his feeling that Yeats had the right to put anything he wanted on the boards and that he had a right to protest against the methods used by the demonstrators — even though, it seemed, those methods were often the only ones that *could* succeed. He felt very definitely, however, that Yeats should have tried to enlist the support of the public rather than the support of the "garrison."[14]

Before the meeting, Skeffington had made known his attitude toward the play itself in an open letter to the *Irish Times.* Written between the first and second performances of *Playboy,* he said later that he considered his comments untarnished since he had written them before "the organised disturbance and the police intervention had clouded judgment."[15] For more than three years he had been a great admirer of Synge's works, he wrote. He had seen *The Shadow of the Glen, Riders to the Sea,* and *The Well of the Saints.* Although others had criticized these plays for their "unreality, morbidity, libelling the Irish character," he had, on every occasion, championed them. He had not liked *Playboy* but he urged that it not be condemned "at second-hand," but be kept on the boards long enough "for theatre-going Dublin to form an opinion independent of any published criticisms."[16]

The letter mentioned that a few years earlier Yeats had predicted that the battle for dramatic freedom in Ireland was destined to center around Synge, and that in twenty years Synge would have a worldwide reputation. Skeffington had agreed with Yeats's assessment then and still did, he said. For that reason, he felt he could take the liberty of issuing a word of warning to Synge, "in the hope that the unfavourable criticism of his admirers may induce him to refrain from wasting his capacities on work unworthy of him, and thus retarding the fulfillment of Mr. Yeats' prophecy."[17]

Launching into his own evaluation of the production, Skeffington wrote, "*The Playboy of the Western World* is described as a comedy, but its 'humour' is of such a low and vulgar type as to disgust, not to amuse, any mind of ordinary refinement and good taste." To him, not only did the play seem badly constructed and too thin for three acts, but it showed "in a marked degree that obsession by the sexual idea which is the obverse of one of Mr. Synge's qualities; it overdoes the grotesque in character and incident."[18]

The audience's reception of what they considered Synge's "strong language" climaxed when "one particularly objectionable phrase" (the word *shifts* was not used in polite society) was uttered near the end of the third act. "I am not squeamish, and have no puritanical objection to strong language on the stage, provided it can be made to subserve an artistic purpose," Skeffington wrote. "But here it appeared to be gratuitously dragged in, as if the author had set himself to find out exactly how much his audience could stand. If that was his object, he achieved it." From then on, the play was "only audible in fragments above the noise of vigorous groaning and counter-cheering." Skeffington took no part in either, his "predominant feeling being one of regret at Mr. Synge's bad taste; but I must say that, in my opinion, the hostile demonstration, manifestly spontaneous and sincere, was thoroughly justified and distinctly healthy."[19]

A sound critical appraisal of *The Playboy of the Western World*, as well as the play's undeniable success, indicated that Skeffington's judgment was flawed. To a certain extent, this was, contrary to what he said, due to his squeamishness and a puritanical streak. "Must conquer baser emotions" and "must work hard" vied for first place in Skeffington's admonitions to himself. This rigorous moral code affected his relationship with Hanna. In his estimation, her beauty was unsurpassed; he noted often in his diaries how she wore her hair and how she dressed, and commented on her physical beauty. Yet he seemed to feel guilty about his interest in her physical attributes. He and Hanna talked often of "men's impurity" and he considered her "pure-minded" because of her "shrinking from her own beauty." These puritanical values affected both their courtship and the early years of their marriage, which, as a consequence, were not totally idyllic. Their relationship was close and tender — they complemented and needed each other — but both believed that sexual desire was something to be "conquered." The climate of the times explains this only partially. The great emphasis placed on religion in both their families and the teachings of the Catholic Church itself were heavily contributing factors. Hanna's convent training had stressed the shamefulness of her body; in fact, as Skeffington noted in his "Facts and Fancies" notebook, "Religious instruction in Eccles St. Convent is given by an aged nun Mother Theresa . . . who was so disgusted with Hanna because she didn't feel loathing at the idea of marriage."[20]

Another obstacle in the path of marital bliss was the lack of money. Aside from the obvious enjoyment that Skeffington's work was affording him, it was providing the young couple with only an intermittent source of income, but with continual friction. In May 1906 he recorded in his diary, "Debts closing in, position becoming impossible." He speculated on the possibility of asking his father for a loan to finance a literary review that Tom Kettle had suggested they launch, with Skeffington as its editor;[21] apparently, though, he ruled that out. That same month he wrote in his diary that a priest, Father Browne, had said to his brother-in-law, Richard Sheehy, that Skeffington was a "lost man," "too independent to work," and living on an "allowance from father." Although Skeffington's comment on this was that "these Jesuits are implacable!" he noted that Hanna had been extremely distressed by the whole incident.[22]

More can be learned of Skeffington's financial situation from an exchange of letters with J. F. Byrne, whose college friendship with him had persisted and strengthened. Late in January 1907, Byrne wrote "Skeff" asking if he had any money for which he had no immediate use. If so, Byrne would like to borrow ten or fifteen pounds. "Don't offer as you offered when once before I asked you for a loan, to get the money for me," he said.[23] Skeffington replied immediately. Once more, he said, he had to turn Byrne down. "You know I lost pretty heavily — that is to say, heavily for *my* resources — over the *Dialogues*. I don't regret that, because the enterprise has *paid* me in other ways, — & even pecuniarily I believe it will prove to have paid me in the long run, — but meantime the fact remains that my scanty reserve funds were depleted by that journalistic debauch, & have not since been replenished." If the *Irish Peasant* had survived, he said, he might have been in a better position. "The stoppage of that paper meant the loss of a guinea a week to me, &, although I am steadily forging connections with the English press, you will readily understand that I am not yet in possession of an income in which a guinea a week is a negligible quantity." He was extremely regretful, for "inability to oblige one's best friends is, I think, quite the worst consequence of poverty. But I hope that, sometime or other, you may be in need of money when I have it."[24]

Byrne found Skeffington's reply almost as acceptable as a loan. He agreed that inability to help a friend was one of poverty's worst features, but he did not agree with the "pious expectation that I may be in need when you have plenty. You know very well that the reverse is much the more likely." He added, less facetiously, that he thought Skeffington would never be a rich man, but "you will be a happy one; for you find your happiness, at least as much happiness as you can hope for, in pursuing your ideals, and you will sacrifice everything for them. I wish *I* had ideals to pursue."[25] Byrne's remarks were percipient and prescient. For the most part Skeffington was a happy man and, for the most part, poverty did not have too serious an effect on his marriage. Louie Bennett, a close friend of both Skeffington and Hanna, once wrote of their marriage, "It was a sort of revelation and an admonition to find two people, who seemed to live literally in the spirit of the text, 'Take no heed for the morrow,' surrendering personal aims and ambitions, and giving themselves with almost reckless selflessness to the service of humanitarian causes. But there was a joyousness in their manner of living which the more worldly and more outwardly comfortable people entirely miss."[26] She was right — but there were also periods when poverty weighed heavily on them.

When it became necessary for Skeffington to write his friend Lindsay Crawford that the *National Democrat* was discontinuing publication "for the present at all events," he said that it was not a question of money but simply lack of time: he and Fred Ryan were involved in too many other things.[27] Regardless of his claim, however, money must have played a large part in the decision. The paper had not grown as the editors had anticipated. One of the factors contributing to its lack of development was the reappearance of the *Irish Peasant* — this time called simply *The Peasant*. Although the *National Democrat* hailed the paper's appearance, it was obvious that circulation would suffer because of competition for the same audience.

Lack of time, however, was an important factor in the demise of the *National Democrat*. A check of the press in 1907 reveals that both Skeffington and Hanna managed to receive a hearing — either from the platform or the audience — at most of the meetings concerned with the significant issues of the day. A July Sinn Fein meeting was reported at great length in *The Peasant* and the *Freeman's Journal*. The meeting, whose purpose was to denounce the right wing of the Parliamentary Party, was attended by perhaps five hundred, many of them women, and speeches were delivered from a wagonette. Speaker after speaker praised the efforts of the Sinn Feiners; without them, they claimed, there would have been no Land Acts, no Arrears Act of 1882, no prospect of an Evicted Tenants Bill. Bulmer Hobson, a Sinn Fein organizer from Belfast, made a persuasive speech urging that everything English be boycotted and that the practice of recruiting Irishmen for the English armed forces be denounced. Then Francis Skeffington appeared on the platform. After being assured that he would get a fair hearing, he proceeded to express his disappointment with the preceding speeches. The Irish Party was doing its work both in Ireland and at Westminster, he said, which was as it should be. To ask the Parliamentary Party to withdraw its support from Westminster was, he felt, foolhardy. He pointed out inconsistencies within the Sinn Fein Party; for example, had John Sweetman and Edward Martyn, good Sinn Feiners, refused to pay their income taxes? No. When a member of the audience asked Skeffington whether he believed it was right for members of the Irish Party to take the oath of allegiance to the Crown as they had done, he replied that it was "a mere formality necessary in order to let the Parliamentarians get at their work." He concluded by urging the Sinn Feiners to work with the Party, not to obstruct it. As usual, his speech was interrupted by shouts, laughter, and groans. But, also as usual, he was effective. A letter from Michael O. Dempsey in Enniscorthy said, "I am so glad you put in your word against Sinn Fein on Sunday. A man from the Wexford Press is doing an interview with me for next Friday's issue in which I commit the Branch [Young Ireland Branch] to a most idealistically practical policy and repeat your dictum about the oath of allegiance."[28]

A lengthy article in Dublin's *Evening Telegraph* late in March reported a lecture by Skeffington before the University College Literary and Historical

Society, Tom Kettle presiding, which gave his views on "Ireland and the Drama." It seemed to Skeffington that the Abbey Theatre, which had opened in 1904 with great expectations, had realized them only during the very early years of its existence. His thesis was that the directors of the Abbey — and Yeats in particular — were not clear in their own minds as to whether they wanted a "literary" theater or a "national" theater. Consequently, dramatists such as Edward Martyn, George Moore, Alice Milligan, AE, Frederick Ryan, and Padraic Colum were no longer writing for the Abbey and only Yeats, Lady Gregory, and Synge remained. There were two roads for the theater to take, as Skeffington saw it. It could either produce plays by lyric poets and dramatists who were indifferent to stage success and who voiced ideals not embraced by the masses, or they could produce plays by dramatists who wanted to see them staged in their own lifetime amid the applause of their own countrymen rather than the applause of a clique. Of Yeats, Skeffington said that, though without him there would be no Irish theater at all, he did not seem to "possess the strictly dramatic gifts in proportion to his lyric genius." Of Lady Gregory, he said that her "farcical comedies are delightful, but cannot of themselves lead us much further along the road to great drama." And he called Synge "the most powerful dramatic genius in the Society." Lately, however, he added, he had "lost himself and wasted his talents in repellent studies of the morbid." He had, of course, *Playboy of the Western World* in mind.[29]

A July meeting in Tara Hall of the United Irish League at which Joseph Devlin, M.P., spoke was covered in typical *Leader* style. The editors had read, the item indicated, in Mr. William Murphy's "Nationalist organ," the *Irish Independent*, that

« « « « « « « « «

The speaker (Skeffy) wished to deprecate the fact of running the risk of an open breach with the Liberal Party, and the surrender to the arrogant type of clergymen, who, he said, were "never satisfied unless they had the laity under their feet." This tilting at the "arrogant type of clergymen" did not agree evidently with the humour of the meeting. There were cries of "Sit down" and "Withdraw" and "Shut up." Skeffy, clad in the mantle of Michael Davitt, appears to have drawn in his horns promptly. That is a rather mixed sort of a picture; but a hyphened picture admirably suits a hyphened democrat. Skeffy is reported to have expressed sorrow if he had touched on any objectionable matters! What a robust democrat, to be sure — if you don't like my views I'm sorry I mentioned them![30]

» » » » » » » » »

And so it went: account after account of the Skeffingtons' activities. Francis Sheehy-Skeffington — his name, his garb, his rather high-pitched voice — was becoming an important part of the Dublin scene. There may have been laughter at his expense, as indicated by *The Leader's* derisive tone, but he was being listened to and this was his main objective. When, in 1908, his biography of Michael Davitt appeared, his place as a Dublin personage was assured.

Before the Davitt biography appeared, however, Skeffington had revisions to make, proofs to read, an index to prepare, and editorial problems to resolve. All this, plus making speeches, writing articles, and attending a vast number of meetings took its toll. In May 1908, Skeffington fell ill with diphtheria and came close to death. As Hanna wrote him during his convalescence: "I've had a very bad fright — I may say when all is over — & I won't forget how near I felt to losing you — it's like a bad dream when I think of those days of anguish at first."[31] Her father, not surprisingly, turned to religion for help. Writing to her from the House of Commons in mid-May, he expressed his shock at "poor Frank's serious sickness," but was happy to hear "that the throat trouble was no longer dangerous." He realized how anxious Hanna was, he said, but "all I can do is to offer the Masses which I attend, for his recovery.'[32]

Early in June he went to Youghal, County Cork, to recuperate. A letter to his father from there brought money to help cover his expenses, as well as the usual advice. He was not, his father cautioned, to bathe too much: "I don't think it is good — a wash once a week in tepid water or in summer fairly cool water may be useful for cleansing. But as a stimulant it is bad — bad for the heart especially."[33] His mother, too, was concerned and instructed him to write her at least once a week,[34] though he assured her that he was "pulling up fast; doing nothing but eating & sleeping, & loafing in the open air."[35] Skeffington's friends were also worried. Fred Ryan, writing from Cairo where he was now employed, urged him not to bother replying until he was "thoroughly well." The best thing Skeffington could do for himself and his friends, Ryan wrote, would be "to take a good long rest, read no newspapers, & let humanity & its problems in Ireland & elsewhere go hang. Three months hence, it is to be sadly feared, the problems will still be there to tackle."[36]

Hanna, meanwhile, had been left to move them from Airfield Road to 21 Grosvenor Place, Rathmines, singlehandedly. She had managed to do so without too much difficulty and was settling them comfortably into their new home: an attractive, two-story brick house with the usual front garden. The move had caused Skeffington much concern, for Hanna was not feeling too well. Though almost every letter from her during his convalescence urged him not to worry, his anxiety was great enough to cause him to write to her doctor, Elizabeth A. Tennant. The doctor's reply assured him that there was no cause for anxiety. She had simply told Hanna the truth, she wrote, and had not dissembled, but there was nothing seriously wrong with her. Apparently the problem was gynecological for she added that treatment would be required for a short time and "during treatment it will be advisable to abstain from marital relations — but you both may feel quite at rest &

content that . . . there is nothing to prevent her in due course having a family." [37]

Free of that worry, Skeffington turned to the more familiar worry about money. Hanna had written him not to be disturbed: "I'm just paying nothing save milk or bread & the ordinary calls. . . . I notice people for some weird reason never press you if you only go on buying." [38] Despite her reassurance, Skeffington turned to his father for financial assistance, reluctantly but not for the first or last time. His father was quite gracious about it and assured Francis that he could have the money he needed "on whatever terms you choose to consider — I don't mind." He had been doing well with stocks and "but for the War Scare," which he hoped would soon pass, he might have done even better, he wrote. "It did a lot of harm to stocks . . . there seems a lot of explosive material still about the Balkans." [39]

By mid-July Skeffington was home from Youghal. "I am feeling quite strong & everyone says I am looking better than before I took ill," he wrote his mother. "Hanna is very busy with the intermediate papers, & will be till the end of the month." [40] He added that Hanna was too busy to write but, before the end of the month, she did. Skeffington had gone over to London and she was to join him for a long holiday. "He is looking very well now & has a good appetite. He ought to be well built up now that we are getting August away," she wrote. "But he will want it all, for he had got very much pulled down in this last fit. . . . There is a very good notice of "Davitt" in a weekly called the "Nation" this week. He is getting plenty of notices in every direction." [41] Skeffington's father differed with Hanna on this latter point. It was his impression — which he did not hesitate to communicate to his son — that the Davitt book was not receiving much attention, but "I hope you will get enough to keep going — if not let me know." [42]

But J. B. was wrong. Thanks in no small measure to the Davitt book, the British left was beginning to take note of Francis Sheehy-Skeffington. As a consequence, he was being sought out more often to write articles and reviews for such publications as *New Age*, the *Nation*, and others. His voice was helping establish the essential ties between the progressive movements in both countries. In Ireland, he was becoming more and more involved in labor politics and was being mentioned as the natural leader of an evolutionary socialist group that might emerge in a Home Rule parliament.

NOTES TO CHAPTER 5

    1. Francis Sheehy-Skeffington, "A New Life of Moore: A Review of Stephen Gwynn's 'Thomas Moore,' " *New Ireland Review*, Vol. XXIII (March 1905), pp. 34–40.
    2. Ellmann, *Selected Joyce Letters*, p. 99.

3. *The Leader*, 2 February 1907.
4. Ibid.
5. Diary of F. Sheehy-Skeffington, 25 December 1906.
6. *National Democrat*, Vol. I, No. 1 (February 1907), pp. 10–12.
7. Ibid., pp. 2–3.
8. Ibid., Vol. I, No. 3, pp. 43–44.
9. Ibid.
10. F. Sheehy-Skeffington to Augustine Birrell, 28 January 1907.
11. *National Democrat*, Vol. I, No. 4 (May 1907), p. 64.
12. Diary of F. Sheehy-Skeffington, 9 December 1905 and 20 January 1906.
13. "Parricide and Public: Discussion at the Abbey Theatre," *Freeman's Journal*, 5 February 1907.
14. Ibid.
15. F. Sheehy-Skeffington to James Cousins, 13 December 1914. Cousins had asked Skeffington for his impressions of *Playboy*. In reply Skeffington sent him a copy of his letter to the *Irish Times*, 29 January 1907, saying "I find it very interesting reading, after nearly eight years."
16. *Irish Times*, 29 January 1907.
17. Ibid.
18. Ibid.
19. Ibid.
20. "Facts and Fancies," 8 February 1903.
21. Diary of F. Sheehy-Skeffington, 11 May 1906.
22. Ibid., 15 May 1906.
23. J. F. Byrne to F. Sheehy-Skeffington, 27 January 1907.
24. F. Sheehy-Skeffington to Byrne, 28 January 1907.
25. Byrne to F. Sheehy-Skeffington, 29 January 1907.
26. Owen Sheehy-Skeffington, in "Francis Sheehy-Skeffington," p. 138.
27. F. Sheehy-Skeffington to Lindsay Crawford, 24 August 1907.
28. *The Peasant*, 27 July 1907; *Freeman's Journal*, 22 July 1907.
29. *Evening Telegraph* (Dublin), 25 March 1907.
30. *The Leader*, 27 July 1907. The "Nationalist organ" referred to was the *Irish Independent*, owned by William Martin Murphy, the wealthy industrialist who had formerly been a member of the Parliamentary Party.
31. H. Sheehy-Skeffington to F. Sheehy-Skeffington, 8 July 1908.
32. David Sheehy to H. Sheehy-Skeffington, 18 May 1908.
33. J. B. Skeffington to F. Sheehy-Skeffington, 26 June 1908.
34. Rose Skeffington to F. Sheehy-Skeffington, date unclear but sent from Ballykeel where she was visiting.
35. F. Sheehy-Skeffington to Rose Skeffington, 10 June 1908.
36. Fred Ryan to F. Sheehy-Skeffington, from Cairo, 25 May 1908.
37. Dr. Elizabeth A. Tennant to F. Sheehy-Skeffington, 17 July 1908.
38. H. Sheehy-Skeffington to F. Sheehy-Skeffington, 23 June 1908.
39. J. B. Skeffington to F. Sheehy-Skeffington, 21 October 1908.
40. F. Sheehy-Skeffington to Rose Skeffington, 12 July 1908.
41. H. Sheehy-Skeffington to Rose Skeffington, 28 July 1908.
42. J. B. Skeffington to F. Sheehy-Skeffington, 21 October 1908.

6

Tilting at Windmills   1908–1910

Like many members of the Young Ireland Branch of the United Irish League, Skeffington was growing more and more critical of the Parliamentary Party. This was one issue about which he and his constant critic, *The Leader*, agreed. Late in 1908 the paper reported, "Judging by the very brief newspaper report of the last meeting of the Young Ireland Branch . . . the Irish Parliamentary Party came in for a good deal of candid criticism. It is seldom we agree with anything Skeffy says, but he was not far short of the mark when he said that Mr. Sweetman's party was going on steadily doing nothing."[1] The dissidents in the Young Ireland Branch — the "ginger group," as they were called — had fought hard against the Irish Council Bill, offered in 1907 as a Liberal devolution scheme to substitute for Home Rule. Although John Redmond, as head of the party, had been successful in having the bill withdrawn, to Skeffington and the ginger group the whole affair was indicative of the precarious position of the Parliamentary Party and its relative lack of strength.

More than a year earlier, James O. Hannay had written to Skeffington that he had "a sort of hope that you may see the futility of continuing to support a party which has so obviously offered itself as a door mat to an arrogant & exacting clericalism." He went on to say that "liberty of speech & thought" would be safer "in an Ireland governed by Dunraven and Horace Plunkett than in one governed by the present parliamentary party. . . . The really terrible thing in government is not the ascendancy of this class of the community or that — some class under any conceivable system must be in the ascendant — but the domination of a coterie opposed to individual liberty."[2] Skeffington, while finding Hannay's sentiments provocative, thought it wiser to stay on the inside and fight.

It was not only the Home Rule issue that caused both Skeffingtons to be discontented with the party. It was the party members' apparent lack of interest in the suffrage movement as well. Need for concrete action to win the vote was beginning to be obvious to both of them and, before the end of 1908, they had met another couple who shared their belief. James and Margaret ("Gretta") Cousins were members of the Philosophical Society, as were the Skeffingtons, and their interests were quite similar — they were pacifists,

socialists, and even vegetarians. The Skeffingtons found them fascinating.
James, who had taught stenography in Belfast, wrote poetry, and plays in the
style of the Celtic bards. Gretta was a practicing medium. She was also a
proficient pianist. In fact, at a much later date her claim to fame might well
be that she occasionally acted as accompanist for James Joyce, then known
only as a young local tenor. But Gretta's main attraction for the Skeffingtons
was her militant stand on suffrage. Late in 1906, while in London, she had
attended a meeting of the National Council of Women. Fired with enthusiasm, she returned to Dublin and joined the Irish Women's Suffrage and
Local Government Association, which had been formed in 1876 by a
Quaker couple, Thomas and Anna Haslam. The Haslams were now elderly
and, although people like the Sheehy-Skeffingtons were members of the
organization, it was far from a moving force. For Gretta, it was not enough.

Both Hanna and Gretta were thoroughly convinced that militancy was
the only way to deal with the Parliamentary Party — a belief shared by the
"ginger group" — and that it was time to form a new organization to wage
the battle. Accordingly, definite plans were made at the Skeffington home in
early November 1908. One week later, the Irish Women's Franchise League
came into being, with Hanna as its secretary. They had a splendid model in
the Women's Social and Political Union in Britain, which had been formed
in October 1903 by Emmeline Pankhurst. With leaders such as Emmeline
and her daughters, Annie Kenney, and the Pethick-Lawrences, the organization had taken much action during the previous three or four years —
deputations, meetings throughout England, and the organization of workers'
groups. Like the British Women's Social and Political Union, the Irish
Women's Franchise League confined its membership to women but men
could become associate members.

Immediately upon the formation of the League, Skeffington became
an associate member. He was joined by James Cousins, Thomas Mac-
Donagh (a poet and university lecturer), and Francis Cruise O'Brien, a regular attendant at the Sheehy Sunday evenings. O'Brien's ticket of admission
had been his position as auditor of the Literary and Historical Society. The
Skeffingtons liked his ideas — his joining the I.W.F.L. was typical — but
Bessie Sheehy disapproved of him and of his obvious attraction to her youngest daughter, Kathleen. Her disapproval stemmed from the twin evils of poverty and agnosticism, which to her was almost as bad as being a Protestant.
Furthermore, he was physically unimpressive and, although he had attended
Christian Brothers School on Synge Street, talked with what amounted to an
English accent, which Bessie was sure was affected. David Sheehy was not
very fond of him either, and he had an additional reason: Cruise O'Brien was
extremely critical of John Dillon, David Sheehy's leader in Parliament and
someone he regarded highly. O'Brien's son, Conor Cruise O'Brien — a
renowned writer in Ireland and a grandson David would never really
know — writes that David Sheehy thought Cruise O'Brien "one of the most

obnoxious of the new intellectuals in the party organization . . . rich in, if little else, the power to say wounding things in a memorable manner."[3]

Until now, Bessie Sheehy had been fairly content with the men her daughters had chosen. In 1907, Margaret had married Bernard ("Frank") Culhane, whose family was "in trade" but who could be forgiven that because they were prosperous and strongly Catholic. She was quite pleased, also, that Mary and Tom Kettle were planning to marry.[4] Kettle was Mrs. Sheehy's favorite — tall, handsome, and well mannered, he was a good Catholic, a writer, a member of Parliament, and already acquiring an international reputation. Of course, Kettle drank rather heavily and smoked and she was pleased that Skeffington did neither — but then one didn't go to Mass and the other did. Obviously, you couldn't have everything. Kathleen, however, was proving a great worry. Ordinarily so sweet, gentle, and tractable, she was obstinate on the subject of Francis Cruise O'Brien. The Sheehy-Skeffingtons were fully and openly on Kathleen's side and a rift developed in the family.

Skeffington was enjoying the whole affair since it contained the excitement of the clandestine as well as a chance for him to advise and guide. A note, written early in 1909, to Cruise O'Brien reads, "You are requested to meet Dick [undoubtedly Richard Sheehy, Kathleen's brother] on the Library steps at half-past seven. After the interview, you are further requested to come out to 11, Grosvenor Place; Kathleen will be there."[5] The situation grew so bad that Kathleen, who was giving Skeffington Irish lessons, was forbidden to continue with them. When she told him that she was awaiting a favorable opportunity to ask her parents to drop the prohibition, Skeffington urged her not to do so. He thought Bessie might "be prepared to overlook in silence a breach of the prohibition by you, to let judgement go by default. That would be, from her [Bessie's] point of view, a less humiliating surrender than a verbal one."

To maintain the peace, Skeffington felt, Kathleen should simply continue to give him the Irish lessons and say nothing about it. It was best that she save her strength for the "open fight" with her family that he felt sure would occur, he wrote her. This would be "a sufficient, though a quiet" method of asserting her individuality.[6] Kathleen followed his advice for a time, but a month later she began to break engagements with the Skeffingtons; he was furious. At one point he had cautioned her, "Keep your heart up! We'll pull you through, if you make but the slightest effort for yourself."[7] Now he wrote, "Ours is the one place you were forbidden to visit; ours is therefore the one place you conscientiously avoid." If, he said, she had "a spark of spirit," she would have done just the opposite. She should have learned from her experience in the matter of his lessons that the road he had urged on her did not greatly endanger her peace at home. But since she refused to endure even "a little temporary discomfort," he was withdrawing from the fray.[8]

When, a fortnight later, Kathleen informed Skeffington that she was not strong enough to revolt openly, he wrote her a long and loving letter. Her decision, he said, was not one that he would have advised. However, since she was being so frank and honest with him, he promised not to be unsympathetic with "what I may regard as errors. He then went on to advise her on the benefits of contemplation and the virtues of truth. She should, he said, set aside a certain time each day — possibly a half-hour in the morning and another at night — "for steady & concentrated thought" about her life. Do this so as to "attain by degrees the power of altering your own course in great things & in small instead of drifting with surface currents," he told her. Further, he suggested that she should avoid telling lies at home. This was not because she need have any scruples about deceiving the family, but purely because of the "degrading effect" lying would have on her character. Skeffington had the grace to apologize for all this preaching. "I am of a didactic temperament," he wrote Kathleen, "and personal affection is apt with me to express itself in crudely didactic forms."[9] The similarity with his father is readily apparent. The difference is that J. B. would not have apologized for his preaching.

Skeffington put aside Kathleen's problems and his work with the newly formed Irish Women's Franchise League, however, when his mother became gravely ill early in 1909. The senior Skeffingtons had been living in Ranelagh, a Dublin suburb, since around 1900. Since J. B.'s work as a school inspector involved travel, Skeffington spent as much time with his mother as he could spare. Thus the full burden of his mother's illness and death fell on Skeffington. He visited her daily, conferred with her doctor and nurses, and kept up her not inconsiderable correspondence with relatives in the north when she was no longer able to write. It seemed that she wanted it that way and that she felt her husband's presence would place an added strain upon the household. Consequently, it was not until ten days before her death that Skeffington summoned his father home.

When Rose died in April 1909, he missed her a great deal, for his affection for her was very deep. But J. B. missed her even more. Although he was much younger than his wife and seemingly so independent, he seemed unable to adjust to the void that her death left in his life. It is obvious from his letters that J. B. wanted to be near his son. Writing to Francis from Belfast, he said, "Sometimes I have an idea of taking a house in Dublin . . . that would do you & me both."[10] A few days later he wrote again to say that he did not like staying in Belfast for very long and mentioned once more the possibility of buying a house. "It would be a sort of investment — Rents are so high in Dublin."[11] The solution Skeffington offered was that he write a book. That, he wrote his father, would not tie him down to any particular "place or time."[12]

Shortly after his mother died, Skeffington summed up his own situation in a letter to a friend: "I am still alive, and comparatively flourishing — in spite of influenza (one month), diphtheria and its sequelae (three months), a storm provoked by the publication of my 'Life of Davitt', an exceptionally full winter of political and other work, and finally (within the last few weeks) the death of my mother. The last, in spite of her age, was a considerable shock, from which I have not yet fully recovered."[13]

Skeffington was understating the case when he called that winter exceptionally full of political and other work. His main preoccupation during that period, however, was Hanna's pregnancy. Dr. Tennant's assurances had proved not without foundation and on 19 May Hanna gave birth to a son, Owen. It had not been an easy pregnancy or birth, and for a time Hanna's life had been threatened. Gretta Cousins wrote to Skeffington expressing her shock "to hear how near we all were to losing our dear Mrs. 'Skeff'." Always the feminist, she added that it showed "the absurdity of saying women can't fight when every day many of them are going into the 'valley of the shadow' willingly for the future of the race & country & that without all the excitement of war but almost as one might say in cold blood."[14] Soon, however, Skeffington was able to write a cousin in the north that Hanna was "progressing very satisfactorily" and was in a nursing home for a fortnight. Owen, he added, was "thriving."[15]

The baby was a source of great delight to his parents, to J. B., and to the Sheehys. The grandparents' joy would have been tempered considerably had they realized that their grandson would be brought up outside the Catholic faith. As early as 1905 Skeffington had indicated in his diary that he was attending Mass at Christmas because Hanna was "dreading gossip!" He was also making notations that indicated that he was doing his best to wean the younger members of the Sheehy family away from the church. One triumphant entry reads, "K. [Kathleen, presumably] growing more & more anti-Catholic. Can't accept physical resurrection of Christ . . . Things are moving!"[16] Many years later Owen wrote in a brief biography of his father that his parents "were married as Catholics, and practised that religion for some years afterwards, but two or three years before I was born, in 1909, they had thought themselves out of it — not drifted out — and became convinced rationalists and humanists, with a consequent determination that their son should be brought up with a free mind and without formal religious instruction." It was a decision, he wrote, "for which I never cease to be grateful to them." When Owen was very young, one of his friends asked him whether he was a Catholic or a Protestant. He faced his father with this problem and was told to tell his friend: "I am an Irish boy." Owen writes, "This did not seem theologically satisfactory to my friend, but it seemed all right to me."[17]

Newspaper accounts indicate that Hanna's difficult pregnancy did not limit her activities appreciably. A paper that she read before the Young Ireland Branch of the United Irish League, "Women and the National Movement," received a great deal of attention and was carried in three successive issues of the *Irish Nation*. She talked of the early days of the U.I.L. when she and other women students attended a League meeting, paid their entrance fees, and insisted on being formally enrolled as members. They simply disregarded the official in charge, who suggested a "Ladies Branch" would be more suitable. To emphasize the importance of votes for women, Hanna summarized the Ladies' Land League's history. In her opinion, the death of that organization, brought about by Parnell, had proved positively that the women of Ireland must not simply throw in their lot with parliamentarianism or devote themselves exclusively to the language movement and Sinn Fein. "To make their help and cooperation in any cause permanent and solid, and not a mere parasitic growth on male strength," she told her audience, "they need before all to build, not on the shifty quicksands of men's sufferance, but on the basic rock of citizenship. . . . Till armed with vote, women, after all, are but timid watchers of the fight from behind buttressed walls." Politicians have little time to waste on the voteless, she said. Before an audience, the gentle, soft-spoken Hanna became forceful and dynamic; those who knew her well were always surprised at her platform manner. On this occasion, she concluded by reciting Parnell's sister Fanny's stirring "Hold the Harvest" — a poem that Davitt had called the "Marseillaise of the Irish Peasant." [18]

> Oh, by the God who made us all —
> The seignior and the serf
> Rise up! and swear this day to hold
> Your own green Irish turf;
> Rise up! and plant your feet as men
> Where now you crawl as slaves,
> And make your harvest-fields your camps
> Or make of them your graves. [19]

Both Skeffingtons were devoting a great deal of time to the Irish Women's Franchise League. Its activities were increasing, its scope was broadening, and, inevitably, it was beginning to come under attack. As reported in the *Irish Nation*, an article called "Free Women in a Free Nation," indirectly criticizing the I.W.F.L., had appeared in the March issue of *Bean na h-Eireann* (*Woman of Ireland*), a journal devoted to Irish women's nationalist activities — the first and only journal of its kind. The author took the position that Irish women, while wishing their British sisters every success in their struggle for the vote and aiding them whenever possible, should not join their societies and should think twice before crossing the Channel to demonstrate with them. "We must always bear in mind that though they are with us in our sex's war for freedom, yet in our national struggle they are with the men of England and against us." The women of Ireland were urged not to split on this issue but to work together in public life, to serve on committees and boards wherever they were permitted to do so, to prove themselves by working hard and well, and to spend the family's money on Irish goods and teach others to do the same. To use the mottoes and badges of the British movement, to sell their literature, or to shout "Votes for Women" with them would be self-defeating, the article concluded. The *Irish Nation* approved of this stand and commented editorially: "Here is the basis of a true national women's movement that will take its place within the nation, instead of being a disintegrating force. There are enough of them already. It may not be so showy, but it will be a national asset instead of an added national weakness and cause of division."[20]

Another voice was raised in opposition to the I.W.F.L. The fiery rebel, Constance Markievicz, a frequent contributor to *Bean na h-Eireann*, sent an "Open Letter" to *Sinn Fein* headed "Irishwomen and the Suffrage." She began deceptively: "We hear a great deal just at present of a league that is being started in Dublin called the Irish Women's Franchise League. This league appears to be a very vague organisation, but we see no reason why, when its members have gained a little experience, it should not become something definite and something useful to Irishwomen, and — bar consequence — useful to Ireland." But, she continued, she begged the group to reexamine its propaganda, for she feared it had a British-made stamp on it. The I.W.F.L. had distributed a leaflet and, although Mme. Markievicz found it an admirable one, she questioned whether it was a reprint from one sent out by the English suffrage societies. In addition, she was critical of the phrase "We demand the vote on the same terms as it is or may be granted to men"; rather, for Irish women, it should be changed to "We, the women of Ireland, declare that Ireland is a free nation, and we as an integral part of that nation are entitled to the rights of free citizens." To the claim made in the leaflet that the possession of a vote would of itself raise the status of women, she pointed out that in Ireland the national heroes were men who were as much without the vote as were women: they were felons and convicts. "Our martyrs and saints are those who were hung and their bodies desecrated because they would not admit the right of England to govern them," she wrote.[21]

Arthur Griffith, the *Sinn Fein* editor, did not agree with Mme. Markievicz's stand on the I.W.F.L. and felt called upon to add an editorial note to her piece. In no way, he wrote, did the constitution of the I.W.F.L. violate Sinn Fein principles and, until it did adopt a policy that would be repugnant to Sinn Feiners, any organization that helped "awaken civic and national consciousness in Irishwomen" was worthy of support.[22]

But there was no changing Constance Markievicz's mind. She could not join the Irish Women's Franchise League, and this was the stand of Inghinidhe na b-Eireann (Daughters of Erin) as well. Although Hanna considered Mme. Markievicz neither a feminist nor a socialist, her admiration for her was always great. "Madame," she once wrote, "had a way of appear-

ing when storms blew."[23] Although she finally did attend I. W. F. L. meetings
as the years went on, Mme. Markievicz never altered her opinion that the
group was simply not going far enough in its nationalist demands and that
rather than sending its members to press their claims in the English Parliament it should be confining its efforts to work at home.

An impassioned letter, signed "Member of the I. W. F. L.," appeared in
late May in *The Leader*. It attacked that paper for its criticism of the Irish
Women's Franchise League for having as one of its speakers an English
suffragette who had reported on the movement's progress in England. *The
Leader* entirely ignored, said the writer, the fact that only Irishwomen and
Irishmen had participated in the ten highly successful meetings held since
the formation of the I. W. F. L. As for the paper's point that the I. W. F. L.
should campaign against the treatment of women on the stage — the
musical comedy heroine — when the vote for women was obtained on
the same terms as for men, the writer continued, "the disappearance of the
'stage-woman' will be one of the inevitable results of the struggle." So would
the disappearance of "the 9½d. per dozen payment for making blouses,
given to Belfast women," and other "surface evidences of a disease with the
very root of which all women suffrage societies are directly and indirectly
grappling."[24]

All this controversy was actually helpful to the I. W. F. L., and the early
months of 1909 saw well-attended weekly meetings held in Phoenix Park
that received wide coverage in the press. Speakers who were sent outside
Dublin managed to deliver their message successfully even though they
received much less sympathetic receptions. Weighing all factors, the Skeffingtons and Gretta and James Cousins were satisfied with the results of their
not inconsiderable labors.

Had the I. W. F. L. launching gone smoothly, Skeffington would have
been surprised, for most of his battles were beset with pitfalls and disillu-
sionments. In his "Introduction" to the 1967 edition of Skeffington's book on
Davitt, F. S. L. Lyons writes, "Davitt the champion of unpopular causes
drew Sheehy-Skeffington like a magnet, for he too spent his short life tilting
at the same windmills with the same quixotic prodigality."[25]

Never was there a paucity of windmills. In 1909, for example, Skeffington's letters to the editors of various papers covered such diverse subjects as
the teaching of Irish, equal education for women, and temperance — not to
mention Home Rule and women's suffrage. As a strong supporter of temperance legislation, he was also heartily in favor of the Children's Bill — a
bill that was, according to him, "the beneficent regulation which will
henceforth prevent English children from entering licensed premises."[26]
The Irish Party had voted to exempt Ireland from the bill, reasoning that in
Ireland it was impractical to forbid any child under fourteen from entering,
for any purpose whatsoever, premises licensed to sell spirits. Many licensed
shops sold general goods as well as spirits and thus children had to enter those

shops to purchase groceries. Skeffington remained unconvinced, clinging tenaciously to his belief that Ireland should not have been exempted. It was a losing battle, however.

He was fighting hard also against a campaign that was being waged for "essential Irish" in the National University. Granted, he was taking Irish lessons from Kathleen Sheehy. He felt he should know the language, but nevertheless he was strongly against making learning it mandatory. The fury of the Gaelic League on the subject indicated to him that they did not actually believe their own claim that it was "impossible to kill Irish." In a rough draft of a letter to the editor, written in 1908, Skeffington stated, "I hope the present ignorant clamour will not be allowed to irritate the Senate into overlooking the need to create in the National University a great school of Irish studies, where not merely the Irish language, but in especial the scandalously neglected Irish history will be taught to all who wish it. But let there be no compulsion."[27] Now, a year later, he had not changed his mind. However, he did write his father, "I am keeping altogether quiet on the Irish-in-the-University discussion; the Gaelic League and the Bishops may fight it out."[28]

Not without skepticism, the Skeffingtons had been looking forward to the National Convention of the United Irish League, scheduled for February 1909. Early that month the *Irish Nation* carried an article by Skeffington, in which he forcefully outlined his thoughts about the upcoming meeting. His impatience with the Irish Party was manifest. Although his belief in the parliamentary procedure was unshaken, he asserted, he felt that if the party had pursued vigorous methods, it could have accomplished something to bring Ireland closer to Home Rule. He saw missed opportunities and blunders at every turn:

«   «   «   «   «   «   «   «   «

> Well, it is all going to be brought up at the Convention — the virtual desertion of Home Rule, the virtual alliance with the Liberals, the scandal of the National Liberal Club, the whole miserable situation which, I fear, delights some Sinn Feiners (though it shouldn't) and which pains the thoughtful rank and file men in the Parliamentary movement. And to me the question of the moment, far bigger than compulsory Irish, is whether the Convention will show even a moderate firmness in dealing with the Party? Will the Party be frightened into a change of heart, late in the day as it is? Or will a formal vote of confidence in them mark yet another stage in their descent into the pit of a dishonourable extinction?[29]

»   »   »   »   »   »   »   »   »

The convention proceedings did nothing to allay Skeffington's fears, as can be seen from an article he wrote that appeared in the *New Age* after the convention. Cruise O'Brien, president of the Young Ireland Branch, had introduced a resolution calling for a return to the old policy of strenuous opposition in Ireland, in Parliament, and in every British constituency to any British government that refused to grant Home Rule or suggested that the question be postponed. There should not be abstention from Westminster, as Sinn Fein requested, but neither should the Irish Party fight for minor reforms, such as land bills and university bills, while giving general support to any government that refused to introduce a Home Rule bill at once or to agree to have a Home Rule plank in the Liberal platform at the next general election. O'Brien's resolution was placed on the agenda but in the form of an amendment to the official vote of confidence in the party — an old dodge, according to Skeffington, and one that he labeled the "no confidence" trick. He maintained that the United Irish League had known the Young Ireland Branch's position for months but that the League's leaders had ignored it. "We were only a small band of 'young and rather ignorant politicians,' — 'unthinking enthusiasts' is another name for us — and we could be safely ignored," he wrote.[30]

The resolution and the speeches supporting it did, however, make a marked impression, for Joseph Devlin, secretary of the League, felt called upon to respond, calling for the defeat of the Home Rule resolution. Skeffington called Devlin's reply "intellectually and ethically contemptible," saying that Devlin evaded the points raised, sneered at the Young Irelanders, and used his personal power (he was an outstanding public speaker) unscrupulously. So effective was his oratory that the resolution was defeated "by an overwhelming majority."[31]

At the request of the Irish Women's Franchise League, the Young Ireland Branch agreed to sponsor a resolution calling for women's suffrage, to be presented to the convention. Skeffington was to make the first motion for the resolution and Tom Kettle to second it. At the last moment, however, Kettle refused.[32] Skeffington called Kettle's failure to keep his promise "Mr. Kettle's first breach of faith with the women's suffrage party."[33]

Without Kettle, the motion was still made and seconded. Although it was placed last on the convention's agenda and both Skeffington's speech and the seconding speech limited scrupulously to five minutes each — indeed, although it was rejected — Skeffington felt that simply having it introduced amounted to something of a victory for the women's cause. After all, this was the first time that such a resolution had been placed before such a convention. Since the suffrage movement had made little headway in Ireland, even in Dublin and Belfast, and since the bulk of the delegates were "conservative agrarians," suffragists were pleased by the amount of support the resolution did receive and were "not disposed to regard its rejection, though unsatisfactory, as at all disheartening."[34]

Skeffington, ever hopeful, saw some good coming out of the introduction of the defeated Home Rule resolution as well. Though the dynamic Devlin had defeated the Y.I.B. resolution, his arguments, when seen in print, did not seem so persuasive. It amused Skeffington to see that John

Dillon felt called upon to threaten the Liberals with lack of support if something were not done to push Home Rule legislation soon. This, of course, was what the Young Ireland Branch had called for in their resolution — strenuous opposition in Ireland and in Parliament to any government that refused or postponed Home Rule. He noted also that John Redmond had made a great show of withdrawing his support from the government on the Tariff Reform amendment. Though Skeffington realized that these were only small steps, still, as he pointed out in his *New Age* article, "We may yet succeed in revivifying the Home Rule flame in an apathetic Ireland, lulled to sleep by a party which has lost its enthusiasm."[35] It was Y.I.B. pressure, he knew, which had forced action. This was reason enough, as he saw it, for that group not to withdraw from the United Irish League but to continue to exert pressure from within.

As his part in the Convention proved, Skeffington was adept at political maneuvering. He was not reluctant to point out his "personal triumph" to his father. He wrote: "Redmond was just going to put the motion [the Y.I.B. resolution], without deeming it necessary to call on anyone to reply for the Party, when I insisted on speaking. I produced such an impression on the Convention, as the *Irish Times* correctly said, that Devlin had to get up to counteract the effect." He added, "Dillon said in private that my forcing a reluctant Convention to listen for so long was a remarkable display of ability of a rare kind."

In letters to his father, to Tom Kettle, and to his friend Lindsay Crawford, Skeffington gave his opinion of some of the Party leaders. John Dillon he saw as an "obstinate man," bitter, but honest.[36] Devlin was quite another matter; Skeffington felt strongly that the Young Ireland Branch should not have "any further truce or truck" with him. "He must go down and out. There can be no safety or health, not to speak of progress, in the organisation or the movement so long as this brainless bludgeoner retains any official position within them."[37] He considered Devlin "the worst foe of the ideals of the Young Ireland Branch."[38] As for Redmond, he considered that he could be manipulated more easily than either Dillon or Devlin. He had talked with Skeffington at the Convention, saying that he saw very little disagreement between them — but, of course, Skeffington noted, it was "his forte to be smooth and suave." Redmond had said that he hoped the Y.I.B. and the U.I.L. could come to some agreement.[39]

Skeffington did follow up on this. He wrote Redmond asking to have a date set for a meeting, which he was sure would be "productive of much good." He also suggested that branches of the United Irish League might be set up in Dublin, and complimented Redmond for seeing the advantages in keeping in touch with "the younger generation of Nationalists," and for, on occasion, recruiting from its ranks. They, in turn, he wrote, would "welcome the opportunity to remove, by actual contact with the working of the political machine, that inexperience of matters political which, in default of other reproach, is frequently alleged against us." Skeffington, though becoming an able strategist, was not losing his flair for sarcasm.

In Skeffington's view, politicians like Devlin, Dillon, Redmond and others threatened his efforts to reach the goal of setting Irishmen free. All around him he saw the individual debased by the by-products of poverty — disease, crime, drunkenness, and despair. Conditions in Dublin, circa 1908, were scandalous. Approximately 30 percent of the population lived in abject poverty in the shells of the Georgian mansions. More than two thousand families lived in single-room tenements without heat, light, water, or adequate sanitation. The death rate in the city was the highest in the country, and infant mortality was higher there than anywhere in the British Isles. Tuberculosis was common, and malnutrition was simply part of the general scene.[40] For Skeffington, with his compassion for oppressed workers, suffering masses, and hungry children, this plight of the individual, a basic evil of capitalism, had to be eliminated. He was ready to support any movement that he felt would work toward that end. When, in 1909, Fred Ryan returned to Dublin and resumed his friendship with the Skeffingtons, Francis was receptive to his talk of joining an organized socialist group.

Ryan had at one time been a member of the Irish Socialist Republican Party (formed by James Connolly in 1896). Its many splits and reconciliations had been disillusioning, however, so he broke away. In 1903, when Connolly went to America, the party split into two factions — the Socialist Labour Party and the Irish Socialist Republican Party. In 1904, they were reunited as the Socialist Party of Ireland. Although members were few, originally about sixty, the party somehow managed to survive until June 1908, when William O'Brien, dedicated trade unionist and Connolly's close friend, began trying desperately to revive the organization on a much broader basis. In mid-June 1909 the *Irish Nation* carried a notice calling on all those who might be interested to attend a meeting in the Trades Hall, Capel Street. Much to O'Brien's delight, both Skeffington and Ryan did. This, O'Brien felt, was a sign that the membership would be "very different to what we had been in the habit of getting in the socialist movement prior to that."[41]

It was an enthusastic meeting, with approximately one hundred and fifty people attending, including several women — Hanna was doubtlessly among them. William O'Brien, in the chair, gave a brief history of the socialist movement in Ireland, stressing that the time had come for a new organization that had as broad a base as possible. After a lively general discussion, Fred Ryan rose to propose "that this meeting affirms the necessity of a Socialist Party for Ireland embracing Socialists of all shades of opinion, and that membership shall be determined by the applicant declaring his acceptance of Socialism as the only remedy for the evils of society."[42] The motion was adopted, not without the usual heated discussion, and a provisional committee was elected to draw up a constitution. This committee, which had Skeffington, Fred Ryan, and William O'Brien among its members, was to report to a general meeting two weeks later. Reflecting the growing interest in a Gaelic revival, one Peter Macken moved that the name of the organization be in Irish, to which O'Brien replied that this should not concern them too much since they had been known by many different names, some "by no means complimentary."[43] As a compromise, the name chosen was "The Socialist Party of Ireland — Cummanacht na h-Eireann."

Before the conclusion of this planning meeting, the goal of the organization was clearly spelled out: "to replace the present chaotic state of Society by the establishment of an organised commonwealth in Ireland in which the land, railways, and all other means of production, distribution and exchange shall be owned and controlled by the whole people." This ambitious goal would be achieved by "(a) The education of the people in the principles of Socialism; (b) the independent representation of Socialist principles on all public bodies in Ireland."[44] All future meetings were to be held in the Antient Concert Rooms in Brunswick Street.

A handbill announcing the first public meeting, to which "Members, Friends, Inquirers, & Opponents" were invited, was sent out and O'Brien's diaries report that it was the "most enthusiastic soc. meeting" he had ever seen in Dublin. He concluded, "The future looks bright if we only handle the new organ. in the right way. Peter Macken who was to speak in Irish failed to show up."[45] This same Peter Macken had been instrumental in drafting a plank in the party's platform advocating the revival of the Irish language. He was determined that the Socialist Party of Ireland would push Irish more vigorously than any other organization had, and, through his efforts, an Irish language class was established. It was inevitable that Skeffington, who never was able to fit completely into any organization, should have some differences with the platform of the S.P.I. — and this was one of them. In general, however, he was satisfied and optimistic about the party's chances for success and growth.

Conversely, Skeffington was pessimistic about Sinn Fein. As he said in an article in the *New Age*, he attributed much of Sinn Fein's trouble to its leadership rather than to the impracticality of the group's proposals. Edward Martyn, the first president of Sinn Fein, was extremely well-meaning — a serious dramatist, a patron of the arts — but no politician. John Sweetman, the second president and the one in office in 1909, was also well-meaning, but he was a country gentleman who actually declined to support a strike against income tax — one of the Sinn Fein proposals — because his furniture might be seized. In Skeffington's opinion, Sweetman was a "narrowly clerical" Catholic and, even though Sinn Fein admitted women to membership (and even to the executive board), an antifeminist. As for Arthur Griffith, editor of *Sinn Fein* and creator of the Sinn Fein policy, his posing as another leader like Parnell seemed to Skeffington unjustified. While admitting that Griffith was undoubtedly the brains of the party, and an earnest and forceful character, Skeffington felt that Griffith's outlook was narrow, and his inability to engage in controversy with honest opponents without venomous bitterness more than unfortunate.[46]

As proof of the fact that Sinn Fein was losing its power, Skeffington's article noted that there were only 106 branches in all of Ireland and that many of these seemed to exist merely on paper since no reports were forthcoming from them. Although membership dues were only one shilling annually, only 581 people had paid up throughout all of Ireland by the end of 1909. As a basis of comparison, one Dublin branch of the United Irish League had five hundred paid-up members during the same period. To those who pointed to the success of the organ of the party, *Sinn Fein*, which developed from a weekly to a daily with a circulation of more than three thousand, Skeffington replied that the number of those who sympathized with Sinn Fein ideas was far in excess of those who wished to join the movement. There existed a block of parliamentarians who actually sympathized with the Sinn Fein goals but who felt that the place for those who were fighting for Home Rule was *within* the Parliamentary Party — and, for that matter, within other organizations whose aims were somewhat similar. W. P. Ryan's paper, the *Irish Nation*, had now adopted this view. To Skeffington's mind this meant that those who agreed — and he felt their numbers were great — would now rally round the *Irish Nation*, thus causing the collapse of *Sinn Fein* and with it the Sinn Fein organization. It was his hope that a certain number of these people would gravitate toward the Socialist Party of Ireland as well.[47]

As pointed out earlier, Skeffington was one of those who felt his place to be *within* the Parliamentary Party. He had no trouble reconciling his membership in it with his membership in the new Socialist Party of Ireland and in the Young Ireland Branch of the United Irish League. Until Home Rule was won, it seemed to him, the fight must be carried on through the Parliamentary Party. He felt, too, that it was healthy to have a socialist voice raised at Young Ireland Branch meetings; apparently he convinced Fred Ryan, for he joined the Y.I.B. also.

A September note in William O'Brien's diaries indicates that membership cards were issued to James Connolly and to Skeffington. Another, that same month, yields the information that Connolly, then residing in the United States, was eager to return to Ireland if money could be raised by the Transport Workers Union to employ him as an organizer. He also asked O'Brien if Skeffington could do something about getting his manuscript, *Labour in Irish History*, published. This request O'Brien dutifully passed on to Skeffington, who agreed to speak to the manager of Maunsel's about it. He did not think that he could do much good but he promised to do anything in his power. Thus the paths of Connolly and Skeffington crossed once more.[48]

(The paths of Joyce and Skeffington crossed about that time, too. An

August 1909 letter from Skeffington to Joyce read, "This is to remind you that we expect you about 8:30 tomorrow evening."[49] Joyce did not go. This must have been a second rejection, for Joyce had written Stanislaus earlier that "Mr. and Mrs. Skeffington invited me to their house: I did not go."[50] The two old friends had met on the street and, although Skeffington was extremely cordial, Joyce was cool — as, says Richard Ellmann in *James Joyce*, "befitted an old debtor with an old creditor."[51])

The Socialist Party of Ireland took a great deal of Skeffington's time and attention in late 1909. At an October public meeting, he and Fred Ryan were elected to the general committee — Ryan as secretary and Skeffington, with two others, in charge of press and publications.[52] As always, Skeffington took his duties very seriously. Unable to attend one of the committee meetings, he asked Ryan to propose that A. R. Orage, editor of the *New Age*, be invited to deliver a lecture sometime in the spring. "His lecturing fee is one guinea. His expenses would also have to be paid; but he is in negotiation with the National Theatre Company with regard to delivering a lecture for them; and I understand that the Irish Women's Franchise League would probably be prepared to stand in if he came, and get a lecture from him; so that the expenses could be shared by three societies." Skeffington had heard Orage speak in London and thought him an admirable lecturer. "Those who read the New Age will have no doubt of the stimulating effect his visit would be likely to have on the S.P.I. And I have no doubt that it might be made the source of considerable profit as well, if it is worked on a business footing and not as a philanthropic enterprise. With sixpenny and shilling tickets, judicious advertising, and *no free list*, it ought to pay well."[53]

The letter proves Skeffington's devotion to duty but it also proves what many people, including J. B., would not have conceded — when sufficiently motivated, he could be very practical and businesslike. This aspect of his character had also emerged when, late in August, he had applied for the position of Secretary and Bursar of University College, Dublin. Writing to the Dublin Commissioners, he stated that he had held a similar post as registrar for three years (1901–1904) and referred them to the College Council for information about his record. Again, he spared them the "fatuity of testimonials."[54]

He did not let the matter rest there but proceeded to send a series of letters to people of influence, asking for their support when "the question of recommending for the position comes before the Governing Board of the College."[55] For example, to Mary Hayden, well-known educationist and nationalist, he wrote asking that she propose his name for the position, "if there is anything in the nature of a formal proposing of names." He had not, he wrote, asked anyone else to do this "as I dislike intensely the kind of canvassing usually necessary for such favours; but I feel that I can approach you without fear of being misunderstood." He concluded, "If the claims are considered on the merits, I have no doubt of the result, — at least against any other candidate of whom I have knowledge. That being so, I should not like my application to fall through merely because I had omitted to ask anyone to propose me."[56] Also, in a letter to the Lord Mayor of Dublin on another matter, he appended a postscript telling the Lord Mayor of his candidacy for the secretaryship of the new University College, Dublin, reminding him that the "date of appointment is drawing near. . . . I think I am correct in saying that none of the other candidates — certainly none of those who are mentioned as favourites — ever took any prominent part in Nationalist politics." Apparently Skeffington felt this was no time for modesty.

Writing to his father early in September, Skeffington was able to report, "I have put in a good canvass, and I believe I have a fighting chance. Of course, I am not counting on it. In any event, I am looking forward to a prosperous winter, as I feel in excellent form for work, and have in addition some work by me which I hope to market soon."[57] J. B. did offer to intervene but Skeffington declined the offer, saying that he had made a complete canvass of the Governing Board "except of the clerical members . . . and also excepting the Chief Baron, canvassing of whom is fatal." There were, he told his father, two hundred candidates for the position.[59] He was right not to count on the position for he was not awarded it.

A measure of success was, however, being achieved by the Socialist Party of Ireland, due in no small part to the efforts of Skeffington, Fred Ryan, and representatives of such organizations as the League of Progressive Thought, the Irish Women's Franchise League, labor groups, and even the Abbey Theatre (in the person of Arthur Shields). A series of lectures given by the S.P.I. during that winter were, in terms of both attendance and interest, the most successful Dublin had witnessed in some time. Some of the topics discussed were "Unemployment: Its Cause and Cure," "Christian Socialism," "Some Objections to Socialism Answered," and "Wanted — An Irish Labour Party."

Two lectures in the series — "The Spirit of Socialism" and "Utopianism" — were given by Skeffington. In both he displayed clearly his inability to go with the crowd, and in neither did he show any tendency to adhere to any particular socialist theory, except for the policy of land nationalization. "Indeed, he was quite impatient with doctrinal hair-splitting," says Ken Hannigan in his undergraduate thesis on Skeffington.[59] In his lecture on utopianism, Skeffington described four utopias, those envisioned by Edward Bellamy, William Morris, H. G. Wells, and Anatole France. He criticized all of them — primarily because they ignored human individuality, which to Skeffington was of first importance. Bellamy's utopia he found too hard and cold — the progress of society through companies to trusts and from trusts to public control. Morris depicted a system of anarchical communism, rather than socialism. Wells, on the other hand, Skeffington felt, combined order and liberty with the power and beauty of Morris's world but showed a certain distrust of democracy. And Anatole France did not seem to recognize equality of the sexes. [60] For Skeffington, socialism was the noblest expression of the spirit of liberty and, to him, that meant liberty of the individual. It could not be forced on anyone; it was necessary to obtain free cooperation — "the true reformer does not seek to do good to his neighbour, but to awaken his neighbour's conscience." [61]

This belief was the cornerstone of the Skeffington philosophy, beyond a doubt. He detested all forms of compulsion, and surely he would have fought just as hard against an authoritarian socialist state as he did against the established order in Ireland. His son Owen wrote many years later that his father had told him that nobody could ever force a person to do anything that he didn't want to do. When Owen had argued that they could, saying "they could kill you," Skeffington replied, "Yes, they could kill you, but they could not make you do it." [62] But it was clear to him that those ideals for which the socialists stood were his: nationalism was not sufficient, and exploitation and class privileges would have to be wiped out in Ireland if there was to be genuine freedom for the Irish people.

In its attitude toward the Socialist Party of Ireland, Moran's *Leader* was as venomous as ever. Moran seemed to be concerned that the S.P.I. might be confused in people's minds with the Gaelic League both because of its Gaelic name — *Cummanacht na h-Eireann* — and because it favored the revival of the Irish language. The paper prophesied that socialism would never take hold in Catholic Ireland, although obviously it was not certain enough to avoid fighting it. An early October issue took consolation in the fact that the "hyphenated Democrat" was on the platform during the inaugural meeting. The paper commented, "We don't know what Skeffy said, but if he sided with Socialism, that should be enough to kill Socialism in Ireland." [63]

Members of the Socialist Party of Ireland were not content simply to conduct a series of lectures — they spoke before other organizations and, whenever possible, engaged in debates. Late in 1909 the S.P.I. issued a manifesto to the Irish voters in Great Britain, urging them to support the Labour Party, and S.P.I. members campaigned for sympathetic candidates in Ireland. Skeffington campaigned for the United Irish League candidates but not in his own South Dublin district. There he found neither the Unionist nor the Nationalist candidate acceptable. *The Leader* was quick to note this editorially:

« « « « « « « « «

In the course of a discussion after a lecture by J. H. Hutchinson on 'The Crank in Politics,' Skeffy, the hyphened democrat, declared that he could not, and would not, vote for Alderman Cotton in South Dublin. As Skeffy resides in Rathmines, we assume that he is enfranchised. Mr. Hutchinson remarked that he thought that Skeffy's attitude was that of a crank. If we were to say what we thought of Skeffy's view on that particular matter, and of Skeffy generally, we would not waste as many letters of the alphabet as are in the word 'crank.' [64]

» » » » » » » » »

Skeffington had developed a stock answer to the charge of being a "crank." "Yes," he would say, "that's right, and a crank is a small instrument that makes revolutions."[65] *The Leader's* memory was long, for as late as June 1912 it was to remind readers that Skeffington had fought for votes for women although he himself had failed to vote in 1910. "Skeffy had a little vote and Skeffy didn't use it," said *The Leader.*[66]

That paper and its followers were not alone in fearing the growth of a socialist movement in Ireland. At the Catholic Truth Society's conference in Dublin in October, a discussion of socialism was on the agenda. Several religious journals published articles condemning socialism, and the *Irish Ecclesiastical Record* ran a series of articles on the subject.[67] How much of this furor was due to the threat posed by the Socialist Party of Ireland is difficult to say, but surely the uproar had its effect on that organization, for it began to lose ground steadily. The party's weakening may also have been due to the Irish workingman's inability to reconcile his strong faith in Catholicism with a militant socialist movement. After the first flush, a built-in fear may have taken over. At any rate, early 1910 found membership morale low as attacks were launched on the S.P.I. meetings by mobs purported to be inspired by the Catholic and conservative Ancient Order of Hibernians.

While hopes for the Socialist Party of Ireland were still running high, it had been suggested that James Connolly be hired as a full-time organizer. Now back in Ireland, he was holding a series of meetings for *Cumannacht na h-Eireann,* which were well attended. He was an impressive speaker, and his wide experience in Ireland and America in the labor movement made a strong impression on his audiences. He outlined a series of goals with great clarity: issue popular publications dealing with particular phases of the worker's everyday life in terms of socialist thought, as was being done successfully in other countries; explain social, economic and other forces in the light of Irish history and tradition; discuss issues of the day such as the Poor Law, the police, education; stress the need for freedom of contract for workers — "If you had all the patriotism of Emmet or Tone, all the poetry of a Moore or a Mangan, all the religion of a Father Kane or a bishop, if you are a worker, you cannot live except you can get a rich man to make a profit out of you." The *Irish Nation* gave excellent coverage to Connolly's series and called him a "vigorous and progressive personality . . . an enthusiast in the cause of the people."[68]

The advantages to be gained from employing Connolly as a full-time organizer were obvious. An informal delegate conference of the Dublin, Belfast, and Cork branches of the S.P.I. — the first ever to be held — was scheduled for mid-September 1910, and Skeffington was to chair the meeting. This seemed the appropriate time to discuss the matter. Connolly, although invited, diplomatically did not attend. It was decided, finally, that the party could offer Connolly only thirty-five shillings per week for six months, which was considerably less than he felt he wanted and needed. Fred Ryan suggested that supplementary employment might possibly be found for him. One of the members, knowing that the Transport Union in Belfast needed a secretary, offered to speak with Larkin about appointing Connolly. Skeffington then suggested that a fund be set up to help cover Connolly's salary. He would contribute three pounds, he said, if a hundred pounds could be raised. [69] This offer was surpassed by none and equalled only by one. Although Skeffington could ill afford it, those who knew the Skeffingtons well could testify that they were always ready to deprive themselves in order to contribute to the various causes for which they worked so diligently.

The trouble with this philanthropy, as J. B. saw it, was that it was often with his money. Again and again over the years, Skeffington had to turn to his father for assistance. It was always given but often grudgingly. Skeffington did not find it easy to ask, as an exchange of letters — and words — during 1909 shows. In September a letter from Skeffington informed his father that expenses had been heavy and, because he had had to "take things easy" the winter before, he was "again in straits for cash." Apparently he was given assistance but, in November, he had to write again. This time, in a letter marked "Private," he asked for a loan of one hundred pounds to meet his obligations, which included a bank overdraft. He had no other recourse, he wrote, and went on:

«   «   «   «   «   «   «   «   «

You will probably think my asking for the money as "a loan" is mere impertinence, & that it will in effect amount to a gift. I cannot prevent your thinking so, beyond saying that I have reason to think otherwise. I am so far confident not merely of the future, but of the immediate future, as to be willing to give my ideas of a career only one more year of trial. After that, I shall be prepared to adopt some of the alternatives you have so often urged on me.

»   »   »   »   »   »   »   »   »

If J. B. was not willing to make the loan, Skeffington added, "please say so as briefly as possible. There is no reason why it need be alluded to again." He added that he would accept any terms. [70]

Exactly what J. B. responded is not clear, but Skeffington's reply, just a few days later, was a masterpiece of controlled fury. He had been, he told J. B., reluctant to approach him at all and had been sure, until the very last moment, that it might not be necessary. He was owed a little money for a serial he had sold recently and hoped it would tide them over. He then gave a detailed account of his "total obligations," which amounted to 270 pounds, 100 pounds of which he owed J. B. but "which stands on a different footing from the other advances I have received from you & which will assuredly be repaid." He also assured him that the money was not, as his father suggested, "lent or advanced for the benefit of any other person, but was strictly (& I believe wisely) applied for my own advantage." His list continued — rent, nurses, medical fees, books, coal, and even "balance due for loss on

'National Democrat' in 1907, £15." This sum, he said, would never be demanded of him "but I feel honourably bound to pay it whenever able, so must include it in any full list of my obligations." The listing ended: "I emphatically deny having spent or lent any money for the benefit of other people. The only expenditure of the past six years that remotely approaches that category is paid for wedding present for people who gave us valuable wedding present." He and Hanna had not, he assured his father, lived extravagantly but "indeed as regards our food and furniture, with extreme simplicity." Their "bad position" was simply due to insufficient income, the causes for which were twofold: "First, my deliberate taking things easy last winter — call it laziness if you like — in order to recover fully from the effects of my illness. Second, the expenses directly and indirectly due to Hanna's illness last year." However, thanks to his "present health & vigour" and to seeds he had sown, he felt that during the coming twelve months he should be able to "make good, as the Americans say." He was so sure of this, he said, that "if I do not succeed this year I am quite prepared to abandon as hopeless the attempt to make money on my present lines."[71]

Another letter, dated the next day, indicated that he had received the money from his father. He was grateful for it, but apparently far from grateful for the letter that accompanied it. "As to what you say about myself," Skeffington wrote, "I might make some protest; but I understand your point of view, and, from that standpoint you are perhaps not oversevere. But I must add that I cannot allow you to insult or attack my wife. No amount of pecuniary or other indebtedness would induce me to condone this." He wanted this to be made clear "before anything irrevocable is said." J. B. had accused him of giving money to the Sheehys, and this idea Francis found "too grotesque for discussion." He added, "You had a similar mania with regard to poor mother's people; and I hope, for the sake of your common-sense and dignity, that you will not pursue this will-of-the-wisp further."[72]

Another indication of the Skeffingtons' financial situation that fall is given in correspondence with the editor of *The Native*, a small Irish publication. He had offered Skeffington ten pounds for a lengthy story, which he planned to run serially, called "Jimmie Barrett's Probation." If *The Native* paid a mere ten shillings per thousand words, he told the editor, it would run to thirty-three pounds. If, however, the publication date could be less vague than "at the first convenient opportunity" and he could be paid after the first installment, he might be reconciled to the "exiguous figure." Under those terms, however, he would have to insist that the story be published under his *nom de plume*, "Christopher Francis." If his name were used, that would be five pounds more. A subsequent letter indicates that he accepted the offer of ten pounds with the conditions cited.[73]

Skeffington had not forgotten his promise to intervene with Maunsel, the publisher, on behalf of Connolly's *Labour in Irish History*. They had, indeed, published it and Skeffington reviewed it for the *Freeman's Journal*, calling it a "striking and original book." Connolly's attitude, he wrote, could be summed up in one statement: "Were history what it ought to be . . . the pages of history would be almost entirely engrossed with a recital of the wrongs and struggles of the labouring people, constituting, as they have ever done, the vast mass of mankind." Skeffington did not entirely agree with Connolly's critical assessment of some of the great names of Irish history. He did agree, however, with his wholehearted respect for "the genuine Irish revolutionaries" such as Wolfe Tone, Robert Emmet, John Mitchel, and Fintan Lalor, whom Connolly admired "not solely for their uncompromising hostility to English rule, but also because of the advanced democratic nature of their principles and propaganda." He recommended the book even to those who disagreed with Connolly's views, which Skeffington thought strongly individualistic, and he believed the book illuminated a phase of Irish history that had been neglected. "Cheap at half-a-crown," he concluded.[74]

For a listing of and comments on the activities of the Socialist Party of Ireland, the diaries of William O'Brien are an invaluable source of information, a reflection of the Skeffingtons' devotion to the cause of socialism, and often very amusing. At one S.P.I. lecture, a Professor Houston criticized the methods used by farmers, saying they "only tickled the surface of the soil with a plow and expected it to break forth into smiling grain." In the ensuing discussion, O'Brien reports, a member deplored all this scientific talk about oxygen and hydrogen and "such new fangled ideas." He evidently thought they were "parent manures," O'Brien wrote. Skeffington was chairing that meeting and "gave a fine tone to the mtg," which ended with a piano solo received with loud applause though one member was heard to comment that it was "rotten." "The vote of thanks," said Skeffington, "is carried with one dissentment, who no doubt is a rival performer."[75]

In another early 1910 item, O'Brien reported a "Men's Meeting," with Skeffington in the chair, which took up the question of women's suffrage. One elderly gentlemen, O'Brien wrote, objected to women's having the vote on the grounds that "men are men & women are women." He interrupted James Stephens of St. Enda's College, who was speaking of the necessity of higher education for women, by saying, "But they are a different sex." Stephens retorted, "We are not going to educate the sex out of them." O'Brien concluded his report: "Skeffington (who made an admirable Chairman) asked the man for his name," undoubtedly in the interest of educating him later.[76]

A February meeting, according to O'Brien, was attended by representatives of the Trades Council so that the need for a Labour Party might be discussed. James Larkin and Skeffington participated in the discussion, with Larkin attacking party members who continued to be members of the United Irish League. Skeffington replied in defense of this policy, and apparently very ably, for O'Brien reports that Larkin complained later that he should have been allowed to make the concluding speech. The tone of the report of this controversy reflects O'Brien's dislike of Larkin — both were supreme egotists — and, to a degree, Larkin's feeling toward Skeffington. The latter did not always please O'Brien either. In a March item, O'Brien mentioned that Skeffington had lectured at the Mansion House on Fintan Lalor, whose ideas on land reform had strongly influenced Davitt. "Skeffington told us nothing new about Lalor, and as most of the audience was fairly well acquainted with Lalor's life and work the proceedings were pretty dull," he wrote. [77]

O'Brien's diaries underline the fact that during the latter part of 1910 the *Irish Nation* was in serious financial trouble. [78] Its audience and that of *Sinn Fein*, the organ of the Sinn Fein movement, were much the same. Skeffington had long believed that *Sinn Fein* and the Sinn Fein party would not survive and that the *Irish Nation* would prosper as a result. In fact, he believed this so strongly that, writing in September 1909 to the secretary of a group he was to address some months later, on "A Critical Examination of Sinn Fein," he mentioned that, should the Sinn Fein party no longer be in existence at the time of the meeting, he would change his topic. [79] But he was proved wrong, for it was the *Irish Nation* that was doomed. Even though O'Brien's diaries make it clear that he, Connolly, Skeffington, and others made every effort to save it, the December 1910 issue was its last. *Sinn Fein*, on the other hand, seemed to be flourishing.

There must always be times when those who tilt at windmills are beset by serious doubts that their battles will ever be won. As far as can be determined, those who knew Skeffington were not aware of his feelings — but as 1910 ended, he had reason to be discouraged. Many of his good friends were leaving Ireland and as a result he was saddened and distressed. Lindsay Crawford had returned to Dublin in 1908 after losing his position as editor of *The Ulster Guardian* and being expelled from the increasingly conservative Independent Orange Order. He had tried desperately to find employment in Belfast, but politics in Ulster had taken a strongly conservative turn and Crawford did not fit in. Not only was he an advocate of Home Rule but he had done much to expose the atrocious labor conditions in the linen industry. Dublin proved as sterile a field for him as Belfast, and he was soon being denounced for preaching "all creeds to all classes." In June 1910 he left for Canada.

W. P. Ryan, after getting out the last issue of the *Irish Nation* in December, left for England and for what Skeffington called "the intellectually freer atmosphere of London." Fred Ryan was finding it difficult to get along as well, and soon he left for London, where he took over the position of editor of Wilfrid Blunt's paper, *Egypt*. Earlier, J. F. Byrne, Skeffington's very good friend and chess adversary, had gone to the United States. In a letter to Byrne, Skeffington mentioned another who had gone to the United States. "The American lecturing life will suit him far better," Skeffington wrote of Father Eugene Sheehy.[80] He saw all of this in more than personal terms. To Skeffington, it was a condemnation of Ireland and Irish journalism.

NOTES TO CHAPTER 6

1. *The Leader*, 19 December 1908.
2. James O. Hannay to F. Sheehy-Skeffington, 20 July 1907.
3. Conor Cruise O'Brien, *States of Ireland*, pp. 78–80.
4. Ibid.
5. F. Sheehy-Skeffington to Cruise O'Brien, 2 February 1909.
6. F. Sheehy-Skeffington to Kathleen Sheehy, 15 February 1909.
7. F. Sheehy-Skeffington to Kathleen Sheehy, 15 February 1909.
8. F. Sheehy-Skeffington to Kathleen Sheehy, 16 March 1909.
9. F. Sheehy-Skeffington to Kathleen Sheehy, 27 March 1909.
10. J. B. Skeffington to F. Sheehy-Skeffington, 2 May 1909.
11. J. B. Skeffington to F. Sheehy-Skeffington, 7 May 1909.
12. F. Sheehy-Skeffington to J. B. Skeffington, 5 May 1909.
13. F. Sheehy-Skeffington to John Burns, 20 April 1909.
14. Gretta Cousins to F. Sheehy-Skeffington, undated, but undoubtedly 1909.
15. F. Sheehy-Skeffington to his cousin Mary Rose, 25 May 1909.
16. Diary of F. Sheehy-Skeffington, 4 December 1905.
17. O. Sheehy-Skeffington, "Francis Sheehy-Skeffington," p. 139.
18. *Irish Nation*, 6, 13, and 20 March 1909.
19. Ibid., 13 March 1909.
20. Ibid., 20 March 1909.
21. *Sinn Fein*, 27 March 1909.
22. Ibid.
23. Hanna Sheehy-Skeffington, "Reminiscences of an Irish Suffragette," in *Votes for Women: Irish Women's Struggle for the Vote* (Dublin: A. D. Sheehy-Skeffington, 1975), p. 26.
24. *The Leader*, 29 May 1909.
25. F. S. L. Lyons, "Introduction," F. Sheehy-Skeffington, *Michael Davitt*, p. 10.
26. *The Peasant*, 25 December 1908.
27. Rough draft of letter to the editor, 23 December 1908. Ms 22, 259 (1), National Library of Ireland.
28. F. Sheehy-Skeffington to J. B. Skeffington, 13 February 1909.
29. *Irish Nation*, 6 February 1909.
30. *New Age*, 25 February 1909.
31. Ibid.
32. A letter to the *Freeman's Journal*, written by Skeffington soon after the close of the convention, concerning Kettle and the suffrage cause, was never printed by that paper but it did appear a few years later in the *Irish Citizen*.

33. *Irish Citizen*, 3 August 1912.

34. *New Age*, 25 February 1909.

35. Ibid.

36. F. Sheehy-Skeffington to J. B. Skeffington, 13 February 1909.

37. F. Sheehy-Skeffington to Thomas Kettle, 29 April 1909.

38. F. Sheehy-Skeffington to Lindsay Crawford, 10 May 1909.

39. F. Sheehy-Skeffington to J. B. Skeffington, 13 February 1909.

40. Larkin, *James Larkin*, pp. 41–42.

41. William O'Brien Papers, National Library of Ireland.

42. *Irish Nation*, 19 June 1909.

43. O'Brien Diaries, in O'Brien Papers.

44. *Irish Nation*, 10 July 1909.

45. O'Brien Diaries, in O'Brien Papers.

46. F. Sheehy-Skeffington, "The Collapse of Sinn Fein," *New Age*, 30 December 1909.

47. Ibid.

48. Sean O'Casey, writing to his friend Jack Carney, 15 January 1947, made this statement: "His [James Connolly] best work, *Labour in Irish History*, was largely the work of the modest, saintly Sheehy-Skeffington, that strange pacifist who was one of Ireland's finest fighters; he refused to sanction violence, but allowed himself to be a Vice-President of the I. Citizen Army — the Irish Gandhi!" (*The Letters of Sean O'Casey 1942–54*, Vol. II, edited by David Krause [New York: Macmillan Publishing Co., 1980], p. 437.) It is doubtful that Skeffington had anything to do with the writing of Connolly's work. Sean O'Casey is not noted for his accuracy.

49. F. Sheehy-Skeffington to James Joyce, 29 August 1909.

50. Ellmann, *Selected Joyce Letters*, p. 156.

51. Ellmann, *James Joyce*, p. 287.

52. Report of Socialist Party of Ireland meeting, 16 October 1909, O'Brien Papers.

53. F. Sheehy-Skeffington to Fred Ryan, 1 January 1910.

54. F. Sheehy-Skeffington to Dublin Commissioners, 30 August 1909.

55. F. Sheehy-Skeffington to members of the Governing Board of University College Dublin and others, 31 August 1909.

56. F. Sheehy-Skeffington to Mary Hayden, 6 October 1909.

57. F. Sheehy-Skeffington to J. B. Skeffington, 8 September 1909.

58. F. Sheehy-Skeffington to J. B. Skeffington, 24 September 1909.

59. Ken Hannigan, "Evolution of Skeffy," p. 20.

60. *Irish Nation*, 19 March 1910.

61. F. Sheehy-Skeffington, "Nationalism and Progress," *The Pioneer*, Vol. I, No. 1 (February 1911).

62. O. Sheehy-Skeffington, "Francis Sheehy-Skeffington," p. 139.

63. *The Leader*, 2 October 1909.

64. Ibid., 26 February 1910.

65. O. Sheehy-Skeffington, "Francis Sheehy-Skeffington," p. 137.

66. *The Leader*, 29 June 1912.

67. Hannigan, "Evolution of Skeffy," p. 22.

68. *Irish Nation*, 29 August 1910.

69. Account of Socialist Party of Ireland meeting held 18 September 1910, O'Brien Papers.

70. F. Sheehy-Skeffington to J. B. Skeffington, 11 November 1909.

71. F. Sheehy-Skeffington to J. B. Skeffington, 14 November 1909.

72. F. Sheehy-Skeffington to J. B. Skeffington, 15 November 1909.

73. F. Sheehy-Skeffington to editor, *The Native*, 17 and 21 September 1909.

74. *Freeman's Journal*, 12 November 1910.

75. William O'Brien Diaries, 1910, O'Brien Papers.

76. Ibid.

77. Ibid.

78. Ibid., account of Socialist Party of Ireland meeting held 28 July 1910.

79. F. Sheehy-Skeffington to secretary of Mountjoy Ward of United Irish League, 2 September 1909.

80. Byrne, J. F., *Silent Years: An Autobiography* (New York: Farrar, Straus and Young, 1953), p. 91. Letter from F. Sheehy-Skeffington to Byrne was dated 25 April 1910.

7

The Constant Battle   1910–1911

On the whole, 1910 was a significant year for the feminist movement and, Skeffington thought, for Home Rule as well. A general election early in the year gave the Liberals 275 representatives and the Unionists 273, making them equal in strength. The balance of power, therefore, was in the hands of the remainder of the House of Commons — 84 Irish Nationalists.

On the day that J. F. Byrne left for the United States, early in April 1910, Skeffington went to the police court "to hear the chalking case." Mrs. Garvey Kelly, a member of the Irish Women's Franchise League, had been summoned for chalking an announcement of a Christabel Pankhurst meeting on the pavements. The charge was "causing an obstruction in the public highway by placing thereon some words in chalk." The wily "Tim" Healy managed to get the summons dismissed by arguing that it was impossible for words in chalk to obstruct anyone. "Two columns in all the papers; a good advertisement for the League," Skeffington wrote Byrne.[1] It was, according to historian Margaret MacCurtain, the Irish women's "first brush with the law."[2] The next brush, only four months later, would result in jail sentences.

The meeting that Mrs. Kelly had been attempting to publicize was held in the Round Room of the Rotunda under the sponsorship of the Irish Women's Franchise League. It was, according to the *Irish Nation*, one of the largest meetings held there "for some time"; in fact, people had to be turned away. The principal speaker, Christabel Pankhurst, was forceful and received an enthusiastic response, the paper reported.[3] *The Leader* acknowledged its importance by devoting almost a full page to an account of the meeting. After making it clear that they favored the franchise for women, *The Leader's* editors went on to say that they assumed the question was of interest only to spinsters and widows, for surely married women, "apart from exceptional cases," were not concerned with the vote. There did not, therefore, seem to be much reason to get excited about the matter. "In other words, we are happy to say we are not Skeffys!" The account continued, "Skeffy at the back of the platform wildly waving his handkerchief, would tend to drive any man of sense against whatever he performed these antics for; but on reflection you find that an antipathy to be, as it were, hyphened

with Skeffy in any cause is not a rational reason for going against that cause."
They would, therefore, "remain of opinion that women should have the
franchise," despite Skeffington "and his kerchief."[4]

Leaving Skeffington aside with difficulty, the editorial turned to Christabel Pankhurst, the "English lady." She seemed a bit too much like a
"Salvation" lass addressing "policemen, some urchins and themselves."
Professors Kettle and Oldham — two "real live Professors" — had spoken
as well, but neither of them pleased *The Leader* greatly. Striking a serious
note, the editors felt that the women's movement in Ireland seemed to be
simply an imitation of the English. The Gaelic League, it was pointed out,
was open to women from top to bottom, but apparently it was not as effective
to use power already available as to shout for power still not obtained. "The
movement in Ireland is a little artificial, Skeffy makes it ridiculous, and there
is a suspicion of West Britonism about it." It seemed to *The Leader* that first
Home Rule should be achieved and then women enfranchised. Returning
to a humorous — and contemptuous — tone, the editorial concluded:

«   «   «   «   «   «   «   «   «

> It was a big meeting, and one of the natural consequences was a rush on
> the trams when it was over. The tram we boarded was quickly filled.
> . . . Happily we were up near the top, so that it was left to other men to
> solve the problem — would a mere male be safe and wise in offering his
> seat to a standing militant Suffragette? The conductor of the tram . . .
> pleaded that he might get into trouble if he carried too many . . . .
> "You better mind yourself," said one of the lady passengers to him; "we
> are all Suffragettes here, and if you don't go on we'll turn you off the car
> and drive it ourselves." Unhappy male! Yet even at the end of that tram
> drive, so proof are our convictions against the assaults of anything short
> of reason, we remained in favour of the franchise for women.[5]

»   »   »   »   »   »   »   »   »

The Leader's stand was a popular one; the Irish Women's Franchise
League was under attack from many sources for putting the fight for women's
suffrage ahead of the fight for Home Rule, as well as for being too closely
allied to the British movement. Hanna was one of the ablest defenders of the
I.W.F.L. position. In answering the first charge, she pointed out that, without the vote, women were *unable* to fight effectively for Home Rule; without
the vote they were able only to play the traditional role — to fight men's
battles for them and neglect women's battles. She labeled as a misstatement
the claim that the I.W.F.L. was collaborating with the English suffrage
movement. Irish women would march side by side with women from other
countries only under the banner of Ireland. If taking part in an international
movement was unpatriotic, then surely patriotism was in a bad way. In this
same connection, the I.W.F.L. had been criticized for sending reports to
Votes for Women, Emmeline Pankhurst and Frederick Pethick-Lawrence's
weekly paper. Hanna answered this criticism by saying that publicity for the

I.W.F.L. was needed on every front, both at home and abroad. Since *Votes for Women* was read avidly by militant suffragettes everywhere, it was important that those readers be made aware of the activities of Irish women and of their strength, Hanna contended.

Articles signed by Hanna Sheehy-Skeffington were appearing fairly regularly in the pages of the *Irish Nation*. One replied with clarity and cogency to what she regarded as misstatements concerning the work and scope of the I.W.F.L., which had appeared in several issues. Hanna branded as "loose-thinking" the concept that the vote was a purely British invention that would be inflicted, like the rest of British misrule, on unwilling Irish women. She agreed with the writer that English opinion meant very little to Irish women although, she said, "there is a certain amount of false courage displayed in protesting this overmuch." But she disagreed vehemently with the concept that Irish women, if they so desired, could serve on public boards and councils. To her, this reflected the writer's "naive and cheerful simplicity." The I.W.F.L. was considering publication of a talk by a Dr. McWalter on "Women and the Poor Law," which would give ample proof of the extent to which women were excluded from county councils, technical committees, the Public Health Department, and public libraries through the "arbitrary selfishness of Irishmen, Nationalist and Sinn Fein alike," she wrote.[6]

Continuing her defense, Hanna noted that the I.W.F.L. was accused of being too nationalistic and at the same time too inclined to disregard nationalism in favor of internationalism. This would seem to indicate that the league "has happily preserved the golden mean." As proof that the league did not have an "un-Irish outlook," she listed the names of some of the league's lecturers — Lindsay Crawford (on "Problems of Irish Thinking Women"), Padraic Colum, Mary Hayden, A. J. Nicolls (on "Women and Social Reform"), T. M. Kettle, T. MacDonagh, Padraic Pearse, James Stephens, and Frederick Ryan. In addition, the I.W.F.L. circulated pamphlets that had been produced in Australia, France, the United States, and Britain. "That British is foreign I hope I have always made abundantly clear!" Hanna wrote, but added that the league would continue to stock John Stuart Mill's "Subjection of Women" until an Irish writer turned out something better.[7]

Hanna's *Irish Nation* article was an excellent enunciation of the Irish Women's Franchise League policy — a policy that was followed to the letter. The League was, as its name indicated, an Irish women's organization, and Irish women — and men — took the leading role in its activities. This did not preclude, however, its cooperation with *all* suffrage movements, British and otherwise. For example, when in late July the Women's Social and Political Union held a meeting in London's Hyde Park, an Irish contingent was present. When they marched to Hyde Park, at their head were the pipers of the Parliamentary branch of the United Irish League led by a veteran of the Fenian movement. At the meeting, the "Irish platform" was presided over by the secretary of the I.W.F.L., whose introductory remarks were in Irish, and the women from Dublin and Belfast were joined by Irish women living in London and in other parts of Great Britain.[8]

Judging by increased attendance at its meetings, the Irish Women's Franchise League was growing in strength. Saturday evening meetings were held in Kingstown (now Dun Laoghaire) and on Sundays in Phoenix Park, and the League's literature sold well at both locations. Early in October 1910, under the League's sponsorship, Mrs. Emmeline Pankhurst spoke at the Palace Rink in Rathmines. The hall was filled, and there were a great many men present. Earlier in the day a group of women had paraded through the streets of Dublin carrying placards advertising the meeting. Led by a pony and trap decorated with green flags, the women had followed on foot and on bicycles, carrying banners, making an impressive sight. Hanna presided at the meeting and, as usual, read telegrams from supporters. There was one from W. B. Yeats, "one of our best friends," as well as a letter from G. B. Shaw saying that he would have been happy to attend in order to bear "testimony to the long campaign of public work by which Mrs. Pankhurst had gained the friendship and admiration of all the most earnest and advanced workers in the cause of Labour, and had qualified herself to take the lead in the struggle for the emancipation of women when the need arose for such a leader."[9]

Mrs. Pankhurst began her address by moving that a resolution be adopted emphatically endorsing the claims of women to the parliamentary franchise and calling on the Liberal government "to give full facilities for the passing into law this year of [the] Woman's Suffrage Bill, which has already passed its second Reading by a larger majority than was obtained by any other measure of this session." She then proceeded to give reasons why such a resolution should be adopted. To one of her statements, the Skeffingtons were a living testament. Those in the suffrage movement believed, she said, that "men and women could work together to make the world better and happier than men would ever be able to make it by themselves." Her resolution was passed; only a few noes were heard from the back of the hall.[10]

Before the meeting adjourned, Tom Kettle, on the platform with Mary, his wife, rose to propose a vote of thanks to Mrs. Pankhurst. His remarks underlined the position of those who, despite their devotion to the cause of votes for women, placed Home Rule first. What had first attracted him to the struggle for enfranchisement for women was the similarity between their condition and that of Ireland. For all practical purposes, he said, Ireland was a country without a vote; it had no power to make the laws under which the people of the country lived. When someone in the audience asked whether women would vote for Home Rule if they got the franchise, Kettle answered that, since women moved on a higher plane of intelligence than men, of course they would vote for Home Rule. His response drew loud applause.[11]

The suffragette strategy in England while the proposed Conciliation Bill was being considered was the observation of a period of nonmilitancy. The mild Conciliation Bill, drawn up by a Conciliation Committee for Woman Suffrage, reflected the national mood of peace and goodwill following the death of Edward VII in May 1910 and the keen sympathy toward his widow, Queen Alexandra. Under the provisions of the bill, women householders would have the right to vote for representatives of the county or borough in which their homes were situated. It would also ensure that marriage would not disqualify a woman from being registered as a voter, provided husband and wife were not registered as voters in the same constituency. Though not exactly a far-reaching bill, both David Lloyd George and Winston Churchill spoke out against it.

When Prime Minister Asquith refused to allow time for the passsage of the bill after it had passed its second Reading, the suffragettes resumed their militant tactics. In a moving speech in November, Mrs. Pankhurst declared that constitutional effort had failed and was at an end. She would lead a deputation to Downing Street since the House of Commons was not in session. Thirteen members of the Irish Women's Franchise League took part in the demonstration. As they neared their destination, they were met by a cordon of police, who attacked the women with cruelty and violence. Many, including members of the Irish delegation, were arrested that day and several days later at another demonstration.[12] In a sworn deposition, Mary Frances Earl, one of the Irish women, gave a precise account of the brutality of the police. She testified that she had "received a blow from a policeman's fist on the nose which bled profusely," and that another policeman had bent back her thumbs and twisted her wrist. Also, "he flung me to the ground with great force and proceeded to kick me as I lay." Women friends helped her up and, after she had recovered somewhat, she rejoined the group. Another policeman kicked her and flung her to the ground under the horse of a mounted policeman, to whom he shouted, "Ride over her." He would have done so, Mrs. Earl said, but Hilda Webb "seized the horse's bridle and turned him aside, so I escaped with a kick on the hip from the horse's hoof." Somewhat later she and a group of eight women tried to reach the House of Commons by an underground passage. Here they again had a struggle with the police, who were "brutal and indecent. They deliberately tore my undergarments using the most foul language — such language as I could not repeat. They seized me by the hair and forced me up the steps on my knees, refusing to allow me to regain my footing. I was then flung into the crowd outside." Her deposition continued with the events that took place several days later, on 22 November, when a deputation again attempted to call on Mr. Asquith in Downing Street. Here they were the victims of further brutality, and Mrs. Earl, with others, was taken to Cannon Row Police Station, held for five hours, and then bailed out. The next day they appeared at Bow Street and were charged with obstruction; since no evidence was offered, however, they were discharged.[13]

The folly of the police brutality and intervention was clear to Skeffington. Fully a year earlier, he had written to John Redmond saying that it had come to his attention that organizers of a Mansion House meeting at which Redmond was to speak intended to exclude women. Although no reason had been given publicly "for this insult to the Nationalist women of Dublin," it had been suggested privately that it was feared there would be interruptions by suffragettes. "This idea is too absurd to be seriously entertained," Skeffington wrote. "Anyone who has followed the development of the Suffragette agitation in England must know that interruption at public meetings was only resorted to when all other means of access to responsible public men, and all other opportunities of putting the case for Woman's Suffrage before them, were denied to women." He complimented Redmond — prematurely, it developed — for not following Asquith's "disastrous precedent" but instead consenting to see a deputation from the I.W.F.L. shortly before the scheduled meeting. "In that fact lies your best safeguard against any Suffragette interruption," he wrote.[14] It was obvious then and later that Skeffington's arguments did not convince Redmond.

Arrests continued, as did demonstrations. One, shortly before Christmas 1910, sponsored by the I.W.F.L., welcomed home from Holloway Prison three suffragettes released the day before — Gretta Cousins, Miss Allen and Mrs. Garvey Kelly. According to the *Freeman's Journal*, it was "a very respectable demonstration both in size and quality," with many men present. Hanna was in charge of the procession. A dense but not hostile crowd lined the parade route; according to one newspaper account, the only disorderly group was a "knot of young men, in the hobble-de-hoy state of development."[15]

A reception and meeting followed the parade. Among those present were the Kettles, James Connolly, James Stephens, James and Gretta Cousins and, of course, Francis Sheehy-Skeffington.[16] Tom Kettle presided, as he often did. In his congratulatory remarks to the I.W.F.L., he said the procession had done more to make women's suffrage a live issue than all their propaganda. Mrs. Cousins then spoke of her prison experiences — the loneliness, the lack of fresh air — but noted that conditions were better than they had been when the first English suffragettes were jailed, thanks to their struggles. Hanna also spoke, saying that the college students' counter-demonstration had not detracted from the dignity of the procession nor from the impression it had made. She hoped that, as these boys grew up, their minds would be changed, "if they had minds to change." Much laughter and applause followed.[17]

Tom Kettle may have been beyond reproach to the feminists at this time, but this was not true of Cruise O'Brien. Although still an associate member of the I.W.F.L., he was critical of their tactic of taking the battle to Westminster. An article in *The Leader*, headed "Reply to Mr. Cruise O'Brien" and signed H. S., questioned whether he had been won over by the Sinn Fein Party. "His attitude towards Irish Suffragettes can only be justified logically by similar application to the Irish Parliamentary Party," as preached by Sinn Feiners. "If, however, as Parliamentarians hold, the Irish Party are perfectly justified in going to Westminster to demand self-government for Ireland, then, too, are Irishwomen similarly justified in raiding the British House of Parliament in order to wring from the Government the recognition of their rights as citizens." Would O'Brien be happier to see those women who were arrested confined to Irish jails? Did he really feel he was criticizing as a friend? If so, said H. S., he might better have brought the matter up at a meeting of the I.W.F.L. "Until we women achieve the rights of citizens and are removed from the voteless category of the child, the lunatic and the criminal, we can serve no party." With the blessing of their Irish representatives in Parliament, both Nationalist and Unionist, the writer continued, the women had been passed over "when English, Scottish and Welsh women were declared eligible for County and Borough Councils." Had they been "less party-blind and more solidly sex-loyal," this would not have happened. "The result of that bitter lesson is the non-party Irish Women's Franchise League." [18] It cannot be denied that agitation was proving effective: one proof was the hostility of both the police and the press.

Skeffington's impression that progress was being made on the Home Rule front as well during 1910 was fortified in a year-end report of the activities of the Young Ireland Branch of the United Irish League. The report noted with great satisfaction that the policy that the organization had been advocating for years — namely, concentration on Home Rule and the subordination thereto of all minor measures — had now been fully recognized as the national policy. At the annual meeting at which this report was adopted, Kathleen Sheehy was unanimously elected vice president and Skeffington was proposed for president. In the light of his other activities, he asked to have his name withdrawn in favor of Thomas Dillon.

Although Skeffington refused to stand for the presidency of the Young Ireland Branch, he continued to be very active in its affairs. He was relieved, however, to be free of the duties of secretary of the Branch — a position he held during 1909. He could now devote more time to the Socialist Party of Ireland and the Irish Women's Franchise League. It is a source of wonder that he and Hanna were able to have any home life whatsoever — but letters from friends and relatives indicate that they did indeed, and that Owen at no time felt neglected. Owen's grandfather — J. B. — thought otherwise. In a letter to Francis, he made his feelings clear:

«   «   «   «   «   «   «   «   «

I suppose you will not be greatly surprised to learn that I am about to marry a Southern lady — it of course does not concern you directly, but I hope to be still able to give you occasional help, when and if you require it; though you have no claim on such aid for many reasons.

In the first place *all* your *wants* result from your neglect of my advice and even your opposition to my wishes; second because you have practically given me up, and ranged yourself as a *Sheehy* — under which name (and not Skeffington) you appear in Thom's Directory. Therefore it is the Sheehy's you should in reason look to. Thirdly if your principles and policy could be put in practise, they would sweep away all the results of my life's work (*and study*) and reduce me to a 5/ Pensioner, like all the stupid, lazy, thriftless and extravagant — so that you do not seem to have any right of claim on me.

Still I am so extravagantly goodnatured, and remember you so well as a little child, that I suppose I should have to help you if you needed it — at least, if all else fail you, try me last.

As to dear little Owen I shall not forget him either — he is not to blame, poor child — and indeed I feel greatly grieved at the way he is being brought up — as a mere animal — without any development of the spiritual which is an essential element of *humanity* as distinguished from *animality* — he should learn hymns, Prayers — stories of angels, etc. — and be elevated above mere material thoughts. It is his *right*, and you are unjust to him, and I repeat it distresses me very much —but it is not his fault. With best wishes to all, and love to Owen. [19]

»   »   »   »   »   »   »   »   »

Another letter from J. B., written later in the month, is a reply to a letter from Francis that has not appeared in his papers. In it Francis seems to have used what J. B. considered "ungracious and ungrateful phrases," concerning his father's marriage and his way of offering financial assistance; J. B. wrote that he had simply wanted to make clear that, even though he had remarried, his "financial relations" with Skeffington would not change. So far as his marriage was concerned, he considered his son the "main agency" in driving him to it. J. B. had offered to take a house large enough for him and the Sheehy-Skeffingtons but his offer had been rejected. His son was also fully responsible, he noted, for injuring his father's career and ruining his own by his political activities. At least he did not blame Skeffington for Owen's lack of religious training. He reserved that criticism for Hanna, since, as he said, that was a mother's responsibility. [20]

Throughout this exchange of letters, J. B. lamented his son's disastrous financial state. If he had not given his son enough assistance, J. B. was able to blame his son for that as well. "As to money you only went really wrong when you were best supplied, showing that you would likely have gone to the dogs if better supplied," he wrote. In conclusion, he repeated, "I hope to still be able to afford assistance while hoping you shan't need it." [21] If J. B. had seen the checks received from the *Manchester Guardian*, for example, for Skeffington's contributions, he would have known that his hope was vain — his son was paid five shillings for his March contributions, two pounds for his July items, and two pounds for October's.

Though money was merely trickling into the household from Skeffington's various articles and reviews, for him disseminating his progressive ideas was of paramount importance. He was doing signed work now for the *New Age*, a small British publication, which he considered a brilliant paper. A letter to the editor signifying his desire to contribute articles indicates his attitude. Even though the *New Age* did not pay for contributions, he wrote, "The free lance journalist's natural reluctance to write anything without payment is overcome by a keen appreciation of the advertisement obtainable from inclusion in the NEW AGE galaxy." He added that he hoped, too, that he might do reviewing for them "and thereby indirectly relieve a purse assailed by the wasting fever of book-buying."[22]

This is not to say that Skeffington adopted a completely cavalier attitude toward lucrative employment. Many instances have been cited previously, and correspondence indicates that in March 1911 he attempted, unsuccessfully, to obtain a position as librarian in the Urban District of Rathmines and Rathgar.[23] But publications like the *Irish Nation* were essential to him as a platform, no matter how meager the monetary return. There seemed, fortunately, to be enough men of good will with ideas similar to his to ensure the constant appearance of such publications — as short-lived as they might be.

Early in 1911, *The Pioneer* appeared with an editorial board of ten such people, many of whom held academic degrees. Among the ten were James Cousins, literature editor; Maurice Wilkins, who would play an important role in Skeffington's life, ethics; Lady Sybil Smith, feminism; and Francis Sheehy-Skeffington, politics. The lofty objective of the publication was to "stimulate, organise, and make articulate a growing body of thought which . . . is striving towards the elevation and enrichment of life; and to guide such thought towards a beneficent and effective expression in personal, civic, and national action."[24]

The Pioneer was destined to live only several months, but in that brief time Skeffington contributed several articles and book reviews. One article, "Nationalism and Progress — An Open Letter to an Irish Reformer," examined the customary lack of success of a reformer. The reformer's aims and standards were high. On the social front, he strove to abolish intemperance, obtain better housing for workers, clear the slums, alter the poor laws to make them more humane, improve health, and encourge self-reliance. On the political front, he fought for peace, international arbitration, enfranchisement of women. Why then, asked Skeffington, was he unsuccessful? It was, in Skeffington's opinion, because of his anti-nationalistic attitude — an attitude that did incalculable harm and caused Nationalists, who made up a large proportion of the population, "to associate many much needed reforms with anti-Nationalism, and even to regard them as 'red herrings' drawn across the Nationalist path." As a consequence, this suspicion had defeated the implementation of vital reforms. "Whether you like it or not," he wrote, "there exists in the mass of the Irish people a feeling of separateness from all other peoples, and from the English people in particular." That feeling could not be argued with, he believed. "You must not flout political

Nationalism; you must not oppose it," he cautioned the reformer. "So long as you remain an anti-Nationalist, your work for reform is doomed to futility."[25] Tom Kettle was advancing similar ideas in his National Economics Lectures at University College, Dublin. Economists, he pointed out, were now studying actual conditions in their own countries rather than following set principles as had the classical school of economics. Kettle talked of a notable transformation of Marxism. "Today you have an International that possesses reality because it roots in Nationalism," he said.[26]

Another article that Skeffington wrote for *The Pioneer*, "Peace on Earth," took issue with the enthusiasm with which pacifists everywhere were greeting the interchange of views between U.S. President William Howard Taft and Sir Edward Grey on the subject of international arbitration. Skeffington pointed out that this already appeared, to the small nations particularly, like simply another coalition of the "Great Powers." And to Germany it seemed a new menace to their growth, a fresh attempt to isolate them and keep them from expanding. To conclude such a treaty, he maintained, would be a signal to Germany to step up its building of warships immediately. Undoubtedly the existence of courts of arbitration would tend to lessen the warlike spirit; but if a spirit of brotherhood could be created among nations, then peace would come gradually of itself and there would be no need for elaborate machinery. The article concluded with the thought that an international labor movement might do more in this direction "than all the eminent 'pacific' statesmen with an eye on political combinations and territorial aggrandisement."[27]

In a review of *The Party System* by Hilaire Belloc and Cecil Chesterton, Skeffington called Lawrence Ginnell the only indispensable man in the House of Commons. This was the man who in 1917 would resign his seat in the House of Commons to join the struggle for the sovereign independence of Ireland. Critics of Ginnell had said that he spoiled his arguments by "being personal to the Speaker, instead of attacking the system of which the Speaker is only the instrument." Skeffington countered this with the argument that all bad systems are run by fine men "whose personal virtues become barriers against any assaults on the system itself." These men must be attacked, he said, if a system is to be brought down. "Boorishness is the first essential virtue of the practical reformer," he wrote.[28]

To Skeffington's great delight, his comments about Ginnell brought an enthusiastic letter from his friend Lindsay Crawford, now one of the "leader" (feature) writers on *The Globe*, in Toronto, Canada, where he had gone after leaving Ireland some months earlier. He agreed that the attitude of the Irish Party toward Ginnell was a disgrace, thanked Skeffington for copies of *The Pioneer*, and said that he admired "its platform and independent tone and was cheered not a little by the advent of this much-needed gospel of Irish thought and character." Crawford was enjoying his job on *The Globe*, which he referred to as the "Thunderer of Canada." He was, he said, handling mostly British and foreign affairs. Two items in Crawford's letter pleased Skeffington very much. First, "the feminist movement is very strong on this Continent"; second, "I am getting on well here and can see a future before me. The Globe voices my own views on most questions so I am happy in being able to give rein to my thoughts."[29]

Skeffington's response to Crawford's letter, incidentally, brought a reply filed with nostalgia. It was his opinion that this was the right time to "bring the Irish question to Ireland once for all and allow us to settle our differences in our own way in an Irish Parliament." He felt that he could do good work in England and Ireland along these lines and that it would be worth sacrificing his opportunities in Canada to assist in the fight for self-government. He continued: "It is satisfactory to see that the Ulster Liberals — although from self-interest — have come up to my platform for which they drove me from the Ulster Guardian." Skeffington's letter, he said, had "stirred in me a strong desire to return to the old country and even should the door be closed against me I hope some day to see you all."[30] Skeffington's determination to stay in Ireland, no matter how adverse the situation, must have had this effect on many of his colleagues.

The first issue of *The Pioneer* carried an announcement of a new monthly publication, the *Irish Review*. "On the strength of a whole fortnight's seniority, it said, "we bid our coadjutor a hearty welcome to the work of stimulating and expressing the intellectual life of Ireland."[31] The first issue of the *Review* contained a short story by George Moore, a critical article by John Eglinton, a sketch by Lord Dunsany, a picture by William Orpen, and poetry by James Stephens and Padraic Colum. Since the audience for both publications was limited at best and not dissimilar, the *Review* must have contributed in no small way to the rapid demise of *The Pioneer*. Skeffington, however, liked the publication and was soon contributing book reviews.

His first piece for the *Irish Review* appeared in May and was a critique of a new volume of Shaw plays — *The Doctor's Dilemma, Getting Married,* and *The Shewing Up of Blanco Posnet*. To Skeffington, the prefaces revealed the real Shaw, and these three plays — on doctors, marriage, and censorship — were "among the most incisive work Mr. Shaw has yet done." Two lines in the review were very revealing: "In all ages it is necessary, if society is to grow or even to remain healthy, for some one to take on himself the task of scourging the accepted virtues of his time. Scourges for the conventional vices will never be wanting; but it is by assailing the cherished ideals of a community that the rebirth of society is made possible."[32] A review of J. R. Fisher's *The End of the Irish Parliament* appeared in November. Skeffington took exception to what he considered Fisher's misuse of history in politics as a direct argument for "existing or proposed institutions." He maintained that "too great attachment to evolutionary theories" would produce a "new fatalism" which would impede all progress. "Ireland's need for Home Rule depends not on the merits or misdeeds of the Irish Parliament in the eighteenth century, but on the social condition of the Irish people in the twentieth," Skeffington wrote. "Politics is a science of the future, and the penetrating imagination, not the well-stored memory, is the characteristic of politicians who reach the statesman's level."[33]

In July of that same year, another and quite different publication was launched. This was *The Irish Worker,* or, to use its full name, *The Irish Worker and People's Advocate.* James Larkin was its editor and was in full control of it. Emmet Larkin, the contemporary historian, says that the paper attacked "with a monumental perseverance the sweating, exploiting employers and the corrupt, cynical politicians, who in his [James Larkin's] eyes were responsible for the reprehensible social condition of Dublin."[34] It was indeed a free-swinging paper that never hesitated to name names. During the first year of its existence, seven cases of libel were brought against it. The first issue sold 16,000 copies; within a month the circulation had increased to 19,000 copies, and within two months it was 23,500. It averaged, after that, 20,000 copies per week. Contrast this with *Sinn Fein* which, during its subsidized existence, averaged about 2,000 copies an issue.

Skeffington wrote a year later, in a review of *The Pope's Green Island,* by W. P. Ryan, that "Irish Clericalism will meet its Nemesis at the hands of the Irish Labour movement which, by simply going about its own business and ignoring the fury which the clergy must continue to lavish upon it, will prove an effectively shattering force. It will not be so cultured, or so broad-minded, or so agreeable in all its aspects as Mr. Ryan's attitude; but it will win." He cited the success of *The Irish Worker* as opposed to the failure of the *Irish Nation* as "not without significance in this connection."[35]

Pleased as he was with *The Irish Worker,* he disliked Larkin's personality and distrusted his method of operation. Quick to admit Larkin's ability, he was, nevertheless, impatient with the man's attacks on friends who disagreed with him even slightly and with his inability to control his temper. Skeffington had reason to believe, too, that Larkin was not in sympathy with the cause of women's rights. On one occasion, when James Connolly addressed a meeting of the I.W.F.L., Larkin criticized him for "mixing himself up with a pack of women."[36] Emmet Larkin says that "he could love humanity but he had difficulty loving Tom, Dick, and Harry."[37] This did not endear James Larkin to Skeffington, to whom the individual was of supreme importance. James Connolly shared Skeffington's feelings about Larkin. "Do not pay any attention to what Larkin says," he wrote to William O'Brien in May 1911. Connolly pointed out also that Larkin had claimed to be a member of the Socialist Party of Ireland when, of course, he never had been. "The man is utterly unreliable — and dangerous because unreliable," he added.[38]

Connolly's letter to O'Brien noted that Skeffington was going to be approached to become National Secretary of the Socialist Party of Ireland.

There was no chance that he would accept, Connolly said, since Skeffington would not oppose the United Irish League on a national level. "He wants it to rule the roost politically until we get Home Rule," Connolly told O'Brien.[39] Nevertheless, O'Brien did offer Skeffington the secretaryship, stressing that the work would not be onerous. Skeffington, however, regretfully declined, saying, "Whoever takes such an office should, I think, be prepared to put into it a *single-minded* Devotion which I am not yet in a position to give to the S.P.I."[40] He was, in fact, ready to give single-minded devotion to all his major causes — emancipation of women, socialism, pacifism, and nationalism, and as time went on he became more than ever convinced that militancy was needed to forward them all.

NOTES TO CHAPTER 7

1. Byrne, *Silent Years*, p. 91.
2. Margaret MacCurtain, "Women, the Vote and Revolution," in *Women in Irish Society: The Historical Dimension* (Dublin: Arlen House, 1978), p. 49.
3. *Irish Nation*, 19 March 1910.
4. *The Leader*, 19 March 1910.
5. Ibid.
6. *Irish Nation*, 11 June 1910.
7. Ibid.
8. Ibid., 6 August 1910. The meeting of the Women's Social and Political Union was held 23 July 1910 in Hyde Park, London.
9. *Freeman's Journal*, 5 October 1910.
10. Ibid.
11. Ibid.
12. Ibid., 23 November 1910.
13. Sworn deposition of Mary Frances Earl of 39 Raglan Road in the County of Dublin, 15 December 1910, Sheehy-Skeffington Papers.
14. F. Sheehy-Skeffington to John Redmond, 11 November 1909.
15. *Freeman's Journal*, 26 December 1910.
16. Skeffington, incidentally, wrote Cousins sometime later that the Socialist Party of Ireland was "much more friendly to the suffrage agitation since Connolly took up the reins."
17. *Freeman's Journal*, 26 December 1910.
18. *The Leader*, 17 December 1910.
19. J. B. Skeffington to F. Sheehy-Skeffington, 2 October 1911. The southern lady J. B. married was Hannah Nugent from County Tipperary. In 1914 she gave birth to a daughter, Anna. There is nothing to indicate that Francis ever saw his step-sister or spent time with J. B. and the new family, but it would be surprising if he had not. It should be remembered, however, that Anna was only two years old when he was murdered. In 1976 Anna Skeffington corresponded with Samuel Levenson, and was interviewed at the home of Andrée Sheehy-

Skeffington early in 1977. Anna was living in Clonmel, County Tipperary, unmarried, and employed as a salesclerk, as she had been for many years. She was a very pleasant, rather ordinary woman, most cooperative but knew nothing of any importance. She was not sure of the date of her mother's death but thought it was 1956. She herself died in 1979. Andrée Sheehy-Skeffington, apparently carrying on Hanna's tradition, had been in touch with her through the years, seeing her once or twice a year.

20. J. B. Skeffington to F. Sheehy-Skeffington, 16 October 1911.

21. J. B. Skeffington to F. Sheehy-Skeffington, 16 October 1911.

22. F. Sheehy-Skeffington to A. R. Orage, 28 September 1909.

23. F. P. Fawcett, Clerk of the Council, Urban District of Rathmines and Rathgar, to F. Sheehy-Skeffington, 23 March 1911.

24. *The Pioneer*, Vol. I, No. 1 (February 1911).

25. F. Sheehy-Skeffington, "Nationalism and Progress," pp. 31–35.

26. Thomas Kettle, *The Day's Burden* (London: Browne and Nolan, 1937), p. 135.

27. F. Sheehy-Skeffington, "Peace on Earth," *The Pioneer*, April 1911, pp. 114–116.

28. F. Sheehy-Skeffington, "The Pioneer's Bookshelf," *The Pioneer*, March 1911.

29. Lindsay Crawford to F. Sheehy-Skeffington, 17 April 1911.

30. Lindsay Crawford to F. Sheehy-Skeffington, 16 October 1911.

31. *The Pioneer*, Vol. I, No. 1 (February 1911).

32. *Irish Review*, Vol. I (May 1911), pp. 152–155.

33. Ibid., November 1911, pp. 466–467.

34. Emmet Larkin, *James Larkin: Irish Labour Leader, 1876–1947* (London: Routledge & Kegan Paul, 1965), p. 76.

35. *Irish Review*, June 1912.

36. William O'Brien 1910 diaries, O'Brien Papers.

37. Larkin, *James Larkin*, p. 222.

38. James Connolly to William O'Brien, 24 May 1911, O'Brien Papers.

39. Ibid.

40. F. Sheehy-Skeffington to William O'Brien, 29 June 1911.

8

Crimes and Punishments   1911–1912

I n *If the Germans Conquered England*, Robert Lynd says that Skeffington played the part of "the Socratic gadfly" in the United Irish League,
and that on every front "he became a sort of legend as an interrupter of
the somnolent."[1] Skeffington would have liked that description, for this was
the role that he visualized for himself in the many organizations to which he
belonged. Basically a misfit as an organization man, he was nevertheless
deeply involved not only in the work of the Irish Women's Franchise
League, the Socialist Party of Ireland, and the Young Ireland Branch, but
was also a member of the Incorporated Society of Authors, the Proportional
Representation Society, the Irish Anti-Vaccination League, and the Independent Labour Party of Ireland. None of these memberships was in name
only except for the Society of Authors. He was in demand to speak, write,
and in the case of the Proportional Representation Society, to form a
Proportional Representation Committee in Ireland.

The breadth of Skeffington's interests and involvement can be judged,
too, from a letter he wrote to the editor of the *Morning Leader*, a British publication, in 1910. Here he listed a few of the topics he would like to discuss in
future articles: the breakdown of elector conventions due to the bossism of
Devlin and the Hibernians; the end of Sinn Fein as a force in Irish politics;
the decay of the Gaelic League under the "quiet hostility of the priests"; and
the workings and prospects of the new universities. "Can you use any of these
within the next month or two?" he asked.[2] In addition, Skeffington kept up
an extensive correspondence with friends and relatives. A cousin, writing
from Irish Street, Downpatrick, marveled at the fact that Skeffington could
remember all their birthdays. (Incidentally, he generally sent them books as
gifts.)

Yet when King George V was scheduled to visit Ireland after his
coronation in June 1911, Skeffington was in the forefront of the protest
movement. Sinn Fein, the Socialist Party, and the I.W.F.L. were all taking
steps to see that the king's welcome was a cold one. At a public meeting of the
National Council of Sinn Fein, Skeffington was unanimously elected to
serve on an arrangements committee.[3] The Socialist Party issued a lengthy

manifesto headed "The Royal Visit," with the subhead "The great appear
great to us, only because we are on our knees. Let Us Rise." This was an
impassioned plea to workers not to attend any of the processions or festivities,
or countenance in any way the king's visit. For distributing this leaflet,
Walter Carpenter, an S.P.I. member who had supported the socialist cause
vigorously for years, was sentenced to three months in jail. Skeffington
fought hard for Carpenter's release and, characteristically, sent William
O'Brien some money toward a fund to help Carpenter's family, saying that
he would try to be at the prison gates to welcome him upon his release.[4]

For some time also Skeffington had been involved in what has been
called the "penny dirties" controversy. He had infuriated a great many
people — and certainly *The Leader* — with an article entitled "Dublin &
Sunday Papers" in the British weekly *John Bull*, the tone of which reflected
what must have been his pure joy in writing it. He portrayed Ireland as suffering from one of its periodic bouts of moral indignation — this time in the
form of a campaign against the *Sunday Chronicle* and other English Sunday
papers, which were being labeled as "immoral literature." This campaign,
he wrote, emanated from Limerick, which he considered altogether fitting.
"There is hardly a reactionary movement of recent times in Ireland that
cannot be traced to the Most Reverend Edward Thomas O'Dwyer, Bishop of
Limerick." Skeffington pointed out that "Eddie O'D.," as he was called,
conducted the campaign against the Jews in Limerick some seven years
earlier, led the opposition to equal opportunity for women in the National
University of Ireland, and prevented the foundation of a free public library in
his district — thus checking the spread of libraries "with their concomitant
dangerous habit of promoting thinking."[5]

Purity of morals was the motive for this new crusade. Would it be a bit
awkward, Skeffington asked, to question what clergymen were doing to stop
immorality by raising the social and economic status of women?[6] The
economic necessity that drove women to turn to prostitution had troubled
him for years. As early as 1903 he reported in his "Facts and Fancies"
notebook a prostitute's attempted suicide. "How many of these occur in
Dublin in a year I wonder?" he had written. "On this occasion a constable
'gallantly rescued her'; & she was sent to jail for 3 months! 'The woman had
been 95 times before the Court.' Prostitution is no insignificant evil in
Ireland."[7] He had also written that his attention had been called to an article
in the *Encyclopedia Britannica* on prostitution. "There it is stated that
Dublin is the only city in the Three Kingdoms where brothels are tolerated
by the police; & though in one street only (Tyrone St.) yet there more openly
than in 'the south of Europe or Algeria'!!"[8] He had seen no evidence over the
years that the clergy had made any valiant effort to fight this evil. His
question, therefore, was not a new one for him.

The *John Bull* article pointed out that vigilance committees were being organized and newsagents terrorized in an attempt to wipe out the sale of the "penny dirties." In every parish they were being told to discontinue carrying these Sunday papers or risk being boycotted. "As a Nationalist I trust the Dublin newsagents will rise to the occasion. The clerical attack on their independence places them in the foremost fighting line of freedom," he concluded.[9]

The Leader, to quote one priest, had "espoused the holy and noble cause of clean literature" and joined the war on the Sunday papers. That paper had, in fact, coined the phrase "penny dirties." It was so infuriated by Skeffington's article that it called for him to be ousted from the Young Ireland Branch. As usual, *The Leader's* sheer vituperation was hard to surpass. A December 1911 issue editorialized, "We are all familiar with the carrion crows — some of whom 'carrion' against their country at so much a day in England." This carrion crow, the item read was "a dignified bird" compared to "the hyphenated-democratic Sheehy-Skeffington," who was "a carrion sparrow" and "a sort of spook in whiskers and knickerbockers." *The Leader* had always laughed at him, the editorial stated, and still did, but "now that he has written over to the Big Brother to defame Limerick, the third largest Nationalist city in Ireland, and shouts 'freedom' in the cause of the anglicising and dirty imported penny papers, he is presuming on the immunity he receives in his recognised capacity as a minor oddity. We await the next move of the Young Ireland Branch, U.I.L., of which this champion of English 'penny dirties' is a prominent member."[10] The newspaper continued to urge the Y.I.B. to do something about the "carrion sparrow," although one editorial did attempt a great show of indifference. "It would be a disadvantage to those of us who are fighting for a clean Press to have an oddity like Skeffy on our side; he is more effective for us on the other side. If the Yibs like him, that is their business."[11]

Many months later the battle still raged. An editorial, possibly Skeffington's, in the *Irish Citizen,* reported that one of the "unfortunate dupes" of the campaign against so-called immoral literature had smashed a picture dealer's window in which classical pictures and statues were displayed. The question was raised whether leaders of this campaign, "mostly clergymen," felt justified in destroying private property when their "moral sensibilities" were offended. It seemed to the writer that "male puritans" were failing to get at the roots of immorality — the social and economic degradation of women. "Those who are interested in genuine and firm-based morality had better devote their attention to freeing women; when they are free, they will make surprising changes in the moral tone of the community. Meantime, the valiant male combatters of 'immoral literature' might consider whether gross misrepresentation, such as is indulged in by their pets in the press with regard to the women's movement, is not the most flagrant form of immorality the press can be guilty of."[12]

Without a doubt, Skeffington's words were adversely affecting *The*

Leader's coverage of suffrage activities. Even though in 1910 D. P. Moran, the editor, had said that he sympathized with the women's movement, it had been a half-hearted sympathy, and by early 1912 the paper was editorially condemning "Skeffy and Co." It was willing to admit that *some* of the suffragettes might be Nationalists, but maintained that many of them were "sour non-Nationalists to put it at the mildest."[13]

It was the attitude of the *Irish Times*, rather than *The Leader*, that troubled Skeffington, however. Much space was being devoted to prove that in countries where the vote had been obtained for women, such as Finland and New Zealand, no measures had been passed that would not have been passed without the women's vote. The authority for these views was never clear, he felt, whereas he could cite examples to prove that progressive legislation had indeed followed regularly in both countries. He noted that the *Irish Times* wistfully expressed the hope that "authoritative information" might be made available about the effect of the women's vote in New Zealand, for example. In a letter to the *Irish Times*, he called the paper's attention to the fact that such information had been published many times, showing that, among other things, New Zealand had lowered its "infantile mortality by 50 per cent since women got the vote." He called attention also to the fact that an *Irish Times* article exhorted Unionists not to shrink from amending the Home Rule Bill by inserting in it provisions for proportional representation but refused to apply the same cogent reasoning to the need for an amendment calling for votes for women.[14]

To Skeffington, it appeared that, under a pretense of friendliness toward the suffrage movement, the *Irish Times* missed no opportunity of injuring it. Apparently it was the paper's attitude of sweet reason that annoyed him. But the press attacks were inevitable, for the women's suffrage movement in Ireland was gaining in strength, and the fear was great that it was injuring both the Irish Party and the cause of Home Rule with its call for "the vote first."

Although disagreeing with women like Constance Markievicz who claimed that the I.W.F.L. was dominated by its British sisters, the Skeffingtons were not ignoring the problem. As early as March 1910, Skeffington had written a fellow Y.I.B. member that the I.W.F.L. was extending its operations to the provinces. It was imperative that this be done, he said, since "the Women's Freedom League of England has sent over emissaries, and is trying to run the Suffrage movement in Ireland on purely English lines; and they must be forestalled."[15] It had, nevertheless, been tactically correct for the I.W.F.L. to work closely with those who had more experience, greater funds, and the same aims. For instance, *Votes for Women* had put out a clear, concise leaflet called "The Conciliation Bill Explained" after the second Reading of that bill had passed, and it would have been a waste of time and money for the I.W.F.L. to issue its own.

Conditions were changing, however. The I.W.F.L. Executive Committee for 1911–12 was a strong one, consisting of people who had fought hard — and some of whom had been jailed — for their activities: Gretta Cousins, Hilda Webb, Marguerite Palmer, Mary Frances Earl, Miss Tatlow, Kathleen Sheehy, Mrs. Garvey Kelly, and Helen Laird. They were issuing some informative leaflets giving facts as to why women needed the vote and what voting would mean to them. In Ireland in 1912, there were roughly 3,000 women in the civil service, 2,000 in medical service, 13,000 in education, 4,000 in commerce, 35,000 in shopkeeping, 70,000 in farming and pasturing, and 180,000 in textile industries. In short, there were about 550,000 women workers. Of these, about 320,000 were over the age of twenty-five.[16] This was an impressive block. Very little headway was being made, however, in getting a firm commitment from the Irish Party on the suffrage question; thus as the women's militancy increased, so did their hostility toward the party. They were becoming a source of embarrassment that could no longer be ignored. It was then that publications such as *The Leader* began to step up their attacks.

On Sunday afternoon, 31 March 1912, called Home Rule Day, a massive Nationalist rally was held in O'Connell Street to welcome the introduction of the third Home Rule Bill. That morning Dubliners found "Votes for Women" painted on walls, billboards, and footpaths in Sackville Street. Later that day twenty-three women with placards inscribed with suffragist slogans paraded quietly through the streets. The crowd was courteous, but not so the Nationalist stewards. As the marchers turned onto Dawson Street near the end of their route, posters were knocked out of their hands and they were pushed and shoved ruthlessly. Hanna's glasses were broken in the scuffle. She said later that this was to blind her to the defects of the party.[17] The women retaliated by renting seven windows in Sackville Street and decorating them with flags and posters. Hundreds clustered around the windows and leaflets were distributed among them. "It appears that Skeffy was amongst the girls flinging leaflets at the crowd," said *The Leader*.[18]

Infuriated at the ruthlessness of the stewards, Hanna announced at the next meeting of the I.W.F.L. that she had that day sent in her resignation to the Young Ireland Branch. She called on all I.W.F.L. members to follow her example and resign from any organization connected with the Irish Party. This was the time for militant action, she said. Her friend Isabella Richardson, in an open letter to the *Irish Times*, said that feeling at the meeting rose "to an almost painful degree of intensity" when Hanna made her announcement in an emotion-choked voice. Mrs. Richardson went on to say that she agreed with Hanna's stand up to that point but that she would not support the call for militant action. It was her feeling that violence only injured the women's cause.[19]

John Redmond had consented to meet at the Gresham Hotel with a delegation from the I.W.F.L. the day after the Home Rule Day rally. He insisted that his remarks be off the record but made it clear that he could not support women's suffrage either in the Home Rule Bill or after Home Rule was won. It was a frustrating meeting so far as the women were concerned and many reached the limits of their patience. In a letter to the *Irish Times* in early April, Hanna called on Redmond to make an *open* statement of his position on women's suffrage. She stated that he had publicly announced, through the Press Association, that members of the Irish Party were free to vote as they chose, but it had been learned that at a party meeting he had given an imperative order that no one was to support women's suffrage that year. Her letter concluded with "a word of warning to Mr. Joseph Devlin and the Ancient Order of Hibernians." Since their crusade against indecent postcards, she said, the members had been wearing a halo. "If, in their war against women who are asserting their rights as citizens, the Hibernians carry out the threats which they have been loudly uttering within the past few days, they may rest assured that their halo will be publicly stripped from them." [20]

Incidents of harassment grew more frequent. When Councillor Sarah Cecilia Harrison, the South City Ward representative on the Municipal Council and an avowed Nationalist, spoke before a mid-April meeting of the Irish Women's Franchise League, she was interrupted by a band of about twenty women. Skeffington wrote in the *Irish Worker* that these women, half-drunk and shepherded by a few men "of the bookmaker and 'bully' type" shouted Councillor Harrison down, as she began to speak, with cries of "No Votes for Women," "We Want Home Rule," and "Cheers for John Redmond." They had set out for the meeting from a public house on the north side of town and were to return there after the meeting to be paid off. Ironically, Miss Harrison had come to explain to the members of the I.W.F.L. that, although she felt strongly about women's suffrage, she put Home Rule first, and therefore urged them to support the Irish Party. [21]

A National Convention had been called for 23 April at the Mansion House, Dublin, to consider the Home Rule Bill that had been introduced earlier that month. Since the bill definitely excluded women from any participation in the proposed Irish Parliament, the I.W.F.L. decided this was the right time and place to protest. Gretta Cousins organized a meeting of "Convention Deputation Volunteers" to instruct them how to proceed. She need not have bothered, however, for they were refused admission to the Mansion House even though they waited outside all day. Apparently there was violence, for Isabella Richardson wrote to Hanna saying that she hoped Hanna was all right after what she had gone through the day before. "I was so sorry to see in the morning paper that you fainted & returned again to the fray!" She went on to mention her letter to the *Irish Times*. She had been "hurt & astonished" by the reception it had received from her friends, felt they were being unjust, and wanted Hanna to believe "that it is my consciencious [*sic*] idea the recent methods of the I.W.F.L. are ruining the women's cause in Ireland, and that therefore it is one's duty to oppose them." [22] Hers was an attitude that the Skeffingtons knew well but found difficult to understand. As Francis had said at a mass meeting some months earlier, "In a country which is under foreign rule, the nationalists who believe in its natural destiny and independence, ought to spend a considerable portion of their time, if not in jail, at all events in doing the next best thing which would merit them, in the opinion of these foreign rulers, a term in jail," and also "no progressive movement can be in a healthy state unless its members are prepared to face the risk of imprisonment."[23]

Tom Kettle had agreed to put the women's case before the National Convention but broke his promise at the last moment, as he had done at the Baton Convention (so called because of the violence of the stewards who were influenced by Devlin's oratory). Skeffington, who attended the convention as a reporter, was appalled. Contrite but unbending, Kettle called at the I.W.F.L. headquarters and, not finding either of the Skeffingtons there, left a note for Hanna. "I called to let you abuse me," he said, "but also to make it clear that even if *no amendment whatever* to any clause can be carried I think that the Bill ought to be accepted." With him Home Rule would always come first. Skeffington found his thinking flawed and made that clear in a review of Kettle's *The Open Secret of Ireland*: "His treatment of Ulster is inadequate; but then to treat Ulster adequately would require a faithful handling of clericalism, and that Mr. Kettle has eschewed since the days of the 'Nationist.' Otherwise the full gospel of Home Rule is here." He did underline, however, his admiration for Kettle's style, his brilliance, and the quickness of his wit. He quoted him on Irish administration: "Dublin Castle understands Ireland. Did it not know what the people of Ireland want, it could not so infallibly have maintained its tradition of giving them the opposite." Of Kettle's oratory, Skeffington wrote, "He is the Public Orator of Ireland — our nearest analogue to Lord Rosebery in the ability to frame in faultlessly-cut phrases the thoughts and emotions of the man in the street."[24]

It was becoming obvious to the Skeffingtons at that time that a bad situation was worsening. They could see that the Irish women's movement was being weakened by the growing impression that it was simply an offshoot of the British and by the charge that it was anti-nationalist. One way to fight this, it occurred to Skeffington, was for the movement to have a paper of its own. With this in mind, Francis approached James Cousins. They had always liked each other and worked well together. Cousins's first question was "What will it cost?" As Skeffington saw it, they would need enough capital to be able to lose five pounds per week for a year. By that time they should be firmly established. Although neither of them had any money, Cousins had contacts. Knowing how strongly feminist his good friend Pethick-Lawrence was, he immediately wrote to him outlining the situation and underlining the need for a feminist publication that would make clear the distinction between the Irish and British movements. Within days he had received 260 pounds.

Enough money to get started was finally raised, and early in May Skeffington wrote to Cousins that he had found someone to take over the advertising and handle distribution and circulation. "He is hopeful as to getting advertisements for first month; after that it will depend on circulation," he wrote. "I'm writing 'Notes of the Week'; I shall write some every day till we are ready to print, when the stale ones can be eliminated. Should we not arrange to meet somewhere daily for the present?"[25]

The first issue of the new paper, the *Irish Citizen*, appeared on 25 May 1912. Since Cousins was a full-time teacher, Skeffington carried the burden, doing most of the editing and covering the political aspects of the women's movement in signed and unsigned articles and notes. Cousins wrote on the movement's more general aspects. It was an impressive eight-page publication, and advance publicity promised that it would be a product of "Irish life, Irish initiative, Irish brains, Irish manufacture, Irish labour."[26] This was Skeffington's most ambitious venture to date. It was also to be the longest-lasting, the most time-consuming, and the most rewarding.

The aim of the *Irish Citizen*, as expressed in the lead editorial, was "simple and inclusive; to win for men and women equally the rights of citizenship, and to claim from men and women equally the duties of citizenship." All movements that worked for the fullest development of "a complete humanity" would be assisted; everything that tended to "lower or limit human freedom" would be opposed. Attention would be focused chiefly on the abolition of "the sex-bar to the polling booth." In an all-out editorial attack, the Irish Party was blamed for killing the Conciliation Bill and criticized for its blindness. For example, even though the Irish Party appealed to Americans for support for the cause of Home Rule, they failed to note that at least 10,000 women had demonstrated in New York City to demand the incorporation of votes for Irish women in any Home Rule bill.[27]

Skeffington had resigned from the Young Ireland Branch over the suffrage issue at the same time as Hanna. Regardless of that issue, however, his continued membership seemed no longer necessary. He had always felt that he must support the Irish Party in order to achieve Home Rule but, with the introduction of the third Home Rule Bill, that goal appeared virtually assured. He could now attend Socialist Party meetings more regularly and involve himself in efforts being made to organize a new party. At Easter time he chaired a conference that voted into existence the Independent Labour Party of Ireland, bringing together the Dublin, Cork, and Belfast branches of the Socialist Party of Ireland and four of the five branches of the Belfast Independent Labour Party. It was to be "open to all men and women, irrespective of their past political affiliations, who desire to see the working class of their country organized upon the political field."[28] The inaugural meeting was held in Belfast in mid-May and impressed Skeffington as proving the extent to which labor solidarity could overcome the deep-seated religious and political enmities of that city. The approximately fifteen hundred men and women who attended the meeting belonged to both of the religious groups that had long divided Belfast into two hostile camps. A resolution was passed welcoming the Home Rule Bill as the necessary preliminary to social reform in Ireland and demanding that it include votes for women. There was only one dissenting vote — on votes for women. [29]

Skeffington sent a report of this meeting to the *Daily Herald,* a British labor paper, saying that he would like to submit labor news and comments from Ireland from time to time, "not as a commercial proposition, but as a means of helping my own property (I have applied for a few shares in the Daily Herald)." He added that he thought there should be a good market for the *Herald* in Ireland, and that it would certainly fill a void. "The Irish Press is even worse than the English in its treatment of labour matters," he wrote. "Last year, a strike of 1500 women textile workers continued for some weeks in Belfast without a word about it being printed in the Belfast papers! though they were printing news of much smaller strikes elsewhere." [30]

In response to what amounted to a draft, Skeffington agreed to act as secretary of the Dublin Branch of the Independent Labour Party of Ireland, but only on a temporary basis. His time was limited and he could do nothing half-heartedly. That he could have accepted the secretaryship even on a temporary basis seems incredible. He was producing the *Irish Citizen* almost singlehandedly, writing articles for various publications — both Irish and British — and spending a great deal of time outside of Dublin — both in the north and in London, fulfilling speaking engagements. Of course, his activities did overlap conveniently. Both the I.L.P.I. and the S.P.I. were, on the whole, sympathetic to the suffrage cause, and the *Irish Citizen* carried labor news as it related to suffrage activities. His traveling, too, was a source of material for his articles.

It was indeed the right time for a feminist paper to emerge; Skeffington's instinct had been infallible. The general press had been uncooperative all along — their hostility increasing in direct proportion to the growth of suffrage activity — and an outlet for suffrage news was essential. When the first issue of the *Irish Citizen* appeared, there were five suffrage societies in Ireland in addition to the Irish Women's Franchise League. The oldest was the Irish Women's Suffrage and Local Government Association, founded in 1876 by Anna Haslam, who was still its secretary at age eighty-three. A militant counterpart to that group was the Irish Women's Suffrage Society, founded in 1909. In addition, there was the Conservative and Unionist Women's Suffrage Association, an Irish branch of a nonmilitant British group; the Irish Women's Suffrage Federation, founded in 1911; and the Belfast Suffrage Society, founded that same year. The number of suffragists, both nonmilitant and militant, was estimated at three thousand, with almost one thousand of those members or associate members of the I.W.F.L. [31]

June 1, a Saturday evening, found all the suffrage societies represented at a mass meeting in the Antient Concert Rooms, called together by the I.W.F.L. for the purpose of demanding that the Home Rule Bill, then in committee, be amended to include women. As Hanna put it, "We demand that the Liberal Government shall make itself responsible for this amendment, and we shall not be satisfied with less. . . . If the Liberal Government refuses to respond to our resolutions, there is no further chance for constitutional agitation." Not only were the suffrage societies represented but also such groups as the Women Workers' Trades Union, the Ladies' Committee of the Irish Drapers' Assistants' Association, and the Daughters of Eireann. On the platform, among others, were Constance Markievicz, Kathleen Sheehy O'Brien (she and Cruise O'Brien had married in 1912), Mrs. Garvey Kelly, and Gretta Cousins. Messages were received from such dignitaries as George Russell (AE), the political activist Maud Gonne, Fred Ryan, James O. Hannay, James Connolly, and the by then well known feminists and trade unionists Helena Molony and Louie Bennett. Russell said, "Irish politics, both Unionist and Nationalist, are the most stupid, uninspiring and unintelligent I know of anywhere, and the advent of women into the political arena could not possibly make them worse. It might possibly bring humanity into them." Connolly's message was that "a Home Rule Bill that excluded half of the people of Ireland from the franchise would be an anomaly in this age of progress, and would be a poor recompense to the women of Ireland for all they have done and suffered in the past for the freedom of Ireland." [32]

In an early June issue of the *Irish Citizen*, Hanna gave her impressions of the meeting as seen from the platform. She had sensed a spirit of militancy and of "absolute right" that she found thrilling. Showing signs of a strong female chauvinism, Hanna stated that "women possess the genius for organisation, for skilled manipulation of effect. Their unfailing attention to details give their meetings an element of the picturesque lacking in male-run assemblies." [33]

A resolution was passed at the meeting, calling on the government to introduce an amendment to the Home Rule Bill that would make the local government voting list (which included women) the basis of franchise for the new Parliament. Copies were sent to all Irish members of Parliament, with the demand that they insist on this amendment. No replies were received. Since this was only one of a series of slights, on 13 June eight members of the Irish Women's Franchise League — Kathleen Houston, Marjorie Hasler, Maud Lloyd, Jane Murphy, Margaret Murphy, Marguerite Palmer, Hilda Webb, and Hanna — took action. They broke windows in the General Post Office, the Customs House, the Land Commission Office, and the Ship Street Barracks. Militant action and the resultant arrest were no novelty to these women. Kathleen Houston, a charter member of the I.W.F.L., had a record of three previous arrests for militant action; Maud Lloyd was a landscape painter who had served a week in Holloway for smashing a window in the Local Government Board office in London; Jane Murphy had served two months' hard labor and this was her third demonstration; and Hilda Webb had participated in at least five demonstrations, been arrested twice and discharged, and arrested a third time and sentenced to two months' imprisonment without the option of a fine. All eight were arrested for this latest action, as they knew they would be, and later all sent statements to the *Irish Citizen*, explaining why they had taken militant action and why they should be considered "political" prisoners.[34]

An unedited version of Margaret ("Maggie") Murphy's statement is among Skeffington's papers. In part, it reads:

« « « « « « « « «

> Mr. Justice Denham says "a political offender is one who commits an offence for a political motive, and not for spite or personal gain." I am therefore a political offender, as I committed this action, because I want to put a stop to the sweating of women, which is a prolific cause of the White Slave Traffic, and I realize that no effective Bill can be introduced dealing with these evils, without the intelligent co-operation of the men & women of the country, & the same applies to the Housing question & the Education Bill, also I refuse to be classed with lunatics, imbeciles & children any longer.

» » » » » » » » »

Breaking windows had been her response to being "brutally treated" when participating in "a perfectly peaceful & constitutional deputation," she added. In Hanna's statement, she quoted Henry David Thoreau to the effect that the time might come when prison would be the only place of honor left to an honest man. "Many a brave Irishman has proved the truth of that axiom in the past; it is now for Irishwomen to realise citizenship by becoming 'criminals,' " she wrote.[35]

The windows were broken in the early morning hours. Almost immediately, all eight women were arrested and held in custody until afternoon, pending a hearing. Hanna and Margaret Murphy were charged with breaking nineteen windows and remanded for a week on five pounds bail, which Skeffington paid for both of them. Militancy seemed to be rewarded almost immediately, for that Saturday's meeting of the Irish Women's Franchise League in Phoenix Park was attended by more than a thousand people. It was a busy week for Hanna. Congratulatory messages came in from militants and nonmilitants alike. Emmeline Pethick-Lawrence wrote asking for a "full and detailed account" of what had transpired, with photos of broken windows and the women involved, if possible, for *Votes for Women*. The *Irish Citizen* reported the formation of a special Defence Fund to defray the eight women's legal expenses and stated that so far not one resignation from the I.W.F.L. had been submitted — rather, the league had obtained many new members.[36]

Hanna was among the first four militants to be tried; more than two hundred women attended the trial. The atmosphere in the courtroom was party-like; each defendant carried flowers that had been presented to her by supporters. Hanna had decided to handle her own defense and did so admirably, using the occasion to make a lengthy political speech. Although interrupted constantly by the police counsel and the magistrate, she managed to talk about government perfidy, constitutional methods of protest that had failed, and John Redmond's welshing on his promises. She concluded by stating her willingness to go to jail and her intention of resisting any attempt to treat her as anything other than a political prisoner. Making no secret of their sentiments, her audience applauded. And, when the prosecuting attorney called for the full weight of the law — treatment as ordinary criminals plus payment of trial costs and property damage — some of the spectators hissed. [37]

In handing down his verdict, the magistrate indicated his admiration for the women who had spoken in their own defense. He would have considered them first-class misdemeanants, he said — political prisoners with special privileges — had it been within his powers to do so, but this was up to the Prison Board. The sentence imposed was a forty-shilling penalty with the alternative of a month's imprisonment and a further month in default of bail. When all four chose to serve the two-month sentence, many of the spectators, moved by their courage, rose and cheered. This outburst brought forth an order to clear the courtroom. As the crowd left, they could hear Mrs. Palmer shouting "Keep the flag flying," and Hanna urging them to "Remember Mr. Asquith is coming in July." [38]

Before entering Mountjoy Prison, Hanna gave her husband an item for the *Irish Citizen*. "I hope that during my imprisonment my place as paper-seller for the 'Citizen' will be filled," she wrote. "It is most important that our Irish Suffrage organ should be extensively sold in the streets by volunteers. May its circulation be trebled during our detention!" [39] Its circulation, incidentally, was now up to three thousand.

Pressure on the Prison Board to change the status of the women from "ordinary" to "political" prisoners began immediately, both from outside and within the prison walls. Without delay, Skeffington wired M.P. Lawrence Ginnell, following up his telegram with a letter the following day, asking him to "put a question to Mr. Birrell with regard to the prison treatment of the women Suffragists now in Mountjoy." He asked that they receive full privileges of "political offenders." They were receiving some of these privileges, but they were not allowed to receive visitors or to write letters. "I understand you and Mr. Farrell, while imprisoned, were permitted to see one or two visitors daily," he wrote, adding, "I hope you will be able to interest yourself in the matter, in accordance with that old Nationalist tradition which the members of Mr. Redmond's Party have so largely forgotten." [40] Within days he received a communication from the governor of Mountjoy Prison, which read, "I have to inform you that His Excellency has granted to Mrs. Sheehy Skeffington, and the other prisoners convicted with her, the full privileges of First-Class Misdemeanants, so that they are now entitled to write and receive a letter and to be visited once a day by not more than 3 visitors together." [41]

The *Irish Citizen* carried an editorial listing the privileges granted the women as "first-class misdemeanants" — three hours a day exercise together and an hour's associated work in a special room every afternoon (they used that time to do needlework, making "Votes for Women" handbags); an additional half-hour sleep each morning; lights in their cells, where special incandescent burners had been installed, until 10 P.M.; someone to do the menial work of cell-cleaning for them; and a typewriter if requested. They were also allowed to have a woman doctor attend them. For the benefit of readers who might think the suffragettes were having "too good a time," the editorial mentioned that as first-class misdemeanants they were confined to their cells twenty out of the twenty-four hours, since they were not assigned to laundry, kitchen, or other details as the other prisoners were.[42]

It was difficult for the women to be confined to their cells for such lengthy periods, but their cells were kept filled with flowers from concerned friends. So many people wanted to visit them, now that visits were allowed, that the Irish Women's Franchise League was forced to post a schedule in its office for visitors. So many gifts and letters were received that Mrs. Palmer and Hanna had to ask that a note of thanks be inserted in the *Irish Citizen*. Since the prisoners were allowed to send only one letter a day and since three and four packages a day were arriving for each, they were unable to acknowledge safe receipt. "They have done much more than merely minister to our 'creature comforts'," the women wrote, "they have shown us that a strong spirit of unity and camaraderie prevails in the suffrage ranks."[43]

As scheduled, Prime Minister Asquith came to Dublin on the evening of 18 July. The fact that members of the Irish Women's Franchise League were in Mountjoy must have added to the hostility of his reception, but still the actions of the women were mild. As his steamer approached Kingstown, a group of I.W.F.L. women in a small yacht met it outside the harbor and, using a megaphone, made known their demands for votes for women. During the afternoon, fifteen women had paraded the streets of Dublin carrying posters inscribed with such slogans as "Home Rule for Irish Women as Well as Men," and "Who Is Mr. Asquith?" Those who witnessed the procession seemed amused rather than antagonistic and there was no violence. The peaceful scene was disrupted, however, by members of the British suffrage group, which had come over to Dublin specifically to protest against Mr. Asquith. As his carriage turned into Nassau Street, one threw a chisel at Mr. Asquith, which missed him but hit John Redmond, riding with him, cutting his ear. Later, Gladys Evans and Mary Leigh, two members of the British contingent, tried to burn down the Theatre Royal, where Asquith was to speak the following evening. Given the realities of the English situation —broken promises, repression, mass jailings, and forcible feeding — such violence was understandable and inevitable. As the *Irish Citizen* pointed out, the Irish suffrage movement, even at its most militant, had not yet "reached the extreme of exasperation which had been reached in England."[44]

The following evening, while Asquith was speaking at the Theatre Royal, the Irish Women's Franchise League held a meeting at the Dublin Custom House. The press, which was now reporting that a hatchet rather than a chisel had been thrown at Mr. Asquith, had so inflamed the emotions of some Dubliners by various accounts of the women's violence that a noisy mob drowned out the speakers. For half an hour, with police assistance, Gretta Cousins tried to keep order, but it was impossible. When she and the other speakers tried to leave the lorry that served as a platform, they were attacked by the mob, their hats knocked off, and their clothes torn. Some were knocked down and kicked — Constance Markievicz among them.[45]

Even *The Leader* protested, defending the "corner boys" — if the Irish suffragettes could not be held responsible for the hatchet throwing, then the public "that are thoroughly disgusted with the virago Suffers and the Skeffy gang" could not be held responsible either for the conduct of those who threw stones or attempted other forms of physical violence. The writer did add, however, that the "imitation Suffers" in Dublin had a right to their say and that right should be respected. Heckling was all right, but there should be "nothing but condemnation for anything like physical violence." People who disagreed with the women could listen and harangue or, better still, stay away from the meetings.[46]

Meanwhile Asquith addressed a packed house. It was also a "picked" house, for the audience had been carefully screened through an elaborate system of registration for tickets. Women were admitted to the dress circle only, and every man who was suspected of any connection with the women's suffrage movement was denied admittance. Enlisting the services of Dudley Digges, a Dublin-born actor who was visiting Constance Markievicz, Skeffington succeeded in transforming himself into a meek-looking little parson and passed unsuspected into the meeting. About ten minutes into his speech, when Asquith alluded to the emancipation of Catholics, Skeffington grabbed his opportunity. He rose and shouted, "What about the women of Ireland? Are you going to emancipate them?" He was immediately ushered out of the hall but, perhaps because of his clerical garb, not harmed in any way. Three other protestors were not so fortunate. One, in the dress circle, had his head split open by a blow from a steward's stick.[47] A subsequent letter from J. B. to Skeffington said, "By the way that man Palmer who it appears was so badly hurt at the Asquith meeting should bring an action for damages against the getters up of meeting — if he was attacked by the Stewards . . . the stewards, etc. have no right to attack even if they may exclude."[48]

The only way the women incarcerated at Mountjoy could be part of the anti-Asquith protests was to wear black mourning rosettes they had made. Before Hanna entered Mountjoy, however, she had written an article called "The Women's Movement — Ireland" that appeared in the July *Irish Review* and in which she once more defended militancy. "The stone and the shillelagh need no apologia: they have an honoured place in the armoury of argument," she wrote. As for the I.W.F.L., it had already "run the gamut of constitutionalism, and is now knocking at the prison door." [49]

Its militancy had apparently also increased its effectiveness. The audiences for the regularly scheduled Saturday meetings in Phoenix Park were larger than ever. One at which Skeffington spoke was reported by the *Cork Free Press* as having caused more than the usual excitement because of the "hatchet" incident. His appearance was greeted with much laughter and shouts of questions about his dress at the Asquith meeting and his dress in general. Consequently, he began his speech with "Ladies and gentlemen and members of the Ancient Order of Hooligans" and, after stressing that the current Home Rule Bill must be amended to include women, added that "any party or leader which opposed the rights of women must go down, and if the Irish Party or Mr. John Redmond, or the Ancient Order of Hibernians set themselves against the march of the women's movement, so much the worse for them." At the end of the meeting he was quickly escorted to the main road by the police, where he mounted his bicycle and rode away "waving his cap to those who had rushed after him." [50]

J. B. was one of those attending the Phoenix Park meeting. He circulated among the crowd, he wrote his son, listening to remarks that were being made about rights for women "often very bitter and unfriendly some few indeed violent and even atrocious." In typical J. B. fashion, he tried to take command of the situation, calling "order," and, he wrote Francis, he seemed to have some effect. Also typically, he added "You were specially aimed at in brutal remarks; but those who defy authority cannot expect to be protected by officials — and are thus exposed to the evils of anarchy. [51]

On 9 August and again on the fifteenth, the *Freeman's Journal* printed letters to the editor from Skeffington. In the first, concerned with Home Rule and votes for women, he said that the majority of the Irish suffragists and, certainly, all who were also nationalists, would be satisfied if Redmond were to come to them and say, "For tactical reasons I must prevent the enfranchisement of English women, but I shall see to it that my own countrywomen share in the measure of National liberation." In the second, he pleaded for political prisoner status for Mary Leigh and Gladys Evans, the English suffragette prisoners. The only test, he felt, should be whether or not they acted "with a bona-fide political motive." Calling them pure-souled and noble women, he went on: "If such women are driven by the system of government into protests which the law calls 'criminal,' it is the system against which they revolt that thereby stands condemned. If the fears of evil consciences make it necessary for the law to shut up such women pending the speedy enactment of that reform which will bring society into harmony with their just demands, at least the community must spare itself the shame of treating them as ordinary criminals during their detention." Some days later someone signing himself "Weary Willie" wrote a letter to the *Freeman's Journal* saying that he was tired of seeing Skeffington's "effusions in your columns" and suggesting that Skeffington appear in the advertisement section at the usual rates.[52]

NOTES TO CHAPTER 8

1. Robert Lynd, *If the Germans Conquered England*, p. 142.
2. F. Sheehy-Skeffington to "Christian," editor of the *Morning Leader*, 18 February 1910.
3. Jas. P. O'Duffy, Hon. Secretary of the National Council, Sinn Fein, to F. Sheehy-Skeffington, 21 March 1911.
4. F. Sheehy-Skeffington to William O'Brien, 22 August 1911.
5. *John Bull*, 2 December 1911.
6. Ibid.
7. Diary of F. Sheehy-Skeffington, 13 January 1903.
8. Ibid., 27 January 1903.
9. *John Bull*, 2 December 1911.
10. *The Leader*, 9 December 1911.
11. Ibid., 16 December 1911.
12. *Irish Citizen*, 13 July 1912.
13. *The Leader*, 6 April 1912.
14. F. Sheehy-Skeffington to *Irish Times*, 11 June 1912.
15. F. Sheehy-Skeffington to "Molloy," 26 March 1910.
16. Editorial, "The Domain of Woman," *Irish Citizen*, 25 May 1912.
17. "Irish Suffragists and Home Rule," *Irish Times*, 8 April 1912.
18. *The Leader*, 6 April 1912.
19. *Irish Times*, 4 April 1912.
20. Ibid., 8 April 1912.
21. *Irish Worker*, 20 April 1912.
22. Isabella Richardson to H. Sheehy-Skeffington.
23. *Irish Worker*, 12 August 1911, p. 4. Report of a mass meeting held on 6 August 1911 under the auspices of the Daughters of Erin and the Socialist Party of Ireland.
24. *Irish Review* (Vol. II) March 1912, pp. 54–56.
25. F. Sheehy-Skeffington to James Cousins, 2 May 1912.
26. Undated flier issued by the *Irish Citizen*.
27. *Irish Citizen*, 25 May 1912.
28. F. Sheehy-Skeffington to *Daily Herald*, 21 May 1912.
29. *Irish Worker*, 25 May 1912, p. 4.
30. F. Sheehy-Skeffington to *Daily Herald*, 21 May 1912.
31. Hannigan, "The Evolution of Skeffy," p. 36, n. 4.
32. *Irish Times*, 3 June 1912.
33. H. Sheehy-Skeffington, "An Impression from the Platform," *Irish Citizen*, 8 June 1912.
34. *Irish Citizen*, 22 June 1912.
35. Ibid.

36. Ibid.

37. Ibid., 29 June 1912.

38. Ibid.

39. Ibid.

40. F. Sheehy-Skeffington to Lawrence Ginnell, 23 June 1912.

41. Governor, H.M. Prison, Mountjoy, Dublin, to F. Sheehy-Skeffington, 25 June 1912.

42. *Irish Citizen,* 13 July 1912, cover page.

43. Ibid., 13 July 1912.

44. Ibid., 27 July 1912.

45. Ibid.

46. *The Leader,* 3 August 1912.

47. *Irish Citizen,* 27 July 1912.

48. J. B. Skeffington to F. Sheehy-Skeffington, 18 August 1912.

49. H. Sheehy-Skeffington, "The Women's Movement: Ireland," *Irish Review,* Vol. II, No. 17 (July 1912).

50. *Cork Free Press,* 5 August 1912.

51. J. B. Skeffington to F. Sheehy-Skeffington, 18 August 1912.

52. *Freeman's Journal,* 13 August 1912.

9

Strife on Every Front 1912–1913

he tragedy of the sinking of the *Titanic* on 14 April 1912 brought with it personal grief to Skeffington. One of the 1,517 lives lost was that of the founder of the *Review of Reviews*, William Thomas Stead, a pioneer of modern journalism and a champion of child welfare and other social legislation. In a moving tribute to Stead, written for the *British Weekly*, Skeffington said that it was he who "first directed my attention to the importance of the woman question." Stead had written a character sketch of William Gladstone in which he had stated, "For man, Mr. Gladstone has done much; for women, he has done nothing." Since Gladstone was at that time a hero to both men, Skeffington wrote: "It struck me very forcibly that Stead, who also made a hero of Gladstone, should so soundly reprove him for his antifeminism. From the reading of that article I date my interest in feminism." [1]

Skeffington's tribute described Stead as a man whose vivid personality, as it came through each month in the pages of the *Review of Reviews*, "made it impossible even for those who never met him to feel themselves strangers to him." As a matter of fact, the two had met only seven times over the years. They had, however, corresponded for some years prior to their meeting. "I was just eleven years old when the 'Review of Reviews' was started; I read it with avidity from the first number, and for years it was my Bible," Skeffington wrote. He went on to say that even though Stead's writing style was crude, that crudeness only served to bring "into clearer relief the soundness of his heart, the transcendent moral value of his courage and sincerity." [2]

Stead also helped awaken Skeffington's interest in international peace. When Stead organized a memorial to the czar at the time of the first Hague Conference in 1899, Skeffington recalled trying "not very successfully," to persuade his fellow-students in University College to sign it. "Mr. T. M. Kettle . . . was one of those who refused to sign, because the Tsar's disarmament proposals would mean the stereotyping of England's naval supremacy." [3] James Joyce had also refused to sign the Tsar's Rescript, as mentioned in Chapter 2; it is significant that it was Kettle's refusal and not Joyce's that Skeffington mentioned.

It was shortly after the conclusion of the Boer War in 1902 that Skeffington met Stead for the first time, and, Skeffington wrote, it was Stead's opposition to that war that "roused my enthusiasm for him to the highest pitch." He found Stead to be keenly interested in all things Irish; they talked of the Gaelic League, of the question of teaching Gaelic in the schools, and of the struggle then going on between William O'Brien and the Irish Party. They talked, too, about Davitt, and Skeffington was delighted to learn that Davitt had been one of Stead's best friends.[4]

Skeffington was developing a reasonable tolerance for others' ideas as long as they did not compromise the causes he held dear. In this he had been influenced by people like Stead and Davitt — but certainly not his father. He showed no inclination to scoff, for example, when in 1909 Stead published his then-famous interview with the spirit of William Gladstone, and he was not at all contemptuous when reporting that Stead's conversations with him during that period were "full of spiritualism." Amusement must have been Skeffington's strongest emotion when Stead, with his usual matter-of-fact reference to spirits, informed him that Gladstone had visited him and was tremendously interested in the struggle going on in Westminster over the latest budget.

The last time Skeffington saw Stead, they argued about Joseph Devlin, whom Stead held in high regard and whom Skeffington considered John Redmond's lackey. Skeffington was unable to change Stead's opinion, but before he left, he gave Stead material "bearing on the other side of the question." When, not long afterward, Stead published a character sketch of Devlin in the *Review of Reviews*, Skeffington was not surprised to see that Stead had used some of his material. For Skeffington, it was simply another illustration of Stead's customary impartiality.[5]

Skeffington had occasion to write another obituary — of Patrick Ford — in April 1912, a rough draft of which is among his papers. Obviously, he was not as moved by the death of Ford, who was founder and owner of the *Irish World*, as he had been by the death of Stead. Ford's advocacy of physical force was distasteful to Skeffington, his praise of the Phoenix Park assassinations anathema.[6] "For some years," Skeffington wrote, "his paper was full of dynamite propaganda, advocating the blowing up of London, etc." Nevertheless, in the obituary Skeffington did attempt to emulate Stead's objectivity. Although he pointed out that Ford had been "a fervent and even a bigoted Catholic" and his paper strongly anti-Semitic, he added that "Ford was none the less a sturdy opponent of the more outrageous forms of clericalism." To illustrate, Skeffington wrote, "An attack on an American Bishop, whose princely state he contrasted with Christ riding on an ass, nearly ruined his paper at one time." The conclusion that Skeffington reached was that "the vehement outbursts and vagaries which characterised his paper were the outward relief or safety-valve of a shy and sensitive nature."[7]

Skeffington found tolerance and objectivity much more difficult to maintain, however, when he came to believe that his brother-in-law, Tom Kettle, was weakening the suffrage movement through his inaction. His

Outside Mountjoy Prison, August 1912. Hanna Sheehy-Skeffington leaves jail, escorted by her uncle, Father Eugene Sheehy, left, and her husband, Francis.

liking for Kettle and his respect for Kettle's ability as a writer and an orator had never wavered. For example, in a review of Kettle's *The Open Secret of Ireland* for the *Irish Review*, Skeffington pointed out that while the author often sacrificed "originality in thought, to concentrate on originality of expression," it was not easy to give new life to conventional ideas. At this Kettle was, Skeffington believed, a master.[8] But Kettle had reneged on his promise to make a plea for women's suffrage first at the National Convention, and then at the Baton Convention. He had also resigned from the Irish Women's Franchise League for what seemed to Skeffington hypocritical reasoning. For these actions he was strongly reprimanded in the *Irish Citizen*: "Every time the woman's suffrage movement in Ireland has relied on Mr. Kettle at a crisis, he has betrayed it," Skeffington wrote in August 1912. "This is the kind of trickery that goads women to violent action; and if there were any due proportion between crime and punishment under the law, it is Mr. Kettle, rather than the four window-breakers, who ought to be in Mountjoy Prison."[9]

That was early in August. Later that month a moving letter to the editor by Skeffington, headed "The Imprisoned Suffragists," appeared in the *Irish Independent*. Mary Leigh and Gladys Evans, the British women serving their five years' penal servitude sentence in Mountjoy Prison for attempting to burn down the Theatre Royal, had gone on a hunger strike and were being forcibly fed. The force-feeding, Skeffington wrote, was "at best a risky operation even when performed under hospital conditions" and "literally torture when performed on a strenuously resisting patient under the rough-and-ready conditions of a prison, where adequate hospital equipment is absolutely lacking." It was tantamount, in his mind, to the judge imposing a death sentence on them for "burning a hole in the theatre carpet." He was sure this had not been the judge's intention. His letter asked, in conclusion, "Does the Irish public approve of prison torture?"[10]

Hanna and the Irish women sentenced with her were released on 20 August 1912. For the last four days of their imprisonment, they had been on a hunger strike in support of their British sisters. Consequently, Hanna emerged from prison in a weakened condition. She was greeted by a notice from the Rathmines Technical Committee, dismissing her from her post as a teacher in the Rathmines School of Commerce. The only reason given was the decline in the number of students in her German classes during the preceding term. Ordinarily such a dismissal would have come at the end of the preceding school year; therefore, since it came at the conclusion of her jail sentence, the true reason seemed obvious. Writing in the *Freeman's Journal*, the educationist Mary Hayden deplored the committee's hypocrisy and lack of courage. In a country where men who fought for their political principles were revered and often advanced politically for their courage, it seemed surprising to her that a woman who had shown equal courage should be deprived of her livelihood.[11] Added weight was given to the Hayden statement since it was well known that she was not a militant.

Letters deploring Hanna's dismissal came to the *Irish Citizen* from others prominent in educational circles, including the president of the Irish National Teachers Organization. In November a committee was formed and a petition issued, which stated that "in the interests of education, and to protect the security of tenure of teachers and their rights as citizens," a protest was being made against Hanna Sheehy-Skeffington's "summary dismissal, without sufficient reason." Before the year ended more than one hundred sixty signatures had been obtained from such notables as the Lord Mayor of

Dublin, AE (George Russell), Maud Gonne, four members of Parliament, Alice Stopford Green (the historian), Eamonn Ceannt (or Kent, the militant nationalist), and many other people of stature from Cork, Limerick, and other provincial centers. [12]

One happy result of the Rathmines Committee's action was that Hanna was able to give her husband a strong assist with the *Irish Citizen* and to be more active than ever in the Irish Women's Franchise League. The paper was experiencing fair success in obtaining advertising — at least forty firms advertised in its columns regularly. Still, it was difficult to cover the cost of operation, and in October they announced that publication could be assured only through November unless sales and advertising were to increase. Readers were asked to urge merchants to advertise, to make themselves responsible for selling a certain number of copies each week, and to contribute to a "November Guarantee Fund." The appeal was immediately effective. In early November the *Citizen* was able to report that the advertising columns were growing and that members of the I.W.F.L. had begun to sell the papers routinely in the streets. [13] The growth of advertising in the *Irish Citizen* would, however, always be hampered to a certain extent by Skeffington's refusal to accept advertising from any firm for which he could not personally vouch — and his standards were extremely high.

While nurturing the growth of the *Irish Citizen*, Skeffington had also been acting as the Irish correspondent for the London-based *Daily Herald* since it had been founded by George Lansbury in 1911. Lansbury had been a Labour member of Parliament for the Bow and Bromley district since 1910, and, from the beginning of his political career, a staunch advocate of equality for women. Like Skeffington, Lansbury had been against the Compulsory Insurance Act and he had resisted, without compromise, any attempt to rush it through Parliament. The act would impose a tax on domestic servants to be withheld from their wages; housewives who refused to withhold would be subject to penalties. For both Skeffington and Lansbury, the act constituted taxation without representation. The *Irish Citizen* therefore called on women who employed servants to oppose it, for "when a law is passed without the consent of those whom it affects, and without giving them an opportunity of expressing their opinion on it, it has no moral sanction, and is in no way binding on the conscience of those who have not been consulted." [14]

An incident typical of Lansbury's militancy — and one that endeared him to Skeffington — took place in the House of Commons in April 1912. Prime Minister Asquith had remarked that any suffrage prisoner being forcibly fed would be released when she promised never to demonstrate again. Lansbury, who had seen an intimate friend die as a result of forcible feeding, was infuriated by Asquith's callous and cynical statement. Striding up to Asquith, he called him a disgrace to his country and predicted that he would go down in history as a torturer of women. "I tell you, Commons of England," he said, "you ought to be ashamed of yourselves." For his actions, the Speaker suspended him.[15] After due deliberation, Lansbury decided to resign from the Labour Party and stand for his seat as an Independent in the November election. Knowing that Lansbury would have a hard fight, Skeffington resolved to spend most of November in London to help with the campaign. Fred Ryan, editing *Egypt*, a monthly record of Egyptian and Near Eastern news, in London and in constant correspondence with Skeffington, agreed to work on the campaign as well. Hanna, of course, would hold everything together in Dublin.

Lansbury's campaign engendered the kind of excitement upon which Skeffington thrived. As he described it in the *Irish Citizen*, "The dozens of committee rooms, each the headquarters of an active propaganda; the hundreds of outdoor meetings . . . the torchlight processions, the enthusiasm of the children, the keenness of the working-women . . . all contributed to make the election a unique experience." Bow and Bromley was a typical East End constituency — heavily working-class — and, according to Skeffington, Lansbury made the extension of the parliamentary franchise to women the dominant issue of his campaign. Consequently, even though Lansbury lost the seat, Skeffington felt the cause of women's suffrage had "gained an immense and invaluable impetus and experience."[16]

Hanna could testify that all was not quiet on the home front either. The Snowden Amendment to the Home Rule Bill — a proposal to give the vote to Irish women on the basis of the local government register (or voting list), which included women on the same terms as men — was defeated on 5 November, with the Irish Party members voting against it seventy-two to eleven. On the two days following the vote, windows were broken in the Belfast Post Office and the Dublin Custom House. For the latter incident, Peg Connery and Kathleen Emerson, members of the Irish Women's Franchise League, were arrested. In a letter to the *Irish Citizen*, Mrs. Connery said that she considered the defeat of the Snowden Amendment by the Irish Party to be a "shameful act of political treachery" and a "gross insult offered to Irishwomen." To submit to it passively would have involved the loss of her self-respect, she said.[17]

Her letter expressed the mood of many militants. In addition to breaking windows, they were also using a new tactic that was causing a great deal of concern and much discussion: placing small, open bottles containing a black fluid that resembled treacle in pillar boxes, thus damaging the letters. Sometimes the bottles were labeled "Votes for Women," sometimes they were placed in envelopes addressed to members of parliament who stood in disfavor with the suffragists, and sometimes the liquid was simply poured into the pillar box. In defense of this disruptive move, Hanna wrote an article for the *Irish Citizen* titled "Militant Militancy." It read, in part:

«   «   «   «   «   «   «   «   «

One is asked what justification there is for pillar-box attacks. There is
none — that is precisely the reason of their adoption. Reasonable militancy was regarded as merely playing at being militant. . . . Desperate
diseases need desperate remedies, and if the vote is wrested from
Government by methods of terrorism when five and forty years of sweet
and quiet reason produced only seven talked-out or tricked-out suffrage
bills, why, who can say it wasn't worth a mutilated letter, a cut wire, a
Premier's racked nerves? [18]

»   »   »   »   »   »   »   »   »

In an ideal state, she felt, such methods might be condemned — but an
ideal state did not exist. "We live under a Liberal Government, run by
politicians accustomed to yield only to 'pressure.' "[19]

To those politicians, as the year 1913 began, the activities of the suffrage
movement seemed to be reaching crisis proportions. It was apparent that the
militants, especially in England, were having remarkable success in raising
funds as a result of popular opposition to such measures as forcible feeding.
Accordingly, a new act was proposed, providing that a prisoner could be
released temporarily and conditionally by order of the Secretary of State if
his or her health, due in whole or in part to conduct while in prison, was
such that further detention was undesirable. A date would then be set when
the prisoner must return; failure to do so would make him or her subject to
rearrest without warrant. The sentence would be suspended from the time of
release and resumed upon return. The act was officially called the Prisoners
(Temporary Discharge for Ill-Health) Act, but opponents immediately
labeled it the Cat and Mouse Act. There could be no doubt that the Act was
intended to be a retaliatory measure against hunger-striking suffragist
prisoners.

The first test of the act in England came in April 1913, when Emmeline
Pankhurst was sentenced to three years' penal servitude for "malicious
damage to property." She was released after nine days, so weak as the result
of a hunger strike that she had to be removed to a nursing home. Under the
terms of the act, she was ordered to return to jail before the end of April, even
though the act would not become law until the end of the month.

In Ireland, the first test of the Cat and Mouse Act followed rapidly. The
Irish Party had voted for the act overwhelmingly. Following that, party
members had voted, coerced by John Redmond, against a women's suffrage
amendment to the Home Rule Bill — the Dickenson Amendment. Militant suffragist protest followed and in May, on the eve of a United Irish
League Convention in Dublin at which Redmond was to speak, the fanlight
in the U.I.L. offices was broken, and a bust of Redmond in the Hibernian
Academy was painted with broad arrows. For breaking the fanlight (valued at
two pounds), Marguerite Palmer, Dora Ryan, and Annie Walsh were sentenced to six weeks' imprisonment in default of paying fines and compen-

THE SKEFFYITES AND THE BARREL-ORGAN.

This cartoon, "Suffer Week in Dublin," which appeared in the 17 May 1913 Leader, was, according to the paper, inspired by some "Skeffyites" turning out with a barrel-organ the previous week as part of a protest of the Cat and Mouse Act. Skeffington is caricatured as the monkey on the barrel-organ.

sation. The constable who arrested them testified that Mrs. Palmer had approached him and asked to be arrested. "We were after breaking glass," she said. His report was accurate. It was Mrs. Palmer's method of underlining the political nature of their action. After three weeks in Tullamore Jail and a five-day hunger strike when they were denied the status of political prisoners, the women were released under the Cat and Mouse Act, with orders to return to prison to complete the remaining weeks of their sentence.[20]

The implementation of this act in Ireland caused considerable indignation in the ranks of the suffrage movement. Late in June, a protest meeting with Hanna presiding was held in the Dublin Mansion House to an overflow audience. A motion made by Tom Kettle called the Cat and Mouse Act "a dangerous weapon of political oppression," demanded its immediate repeal, and requested the remission of the remainder of the sentences of the three women against whom the act was being employed. To great applause, Kettle said that he understood that Mrs. Palmer was to "see-saw between prison and her own house because she broke the fanlight of the U.I.L. offices." As a member of the United Irish League, he had helped pay for that fanlight, he said, and she had his permission to break it any time and as often as she felt it would forward her cause. (It was significant that Kettle felt called upon to say that he was "prepared, not to sacrifice, but to postpone, any social or franchise reform for the sake of seeing Ireland mistress in her own household." In response to this, there were shouts of "you're not a woman" and "that's not the women's view.")[21]

Hanna, in her remarks, called the Cat and Mouse Act a genuine incitement to militancy. Ireland would have none of it, she said. "The only precedent for it in Ireland was the half-hanging of the rebels in '98, who were strung up, let down to recover, and then strung up again repeatedly." The fiery Madame Markievicz, after making clear that she was not a member of any suffrage society because she was a separatist and a Republican and did not want a vote for the British Parliament, indicated her sympathy for the martyrdom of these three women for their cause. She was "proud to be a woman; how many men would face the Hunger Strike for any cause on God's earth?"[22]

More protest meetings against the Cat and Mouse Act followed, and both Skeffingtons participated. The I.W.F.L. gathered signatures for a petition to be sent to the Lord Lieutenant at Dublin Castle; set up a special Prisoners' Fund; urged members to attend a conference for repeal of the act to be held in London; and sent a telegram of support to the National Political League in London, which was then demonstrating against the Cat and Mouse Act, "the Infamous Act which Government dare not enforce in Ireland."[23] The *Irish Citizen* also spoke out editorially: "The hideous brutality of forcible feeding is fortunately no longer available as an instrument of coercion. Last year Irish public opinion refused to tolerate it; and Irish public opinion has shown even more emphatically that it will not tolerate this other more insidious but no less cruel abomination of tyranny."[24] Temporarily, at least, the editorial comment was valid: as a result of all the agitation, at year's end the three women were still at large and unmolested.

After a period of comparative calm in the labor movement, 1913 saw deep and bitter labor unrest throughout all Ireland. During the first seven months of the year, more than thirty strikes took place in Dublin alone. To James Larkin goes the credit for organizing the workers. But the root cause of the strikes was the conditions under which these workers were forced to live, thanks to unemployment, temporary employment, inadequate salaries, and lack of middle-class and upper-class concern. In this city of some 300,000, nearly 26,000 families lived in slums. And of approximately 5,000 tenements, more than 2,200 barely met minimum standards for human habitation, and another 1,500 were so neglected that they were beyond reclamation. Water was available only in backyards, baths were unheard of, and toilets — also in the yards — were unfit to use. The Dublin death rate was 24.8 per thousand, primarily due to infant mortality and tuberculosis.[25] James Larkin was fighting these conditions through the *Irish Worker* and in the pages of any other publication that would accept his articles, and in a series of emotional speeches to the workers. By May, employees of six of the largest shipping companies in the Dublin port had signed up with the transport union. Larkin's next move was to attempt to organize the farm laborers and here again he met with great success. By the end of August, the Irish Transport and General Workers' Union was in control of practically all the unskilled labor in Dublin and the surrounding areas.[26]

Two large groups of workers remained unorganized — those employed by Arthur Guinness' Sons and by the United Tramway Company. As far as the Guinness workers were concerned, Larkin's appeal had no effect. The company's management treated them fairly, furnished them with housing at a low cost, and provided them with medical treatment. The company's director, Lord Iveagh, was a philanthropist and a model of paternalism, and there was no cause for worker discontent. The United Tramway Company, however, presented an entirely different problem for a union organizer. The chairman of the company, William Martin Murphy, was extremely wealthy and extremely powerful. He controlled Ireland's largest daily paper, the *Independent*; the largest department store; one of Dublin's finest hotels, the Imperial; and many other interests in and out of Ireland. His method of hiring for the Tramway Company made it virtually impossible for his employees to risk joining a union or displeasing management in any way. He divided his employees into two groups, "permanents" and "casuals." If a "permanent" was late, absent, or suspected of being a Larkinite, he knew that he would be replaced immediately by the first man on the "casual" list. This automatically put the "permanent" at the bottom of that list. It was a system certain to create a great deal of discontent and gradually Larkin began to make headway. Like many tyrants, Murphy considered himself a fair man and a good employer and was antipathetic to outside interference. When rumors reached him that a tramway workers' strike was being scheduled for Horse Show Week, when people from all over Ireland would be flocking into Dublin and when any interference with transportation was disastrous, Murphy began to rid the company of all suspected Larkinites and to fill their positions with non-Transport Union men.[27]

Horse Show Week was late in August and, on the second day, the 26th, at 9:40 A.M., seven hundred of the seventeen-hundred tramwaymen walked off the job, leaving the trams wherever they happened to be. Murphy, however, was prepared and, with the help of the police, service was soon fairly well restored. The strike was not as effective as had been anticipated, but the Larkin–Murphy fight accelerated. Three days after the tram strike, Murphy called together four hundred members of the Employers Federation, an organization formed in 1911 to combat strikes. Together they made a brutal decision: to lock out all employees who were members of the Irish Transport and General Workers' Union, virtually starving them into submission. By the end of September, some 25,000 families were affected by the lockout.[28]

From the beginning of this controversy between capital and labor, Skeffington was deeply involved. Each day he submitted a report of the situation in Dublin to the partisan *Daily Herald*, George Lansbury's London paper; reports of protest meetings generally mentioned him as a speaker or an active participant. Even in the *Irish Citizen*, though it declared that it took no stand on the dispute, a great deal of space was devoted to articles stressing the plight of the workers. Editorially, the paper, explaining its apparent bias, made the point that at one time or another and in one form or another virtually all labor leaders had given aid and comfort to the suffrage movement and thus deserved support.[29] For both Francis and Hanna Sheehy-Skeffington, James Connolly was a prime example of such a leader. Consequently, when Connolly was arrested and imprisoned for attending and speaking at a banned meeting, Skeffington was one of a delegation that approached the Lord Lieutenant to demand his release and, when he went on a hunger strike, Hanna kept Connolly's wife informed of his condition. "Thank you so much for your kind letter telling me of my husband's health," Lillie Connolly wrote Hanna. "I have been very anxious and worried." She had not been surprised, she added, when her husband had gone on hunger strike, and she was very proud of him indeed.[30]

As tension increased in Dublin, a highly augmented police force roamed the streets, their main purpose apparently to terrorize the citizenry. One of the most brutal police attacks occurred at an illegal meeting at the Imperial Hotel at which Larkin spoke. Men, women, and children were clubbed without mercy. Over four hundred people — police and ordinary citizens — were treated in the hospitals, and more than one hundred were arrested. Skeffington was present and was called on to help some of the leaders escape.[31]

Violence in all forms was erupting in Dublin. An explosion in one of the slum tenements, in which two strikers lost their lives, was followed, early in September, by the collapse of a four-story tenement, which municipal authorities had declared to be safe just a few short months earlier. Seven people were killed and many more injured.[32]

Even Arthur Griffith, who did not approve of the union's action against William Martin Murphy, sympathized with the plight of the workers. He refused, however, to associate himself or his publication, *Sinn Fein*, with the dispute since he considered it to be affiliated with an international movement. (A nationalist first — and last as well — he even thought that gifts of food to the strikers from English organizations were insulting.) English sympathizers sent food ships and organizations on the Continent sent funds, but the Irish Parliamentary Party took neither side and the Irish representatives disclaimed responsibility by way of the press.

Finally, late in September, it became necessary for the government to

Street violence was a common scene during the 1913 lockout. Here O'Connell Street on Bloody Sunday 31 August 1913, during the police baton charges.

intervene. A Court of Inquiry was set up and public hearings began on 1 October. The employers were represented by T. M. (Tim) Healy, a close friend of Murphy and well known for his ability in the courtroom and his keen wit. Larkin presented the case for the workers. The Court of Inquiry, while indicating the belief that "sympathetic" strikes were wrong, finally ruled that the document that the employers were asking the strikers to sign, a so-called "yellow dog" contract that stipulated that the worker would not join Larkin's union, infringed on individual liberty. The court's report was just that, however — a report and nothing more. It could not force either side to abide by its findings. The employers promptly announced that they would not accept it as a basis for negotiation. It was then that public opinion began to swing toward the Irish Transport and General Workers' Union.[33]

Even the conservative *Irish Times* came out on the side of labor and, in early October, printed AE's famous "Open Letter to the Dublin Employers"

in which he addressed the "aristocracy of Industry" in Dublin. It was a
masterpiece. Just a few sentences convey the flavor:

«   «   «   «   «   «   «   «   «

> Your insolence and ignorance of the rights conceded to workers uni-
> versally in the modern world were incredible, and as great as your
> inhumanity. . . . You went into conference again with representatives
> of the State because, dull as you are, you know public opinion would
> not stand your holding out. You chose as your spokesman the bitterest
> tongue that ever wagged in this island [Tim Healy] and then, when an
> award was made by men who have an experience in industrial matters a
> thousand times transcending yours . . . you withdraw again, and will
> not agree to accept their solution, and fall back again upon your devilish
> policy of starvation. . . . The men whose manhood you have broken
> will loathe you. . . . The children will be taught to curse you. The
> infant being moulded in the womb will have breathed into its starved
> body the vitality of hate. . . . Be warned ere it is too late.[34]

»   »   »   »   »   »   »   »   »

Aroused citizens were banding together to help supply food and coal to
the workers and the *Irish Citizen* was backing a call for the setting up of a
Committee of Citizens to coordinate their efforts. The paper commented in
an editorial: "We hope some women of leisure will interest themselves in this
project, and that it will not be left to those already overburdened with public
work."[35] Constance Markievicz, ably assisted by Hanna Sheehy-Skeffington,
had set up a soup kitchen in Liberty Hall, for both considered the need to
feed the hungry to be of primary importance.

By October the strikers' situation was becoming so desperate that Dora
B. Montefiori, a prominent social worker, started a movement to send their
children to homes in England where they would be fed, clothed, and
comfortably housed. The clergy immediately attacked this well-meaning
scheme. The Archbishop of Dublin appealed to Catholic mothers not to
abandon their faith or their children by handing them over to families who
might not be Catholic and who might even — horrible thought — have no
faith at all. Reflecting Skeffington's sentiments, both the fiery, left-wing *Daily
Herald* and the *Irish Citizen* backed the Montefiori plan wholeheartedly.

Late in October an attempt was made to send a group of Dublin
children to London. Crowds lined the quaysides to prevent them from
leaving, however, and priests actually invaded the Corporation Baths, where
fifty children were being scrubbed prior to their departure. Mrs. Montefiori,
supervising the operation, managed to escape with nineteen of the children,
but the priests followed them, apprehending all nineteen and arresting Mrs.
Montefiori on a kidnaping charge. Furious, Skeffington commented in a
letter to the *Irish Times*: "In the long history of the attempts to rivet on the
minds of the Irish people the chains of a decaying clerical ascendancy, no
incident surpasses in audacity the hypocritical attack upon Mrs. Montefiori

and the Daily Herald League in which several Dublin clergymen have been busying themselves for the last few days." [36]

The Leader, which bitterly opposed the Montefiori plan, took Skeffington's letter as a signal to attack the *Irish Times*, the *Irish Citizen*, and Skeffington. The *Irish Times* had pointed out that if the children were leaving Dublin with their parents' consent, they had a perfect right to go; it was illegal and an interference with private liberty to obstruct their departure. *The Leader's* response was to call the *Irish Times* both anti-Catholic and anti-Irish, the *Irish Citizen* an "obscure little suffragette paper," and, pointing out that he was now a Socialist, Skeffington "more ridiculous than ever" since he had become a "comrade." [37]

Each night during that period the quays were picketed by priests and irate citizens determined that the children should not leave Dublin. Several days after Mrs. Montefiori was arrested, Skeffington, who was very active in his support of her plan, was assaulted at Kingsbridge Station while attempting to get some of the children out. Two men, Patrick Gerrity and John O'Leary, were charged with the assault. At their trial, Skeffington testified that he had seen a crowd on the station platform led by J. D. Nugent of the Ancient Order of Hibernians and some priests. He noted that he and the children were being pointed out and he heard someone shout, "They won't go. We will put a stop to this sort of thing." When he tried to help some of the children board the train, he was knocked down and "bruised about the head and body." Gerrity, he said, struck him "on the face several times with his fist." Although he refused to identify O'Leary positively, he said he did have the impression that he had been involved as well. Skeffington stated further that the crowd had also attacked him and that there were shouts of "kill him." Roughly escorted some distance from the station, he returned to get his bicycle and was once more struck and kicked by members of the crowd and his bicycle tires slashed. [38]

Skeffington's anger, however, was not focused on Gerrity and O'Leary. Refusing to press charges against them, he said, "These men are merely the dupes of more astute persons in the background. If these more astute persons, Mr. Nugent and the priests, who were in the crowd, cannot be put into the dock I don't want to press for punishment against these men." He added that he had gone to the station as a journalist and a sympathizer with the locked-out strikers who were attempting to save their children from starvation. "I approve," he said, "of taking the Dublin children out of the slums until the labour dispute is over." [39]

When, finally, Mrs. Montefiori was released from prison, it was on the condition that she make no further effort to place the children in homes abroad. Her scheme had collapsed, but not without positive results. At the archbishop's behest, the Dublin's Children's Distress Fund was established. The archbishop also sent a circular letter to all parish priests apprising them of the urgency of the problem. The *Irish Worker*, Larkin's paper, pointed out that this realization of urgency was extremely sudden. "During all this time scarce a single Roman Catholic, cleric or lay, in Dublin displayed any concern for the wellbeing of these children."[40] Like *The Leader*, the *Irish Worker* was not given to moderate statements. Be that as it may, the admonitions of the archbishop resulted in an immediate and substantial increase in the number of meals served to schoolchildren and in offers from many convents to help house them.

For Dublin workers in general, 1913 was a year that would never be forgotten. For the Skeffingtons as well, it had been memorable both personally and professionally. In March James Cousins, because he and Gretta were leaving the country, resigned from the editorship of the *Irish Citizen*, leaving it completely in Skeffington's hands. Assuring his readers that the pages of the paper would still be open for free discussion and that its editorial policy would remain neutral, he added that the paper would be "sadly shaken by Mr. Cousins's departure."[41] So were he and Hanna, but only a month later they were to suffer another and much greater loss.

Early in April, at the age of thirty-nine, Fred Ryan died, leaving an immeasurable void not only in the lives of the Sheehy-Skeffingtons but also in the socialist and feminist movements. Skeffington had spent a great deal of time with Ryan when they were campaigning for Lansbury the previous November and, as he said in his tribute in the *Irish Review*, they had maintained "the closest political, intellectual, and personal relationships until his death, even when they were far apart physically."[42]

So closely did Skeffington and Ryan identify with each other's ideas that friends who knew them both well must have been possessed by the eerie feeling, as they read Skeffington's article, that he was writing his own obituary. The following section in particular could have applied to either man:

«   «   «   «   «   «   «   «   «

A journalist whose clear and forceful style made his writings a model both of exposition and of controversy, he was never able to make a living by journalism in Ireland. And the reason is plain. He never wrote a line which he did not believe; and his beliefs were not those popular with the dictators of Irish journalistic expression. . . . He gave his best, un-grudgingly, for years to struggling movements and struggling news-papers. . . . The editor of Sinn Fein [Arthur Griffith] has thought fit to say that Fred Ryan was not a Nationalist. But for those who hold to the essence of Nationalism and not to its accidentals, it will be enough to know that Ryan was an advocate of Ireland's complete political inde-pendence.[43]

»   »   »   »   »   »   »   »   »

Regarding Ryan's religious beliefs, Skeffington wrote:

«   «   «   «   «   «   «   «   «

His intellectual position was that of agnosticism, his creed that of the Rationalist Press Association. His fearless preaching of this creed earned for him the enmity of the churches; and a noted Canon is said to have declared him to be the most dangerous man in Ireland. So, from the canonical point of view, he was. Passionate truth-lovers — and the love of truth was Fred Ryan's dominating impulse — are always dangerous to established hypocrisies. . . . One of [his] favourite themes was the needlessness of any religious sanction to produce the highest type of character, as exemplified by the noble lives of the great infidels. Of this truth he himself was an outstanding illustration. He might well be called the Saint of Irish Rationalism.[44]

» » » » » » » » »

The tribute concludes:

« « « « « « « « «

Despite his high intellectual attainment, he was free from the least trace of intellectual snobbery. . . . He loved truth, justice, liberty; he spent himself on behalf of high ideals; and in his life, as in his thought, he set a high standard for those who follow. . . . The Ireland of to-morrow will reverence him as one of those who laid its foundations.[45]

» » » » » » » » »

There seems to have been one point on which the two friends did not see eye to eye. Skeffington touches on it only slightly in his tribute: "He [Ryan] lent active aid to the new militant suffragist movement in Ireland, and was a frequent speaker at its meetings as well as a worker for it in many other ways; though it should be added that, with his temperamental shrinking from violence, he disliked some recent phases of militancy."[46] At that point, there was no sign that Skeffington drew the line at any of the "phases of militancy" in the suffrage movement in Ireland.

NOTES TO CHAPTER 9

1. F. Sheehy-Skeffington, "Personal Reminiscences of W. T. Stead," unpublished article, Sheehy-Skeffington Papers. It was rejected for space reasons by the *British Weekly* in a letter to F. Sheehy-Skeffington, 6 May 1912.

2. Ibid.

3. Ibid.

4. Ibid.

5. Ibid.

6. Chief Secretary Lord Frederick Cavendish and his undersecretary, T. H. Burke, were stabbed to death 6 May 1882 in Phoenix Park, Dublin. The assassins belonged to a secret society known as "The Invincibles."

7. F. Sheehy-Skeffington, rough draft of "Obituary: Patrick Ford," dated 17 April 1912, Sheehy-Skeffington Papers.

8. *Irish Review*, Vol. II (March 1912), pp. 54–56.

9. "Professor Kettle and the Suffrage Cause," *Irish Citizen*, 3 August 1912. Skeffington originally wrote his comments as an Open Letter to the *Freeman's Journal*, which refused publication.

.

10. *Irish Independent*, 27 August 1912.
11. Mary Hayden's letter to the *Freeman's Journal* appeared in the *Irish Citizen*, 5 October 1912.
12. *Irish Citizen*, 16 November 1912.
13. Ibid., 2 November 1912.
14. Ibid., 6 July 1912.
15. Midge Mackenzie, *Shoulder to Shoulder: A Documentary* (New York: Alfred A. Knopf, 1975), p. 209.
16. *Irish Citizen*, 30 November 1912.
17. Ibid., 16 November 1912.
18. Ibid., 4 January 1913. Pillar boxes is a term for mail boxes.
19. Ibid.
20. Ibid., 5 July 1913.
21. Ibid.
22. Ibid.
23. Ibid., 12 July 1913. Many members of the Dublin Corporation signed the petition to the Lord Lieutenant, including Cruise O'Brien, Constance Markievicz, and Gretta and James Cousins.
24. *Irish Citizen*, 5 July 1913.
25. Dangerfield, *Damnable Question*, p. 100.
26. Emmet Larkin, *James Larkin: Irish Labour Leader, 1876–1947* (London: Routledge & Kegan Paul, 1965), p. 118–122.
27. Ibid.
28. Ibid.
29. Hannigan, pp. 42–43, and *Irish Citizen*, 6 September 1913.
30. Lillie Connolly to H. Sheehy-Skeffington, undated.
31. Jacqueline Van Voris, *Constance de Markievicz: In the Cause of Ireland* (Amherst: University of Massachusetts Press, 1967), p. 108.
32. Larkin, *James Larkin*, p. 126.
33. Ibid., pp. 131–136.
34. Ibid., pp. 136–137, and *Irish Times*, 7 October 1913.
35. *Irish Citizen*, 20 September 1913.
36. *The Leader*, 1 November 1913.
37. Ibid.
38. *Irish Independent*, 6 November 1913.
39. Ibid.
40. Larkin, *James Larkin*, p. 140n, and *Irish Worker*, 1 November 1913.
41. *Irish Citizen*, 1 March 1913.
42. *Irish Review*, Vol. III (May 1913), p. 117.
43. Ibid., p. 114.
44. Ibid., p. 116.
45. Ibid., p. 119.
46. Ibid., pp. 118–119.

10

"Damn Your War!"

T he winter of 1913 was one of the coldest that Dublin had experienced in years; for the locked-out workers and their families the bitter cold plus the lack of food, adequate clothing, and decent housing made the situation intolerable. Louie Bennett, writing in the *Irish Citizen*, said that over a hundred pounds per day were being spent by the Ladies' Relief Committee (one of the groups organized to aid the strikers) to feed the children, but that they were running out of funds and needed help from the general public.[1]

Conditions being what they were, it was not surprising that labor sentiment should be further aroused when, early in November, James Larkin was sentenced to seven months in Mountjoy Prison on a charge of seditious libel. Within a week after his incarceration, an overflow protest meeting took place in London's Albert Hall. George Lansbury presided, and among the speakers were George Bernard Shaw and AE. James Connolly, who was in charge of the labor dispute in Larkin's absence, spoke also, and it was he who proposed a plan of action that proved completely effective. He urged everyone in those areas where by-elections were being held to vote against anyone — Labour or Tory — who was doing nothing to obtain Larkin's release. Seventeen days after his seven-month sentence was pronounced, Larkin was free.

For those who felt that the suffragists' efforts detracted from the fight for Home Rule, an editorial in the *Irish Citizen* — no doubt written by Skeffington — declared that "the moral for suffragists is obvious." The power of the vote was clearly demonstrated. "It is to be noted that the men who took this action, the leaders of the Irish Labour movement, are Nationalists to a man. But they did not allow any dishonest cries about 'hostility to Home Rule' to affect their position."[2]

The day after Larkin was released, he and Connolly issued a "Manifesto to the British Working Class" describing conditions in Dublin — workers being arrested every day and harsh jail sentences meted out to them while scab labor from England was replacing them in large numbers. The manifesto informed British labor that the strikers had closed Dublin's port and urged British trade unionists to help keep it closed. The closing of the port

The Citizen Army drilling outside Liberty Hall, headquarters of the Irish Transport & General Workers' Union. The spectators seem more interested in facing the camera than in watching the army, resplendent in their uniforms, drill.

was effective, but the ports of Derry and Belfast were still open and goods — as well as scabs — were coming in. In some cases, the scabs were armed; some of the more radical publications were beginning to call for arming the strikers as well.

This was the mood when, early in November, Skeffington joined the Civic League, an organization that had grown out of the short-lived and ineffective Dublin Industrial Peace Committee. Both he and Tom Kettle had served on that committee and, through it, had attempted vainly to bring about a peaceful settlement between employers and employees during the early months of the lockout. It was their hope now that the Civic League could prove more effective in making peace.

The prime mover in the newly formed Civic League was Captain Jack White, a former officer in the British army and the son of a famous Boer War general. He saw as one of its main functions the formation of drilling groups, which, he argued, would teach the workers the importance of discipline. These groups would be designated the Citizen Army. At the first public meeting of the Civic League in mid-November, formal announcement was made of its formation.

Skeffington, who was on the platform at the meeting, apparently had no objection to being a member of an "army." For him, as for Captain White, the Citizen Army "had no clear goal of violent revolution, national or social." In the captain's autobiography, *Misfit*, he says, "The Citizen Army, after teaching the police manners, would be the machine of industrial organization in the new era." Even William Martin Murphy, the leader of the employers, claimed later that Captain White had discussed the idea with him, making the point that when the strikers were drilled they would be disciplined and "their moral tone" would be raised.[3] For Skeffington, who had witnessed and indeed experienced police brutality, the Citizen Army was a group designed to defend the workers against the police. And there is every indication that in many instances it did. The very fact of the army's existence seemed to act as a brake on the police. In Skeffington's eyes, this type of militancy did not in any way conflict with his pacifist views.

At precisely the same time, another group was formed that is often confused with the Citizen Army. Calling themselves the Irish Volunteers, they modeled themselves militarily after the Ulster Volunteers, a group pledged to use force to resist the British government's Home Rule Bill. Their goals, of course, were quite different, since the Irish Volunteers were whole-heartedly for Home Rule. As Roger McHugh phrased it, "the gun was back in Irish politics."[4] It was not a group that Skeffington would find attractive, but as usual he did not reflect popular feeling. At year's end, it was estimated that the Citizen Army had between five and six hundred enrolled; the Irish Volunteers were estimated to have numbers varying from thirty-five hundred to ten thousand, depending on which publication you read.

Meanwhile, Skeffington continued to wage his war for women's franchise. Andrew Bonar Law, M.P., leader of the Conservative Party and Sir Edward Carson, organizer of the Ulster Volunteers, were due to speak at a Dublin meeting in late November. Admission to the meeting was by ticket only and elaborate arrangements had been made to keep any representative of the suffrage movement from attending. Skeffington, however, had managed to procure a ticket. That evening, wearing evening clothes, a bowler hat, and a long overcoat, with his cheeks rouged and his whiskers whitened, he presented his ticket and quietly took his seat. Five minutes after Bonar Law began his speech, Skeffington rose and shouted, "What about the women's conflict? Why don't you meet the women?" Spectators said later that they had no trouble identifying the voice as that of Francis Sheehy-Skeffington. Great confusion ensued, with loud shouts of "throw him out." The meeting was resumed only after he had been forcibly ejected.[5] He said later, "I succeeded in getting in because I was disguised as a gentleman."[6] (It will be remembered that Skeffington succeeded in gaining admission to the Asquith meeting disguised as a clergyman.)

Skeffington's interruption of the Bonar Law meeting was part of an organized campaign devised by two Dublin suffragist societies[7] to point up Law's refusal to meet with any deputation of women while in Dublin and also to force him to make his position and that of his Conservative Party clear with regard to votes for women. It was the suffragists' plan to distribute handbills outside the Conservative Club, where Law and Sir Edward would be lunching; outside Lord Iveagh's house, where they were staying as his guests; and outside the meeting at the Theatre Royal.

Early in the appointed afternoon, Hanna and Peg Connery were on hand when Law and Sir Edward left Lord Iveagh's house in Stephen's Green on their way to the Conservative Club. As they emerged, Mrs. Connery rushed forward to hand them leaflets and, when Law brushed her aside, put one in his breast pocket. A policeman stepped in and ordered her aside, but did not hurt or arrest her. Meanwhile Hanna was trying to approach Law from the other side. She was grabbed by a police sergeant, who twisted and wrenched her arm. In her own words, "The Sergeant's autograph, one purple thumb-mark and four red angry fingernails, did not fade from that arm until Christmas." She struggled to get away, shouting to one of the many press photographers that she was being assaulted. Only when the photographer stepped forward to get a picture did the sergeant release her. She was then arrested.

Chief Divisional Magistrate E. G. Swifte presided at Hanna's trial, as he had at her previous one. She wrote later that his "loyalist soul was wrung by the thought of 'our English visitors' being molested." Looking at the gigantic sergeant and the diminutive Hanna, the court rocked with laughter when the sergeant testified that he "was seized, your worship, and pummelled repeatedly with clenched fist" so that three hours later he could still feel the pain. Hanna conducted her own defense and, although she asked permission to call Peg Connery as a witness, her request was denied. The magistrate ruled that the sergeant had indeed been assaulted and Hanna was ordered to "find bail to be of good behaviour, or go to jail for seven days." As she reported later in the *Irish Citizen*, "I got a week for being assaulted by a Sergeant. I may be thankful that an Inspector or (horrible thought) Superintendent did not hit me, for then no doubt my sentence would have been proportionate to the dignity of the officer."[8]

Hanna chose to go to jail, informing the magistrate that she planned to go on a hunger strike immediately to protest her conviction. The first texts that caught her eye as she opened the prison Bible that night in Mountjoy were "Boast not of to-morrow, for thou knowest not what the day to come may bring forth," and "Let the milk of the goats be enough for thy food." The verses could not have been more appropriate, she wrote, for surely she had not dreamed that morning that she would be sleeping on a plank in Mountjoy that night; and, if the words "waters of Vartry" were substituted for "milk of the goats," she would have "spiritual sanction" for her hunger strike. A second term in prison, according to Hanna, was "like having a second tooth out. The novelty is over and one knows exactly how much it hurts." As for her second experience as a hunger-striker:

«   «   «   «   «   «   «   «   «

One tries to remember the former hunger-strike — was it on the third
day that hunger no longer gnawed? On what night did your heart waken
you with its jumping? . . . As before, the three meals reposed all day
untouched in a corner of the cell — tea and dry brown bread, potatoes
and prison soup, and later a pint of milk was mysteriously added.
The smell of tea or soup slightly aggravates the situation, for the
hunger-striker's senses grow sharper by starvation. I believe the hunger-
strike is growing common among ordinary prisoners, but it has been
found that the poor things always succumb when food is left in their
proximity.[9]

»   »   »   »   »   »   »   »   »

Immediately upon Hanna's removal to Mountjoy, the Irish Women's
Franchise League organized a public meeting to be held at 4 P.M. the next
day in Royce Road, separated only by the canal from the Female Prison.
Since Royce Road was a cul-de-sac, no obstruction could result from the
gathering. The police, however, chose to prohibit the meeting and so
notified Skeffington and other supporters that morning. By 3:30 P.M., a large
cordon of police had taken their stations, and members of the I.W.F.L. were
walking about distributing leaflets. At first the crowd was small, but it was
soon augmented by people coming from the football match in Dalymount
Park. By the time Skeffington arrived "on an outside car" at 4:00, the crowd
was about two hundred strong. They attempted to break through the police
cordon but were pushed back; Skeffington, according to an account in the
Freeman's Journal, was "flung into Phibsboro road." He protested loudly,
saying he was entitled to enter the road, but the police ignored him. Trying
again to break through, he was roughly handled, and one policeman
grabbed him by the throat. The crowd was by then very large and, seeing
his struggles, protested vehemently. Skeffington meanwhile was telling the
police that, if he was doing anything illegal, he should be arrested, not
manhandled. He shouted, "This is a fair example of the attempt of the police
to overrule everything in Dublin." The crowd cheered lustily.[10]

Finally giving up his attempt to enter Royce Road, Skeffington addressed the assemblage from a garden railing in Phibsboro Road, saying that
they were gathered to protest his wife's conviction on what he termed the
perjured testimony of the police. He then said that, having made their
protest, they should disperse and not give the police an excuse for blud-
geoning them. In conclusion, he requested three cheers for votes for
women. The crowd cheered, and then carried him away on their shoulders.
Shortly afterward he addressed another group from a wall in the lane leading
to the Mountjoy Female Prison, but there were no further incidents. When
he returned to Beresford Place, he found Connolly addressing a meeting
from a niche under the railway aqueduct. "We'll see whether they will
attempt to stop us from holding a meeting outside Mountjoy tomorrow. The

Citizen Army will be there and will not come empty-handed," he was saying.[11]

Indeed a meeting was held the next day in Royce Road, and, possibly because it was unannounced, proceeded without police interruption almost until its conclusion. When the police finally did arrive, violence broke out once more, several women were assaulted, and Kathleen Emerson was arrested for assaulting the police. At this second meeting, communication was established with Hanna by megaphone, and she could be seen standing in the window of her cell, waving a white handkerchief. An account of the two protest meetings in the *Irish Citizen* concluded, "The whole week has been noteworthy for its manifestation of police brutality and arbitrariness, and at the same time for the extraordinary public sympathy which has been evoked by the women's protests. Mr. Bonar Law's visit has not been fruitless."[12]

Hanna, weak and ill, was released after five days. Her own physician, Dr. Elizabeth Tennant, reported that the hunger strike might have injured her health permanently, but a report on her condition in the 13 December issue of the *Irish Citizen* mentioned that her heart was showing signs of improvement and that the sleeplessness that was delaying her recovery had abated. Philosophizing on her imprisonment, Hanna wrote that, more than any physical discomfort, she had been disturbed by the knowledge that she was innocent and suffering unjustly because of the false testimony of a police officer. "The helplessness of the victims of the law, the folly of expecting justice from police magistrates, the power of the bully in uniform to swear away the liberty (and how often the reputation and the livelihood) of his victim — these are the thoughts that create anarchists." Suffering imprisonment unjustly "makes every turn of the jailer's key an outrage, and burns into the victim's soul a searing hatred of the whole infamy of our prison system, whose victims cry to heaven for vengeance," she wrote.[13]

The bitter winter, the lack of food, and, finally, the closing of the Dublin Relief Fund sponsored by the British Trades Union Congress made it impossible for the striking Dublin workers to hold out any longer. The brutal strike was over by early February 1914. A statement issued by the Executive Committee of the Dublin Employers Federation late in November 1913 had stated that they were going to fight to the finish, and this they had done. For the strikers, nothing had been gained in the way of higher wages, better working conditions, or the establishment of their right to organize or indulge in sympathetic strikes. There were gains, but not the kind destined to soften the defeat.

The plight of the Dublin worker was now obvious to the world as it had never been before. In addition, many nationalists had gained a clearer understanding of the workers' position. As Padraic Pearse wrote in the October issue of *Irish Freedom*, regardless of how one viewed James Larkin's methods, "there is a most hideous wrong to be righted, and the man who attempts honestly to fight it is a good man and a brave man." There can be no doubt that Skeffington's contributions in the *Daily Herald*, as well as his editorials and articles in the *Irish Citizen*, had been of great assistance in this enlightenment. The employers, too, had learned an important lesson — there was a point beyond which they could not push their employees. Even slaves could revolt. Another result was that Skeffington added an item to his list of grievances against the party. He had seen them betray the suffragettes and now he saw them abandon labor as well, at least in this instance. As he wrote in the *Daily Herald*, "It is a blessing for Ireland that the events of recent months have revealed the bourgeois Nationalist parties in their true colours before Home Rule. For now Labour with open eyes will prepare to attack these so-called Nationalist parties at the first General Election instead of waiting for the second." [14]

Another casualty during that period was the Citizen Army. Early 1914 found it at its lowest ebb, down to one badly demoralized company. It was then that playwright Sean O'Casey, who was extremely active in its ranks, suggested to Captain White that a reorganization was in order. At a public meeting in late March, Captain White became chairman, O'Casey secretary, and Richard Branigan and Constance Markievicz, honorary treasurers. Its vice-chairmen, as George Dangerfield points out in *Damnable Question*, "ranged all the way from the flamboyant Jim Larkin to the pacifist Francis Sheehy-Skeffington." [15]

But soon there was more trouble among the hierarchy. "I hear strange things of your leaving the Citizen Army and joining the Volunteers!?" Skeffington wrote Jack White early in May. [16] The rumor was only slightly premature. Both White and Constance Markievicz had been greatly distressed by the anti-Volunteer sentiment in the Citizen Army. Though he resigned, Constance Markievicz stayed on. She was, however, also active in *Cumann na mBan*, the women's auxiliary of the Volunteers. Her dual loyalty so upset Sean O'Casey that he introduced a resolution asking her to "sever her connections" with either one body or the other and, when this resolution was defeated, he resigned. [17]

Skeffington's resignation from the Citizen Army came somewhat later. James Connolly had assumed command of that group and from that time on the connection between the Citizen Army and the Volunteers became stronger and the former group more militaristic. George Dangerfield says accurately that Skeffington resigned because "this gentlest and most determined of socialists, found that he could not abide the growing belligerence of the I.C.A." [18] But militarism was not Skeffington's only quarrel with the Volunteers. He deplored their lack of a positive position in support of the women's movement. Close affiliation with the Volunteers was, for him, impossible.

Always with the goals of the Irish Women's Franchise League in mind, the Skeffingtons continued their fight against John Redmond and the Irish

Party. Late in May 1914 the Home Rule Bill came up for its third Reading before the House of Commons and was scheduled to come up for Royal Assent in late June. It was imperative that Prime Minister Asquith and Redmond be pressured to include an amendment concerned with votes for women; accordingly, the suffragists bombarded Redmond with requests for an audience. In answer to one plea sent in late May — which included Hanna's signature — Redmond once more refused to receive a deputation, stating that such meetings only led to unpleasantness. He understood their views well, he said, but it was his feeling that "Ireland should decide for herself under Home Rule whether she desires women's suffrage or not."[19]

The Irish suffragists' next move was to send a deputation to London to wait upon Redmond and Asquith in the House of Commons. The groundwork was carefully laid by Emmeline Pethick-Lawrence in London and Hanna in Dublin, and promptly at 3 P.M. on 10 June a deputation of Irish women, carrying copies of the *Irish Citizen* and wearing orange and green badges, assembled at St. Stephen's Hall and sent notes in to members whose names had been supplied by Mrs. Pethick-Lawrence. While they waited for replies, they intercepted a number of Irish and Labour M.P.'s, for the most part unsuccessfully. According to Hanna, the M.P.'s could not stop to talk because they were "too busy escorting parties of fashionably-dressed ladies to the inner sanctuary of the House (no woman can pass nowadays without a member, who vouches for her 'good conduct'), where strawberries and cream awaited them on the terrace."[20]

The women did succeed in talking with a few members, however. One could not remember whether he was for or against votes for women, another felt that the women were too militant, and still another that they were not militant enough. An Irish Unionist M.P. said the Tories would get them the vote; an Irish Nationalist said they would get it only from an Irish Parliament. And so it went for the two hours predetermined as the length of the vigil. At the end of that time, when it was obvious that their notes requesting intervention for an audience with either Redmond or Asquith would not be answered, they stormed the steps of the lobby and began speaking. By the time the police realized what was happening and escorted them off the premises with orders that they were not to be readmitted, they had managed to explain why they had come and how they had been treated. One of the group from Belfast shouted, "They only mind the militants who have guns"; another cried, "Had we been men, they would have heard us."[21]

That evening Hanna, with a group of Irish women who were making their way to the House of Commons, saw mounted police disperse a group of working women from the East End, led by Emmeline Pankhurst's daughter Sylvia, within a mile from the House. The police, she said, "drove their horses upon the pavements, on to the steps even of private houses, flinging the crowd, men, women, and little children, pell-mell before them, pinning them frightened into corners, crushing them together in masses and closing in upon them." Although Sylvia Pankhurst was arrested, some of the women who were able to reach the House of Commons were admitted and allowed to speak with one of the Liberal Party leaders. "So we are getting on," Hanna commented. "But a short while ago such a deputation usually ended in serious violence and sentences of 'hard labour' for those who took part."[22]

The Irish deputation contained both militants and nonmilitants, who had marched side by side in harmony. Among the English suffragettes, however, there was a genuine cleavage. Emmeline Pankhurst's spirited daughter Christabel was vehement on the subject in the *Suffragette*. Nonmilitants, she contended, were the greatest obstacle to securing the vote. In an article in the *Irish Citizen*, Skeffington took issue with her position. Both the militants and the nonmilitants were necessary, he maintained. "Without militant action, the whole constitutional movement in Great Britain would sink back again into the Slough of Despond which engulfed it between 1884 and the rise of the W.S.P.U. [Women's Social and Political Union]." But, he said, "Without the great masses of strictly constitutional sympathy and action at its back, the militant movement would spend itself in vain on the embattled fortresses of prejudice."[23]

As Skeffington saw it, the difference between the militant and the nonmilitant was simply one of temperament and, for most people, there was no conscious choice. "Militancy represents the dominance of Will in the personality, while non-militancy represents the dominance of the intellect," he wrote. The temperaments of some lucky few combined the two harmoniously, but this combination, he felt, was extremely rare. Any great cause, he contended, such as the suffrage movement, needed people of both temperaments to succeed. As an example, he cited the alliance between Charles Stewart Parnell and Michael Davitt — an alliance that made the Land League "irresistible." Parnell was a constitutionalist by temperament who had a genuine horror of violent measures, whereas Davitt was a revolutionary. But Parnell understood the importance of an extreme wing and Davitt learned to "tolerate and to work with" the constitutionalists. Skeffington did believe that it was "natural and healthy" for militants and nonmilitants to organize separately — each would undoubtedly be more effective that way. To separate, however, did not mean to be hostile or intolerant; it did not exclude joint action. He concluded his article by pointing out that any other course would serve only to weaken the suffrage movement and to impede its progress.[24] In the *Irish Citizen*, Skeffington did attempt to present both sides. In his own life, he seemed to be one of those individuals he had cited as "few and rare" whose temperament encompassed successfully the militant and nonmilitant.

But the splits in both the English and Irish suffrage movements were destined to widen rather than narrow. In early August 1914, Sir Edward Grey announced to the House of Commons the government's decision to declare war against Germany. To the consternation of many in Ireland,

John Redmond pledged the support of the Irish Volunteers for the cause. They would guard Ireland's shores, he assured the House of Commons, and British troops could feel free to withdraw from Ireland. On the following day the United Kingdom of Great Britain and Ireland entered the war. An *Irish Citizen* poster, dated 15 August, expressed the Skeffingtons' feelings: "Votes for Women Now! Damn Your War!" A week later an item in the paper's "Current Comment" pointed out that the poster obviously reflected the opinion of the majority of its readers, for there were enough orders for extra copies to warrant a reprinting. (There were, of course, some who took exception to it — chiefly, it seemed, because of the use of the word "damn.")[25]

In an editorial headed "The Crime of War," the *Irish Citizen* stated its position; the style bore Skeffington's unmistakable stamp. "While the war-drums are rattling Europe back to barbarism, it is well for us to consider calmly what war is, and what is the natural attitude towards it of that regener-ative social force which finds its expression in the movement for Votes for Women," the item began. War is "one of the social evils, like drink and pros-titution" that arise from neglect of the feminine point of view and are based on a theory of society "one-sidedly and arrogantly male." When to the hor-rors of war, which increased as man's technical skills improved, was added "the horrible truth, that the men concerned in the actual fighting have in almost every case no clear conception of what they are fighting for . . . then the only conclusion at which one can arrive is that the man, or group of men, responsible for promoting war — any war — ought to be branded as criminal lunatics." The editorial concluded, "We are consequently opposed to this present war and to every war; and, while it is no part of our business to fix the responsibility for its outbreak, it is at all events clear that women, political outlaws in all the States now at war, have none.[26]

The categorical stand of the *Irish Citizen* was applauded by many of its readers — but not, by any means, all. One reader protested the paper's taking any stand at all on the war, since the war had nothing to do with fight-ing for the vote. "I have always admired the way you have steered a very diffi-cult course & kept the Citizen to suffrage," the writer said. She wished, henceforth, to dissociate herself from the *Irish Citizen*. To the objections raised, Skeffington replied that the paper had not editorially expressed any opinion on the merits of the present war; it had simply disclaimed any responsibility while condemning war in general.[27]

Outside the pages of the *Irish Citizen*, Skeffington felt free to speak as he wished, and he did so at every opportunity. So great was his hatred of the war that, when the Socialist Party of Ireland — formerly the Independent Labour Party of Ireland — failed to hold an anti-war demonstration as planned, he resigned. A fellow-member, R. J. Mortished, wrote asking him to reconsider his resignation or at least his decision not to lecture for them. Such drastic action, Mortished felt, was unwarranted. His defense of the organization was simply that the meager numbers available to carry out the necessary tasks made curtailment of some meetings unavoidable. He pointed out that all the meetings since war had been declared had been anti-war meetings. Inaction, he said, did not constitute betrayal — merely inefficiency.[28]

Mortished's point about lack of forces was well taken, for the Socialist Party's strength had declined sharply at the end of the 1913 lockout. They were, in fact, so short of forces and funds that in June they gave up their rooms at the Antient Concert Building and moved to Liberty Hall where, presumably, rent was free. In any case, Mortished's plea was effective. Skeffington lectured against the war and conscription for the Socialist Party of Ireland each Sunday until he was arrested the following May. At each meeting he would put forth a resolution that, as he described it in a letter to James Cousins, declared that Ireland had no quarrel with Germany, urged Irishmen not to enlist to fight England's battle for naval supremacy, and called on the Volunteers to resist every effort to make them a portion of the English Garrison in Ireland.[29] His views were clear. To his friend William O'Brien, he wrote: "This war means the end of the British Empire. If Germany wins, that is obvious. But if Russia wins, Russia will speedily turn on India, and end matters that way. I [am] hoping against hope for a German victory; I fear the Germans are hopelessly ringed in."[30]

By the time Skeffington had written to James Cousins, there was already talk of setting up a Compulsory Military Service, and the Secretary for War, Lord Kitchener, had announced his intention to have every boy, upon reaching eighteen, register for a period of military training. By that time also the British government, apparently fearful that they could not rely upon the loyalty of Ireland during the war unless a Home Rule Bill of some sort were passed, placed on the statute books the Government of Ireland Act, which carried a proviso excluding the Province of Ulster. No sooner was it enacted, however, than a Suspensory Bill was introduced — the Act was not to take effect until the war ended.

Though the Skeffingtons and the Irish Women's Franchise League were holding firm against the war, the Women's Social and Political Union was not. Immediately upon England's entry into the war, Emmeline Pankhurst issued a letter stating that the organization was suspending all its activities temporarily. That Great Britain should take part in this war was inevitable, she wrote, and "with that patriotism which has nerved women to endure torture in prison cells for the national good, we ardently desire that our country shall be victorious — this because we hold that the existence of all small nationalities is at stake and that the status of France and of Great Britain is involved." The W.S.P.U.'s paper, the *Suffragette*, was renamed *Britannia*, with a new dedication, "For King, for Country, for Freedom," thus reflecting the patriotic views of both Emmeline and her daughter Christabel.[31]

Much distressed by the W.S.P.U.'s stand, the Skeffingtons were, nevertheless, not unhappy to see the organization withdraw its forces from

Ireland. In mid-1913, Christabel Pankhurst had written to Hanna from her Paris headquarters about the general suffrage picture in Ireland. At that time, she thought, people in Ulster were becoming sympathetic to the suffrage cause; consequently, the Women's Social and Political Union had sent an organizer, Dorothy Evans, to Ulster. Partly because of the satisfactory results of that endeavor, Christabel had come to the conclusion that "there ought not to be a distinction between the English Movement and the Irish Movement." Accordingly, an organizer was being sent to Dublin. She was nothing if not fair, for she went on to say that she would be "thankful indeed to hear that your League had arranged to institute an English campaign in the interests of the Irish Suffrage Cause." [32]

The Skeffingtons, ever alert to the dangers of too close an alliance with the British organization, had been fearful of what the results of this move would be. Their fears had been justified. By the following spring the *Irish Citizen* reported editorially that the establishment of Women's Social and Political Union branches in Ireland had "done little or no good and some positive harm. They have not taken root, and cannot, in this country, but they have broken up a society in Belfast, and they have attracted some Irish Suffrage workers who can ill be spared from the Irish Societies, where their efforts would be infinitely more fruitful." [33] Now, with the W.S.P.U.'s withdrawal, Belfast was left without any militant suffrage group, since the Irish Women's Suffrage Society had been dissolved earlier in the year. The Irish Women's Franchise League seized the opportunity and in September 1914 an Ulster Centre was opened.

The Women's Social and Political Union was not alone in changing its focus. Other suffrage groups soon followed suit. The Irish Women's Suffrage Federation, the umbrella group for many associations, formed a Suffragists' Emergency Corps and began doing relief work. The Irishwomen's Reform League formally dissociated itself from the *Irish Citizen*. In a great show of patriotic fervor, the Reform League's 16 September meeting concluded with a Mrs. James Duncan playing the national anthems of France, Russia, and England. There were undoubtedly defections in the ranks of the Irish Women's Franchise League as well, for Peg Connery was moved to make an impassioned plea in a letter that appeared in the *Irish Citizen*. Appealing to the women of the I.W.F.L. to "stand steadfast" and to make "Suffrage First" their watchwords as they had in the past, she went on:

«   «   «   «   «   «   «   «   «

> Let the male war-mongers fill their war chests as they may. Let them forego their indulgence in strong drink and tobacco and other luxuries they never deny themselves, and learn what self-sacrifice means. . . . Women, the enslaved and outcast among the peoples, owe no service to the war-mongers anywhere. . . . As for men, let them wallow in the mire they have made for themselves till they turn from it in loathing. Our duty is to our organisation — to make women free and

war impossible! Let nothing, therefore, induce us to turn aside from our great task of establishing "peace on earth, and good will amongst men." Suffrage women, stand fast by your organisation![34]

» » » » » » » » »

The outbreak of war had proved a setback for the suffrage movement in general, but it seemed to be only a temporary one. At year's end the *Irish Citizen* pointed out that although 1914 had "temporarily saved the bureaucracy," Ireland had kept its head better than any other part of the United Kingdom and that the suffrage movement, on the whole, had "a much better grip on the sympathies of the masses of the Irish people than it ever had before."[35]

It was not only in speeches, articles, and letters to editors that Skeffington was making his ideas on the war known. He was also, apparently, communicating them to his father. One such letter (unfortunately not among the available Skeffington papers) so infuriated his father that J. B.'s reply was practically indecipherable. In fact, he even added a postscript saying, "I am not sure you can make this all out." He attacked Francis for not taking care of his health, for neglecting Owen's spiritual education, and for his views on Home Rule. As for his analysis of the war, J. B. wrote: "Germany the Boss and Bully of Europe — nay of the world since 1870 — you speak of as worthy of support — the power that robbed France of territory and of millions of money, and would have bled her to death only for the English — You think Russia the cause of war when the world knows that Austria (as you admit) without adequate cause attacked Belgrade an open city — can you have anyone believe that Austria would have dared to act thus without the sanction of Germany?" And he added: "Your German friends seem to have hypnotised you into absurdity." J. B. saw independence for Ireland as an impossible dream. "If England dropped this Island tomorrow, France, Germany, etc. would soon take it over," he said. "The only policy for Ireland is *union* on fair & mutual terms with England & Scotland."[36]

The remainder of J. B.'s tirade was concerned with his son's personal life. J. B. blamed his son's idealism and his impracticality for ruining both his and his wife's careers and even causing his father financial hardship. His South African mining stocks were now unsalable, he pointed out, his dividends had been suspended, and the mines were in the hands of the Germans "who may do as they please with them. . . . Certainly your acts & words in war time make it very uncertain."[37]

There can be no doubt about the brilliance of J. B.'s mind; Francis certainly was aware of it, for he always said that his father was the best teacher he had ever had. He recognized also the truth and the justice in many of J. B.'s statements. For example, the logic of much of the following, written to Francis when he was experiencing difficulties placing his articles because of his stand against the war, could not be disputed:

«   «   «   «   «   «   «   «   «

By grasping at the impossible you have lost all your power for good — for self help for your own independence — for the good of your family — and now as an absurd Freelance you are stranded as I often foretold — a man who cannot write what others want to publish need not expect to write — unless on the sand of the seashore. . . . It is getting very serious at your time of life to have no solid reliable income salary or wages — no earnings that can be counted on. I am sure business of any kind would be better. Of course teaching you could do but you have put that out of your hands also. [38]

»   »   »   »   »   »   »   »   »

Skeffington's moments of self-doubt must have been many. In January 1914 he confided in his diary, "Shall we do much in our lifetime, after all? If only I had money!" But the very next day he wrote, "No lamentations re lack of personal income!" [39] He knew instinctively that he had no choice. His life had to be lived without any basic compromising of his ideals or of his goals. He knew that his father was wrong when he said that he "trampled on Patriotism, Religion, and all the people hold dear, for a Fanatic notion of sex equality which is as *false* and *absurd* as men's equality." He thought his father might be right when he said, "There is no Equality, no Independence — All is inequality, dependence of all degrees and sorts of complexity." But he knew that he had to devote his life to attempting to change that picture. He might not see it changed in his lifetime but he hoped that through his efforts it would change in the lifetime of his son. J. B.'s letter had read: "I am sorry for Owen. You ought to make him a Christian, a Catholic, a Nationalist." [40] He need have had no worry on one score at least. There was never any doubt about Skeffington's love for Ireland — a love that he and Hanna passed on to their son in full measure.

NOTES TO CHAPTER 10

1. *Irish Citizen*, 11 October 1913.

2. Ibid., 8 November 1913.

3. Donal Nevin, "The Irish Citizen Army," in Edwards and Pyle (eds.), *1916: The Easter Rising*, pp. 120–121.

4. McHugh, *The Shaping of Modern Ireland* "Thomas Kettle and Francis Sheehy-Skeffington," p. 135.

5. *Freeman's Journal*, 29 November 1913.

6. Ibid., 1 December 1913.

7. The Irish Women's Franchise League and the nonmilitant Irishwomen's Reform League.

8. *Irish Citizen*, 3 January 1914.

9. Ibid.

10. *Freeman's Journal*, 1 December 1913.
11. Ibid.
12. *Irish Citizen*, 6 December 1913.
13. Ibid., 3 January 1914.
14. *Daily Herald*, 16 January 1914.
15. Dangerfield, *Damnable Question*, p. 109.
16. F. Sheehy-Skeffington to Captain J. R. White, 1 May 1914.
17. Sean O'Casey, *The Story of the Irish Citizen Army* (London: The Journeyman Press, 1919), p. 46.
18. Dangerfield, *Damnable Question*, p. 109.
19. *Irish Citizen*, 13 June 1914.
20. Ibid., 20 June 1914.
21. Ibid.
22. Ibid.
23. Ibid., 13 June 1914.
24. Ibid.
25. Ibid., 22 August 1914.
26. Ibid.
27. F. Sheehy-Skeffington to "Mr." Manico, 20 August 1914.
28. R. J. Mortished to F. Sheehy-Skeffington, 16 August 1914.
29. F. Sheehy-Skeffington to James Cousins, date not clear except for "1914," but context indicates August.
30. F. Sheehy-Skeffington to William O'Brien, 3 August 1914.
31. Mackenzie, *Shoulder to Shoulder*, pp. 282–283. Sylvia Pankhurst, however, continued her attacks on the government and on what she called "the war of iniquity falsely extolled as the War to end War. The Skeffingtons, always very fond of her, retained her friendship and they continued to correspond. Emmeline Pethick-Lawrence fully supported Sylvia, traveled to America to initiate an international Women's Peace Movement, and succeeded in uniting many women suffragists in Europe and America in an attempt to halt the hostilities.
32. Christabel Pankhurst to H. Sheehy-Skeffington, 26 September 1913.
33. *Irish Citizen*, 30 May 1914.
34. Ibid., 22 August 1914.
35. Ibid., 9 January 1915.
36. J. B. Skeffington to F. Sheehy-Skeffington, 11 August 1914.
37. Ibid.
38. Ibid.
39. Diary of F. Sheehy-Skeffington, 17 and 18 January 1914.
40. J. B. Skeffington to F. Sheehy-Skeffington, 11 August 1914.

11

The Price of Idealism   1914–1915

ccompanied by John Redmond and the Earl of Meath, Prime Minister Asquith was scheduled to appear at the Mansion House in Dublin on 25 September 1914, his purpose to recruit for the British army. Early that month, following the usual procedure, the Irish Women's Franchise League requested that Asquith grant them an audience while he was in Dublin; also following the usual procedure, he refused. The *Irish Citizen* labeled his visit an insult to every Irish woman and suggested that "the resentment of that insult" might find vigorous expression. [1] By that time Skeffington knew that plans had been made by the Neutrality League, of which he was a member, to take over the Mansion House by force on the night before Asquith's speech. According to an account by William O'Brien, members of the Citizen Army and the Irish Volunteers were to join forces, occupy the Mansion House for twenty-four hours, and thus prevent the meeting from being held. O'Brien wrote, "It is interesting to note that one of those who volunteered for the enterprise was Francis Sheehy-Skeffington, a well-known pacifist." [2] But on the designated night, with the Volunteer contingent numbering some eighty men standing by at 41 Parnell Square and the Irish Citizen Army contingent of about forty at Liberty Hall, word was received that the Mansion House was an armed fortress. Accordingly, the entire scheme was called off.

The following day, the day of the meeting, the Mansion House was still heavily guarded. Every precaution had been taken — streets closed and tickets issued only through recognized political organizations and only to men. All approaches to the meeting place were guarded by cordons of police and Dawson Street, upon which the Mansion House stands, was blocked off completely. Hundreds of Royal Irish Constabulary occupied the area surrounding nearby Trinity College. According to one spectator's account, Skeffington, attempting to address a crowd at the junction of Dawson Street and St. Stephen's Green, was brutally beaten by the police. "One I saw raise his fist and strike Mr. Skeffington on the head, while they dragged him from his position and hustled him away. The people around seemed terrorised." The spectator added that Skeffington had been "hustled into a cab and taken off, being afterwards released." [3]

Meanwhile, along all the routes to the Mansion House, Irish Women's Franchise League members assembled and distributed leaflets to those entering the area. At the head of Dawson Street stood Hanna and Peg Connery. When they had finished distributing their leaflets, they climbed the steps of a nearby fountain and began to address the crowd. They were immediately arrested, taken to College Street Police Station, and held until midnight, at which time they were released. Hanna's own account suggests that perhaps the charges were not preferred because Asquith had just "rung up from the Viceregal Lodge that he was in bed and had double-locked his door." In describing their arrest, she said, "Only one hero attacked us; a postman in uniform bravely struck Mrs. Connery full between the shoulders, and came round to deliver a second blow on her face, while the police held her hands."[4]

Shortly after the women were arrested, a labor demonstration was held at precisely the location they had been forced to abandon. James Larkin, James Connolly, and P. T. Daly spoke from a wagonette, vigorously denouncing the Asquith meeting and the recruiting campaign while a group of Citizen Army men guarded them armed with rifles and bayonets. As soon as that meeting was over, the wagonette moved down Grafton Street to another location in College Green. A large crowd followed them and, when they reached their destination, another and larger meeting was held. The *Irish Citizen* asked why no attempt was made to halt either meeting and then answered, "Clearly because they [the police] were afraid. The contrast between the treatment of the Labour protest, backed by armed force, and the treatment of the suffrage protest, made by a few women without any show of force, is sufficiently striking."[5]

In both his actions and his words, Skeffington made his detestation of war — this war or any war — perfectly clear. In a moving article in the *Irish Citizen*, he called war the product of a system that accepted fighting as a satisfactory method of settling disputes between nations. Never, he wrote, had an honest attempt been made to ensure peace. "Pacifists were fooled by the pretence that great armaments would maintain the peace. We now know the folly, or the hypocrisy, or both, of that pretence." He labeled as false "the new cant" preached by H. G. Wells and others that this was a "war to end all wars." As he saw it, "War can breed nothing but a fresh crop of wars. By accepting this war, in any degree whatsoever, we are helping to perpetuate war. If we want to stop war, we must begin by stopping this war. The only way we can do that is to hamper as far as possible the conduct of it. The best way to do that is to stop recruiting."[6]

In the same article, Skeffington launched an attack on Christabel Pankhurst — the woman "who deliberately encourages recruiting." She was, he said, guilty of both a lack of understanding and a betrayal of the women's movement.[7] This was the beginning of a feud between the *Irish Citizen* and Christabel Pankhurst. The paper attempted to be fair, however, printing letters for and against its stand, which the *Irish Citizen* spelled out:

«   «   «   «   «   «   «   «   «

The *Irish Citizen* stands for principles, not persons. Miss Christabel Pankhurst has deserted the principle of "Suffrage First," for which she formerly stood, and for which the *Irish Citizen* still stands. Nothing could be more disastrous to any movement than to follow blindly, out of personal gratitude for former services, leaders who have abandoned their principles in the hour of crisis.[8]

»   »   »   »   »   »   »   »   »

Christabel's mother shared her views, and, when Skeffington reviewed Emmeline Pankhurst's autobiography, *My Own Story*, he again made his quarrel with those views plain. Although he praised the book as a fine history of the suffrage movement and recommended it to "every suffragist and still more, every indifferent," he questioned the premise put forward in the preface. When the war is over, Emmeline had written, women would resume their struggle once more. But would the Women's Social and Political Union be able to do that, Skeffington asked, after being "tarnished by recruiting campaigns and war-mongering speeches"? He concluded bitterly: "As one reads the descriptions of the terrible physical suffering inflicted on Mrs. Pankhurst and other prisoners by the Government, the thought persistently intrudes, Might it not have been better that she had died then? — rather than survive to be guilty of the Great Apostasy, to declare that she wished she were a man that she might take part in the useless, senseless, needless carnage in Europe? to throw over the 'deep and abiding reverence for human life' which, she rightly declares, was the 'moving spirit of militancy' in its great days? Perhaps, who can say? It is not the first time a great political leader has stained the end of a glorious career by going over to the enemy."[9] For Skeffington, Mrs. Pankhurst's position constituted treason. "War and anti-feminism are branches of the same tree — disregard of true life-values," he had written earlier. "It is not a coincidence that all the countries concerned in the war are countries which do not recognise women as citizens, and that those which are most aggressively and unscrupulously war-like are precisely those in which women are held in the least regard. It is no mere coincidence that it is those who support women's claim to freedom who are, in every country, the most active in trying to prevent war or to limit its consequences."[10] Emmeline Pankhurst had indeed gone over to the enemy.

In September 1914 Skeffington himself considered doing an about-face — he thought seriously of joining the Irish Volunteers. At the outset of the war, John Redmond had urged the government to allow the Irish Volunteers to be responsible for the defense of Ireland, thus freeing British troops. As far as was known, he did not plan for these men to serve outside of Ireland, but late in September he made a speech in which he called on the

Volunteers to stand ready to fight outside the country as well. The Irish Volunteers responded promptly by ejecting members of their Executive Committee who had been chosen by Redmond. Equally promptly, Redmond formed a new organization — the National Volunteers. A majority of the Irish Volunteers followed him into the new group; it was only then that Skeffington considered joining with the remaining Volunteers who did not.

Should Skeffington's flirtation with the Volunteers have caused his pacifism to be suspect? To some it seemed so, but in truth, the Volunteers' objectives were not clear to him or, for that matter, to many members of their own Executive Committee. When, at an Irish Women's Franchise League meeting, Thomas MacDonagh — poet, teacher, and a forceful leader in the Irish Volunteers — was asked if the Volunteers were in danger of developing an "Irish militarism," he replied rather vaguely that he did not know exactly how far they would go on that road, but that he saw no such danger since they were purely a defensive body organized for the protection of Irish liberties.[11]

On one point, however, Skeffington had no doubts. The Irish Volunteers lacked courage in their stand on women. The day before the Volunteers held their convention in October 1914, he wrote to Thomas MacDonagh asking for changes to be made in their constitution. He would like, he wrote, to have the words *rights* and *liberties* defined. It would simply mean adding the defining words "without distinction of sex, class or creed" to the clause in which those words appeared. He continued:

«   «   «   «   «   «   «   «   «

If this cannot be done, the next best thing would be for some member or members of the Provisional Committee, in the course of the Convention . . . to explain clearly that he intended these rights and liberties to be extended without distinction of sex, class or creed. If that were done clearly . . . and if it met with obvious approval at the Convention, and were not contradicted by any other member of the Provisional Committee, it would virtually have the effect of an official declaration. I hope this opportunity will not be missed — as other opportunities have been — of winning for the Irish Volunteers the support of the women's movement.[12]

»   »   »   »   »   »   »   »   »

It was a vain hope. Skeffington's suggestion was not accepted; consequently, he did not join the Volunteers. In an "Open Letter to Thomas MacDonagh," written many months later, he said that he was glad that he had not.[13]

Skeffington's strong stand both against the war and for votes for women — before home rule — as expressed in the pages of the *Irish Citizen*, won friends not only throughout Ireland but in Great Britain and the United States as well. His views also won their share of enemies; as a result, the *Irish Citizen* faced serious financial trouble. In November 1914, Skeffington sent letters of solicitation to various women in an attempt to raise enough money to keep the paper from folding. Even small sums, they were told, would be welcome "to surmount the present period of exceptional stress." [14]

Throughout this difficult period, Skeffington's creativity, zeal, and optimism did not wane. In a reply to one of his father's "doom-and-gloom" letters, for example, he was able to say, "In spite of what you say, I think things are improving with me. Nous verrons!" [15] When one of the paper's staunch supporters wrote complaining of difficulty selling the paper in the North because " 'Irish' connotes Nationalism to hyper-sensitive Ulster souls," he asked, "Would the North buy a paper with 'Ulster Citizen' on the title page?" It would be possible, he thought, to bring out a special edition for Ulster, "with only the front page different," containing news about the North. (He also took the opportunity to ask for a small contribution.) [16]

Among those Skeffington approached for financial assistance was George Bernard Shaw's wife, Charlotte, since earlier she had offered to send the *Irish Citizen* a small contribution. Now he informed her that he needed "about £5 a month to keep the paper afloat; and it is very difficult to raise even that small sum under present conditions in Ireland." He hoped that she was reading the paper and approved of its suffrage-first policy, he said, and sent his regards to her husband. Diplomatically, he mentioned that he had seen a Dublin Repertory Theatre production of Shaw's *Mrs. Warren's Profession.* He thought the company had done it quite well, he said, but that it had been unfairly reviewed. [17]

Charlotte Shaw's contribution, and the letter that accompanied it, evoked an interesting response. After thanking her for both the donation and her "appreciation of the paper in these chaotic times," Skeffington made some of his own views clear:

«   «   «   «   «   «   «   «   «

You are, of course, quite right in saying that there is nothing "pro-German" in the *Irish Citizen* — though the very fact that it advocates peace has been made the basis of such a charge! But as regards my personal attitude, outside of the Suffrage Movement, there is more excuse for the attachment of that rough and ready label. I want Peace, first of all, no matter who wins; I cannot conceive of any result more disastrous than the continuance of the present barbarism. If that cannot be achieved, then I want a drawn war, with no decisive victory on either side, and with German Militarism and English Navalism equally chastened. Because if *any* Government can point to a decisive victory, the subjects of that Government will have a very bad time after the war; Imperialism will be rampant. A German defeat might bring good to the German people; but an English victory would, I think, bring evil and oppression to the English people, and would, I am certain, bring another period of repression to Ireland. Accordingly the issue of the war which I should most dislike would be a decisive victory for England — and Russia. If France could win in the West, while Germany won in the East and also humbled English naval power, that would seem to me as satisfactory as any outcome of this carnage can possibly be.

No doubt this is "pro-Germanism" as the term is commonly used. But of course I don't put these views into the *Irish Citizen*, which approaches the war solely from the feminist standpoint, and for which I personally write very little, merely keeping it going as a medium of expression for Irish women suffragists. [18]

»   »   »   »   »   »   »   »   »

Skeffington's own financial situation was no better than the *Irish Citizen's*. Among others, he was in debt to T. Fisher Unwin, the publisher of his biography of Davitt. In mid-November he wrote to Unwin that he could do nothing to settle the debt then, "owing to the exceptionally unfavourable financial situation in which I, in common with most free lances, have been placed by the war." When, in the spring, he returned from an American lecture tour, he would clear up the matter immediately, he wrote. (This is the first intimation that such a tour was being planned and the idea seems to have aborted, possibly due to Skeffington's deep involvement in anti-war activities.) He went on to suggest that a "cheap edition" of *Michael Davitt* might be prepared for the United States. "I could dispense of a substantial number of copies in the course of my tour," he wrote. [19] Unwin was charmed with neither the explanation nor the suggestion. His reply pointed out that the overdue account should have been paid long before war broke out. And he had no wish to bring out an edition of the book for the United States. Dana Estes, Boston publishers, had bought two hundred copies on publication and, said Unwin, if he had an order from them or any other publisher in the States, he would gladly fill it. [20]

The war was proving an excellent excuse for the government to introduce many restrictive measures, as witness the difficulties encountered by Irish women in their attempt to participate in the International Women's Congress to be held at The Hague. The *Irish Citizen* had carried an article by Louie Bennett and a lengthy editorial hailing the congress and urging the suffrage societies to support it. [21] The Irish Women's Franchise League decided to send a delegate, but many other suffrage societies refused in the name of patriotism to send delegates or to support the congress. [22] Hanna was so persuasive on the subject that, when she spoke before the Irishwomen's Reform League, of which she was a member, two women volunteered to go as representatives and to pay their own expenses despite some members' strongly worded objections that attendance at the congress might seem like disloyalty to the nation. [23]

The opponents of the congress need not have been concerned. When 180 women applied for passports to attend the meetings, the government at first refused all permits to British and Irish women. Under pressure, they granted permits to twenty hand-picked women — only one from Ireland. In a final move against the Women's Congress, the North Sea was suddenly closed to all traffic and kept closed until after the meetings. The Dublin Trades Council had passed a resolution in support of the congress and of an Irish delegation. Skeffington wrote to William O'Brien to be sure that the supportive resolution had been sent formally to both the Chief Secretary and the Home Secretary, but he was pessimistic. "It is now unlikely that any will be allowed to get through, *but* we want to give them all the trouble possible," he wrote. "Mrs. Despard, Sylvia Pankhurst, every militant except Mrs. Cobden Sanderson, every Irish delegate except Miss Bennett, have been refused permits. Mrs. Skeffington is [in] London, worrying officialdom all she can!" [24] According to an article by Hanna in the *Irish Citizen*, she and the other Irish delegates besieged the House of Commons and the Home Office for a full week. Thanks to the excuse of the North Sea being closed, however, even Louie Bennett, the approved delegate, was prevented from attending the congress and only two delegates from Great Britain got through. [25]

A meeting protesting the government's sabotaging of the peace conference was held in May, at which Thomas MacDonagh was the principal speaker. It was his speech that prompted Skeffington to write the Open Letter mentioned previously. His letter illustrated the difficulties that the pacifist and the humanitarian face always and that are intensified in time of war. It illustrated as well Skeffington's understanding of the ambivalence of MacDonagh's position — an ambivalence that he felt he largely shared. His respect and affection for MacDonagh had been in no way diminished by the speech, which he called "a remarkable one" and "a vivid example of the kind of tangle we have all got ourselves into under the existent militarist and de-humanising system." He went on:

«   «   «   «   «   «   «   «   «

You spoke vehemently and with unmistakable sincerity in advocacy of peace. You traced war with perfect accuracy, to its roots in exploitation. You commended every effort made by the women to combat militarism and establish a permanent peace. And in the same speech you boasted of being one of the creators of a new militarism in Ireland: you described your "disgusting" duties as instructor of bayonet-fighting; you spoke of "hoping" to have "a better opportunity than voting" to show that the Irish Volunteers stood for the freedom of women as well as of men. And then, again, you hoped that it would never be necessary to use the arms with which you had helped to provide thousands of Irishmen; and that we should never see war in this country. You yourself said your position was somewhat anomalous at a peace meeting. . . . We are all in the same tangle.

»   »   »   »   »   »   »   »   »

His next paragraph leaves no doubt about how very close he was to joining the Volunteers in 1914:

«   «   «   «   «   «   «   «   «

As you know, I am personally in full sympathy with the fundamental objects of the Irish Volunteers. When you shook off the Redmondite incubus last September, I was on the point of joining you. Had your Executive accepted my suggestion — to state definitely that it stood for the liberties of the people of Ireland "without distinction of sex, class, or creed" — I would have done so at once. I am glad now I did not. For, as your infant movement grows towards the stature of a full-grown militarism, its essence — preparation to kill — grows more repellent to me.

»   »   »   »   »   »   »   »   »

Long ago, J. B. had extolled the virtues of "marching," and now his son told MacDonagh that he could see the merits of this "clean open-air movement," which gave the men "something better to do than cheer at meetings and pass resolutions." However, he added:

«   «   «   «   «   «   «   «   «

It is militarism at its best. But it is militarism. It is organised to kill. High ideals undoubtedly animate you. But has not nearly every militarist system started with the same high ideals? You are not out to exploit or to oppress; you are out merely to prevent exploitation and to defend. What militarism ever avowed other aims — in its beginnings? You justify no war except a war to end oppression, to establish the right. What warmonger ever spoke otherwise when it was necessary to enlist the people?

»   »   »   »   »   »   »   »   »

Skeffington's letter went on to say that, although MacDonagh was sincere in his attitude, there was the question of the sincerity of his colleagues. "How many of them share your horror of war, your aspiration for a permanent peace?" he wrote. "Are not the bulk of the Irish Volunteers animated by the old, bad tradition that war is a glorious thing, that there is something 'manly' about going out prepared to kill your fellow-man?" As for his own position:

«   «   «   «   «   «   «   «   «

I advocate no mere servile lazy acquiescence in injustice. I am, and always will be a fighter. But I want to see the age-long fight against injustice clothe itself in new forms, suited to a new age. I want to see the manhood of Ireland no longer hypnotised by the glamour of "the glory of arms," no longer blind to the horrors of organised murder.

»   »   »   »   »   »   »   »   »

Continuing, Skeffington discussed the program of the Volunteers point by point. Their objective of training and equipping a body of volunteers "to maintain and secure the right and liberties common to all the people of Ireland" he found praiseworthy, but he questioned whether the phrase "without distinction of sex, class, or creed" should not be added. Why were women omitted? "Consider carefully why; and when you have found and clearly expressed the reason why women cannot be asked to enroll in this movement, you will be close to the reactionary element in the movement

itself." He questioned also whether the training and the discipline needed to
be of a military nature. "Must the arms and equipment be the arms and
equipment of war?" he asked. He then summarized his view of the overall
picture:

«   «   «   «   «   «   «   «   «

> We are on the threshold of a new era in human history. After this war,
> nothing can be as it was before. The foundations of all things must be
> re-examined. Things which we might have let pass, lightheartedly, as
> unimportant, now come to us charged with a tragic and intense signifi-
> cance. Formerly we could only imagine the chaos to which we were
> being led by the military spirit. Now we realise it. And we must never
> fall into that abyss again.
>
> Can you not conceive an organisation, a body of men and women
> banded together to secure and maintain the rights and liberties of the
> people of Ireland, a body animated with a high purpose, united by a
> bond of comradeship, trained and disciplined in the ways of self-
> sacrifice and true patriotism, armed and equipped with the weapons of
> intellect and of will that are irresistible? . . . an organisation that will
> not lay it down as its fundamental principle, "We will prepare to kill our
> fellow men?"
>
> Impracticable? Not if you have the vision to conceive it, the will to
> execute it. Whatsoever the mind of man can plan, that the executive
> brain of man can carry out.
>
> At any rate, it is the only way out of the tangle. It is the only way in
> which we, the oppressed and exploited, can reconcile our hatred of the
> oligarchies and our hatred of organised bloodshed.

»   »   »   »   »   »   »   »   »

Skeffington concluded with a plea to MacDonagh. "Think it over," he said,
"before the millitarist current draws you too far from your humanitarian
anchorage."[26] Future events proved that his plea was in vain. Thomas
MacDonagh was one of the leaders of the Easter Rising and was executed for
his part in it on 3 May 1916.

The impression should not be left that Skeffington was fighting only
against the war and for women's suffrage. In an *Irish Citizen* editorial he
addressed the problem of temperance. Apparently the British government
was contemplating total prohibition, believing that drinking and subsequent
absenteeism was impeding wartime production. Whatever England may do,
the editorial pointed out, it was highly unlikely that total prohibition could
be imposed on Ireland. "Ireland has been called a clerically-ridden country;
it would be much more corrrectly called a publican-ridden country," read
the editorial. Proof is offered. Heads of the various Christian churches in
Ireland had issued an appeal for mild restrictions to be placed on drinking
establishments. The press had not a good word to say for the appeal and, in
many cases, simply disregarded it. "On no other subject could an appeal

signed by Cardinal Logue have been treated so contemptuously. The publican is stronger than the priest in his influence on official Nationalism," the editorial stated. Some weeks later the *Irish Citizen* reported that a petition had been sent to Prime Minister Asquith, signed by more than thirty women's organizations, including the I.W.F.L., urging that "vigorous measures" be passed to curtail the sale of drink in Ireland.[27]

The *Irish Citizen* raised another issue in the 20 March issue, which some might have considered to be allied to the drinking problem. Although a great deal of money had been spent on public lavatories for men, not one penny had been spent for lavatories for women. The claim by the Dublin Corporation was that respectable Dublin women would be too modest to use these facilities. The *Irish Citizen* pointed out it was only because public lavatories for women were a need of the poor that the issue had been pushed aside. Factory workers, flower vendors, and other working women had protested without result. Every women's organization in Dublin was urged to "bombard the Corporation with letters, resolutions and deputations, until the scheme is definitely under way."[28]

There had never been any doubt in Skeffington's mind that he was facing eventual arrest because of his anti-war activities. He indicated this in diary items, in letters to friends, and even in the anti-war and anti-conscription speeches he had been delivering Sunday after Sunday in Beresford Place for the Socialist Party of Ireland. He summarized succinctly his purpose in speaking faithfully week after week in a letter to a representative of the Union of Democratic Control who had spoken in Dublin, giving the Christian pacifist view. "In your speech . . . you said you were not going to dissuade anyone from going to the Army if he felt he ought to," Skeffington wrote. That sounded fine, he admitted, but people, "especially ignorant people," were not really free to choose. "Press, platform, politicians, and sometimes pulpit, are thundering exhortations to enlist." He pointed out that it was, therefore, the duty of those on the other side to counterbalance this propaganda. Since any attempt to do so in print was being suppressed, public speech was essential. In his own speeches, he added, he hoped to give his audience "some rational grounds for their instinctive attitude [against war], so as to strengthen them against the unfair pressure to which they are being subjected. The meeting pledges itself, every Sunday, to resist Conscription *passively*."[29]

Skeffington delivered forty speeches before he was arrested. His last was on 23 May 1915. His arrest took place on 29 May by order of the Commandant of the troops in Dublin, Brevet Colonel H. G. H. Kennard. The charge stated that "Francis Sheehy Skeffington, on the 23rd May 1915, at Beresford Place, Dublin, did make statements likely to cause disaffection to His Majesty, the King, and likely to prejudice recruiting for His Majesty's Forces." He was, read the order, to be lodged in His Majesty's Prison, Mountjoy.[30]

In his prison cell, Skeffington began corresponding with the authorities. No sooner was he jailed than he applied to the chairman of the General Prisons Board for permission to continue to edit the *Irish Citizen* during his incarceration. Granted permission, he again wrote, complaining he could not avail himself of this privilege since he had not been allowed to have the latest edition of his paper.[31]

On 8 June he informed Hanna that he was to appear in court the following day. He told her that he was in excellent form and that he expected his case would be heard first. He had decided to conduct his own defense, and it is doubtful whether he could have had a better advocate. In his cross-examination of Major W. Moulle who was sworn in by the Crown as "a competent authority for the military, to direct prosecutions in such cases," he scored his first point. "You are authorised to suspend trial by jury and enforce summary jurisdiction?" he asked. Upon receiving an affirmative reply, he continued, "Therefore as a military authority you are entitled to suspend the liberty of the subject and enforce military law under this Act?" Again receiving an affirmative reply, he said, "That is all I ask you. It is an eloquent commentary on the present condition of things in Ireland."[32]

Chief witness for the Crown was Constable Patrick McCarthy, who had attended and taken notes at many of the Sunday lectures. At Skeffington's request, his entire transcription of the 23 May speech was read into the record. In his cross-examination of the constable, Skeffington was able to prove conclusively that the notes were faulty and that the speech was not essentially different from the previous thirty-nine. He was also able to force the constable to admit that the tone of the meetings was essentially Irish Nationalist, that, throughout, the stress had been on the interests of Ireland as apart from those of any other country — either Germany or England — and that Skeffington had attempted to impress upon his audience that Ireland had no quarrel with Germany and that no Irishman should enlist to fight England's battles.

Reference had been made during the testimony to recruiting meetings held each Tuesday in the vicinity of Beresford Place. Skeffington, however, pointed out that these meetings had not been successful and that there was a strong possibility that his arrest and subsequent prosecution were an attempt to bring new life to them. In his cross-examination of Constable McCarthy, Skeffington forced the constable to admit that the fortieth meeting had been no different in tone from any previous meeting and that the timing of his arrest, therefore, would seem to coincide with the lack of success of the recruiting meetings. He was also able to set the record straight as to the main thrust of his speeches — passive resistance. Asking the constable to reread parts of the transcript of the latest Beresford Place speech, he brought out that the pledge which he called upon the audience to make at each meeting was that, in the event of conscription becoming law, they would not go and would smash any such act by resisting passively. The constable agreed that

Skeffington had said in his speech that, though the Volunteers and the Citizen Army might use some other means, those who were not members of the Citizen Army should employ passive resistance.[33]

Skeffington's speech in his own defense is such a well-written polemic that it is given in its entirety in the Appendix. Suffice it here to give his conclusion.

«   «   «   «   «   «   «   «   «

This prosecution would be intelligible in a country ruled by an autocrat, in a country under the iron heel of military despotism; in a country ruled by a narrow oligarchy fearing the smallest breath of criticism. It would be intelligible above all in a country held by force by another country, the rulers of which would fear to allow any expression of opinion amongst the subject people. If you condemn me, you condemn the system you represent as being some or all of these things. Any sentence you may pass on me is a sentence upon British rule in Ireland.

»   »   »   »   »   »   »   »   »

The sentence imposed by Magistrate Mahoney was the maximum penalty in his power — six months' hard labor and six additional months in default of bail. The magistrate refused to consider the question of political treatment. As sentence was passed, Skeffington rose, saying, "I will serve no such sentence. I will eat no food from this moment, and long before the expiration of the sentence I shall be out of prison, alive or dead!"[34]

The severity of the sentence must have shocked Skeffington, even though he had expected to be arrested. At the 23 May meeting, he had told his audience that he might not be free to appear the following week. Both Sean Milroy and John MacDermott, two active Socialists, had been arrested for making anti-conscription speeches from that same platform during the previous weeks and both were in Mountjoy awaiting sentence. As it transpired, all three were brought before Magistrate Mahoney on the same day. In *Memories of Mountjoy*, published in 1917, Milroy recalls that his case was taken first and that though the account of his Beresford Place speech, as given by Constable McCarthy, "Crown witness note-taker," was on the whole fairly accurate, it did attribute atrocious grammar to him. "That was unkind of you, Constable," he wrote. "You might have charged me with high treason and I would not have grumbled, but attempt to father that awful jumble of English as she is spoken on me! Oh, McCarthy, McCarthy, may heaven forgive you!"[35]

Milroy gives a vivid account of the events that took place in Mountjoy after the sentencing. When it was Skeffington's turn to be searched, examined, and assigned prison attire, he simply buttoned up his coat and said, "I'll facilitate you in no way, I'll obey no prison regulations, and I'll take no food until I am released." A "Votes for Women" badge he was wearing was taken from him. The next day Skeffington told Milroy, when they were able to talk with each other surreptitiously for a few moments, that he had not eaten but that the doctor had threatened to feed him forcibly. Skeffington was going to "ask the visiting justices to restrain him from so doing." He also said that he was told he could continue wearing his own clothes until the Prisons Board made a decison.[36]

The Prisoners' Record Sheet at Mountjoy listed Skeffington's age at conviction as "Appears about 50 years." In answer to the question of registered religion, he had "declined to state."[37] A letter from the medical officer to the chairman of the General Prisons Board listed his height as 5 feet, 4½ inches and his weight as 124¼ pounds, and stated that he was found to be "in good bodily health and of sound mind," and "fit for hard labour of a suitable kind." Because, said the doctor, he was planning to refuse all food, they would begin to feed him artificially the next day, "by force if necessary."[38]

Hanna was not standing idly by. She had wired her father, seeking his intervention, and he had replied expressing his horror at the situation. "I hate the idea of that hunger strike and his suicide," he wrote. "The sentence itself reads murder to a frail man like Frank." He planned to see Chief Secretary Augustine Birrell to try to have the sentence modified, but he was not hopeful.[39] Hanna was receiving letters from her father-in-law as well, but they by no means gave comfort. Before Skeffington was sentenced, J. B. wrote:

«   «   «   «   «   «   «   «   «

The fact is Joseph [the second of his son's given names] deserves all he gets, in fact he courted all this and even said he rather liked a while in gaol, probably to rival your heroic deeds for *you* are no wiser than he is, in action at least, and I am afraid set him a bad example, instead of being a restraining influence and when the house is on fire at both ends, it is as bad as candle burning at both ends.

»   »   »   »   »   »   »   »   »

He went on to complain that the brunt of his son's "absurdities" always fell upon him. As a result, his health had been injured and, possibly, his life shortened. As for his son's financial indiscretions:

«   «   «   «   «   «   «   «   «

I learn . . . that he has his life ensured for a considerable sum, also news to me, showing further deceit and more silly finance — for that takes a constant annual *drain* and with Rent and bank interests could sink a strong earner. It is absurd save as a provision for Owen who might not need it and who could be better provided for. He should sell that Insurance, or get its *value* from the office, and thus free himself from that load — It is right to speak of these things — it is never too late to mend — It is a time for him to take stock of his business and try a new course. He has fallen to the bottom but he need not *stick in mud* always.[40]

»   »   »   »   »   »   »   »   »

Having bolstered Hanna's morale in his typical fashion, J. B. — again typically — enclosed a check for ten pounds. (According to Owen Sheehy-

Skeffington's account, his father had indeed insured his life for five hundred pounds in order that, should anything happen to him, the *Irish Citizen* could continue to appear. Owen recalls that his mother "always remembered with gratitude" that the insurance company had "paid up at once and without question" at the time of his father's death.[41])

When Hanna wired her father-in-law the verdict of the trial, his reply informed her, once more, that his son was getting just what he could expect. "No one but a Monomaniac would act so," J. B. wrote. "How could any sane person praise Germany, the most degrading tyranny of mind and body at peace and the most brutal savagery at war. Besides so many in Ireland are mourning lost ones. It was a wanton outrage on the Majority." He did feel that the hard labor part of the sentence might be mitigated on the grounds of poor health if a petition, "strongly signed," were sent to the Lord Lieutenant or to the Chief Surgeon. "But he has so attacked Ministers and even Irish M.P.s that I suppose even your own Father would hardly sign for him." He was sure, also, that "the Labour men" would not stand behind him, which showed "the Silliness of working for them, yet he threw up his positions and risked his life for them — he is a *fool*." His conclusion:

«   «   «   «   «   «   «   «   «

He may commit suicide by Starvation, a mean and low trick. Better he was out in Belgium fighting against the Modern Huns, and die a heroic death. . . . They will feed him forcibly, which means destruction in one form or other, Throat, Stomach or Brain — he may lose his reason though it is not much use to him. . . . He can hurt only *himself* and his friends, me especially, for you don't care and you lead him on to this by example and speech. His own child seems nought to him compared with Larkin & Co. I am writing to Dr. Jordan to see if he can do anything on the score of his health. If he made such a speech in Germany, he would be shot like a dog.[42]

»   »   »   »   »   »   »   »   »

An extract from the medical officer's journal for 11 June reported that "Prisoner F. S. Skeffington has been on hunger strike since his committal to this prison on the evening of 9th (Wednesday); he has drank [sic] some water. His weight on committal was 124½ lbs. I have admitted him to hospital for the purpose of special observation."[43] On the following day the medical officer wrote again to the chairman of the Prisons Board to report on Skeffington's condition. Skeffington had told him, he said, that he had slept fairly well during the night. He had taken no food during the past twenty-four hours but had had a glass of water. His weight was now down to 118 pounds, including clothes. The doctor found his temperature normal, his heart free of organic disease, and his pulse full and regular. "The bowels and kidneys are acting regularly, and there has been no vomiting since midnight on Thursday last. . . . The prisoner sits out during exercise hours daily. His conclusion was that Skeffington's general condition was "satisfactory under the circumstances."[44]

David Sheehy, J. B., and Hanna were trying every possible means to get the sentence changed and Skeffington released from Mountjoy. Hanna sent George Bernard Shaw a letter and a transcript of Skeffington's speech from the dock. His reply is a masterpiece of rationalization for doing nothing, but it does make his own position on the war clear. "There is nothing to be done," he wrote. "The Defence of the Realm Act abolishes all liberty in Great Britain and Ireland except such as the authorities may choose to leave us." He informed her that sentences of six months' hard labor were not uncommon "for the most trivial oversights," and that he felt Skeffington had made a grave error in taking the chances he had. "Something can be done with a tyrannical Government: nothing can be done with a terrified Government and a cowed people," he told her. His final justification for taking no part in the matter was that he was considered by the government to be pro-German, and "if they knew that I sympathized with your husband they would declare that nothing but his imprisonment for life could save England. I can fight stupidity; but nobody can fight cowardice."[45]

Despite J. B.'s acerbity and his constant lecturing, he was doing everything in his power for his son. For instance, he asked Dr. MacMahon of Terenure ("he is the son of the Master of Waterford Model School") to examine his son in prison and to give J. B. a candid opinion of his condition. Unfortunately, the prison authorities refused to allow McMahon to visit Skeffington, even though he assured them that he would be willing to have the prison doctor and any other officials accompany him. J. B. also wired as many of his influential acquaintances as possible. One, A. Purser — whom J. B. described to Hanna as "a mild type of Tory" — replied that, though he would make some attempt to talk with the police, he wanted to make his position perfectly clear. "I do not feel any sympathy with your son's politics regarding recruiting. . . . I see no objection to allowing people to commit suicide by hunger-striking or any other means. Few things have, in my opinion, been more injurious to the nation than the shilly shally treatment of such matters by the late Liberal Government."[46] Purser reflected, in J. B.'s opinion, Tory thinking and the thinking of many of the Liberals as well.

Hanna kept J. B. fully informed as to his son's condition. She seemed able to accept his tirades and to understand fully that they represented genuine concern. A letter that she received several days after Skeffington had begun his hunger strike reflected that concern. He said, in part: "You should write in to him to take food. . . . If he kills himself no one will be affected only his relations. . . . It's a terrible business, that he would destroy himself, and worry his relatives, merely to please and gratify his enemies. The force of folly could no farther go — and, you set him the bad example. God help you and poor Owen."[47]

On the seventh day of his hunger strike and in a state of collapse, Skeffington was released, under the Cat and Mouse Act, until 30 June. His son Owen wrote, "I remember him, a pale skeleton of his recent self, being slowly helped by a cabbie up our garden path. . . . Even his voice was almost gone as he tried to greet me: 'Hello laddie.' "[48] Upon hearing the news, J. B. wrote Hanna, "Glad he is alive. Let him get slow careful treatment." It was his belief that at least a month would be needed for recuperation and he enclosed a check for twenty pounds, saying: "I will not see him want for money when he is down."[49]

J. B. was very well aware that under the Cat and Mouse Act his son was subject to rearrest at the end of June; to Hanna, he outlined the steps that should be taken. First, an attempt should be made to get an extension of time by procuring certificates from two or three doctors testifying to his son's poor health. These certificates should be duplicated and sent to the governor of the jail, the chairman of the Prisons Board, the Chief Secretary, and the Under Secretary. If necessary, copies should be sent to the newspapers as well. Meanwhile, Skeffington should go to Wales to recuperate. When he felt perfectly well once more, he should give the authorities the slip and go to America.

Letters to Skeffington during his convalescence reflect the popular feeling against the Cat and Mouse Act, as well as his friends' and acquaintances' affection and concern. James Cousins wrote from Liverpool expressing the hope that the Cat and Mouse "imbecility" would not be enforced and regretting that he was not close enough to be able to help publish the *Irish Citizen*. Frederick Pethick-Lawrence wrote to say that he hoped the authorities would not be "so brutal or so stupid" as to put Skeffington in prison again, and a letter to Hanna from Constance Markievicz expressed the hope that Skeffington would soon be "fit and strong." The press was, on the whole, sympathetic as well. *The Leader*, even referring to him as "Mr. Sheehy-Skeffington" — "in view of the serious condition in which he lies we naturally refrain from referring to him in a more familiar way" — asked what action the government and the Irish Party were planning to take. "Is Mr. Skeffington to be allowed to die? He publicly told Mahoney the magistrate that long before his sentence expired he would be out of prison dead or alive. And certainly he made good his words. Will Birrell fetch him back on June 30th to another Hunger Strike?"[50] Hanna, in a letter to the editor of *New Ireland*, asked the same question. Under his suspended sentence, she wrote, he was "condemned, in order to complete his year's sentence, to fifty-two weeks of hunger strike, plus two years, in fortnightly periods, for recuperation." Would his "permanent disablement or death" as a result promote recruiting in Ireland? Eighteen days' imprisonment which included seven days' hunger strike, it seemed to her, was surely sufficient expiation.[51]

One small indication of how public opinion had been affected by Skeffington's imprisonment was the revival of his play, *The Prodigal Daughter*. Pure propaganda, it had previously been performed late in April 1914 during a Daffodil Fete sponsored by the Irish Women's Franchise League. And not only was the play revived; it was also reprinted as a leaflet. A reviewer in

Nationality felt that all Irish women and men interested in votes for women would do well to read it. "In it we find the women's case put with the directness and cogency with which Mr. Sheehy-Skeffington urges any cause in which he has faith." After referring to Skeffington's courageous fight against conscription and for women's suffrage, the review concluded, "Irish Suffragists when selecting plays for production have up to now usually got them over the water. They have now no further excuse for so doing, as 'The Prodigal Daughter' supplies the want."[52]

Shortly after Skeffington's release from Mountjoy, he spent a month at the seaside in Wales recuperating and making plans for a trip to the United States, as his father had suggested. If rearrested, he planned to resume his hunger strike immediately, but no attempt was made to rearrest him. (As he told an American reporter some months later, "I think they were glad to get me out of the country, so I'm going back in November.")[53] By the end of July 1915 he was on his way to the United States.

Skeffington's ostensible reason for going to the States at that time was to raise money for the *Irish Citizen*. He hoped also that he might book his return passage on Henry Ford's "peace ship," *Oscar II*, which was due to sail from New York to Europe with a group of peace advocates. But his good friend, J. F. Byrne, whose home in Long Island City, New York, was to be his headquarters during his stay, says that "these reasons were subordinate to a purpose which he did not express."[54] This was to carry out an underground assignment for the Neutrality League — namely, contact with Germany. Byrne wrote in *Silent Years*, published in 1953, that Skeffington, "acting according to his lights as a patriotic Irishman, had been engaged, as far back as August 1914 in activities for which he, as a British Subject, could have been tried for his life." He added that what he said was not based on "hearsay or assumption," but on "a knowledge I possessed from the time of the beginning by Skeffington of the activities to which I refer." Further, he was "acting only in accordance with Sheehy-Skeffington's expressed wish to me that some day I would give, or bequeath, testimony to this effect."[55]

John Devoy went even beyond this in *Recollections of an Irish Rebel*, published in 1929. His truthfulness was sometimes open to question as Byrne's was not, but, according to him, he had seen a letter written by Skeffington asking the Germans for assistance; he had not seen it, however, until after the request had been denied. "It was written in a small town in Belgium and handed to the German commander with a request that it be forwarded to the proper authority," Devoy wrote. "It was referred by the German foreign office to Van Bernstorff, and shown to me by Van Skal." The letter was in English and was "very clear and precise." In it Skeffington said, according to Devoy, that he did not belong to the "Irish Revolutionary Organisation" but that its leaders trusted him. He mentioned the effective work that the anti-recruiting movement was carrying out, as well as the importance of that work to the Germans. In addition, he estimated the cost of continuing this work. "I don't remember the amount he named, but it was very modest," Devoy commented, and continued to give his own assessment of Skeffington's actions: "Although violently opposed to all war Skeffington evidently wanted England beaten in that particular war and was willing to make a pacifist's contribution towards bringing about that result. . . . Had the English Government the smallest scrap of evidence that Skeffington had written that letter or held any sort of communication with the Germans in Belgium, he would doubtless have been executed long before Easter Week."[56]

NOTES TO CHAPTER 11

1. *Irish Citizen*, 26 September 1914.

2. William O'Brien, *Forth the Banners Go* (Dublin: The Three Candles Limited, 1969), p. 272. Plans had been made by the Neutrality League, of which Skeffington was a member.

3. *Irish Worker*, 3 October 1914.

4. *Irish Citizen*, 3 October 1914.

5. Ibid., cover page, 3 October 1914.

6. F. Sheehy-Skeffington, "War and Feminism," *Irish Citizen*, 12 September 1914.

7. Ibid.

8. *Irish Citizen*, 3 October 1914.

9. Ibid., 30 January 1915. Review of Emmeline Pankhurst, *My Own Story* (London: Eveleigh Nash, 1913).

10. "The Writing on the Wall" (editorial), ibid., 8 August 1914.

11. *Irish Citizen*, account of activities of Irish Women's Franchise League, 12 December 1914. The meeting at which Thomas MacDonagh spoke was held in December 1914; his topic was "Ireland, Women and the War."

12. F. Sheehy-Skeffington to Thomas MacDonagh, 24 October 1914.

13. *Irish Citizen*, 22 May 1915.

14. Skeffington's series of letters soliciting funds for the *Irish Citizen* were dated 17 November 1914 and requested sums as small as "even £5."

15. F. Sheehy-Skeffington to J. B. Skeffington, 9 May 1914.

16. F. Sheehy-Skeffington to "Mrs." Metge, 17 November 1914.

17. F. Sheehy-Skeffington to Charlotte Shaw, 17 November 1914.

18. F. Sheehy-Skeffington to Charlotte Shaw, 14 December 1914.

19. F. Sheehy-Skeffington to T. Fisher Unwin, 17 November 1914.

20. T. Fisher Unwin to F. Sheehy-Skeffington, 19 November 1914.

21. "A New Move for Peace" (editorial) and Louie Bennett, "Women's Opportunity," *Irish Citizen*, 6 March 1915.

22. Two of the suffrage societies that refused to send delegates to the Hague peace conference were The National Union of Women's Suffrage Societies and the new Constitutional Society for Women Suffrage.

23. *Irish Citizen*, 20 March 1915.

24. F. Sheehy-Skeffington to William O'Brien, 26 April 1915, cited in O'Brien's *Forth the Banners Go*, p. 292.

25. *Irish Citizen*, 8 May 1915.

26. "Open Letter to Thomas MacDonagh," ibid., 22 May 1915.

27. *Irish Citizen*, 3 April 1915.

28. Ibid., 20 March 1915.

29. F. Sheehy-Skeffington to "Mr. Douglas," 5 February 1915. Italics added.

30. State Papers Office, Dublin, G/1137/i.

31. F. Sheehy-Skeffington to Chairman, Prisons Board, 7 June 1915.

32. Incomplete typed trial notes, Sheehy-Skeffington Papers.

33. Ibid.

34. F. Sheehy-Skeffington, *Speech from the Dock: With Letter from George Bernard Shaw* (Dublin: Irish Workers Cooperative Society, n.d.).

35. Sean Milroy, *Memories of Mountjoy* (Dublin: Maunsel, 1917), pp. 14–17.

36. Ibid.

37. State Papers Office, Dublin, Prisoners' Record Sheet, File 2826/15.

38. Ibid., Letter from R. G. Dowdall, M.D., 10 June 1915, G.P.B. No. 2907/15, C.S.O. No. 9328/15.

39. David Sheehy to H. Sheehy-Skeffington, 10 June 1915.

40. J. B. Skeffington to H. Sheehy-Skeffington, 5 June 1915.

41. O. Sheehy-Skeffington, "Francis Sheehy-Skeffington," p. 144n.

42. J. B. Skeffington to H. Sheehy-Skeffington, 10 June 1915.

43. State Papers Office, Dublin, Medical Officers Journal, 11 June 1915, File 2921/15.

44. State Papers Office, Dublin, Letter from R. G. Dowdall, M.D., 12 June 1915, no file number.

45. George Bernard Shaw to H. Sheehy-Skeffington, 14 June 1915.

46. J. B. Skeffington to H. Sheehy-Skeffington, 12 June 1915.

47. J. B. Skeffington to H. Sheehy-Skeffington, 15 June 1915.

48. O. Sheehy-Skeffington, "Francis Sheehy-Skeffington," p. 143.

49. J. B. Skeffington to H. Sheehy-Skeffington, dated only "Wed. noon." He was writing to her almost daily during this period.

50. *The Leader*, 26 June 1915.

51. *New Ireland*, 26 June 1915.

52. *Nationality*, 7 August 1915.

53. *Catholic Herald* (London) 9 October 1915. Report of Skeffington's remarks to a reporter from the *New York Sun*.

54. Byrne, *Silent Years*, p. 97.

55. Ibid., p. 138.

56. John Devoy, *Recollections of an Irish Rebel* (New York: Charles P. Young, 1929), p. 443.

12

Pilgrimage to the United States

There was speculation and possibly skepticism about the true purpose of Skeffington's visit to the United States, but for him — this man who was "enjoying a holiday from the Cat and Mouse Act," as he told reporters[1] — his motives were clear. He had to give the Americans a true picture of the situation in wartime Ireland, he had to point out the importance of striving for peace, he wanted to study the suffrage movement in the United States, and he needed to raise money for the *Irish Citizen* and for himself. News of Ireland's attitude toward conscription, for instance, was being filtered through England and, as Skeffington saw it, badly garbled. There was also a misconception of Ireland's pro-Germanism. At the same time he could, so to speak, work both sides of the street: he could convey to Ireland a picture of the situation in the United States through the *Irish Citizen* and other publications.

He spent almost four months in the States, striving to set the record straight through articles, speeches, and interviews with leading members of the press and prominent figures in the labor and suffrage movements. As always, the hectic schedule and the excitement stimulated him. His health was much improved; he seemed able to do a prodigious amount of work. He was, as he would have said, in rare form.

Skeffington's stay in the United States is well documented, for he attempted to send an article to the *Irish Citizen* each week. In addition, the Sheehy-Skeffington Papers contain twenty-one letters from him to Hanna, written during that period. (Twenty-one more — the first twenty-one he wrote, in fact — are missing and may possibly have been confiscated by the British when they searched and ransacked the Skeffington home after his murder. That they did exist is obvious, since the first available letter, dated 15 October, is marked "22nd letter.")

Toward the beginning of his stay, Skeffington reported that much excitement had been generated in New York City by a move to have women stay off their jobs for one day to prove their strength in the labor market. The instigator of the plan, Mrs. Norman Whitehouse, claimed that she had the backing of a great many women in professional and trade unions. She visualized, as a result of the stoppage, crippled restaurants, closed-down switchboards, chaos in the textile and dressmaking trades, deserted department stores, and offices deprived of stenographic services.[2] For a week the newspapers, while maintaining that the idea was not to be taken seriously, were filled with news of the possibility of the walk-out. Finally, however, the women dropped the scheme. They felt that the publicity alone had accomplished their aims — to show the absurdity of the belief that "woman's place is in the home" and to make known important facts about women workers. One revealing statistic emerged, for instance — 500,000 women in New York City (which then had a population of over five million) alone worked outside the home.[3]

Skeffington had not been in the States for much more than a month when Leo Frank was lynched in Georgia. Frank was a Jew whose death sentence — imposed for the murder of Mary Phagan — had been commuted because of doubt that he was guilty. Much moved, Skeffington wrote to the *Irish Citizen* that the lynchers had simply assumed that Frank was guilty of the murder and were claiming to have avenged Georgia womanhood. Prominent men in that state — mayors, editors — were talking of southern chivalry. To Skeffington, the action of the lynchers was race hatred and nothing more. He reported that a leading feminist, Dr. Anna Shaw, had published a "scathing" statement blasting the southern chivalry myth. She had pointed out that Georgia was one of the most backward of the states in its attitude toward suffrage, that it had no compulsory education law, and that the state sent thousands of children, girls as well as boys, into mills and factories at the ages of seven and eight — several years younger than the age of consent — "to enrich its chivalrous gentry."[4]

"Suffrage is very much in the air," he reported. The states of New York, Pennsylvania, and Massachusetts were all to vote on the Woman Suffrage Amendment to the Constitution in November and New Jersey late in October.[5] After the latter vote was lost, he wrote Hanna that he had attended a suffrage parade that was "the finest I have ever seen. . . . About 30,000 marched, up Fifth Avenue in the teeth of a bitter wind, which swept down their banners remorselessly. It took them over three hours to pass any point. Some 5,000 men were also in the march." The women had not been disheartened by the results of the New Jersey vote, he told Hanna, for they saw it this way: "The 135,000 votes they polled is a great achievement for a first vote in a conservative State."[6] An "extraordinarily persistent and systematic canvass" of New York City voters was being conducted by the suffragists to induce them to vote for the suffrage amendment, and a majority of the press was supporting them. The only serious opponent was the *New York Times.* But despite the suffragists' hard work, the ostensible cooperation of the press, and the fact that public opinion seemd to be behind the women, Skeffington felt that "secret and subtle forces . . . in the drink trade" and corrupt politicians were working against them and, at the last moment, would sabotage the vote.[7]

Skeffington's optimism obviously clouded his powers of prediction when he wrote in the *Irish Citizen* that "the war-madness is passing away, and it is now practically certain that the Government will not commit the great crime of plunging this nation into the European War."[8] He saw the field of American politics as dominated by Woodrow Wilson, William Jennings Bryan, and Theodore Roosevelt. Roosevelt was the "war at any price" advocate, Bryan was the spokesman for the peace party, and Wilson stood between the two. A master diplomat at handling the situation between Germany and the United States, Wilson was at that time, "the most popular and the most respected personality in the United States." All three men professed sympathy with the suffrage movement, but the "more clear-sighted suffragists," he said, did not completely trust them. This applied particularly to Roosevelt, who was suspect because of his general philosophy. But, for Skeffington, the mere fact that all three at least paid lip service to the suffrage movement indicated its strength in the United States.[9]

Skeffington's comments in the *Irish Citizen* give little intimation that he was critical of the American suffragists. But in a letter to Hanna, with which he enclosed a leaflet by Carrie Chapman Catt, president of the American Woman Suffrage Association, he said, "Just what is weak about the big suffrage movement here, — its timidity" she could see from that leaflet.[10] He had seen what the outbreak of war had done to the suffrage movement in England, and it is very possible that he thought war hysteria might have a similar effect on the American movement. He may have feared that timidity — in the form of decreased militancy — might water down the fight for the vote and that patriotism might slacken the fight for peace.

Skeffington's articles on the suffrage movement in the United States were appearing regularly in the *Irish Citizen*, and his articles on Ireland's situation and the need for more truthful reporting of it were beginning to appear in the U.S. papers. Typical of the latter was a lengthy "Letter to the Editor" in the *New York Times* early in October. Under the title "Freedom Was in Ireland's Lap," Skeffington set forth clearly and concisely what he considered to be John Redmond's sell-out of his constituency. Had Redmond, when England entered the war, "risen in the House of Commons to say simply: 'I have no mandate from my constituents with regard to a European war. I and my colleagues will now return to Ireland to consult the Irish people as to what our attitude should be,' " Skeffington wrote, "the effect would have been electrical." Had Redmond done this and then walked out of the House of Commons, Skeffington contended, the world would have realized that Ireland was "indeed a nation, not a mere province of England." Such a stand might have obtained for Ireland a full measure of autonomy similar to Canada's rather than what it had: "a shackled Home Rule act 'on the Statute Book' but not to be put into operation till the end of the war, and then not until it has been mutilated." Instead, Redmond had committed Ireland to support England and had called for loyalty to the

Empire. It was a position, according to Skeffington, from which Redmond had attempted to retreat ever since.[11]

As clarification of Redmond's retreat, Skeffington wrote, "Instead of 'It is your duty to man the trenches in France and Flanders,' the keynote of Redmondite oratory now is, 'Ireland has done magnificently in this war, and has already given more than her share of recruits,' " Not only was this a retreat, but it was false, Skeffington maintained, for the total number of recruits did not exceed 60,000 — 25,000 of them from the Unionist fourth of the population — whereas six to seven times more might have joined. "But that is how Mr. Redmond saves his face with his English friends while desperately struggling to retain the confidence of his followers in Ireland."[12]

To prove his case further and also to show how distorted the picture of Ireland's affairs was in the American press, Skeffington gave an example. The preceding Easter the *New York Times* had published an account of a parade of Redmond's Volunteers in Dublin and had summarized a speech purported to have been made by Redmond at that time. According to Skeffington, Redmond had not given that speech because of hostile crowds; instead, he had handed out a written statement to the British press, which was eventually wired to the States. "How many people in America know that, since Mr. Redmond committed himself to the English side of the war he has been unable to address a public meeting in the City of Dublin?" he asked.[13] He was troubled as well by the distortions of the *Gaelic American*, John Devoy's paper and the most important voice of the Irish Americans. "It's inaccurate and biassed [sic], and chiefly of interest as illustrating the Devoy point of view," he said of a report in that paper of a *Cumann na mBan* meeting.[14]

Skeffington's letters to Hanna from the States are vivid proof of his love for her and of the intellectual stimulation that each derived from the other. Their letters to each other were filled with items clipped from newspapers and accounts of meetings and other events. Skeffington found particularly interesting one handbill that Hanna sent, announcing a "Monster Public Meeting," since it was to "protest against the unwarranted and unjust invasion of the rights and liberties of the Irish people" under the Defence of the Realm Act. The leaflet demanded the release of the leaders of the Irish Volunteers "and others now imprisoned without proper trial or charges being preferred against them." A clipping from *Nationality*, sent subsequently, indicated that more than ten thousand attended the meeting, at which Hanna was one of the speakers. A detachment of the Irish Citizen Army, fully armed, had assisted in the demonstration, and a resolution had been passed protesting against deportations, arrests, and imprisonments under the Defence of the Realm Act, demanding the immediate release of those now imprisoned under it and declaring "the people's right to liberty of opinion and free speech." In the same issue, *Nationality* deplored the effect of the war on the "Ireland-for-the-English journalists," as shown by the *Irish Times*' description of the meeting as being of "moderate proportions."[15]

Hanna also sent a copy of the *Irish Volunteer* containing an article, "Thinking Militarily," which Skeffington said he found revolting. "I am increasingly disgusted with the Irish Jingoes and Militarists, who in this country [the United States] are more rantingly pro-German than the Germans, and, as Dr. Gertrude Kelly puts it, seem ready to make the same mistake that was made in blind allegiance to the Stuarts." [16]

According to his good friend J. F. Byrne, even though Skeffington was doing a great deal of writing and his contributions could be seen in many publications both in the United States and abroad, he was deriving very little income from them — not even enough to cover the expenses of his trip. He was being paid by the *New York Times* for his so-called letters, but the rate was only ten dollars for a column. [17] Money had indeed become a great worry, and Skeffington was afraid that it might be affecting Hanna. Midway through his trip, he wrote her, "I'm sorry to hear of your being depressed again, Hanna sweetheart; I thought from your last that you were in good form again. For fear cash may have something to do with it, I am enclosing 20 dollars (about £4), in the hope that it may help you to tide over; . . . though I am doing quite satisfactorily here, there won't be so much of a profit when all expenses are paid; and it's as well not to increase debts." [18]

In addition to her duties on the *Irish Citizen* and her many speaking engagements, Hanna had taken a teaching position at a technical school. This too concerned her husband, for in the same letter, after reporting on his own health ("better than it has been for a long time"), he wrote, "*You* are a much more appropriate cause of anxiety! I hope you're not letting yourself get sweated in that technical place; evidently it takes a lot out of you, and you should at least insist on proper pay, — *not less* than 5/0 an hour." [19]

Hanna was carrying on valiantly with the *Citizen* and writing to Skeffington regularly. Often she sent as many as nine copies of their paper, which he found "specially useful" for distribution. She also enclosed letters from Owen, then six years old. Skeffington, in one of his letters, commented that Owen's writing was "quite good" and said he was enclosing a card for him in case he could "*read* writing; but I suppose he can't yet." He continued, "Putting paper in the butter doesn't sound very bad! It is merely a misdirected zeal for chemical experiment! The punishment I would suggest is to make him eat it!" [20] The method of punishment that he preferred in dealing with Owen was to ignore him. In one letter to Hanna he wrote, "No card to Owen this time — because of reports of his bad behaviour, tell him." And in another, "I'm sending Owen a card, I had it written before I heard of his misbehaviour!" In the same letter he says once more that he wishes Hanna would not send Owen to bed to punish him, for he considered it "a most objectionable and degrading form of punishment." [21]

It seems surprising that Hanna, capable and well educated, needed constant reassurance — but she did and Skeffington did not hesitate to provide it. "The paper continues to be very good," he wrote. "You are getting into writing editorials excellently, as I knew you would when you had to!" He added, "I love you, sweetheart, and I wish you were not so rushed! Try to take things a little less strenuously, and in particular to get the I.C. [*Irish Citizen*] into a routine; you need not think you're not doing well, because you are! So don't let it worry you; it can stand a lot of neglect yet! . . . After I get back, would you rather continue to do the writing *or* the editing? You can take your choice!" [22]

Skeffington was feeling extremely well physically, as he continually mentioned in letters to Hanna. The October weather in New York City was very much to his taste. Walking had always been one of his great pleasures and he assured Hanna that he was finding time for it; one walk in Central Park included a visit to the zoo, during which, he said, he "spent some time watching the snakes and beating down my aversion to them! not without success." [23] He was also enjoying a hectic social schedule. There were dinners and teas with friends of the Pethick-Lawrences; with former Dublin friends like Francis Hackett, "my old Kilkenny acquaintance," now on the *New Republic* staff; with the short-story writer Donn Byrne, "who was known as Bernard O'Byrne when he was in the Y.I.B. [Young Ireland Branch]"; and with Padraic and Mary Colum. When he heard that James Larkin was in the States, Skeffington tracked him down and spent an afternoon with him. He found him "in excellent form" and "having a most adventurous time," he told Hanna. He says that he is still a suffragist, in spite of the suffragists!" [24]

But business engagements were not neglected. J. F. Byrne had introduced Skeffington to a great many representatives of the press: John Devoy of the *Gaelic American*, Robert Ford of the *Irish World*, and many members of the *New York Times* editorial board. He was Irish correspondent for the *Call* and, as he wrote Hanna later, he was seeing the members of that staff regularly.

Skeffington carefully numbered all his letters to Hanna, dated them when written and also when posted, and listed all enclosures. He kept a carbon of every letter, for he was worried that the mail might not get through to her. Often his letters were sent on munition-carrying ships, which, he said, "I'm sure will be torpedoed some time or other." Censorship was also a problem. A late October letter to Hanna concludes, "Goodbye now, dearie. I'm afraid my letters are doubly scrappy — both of news and of sentiments — but the censor accounts for both. I think your last letter — the one I got this morning — had been opened. Much good may it do them!" In the twenty-fourth letter he reprimanded her, sounding a great deal like his father: "I gather, from your letter of Oct. 5th (here this morning as I mentioned in last) that you have got *both* my 15th and 16th letters; but you don't say so expressly, and I can only reach my conclusion by a process of deduction, as you only mention receipt of one letter since you last wrote. I wish you'd acknowledge everything specifically, as I do." The similarity to J. B. can be seen even more clearly in an excerpt from another letter: "I disapprove of sending Owen to bed; it's in many ways a more objectionable punishment than beating; but as you are clearly unable to manage him, you must just do the best you can till I take a hand again."

Although Skeffington never did develop any great affection for New York as a city (he said later that he much preferred Boston), the rapid pace of life there suited his temperament admirably. On one day, which seems not to have been untypical, he wrote letters and paid calls in the morning, met with Mrs. Eastman Benedict, the sister of Max Eastman (then editor of the *Masses*) in the afternoon, and went on to a *Cumann na mBan* reception in the evening, where the discussion continued until well after midnight. He told Hanna that he had found Mrs. Eastman, the mainspring of the Women's Peace Party in New York, a "congenial spirit" and that he had succeeded in interesting her in the cause of Ireland.[25] She was, incidentally, at the evening reception where Skeffington made "three or four speeches." Possibly as a result, she had accused him of "being an opportunist and of playing for popular applause!" As he told Hanna, for him it was "quite a new sensation to get *that* kind of criticism!"[26]

On another day, just before the November elections, Skeffington had morning appointments with the manager of a press syndicate, the editor of a paper, and the owner of a publishing firm. He also called in at the *Irish World* and the *Call*, he told Hanna, but he did not count those since "they happen so often." He had then spent a restful afternoon with the Colums and went on to speak at an open-air meeting near his lodgings that night. "I gave them a rousing, rhetorical, eve-of-the-poll sort of speech," he wrote, "and got them all right." The main speaker was a woman from the state of Washington, where women had the vote, and Skeffington thought she gave an "excellently logical and carefully documented" account of what the vote meant to the women and what they had done with it. But he thought her speech completely unsuited to an outdoor rally: she "chilled" the audience. He voiced once more to Hanna his objection to the "big" women's association in the States — the National American Woman Suffrage Association. "These women work very hard and organize with great efficiency," he wrote, but he felt their approach was not "militantly pacifist," enough, to use Mrs. Eastman Benedict's expression. He added, "The few members of the Women's Political Union that I have met seem to have more giz and gumption." Finally, after what he described as a "fairly full day," Skeffington went back to his lodgings and to bed.[27]

Skeffington's first impression had been that *all* the U.S. newspapers were fiercely anti-German, but he found this not to be true of the Hearst chain. To his great surprise, William Randolph Hearst was fighting for peace, and many who had previously denounced him for his "yellow journalism" were now, uncomfortably, on his side. The astonishing thing — from the suffragists' point of view — was that Hearst's newspapers, and Hearst personally, were taking the same stand on the League of Neutral Nations and on a proposed boycott for peace as the Women's Peace Party and the Women's International Congress at The Hague.[28]

Skeffington summarized the Neutral Nations plan in this way for the *Irish Citizen*: Neutral nations were to form a permanent representative conference, whose purpose would be to urge continuous mediation upon the belligerents "until such time as they are compelled by increasing exhaustion or returning sanity to give heed to the voice of reason." The result of this would be the establishment of a body that, at the proper time, could be responsible for the recovery and maintenance of peace. The boycott that the peace groups had called for would isolate all belligerents: no nation was to trade with them or communicate with them. This idea, Skeffington wrote, was particularly popular in Irish pacifist circles.[29]

The boycott idea was also extremely popular with William Randolph Hearst. "Boycott Europe," he urged. "Let no supplies of any kind, whether it be of munitions or of food, or of the money to pay for food and munitions, be sent from neutral America to the warring countries." Here he parted company with President Wilson, who felt that in any future wars the United States would have to import munitions and, consequently, that to impose an embargo at this period would be impractical. Regardless of Wilson's views, as Skeffington pointed out in the *Irish Citizen*, the idea of the embargo was being sold to the American public quite successfully by the Hearst chain, "with all the resources of headline and big type that the American newspapers, and the Hearst papers in particular, know so well how to use."[30]

He was perfectly satisfied, too, with the stand taken by the Hearst papers on suffrage. Of course, as he had said earlier, most of the U.S. newspapers were mildly in favor of women's suffrage. The Hearst chain, however, was vehement on the subject — both in editorials and in cartoons. It was as though, he explained for his Irish audience, the Northcliffe newspaper chain, the great British newspaper combine, had suddenly decided to push votes for women "with the same relentless vigour as it pushes Standard Bread, Sweet Peas or Conscription." He believed firmly that if the suffrage amendment carried in New York state, "no small share of credit for that success must be accorded to the written and pictorial appeals of the *New York American* [a Hearst paper] to the common-sense elements of the case."[31]

Skeffington was correct, though, in his prediction of defeat for the 1915 vote on suffrage. President Wilson had announced that he would vote for the Woman Suffrage Amendment in New Jersey as a private citizen, though not as president or head of the Democratic Party. Most of his Cabinet followed his lead. As events proved, these endorsements did no good. The amendment was defeated in New York, Massachusetts, and Pennsylvania. In Pennsylvania the amendment had carried the rural districts, which were heavily Quaker, but in Philadelphia the vote against it had been overwhelming. Skeffington attributed the vast difference between rural vote and city vote to the party machine and the liquor interests, both strong in large cities. On election night he and J. F. Byrne went into New York City to watch the election returns. He wrote Hanna later that there had been "weird forms of amusement, horn-blowing, bell-ringing, confetti-throwing, etc.," and that "these people are amazingly childish and frivolous."[32]

The suffragists in New York state recovered rapidly from their defeat and, two days after the election, held a rally in Cooper Union — a hall that held two thousand people — to a capacity audience. Approximately $100,000 was raised that night for a new campaign. Skeffington was stunned by the number of shouted pledges. Because there were so many, all the speeches had to be cut — except for Carrie Chapman Catt's, which she gave before the collection. 'I have never before seen an audience refusing to listen to speakers in its eagerness to continue giving money!" Skeffington wrote.[33]

The defeat of the suffrage amendment, Skeffington believed, would lead the suffragists to use different methods and become more politically aware. Judging by Carrie Chapman Catt's words, the new tactics would be less conciliatory toward the politicians, for she had declared flatly that the political machines and those who controlled them had betrayed the women; their declared neutrality had been a myth. New York's Tammany Hall organization was one of the political machines under grave suspicion of having violated its neutrality. As Skeffington wrote in the *Irish Citizen*, Tom Foley, one of the leaders of that "great Democratic machine run largely by the Irish," had admitted that he had thrown his influence against the women "to save the poor devils from themselves." It was that kind of contemptuous phrase, Skeffington was convinced, that was already causing leaders such as Mrs. Stanton Blatch, the head of the Women's Political Union, to declare that she, at least, was going to make no more street-corner speeches but was going to try other methods.[34]

Conversations with some of the Irish-Americans and attendance at numerous rallies was causing Skeffington to speculate on the role of the Irish-Americans in politics as well as in the suffrage movement. He was amused that some of those he talked with were saying that Joseph Devlin had learned his methods of organization from people like Tom Foley. Devlin had, they said, greatly admired the Tammany Hall tactics when he was in the States. Whether the imitation was deliberate, or merely the outcome of similar thinking, Skeffington was not sure. He might also have thought that there was a distinct possibility that it was the other way around: Foley might have learned from Devlin and other politicians in Ireland. At any rate, he took comfort from the fact that many Irish-Americans were playing a significant role in the suffrage movement. The chairman of one suffrage meeting he attended was Leonora O'Reilly, secretary of the Women's Trade Union League of America, who was second-generation Irish. The main speaker was Frank P. Walsh, chairman of the Federal Industrial Commission, who was also second-generation Irish. And in a recent issue of the *New Republic*, Francis Hackett of Kilkenny presented the whole case for women's suffrage succinctly. To these could be added such lights as Edmond McKenna of the staff of the *Masses* and K. D. Blake, head of the Women

Teachers' Organization for Suffrage. On the whole, it seemed that the Irish-Americans were playing a creditable role in the struggle for women's freedom.[35]

Skeffington was well aware of the difficulties he would face upon his return to Ireland. His father was urging him to stay on in the United States, as were others, but, he told Byrne, he was determined to go back to "face the music."[36] He was sure that his moves were being checked, his speeches and writings monitored, his mail scrutinized more closely than it would ordinarily have been. As he wrote Hanna, "I don't announce my plans, only achievements — for obvious reasons."[37] This did not deter him from speaking his mind, however; it merely ensured that his words were carefully directed. Thus, when he addressed a letter to President Wilson in early November, he was careful to see that copies of it were circulated widely. A compelling plea for consideration of Ireland's national position, it began:

«   «   «   «   «   «   «   «   «

> Your historic speech yesterday, addressed though it was primarily to Americans, contained passages which thrilled the stranger within the gates. You reasserted, with your accustomed insight and mastery, the fundamental principles of liberty and democracy. You said: — "We believe in political liberty . . . the liberty of men and of peoples — of men to choose their own lives and of peoples to choose their own allegiances." . . . Nor is this American belief to be barren of action, for you also said: — "Our ambition . . . is not only to be free and prosperous ourselves, but also to be the friend and thoughtful partisan of those who are free or who desire freedom the world over."[38]

»   »   »   »   »   »   »   »   »

Skeffington continued in general terms, pointing out that various peace organizations had already done much to "throw open to oppressed nations a way to freedom other than the bloodstained path of war." He saw no reason why Ireland, "as a historically distinct nation," should not be entitled just as much as Belgium to recognition at any peace conference. He did not ask the United States to issue a declaration for Irish independence nor, even less, to go to war for it. But, he asked, if Ireland demanded a plebiscite, "under international and impartial auspices," to determine whether or not the Irish people wanted independence, would the United States support that demand? Would it be too much to ask of the United States to "insist that England, the self-vaunted protector of small nationalities," abide by the result of such a plebiscite? His letter emphasized that if Ireland continued to be regarded as merely "a province of England, simply because depopulation, impoverishment, and disarmament have so far prevented Irishmen from expressing their real feelings in insurrection," Irish nationalists would come to the conclusion that only force could win them freedom, "and will continue their already well-advanced preparations to fight at the first opportunity." (This last statement would seem to indicate rather conclusively that Skeffington knew of the preparations being made by James Connolly for what would be the Easter Rising of 1916.) On the other hand, if at the end of the war Ireland could take its place as a free nation allied with other free nations and with the United States at its head, it could begin the task of building up once more its "long-destroyed civilization in the 'kindly and wholesome atmosphere of peace.' " He concluded, "I am in this country in an interval between two imprisonments for the crime of asserting Ireland's national position. If I can but succeed in awaking your interest in that position, I shall return to re-arrest in Ireland with perfect contentment." [39]

At first it seemed that the letter was going to receive very little attention in the United States. The *Call* printed it, the *Sun* published part of it — that was all. Finally, however, the *Tribune* took note of the letter and Skeffington wrote to Hanna that, in spite of the press boycott of it, it "has stung our friends the enemy more than anything else." An interesting sign that he was giving the enemy trouble had occurred a few days earlier, he said, when he was approached by a man who claimed to be in the confidence of the British Secret Service. Being careful to say that he was simply making a personal suggestion and not acting on any authority, he made a proposition "to the effect that, if I abstained from any further anti-British propaganda while here, there would be 'no trouble' on the other side; otherwise, I would not be allowed to land upon my return!" Skeffington had been happy to refuse, saying that he was not open to any deals. [40]

Skeffington may have been courageous, but he was not foolhardy. He was not reluctant, therefore, to suggest to Hanna that her father, since he was an M.P., intercede for him with the Crown authorities in Dublin. David Sheehy did turn to Sir Matthew Nathan, the Under Secretary who was in charge while Chief Secretary Augustine Birrell was out of the country. Nathan, however, informed Sheehy that Birrell believed that Skeffington's speeches in the United States had "aggravated the original offence." [41] As a consequence, they could give no assurances as to what action would be taken if Skeffington insisted on returning to Ireland during the war.

J. B. continued to urge his son to stay in the United States, although he was sure his appeals would be fruitless. As he wrote to Hanna, he had suggested to Skeffington that he go to the southern states for the winter — "but doubtless he will take his own way." He thought Skeffington's letter to President Wilson a good one but could see, quite correctly, that it would add to the score against him with the Dublin Castle people. "He can do nothing here neither speak nor write, etc., while there he is free and can do a lot — as papers do publish him, etc. . . . and as he can earn nothing here I don't see why he should return till the war is over or things clear up," he told Hanna. He had received cuttings from Skeffington and announcements of lectures but "nothing about the success or result in a pecuniary way — if he's paid for all he writes he should do well enough but I am doubtful of that." [42]

J. B.'s evaluation of Skeffington's opportunities in the United States was correct. So was his opinion that his son would "take his own way." In Skeffington's thirtieth letter to Hanna, he told her that Robert Ford of the *Irish World* had offered him a good job at thirty dollars a week (about six pounds at that time) to start. "Not having any!", he told her. [43]

Skeffington was due to leave for Massachusetts on a lecture tour in mid-November, but his days in New York City remained full. He saw, he wrote Hanna, the movie *Twilight Sleep*, [44] which "they show here at special times to men only, at other times to women only! The way that audience of men took those pictures made me thoroughly ashamed of my sex; I am getting more and more disgusted with men!" An afternoon and an evening were devoted to the Women's Peace Party. He met Norman Angell, the famed British economist, internationalist, and pacifist, who would in 1933 be awarded the Nobel Peace Prize, and was not impressed. "A very dry and uninspiring person; well-meaning but unimaginative; a sort of English [Arthur] Griffith, effective in a quiet way. But he had to be hauled up on Ireland," he wrote Hanna. That same evening he attended a large meeting in Cooper Union at which a "ranting anti-German tirade" was delivered by a socialist speaker. In the discussion that followed, Skeffington said he "had to slay him, and did it to the great delight of the audience, which, being working-class, was genuinely neutral. Few of the Socialists are as bad as that. But the Women's Peace Party is not much good in New York." It was, he found, decidedly pro-English; "well-meaning people, most of them, but ignorant." [45]

Lunch with the liberal pacifist Oswald Garrison Villard, then owner and editor of the *New York Evening Post*, he found most informative, for Villard was a close friend of President Wilson. He volunteered the information that he had just broken with Wilson politically over his new militaristic program, which Villard believed would inevitably lead to war with Japan. Skeffington also met Mrs. O. H. P. Belmont, "a good militant but, as befits the mother of the Duchess of Marlborough, very anti-German and therefore Pankhurstian." She had, however, suggested to Emmeline Pankhurst that she cancel plans for a U.S. tour. "American Suffragists have too much of their own business to mind! and as I gather — though Mrs. B. of course did not say so, — are rather tired of Mrs. P." [46]

Skeffington continued to worry about the burden Hanna was bearing and did his best to help her with the *Irish Citizen*. He commented on the ads, the finances, and methods of building circulation and, as often as possible, sent material in addition to his weekly report. In his twenty-fifth letter home, he suggested that it might be wise to reprint some of the material previously published on the horrors of forcible feeding, "in view of the hypocritical outcry about the shooting of Miss Cavell." Edith Cavell, an English nurse who was head of the Berkendael Institute in Brussels, had been executed by the Germans in October on a charge of harboring and aiding allied prisoners and helping 130 of them cross the Dutch frontier. G. B. Shaw had written on the matter in the *New Statesman* and Skeffington sent the item to Hanna for possible use in the *Irish Citizen*, commenting, "I see Shaw has said the right thing about Edith Cavell." Shaw's article was a cogent plea for women's suffrage; Hanna used it in the editorial comment section under the heading "Thanks, 'G. B. S.'!" Shaw wrote:

«   «   «   «   «   «   «   «   «

Finally, concerning Miss Cavell. As what she did and suffered was done for us, it is right and natural that she should be a heroine to us; and it would be disgraceful for us to dishonour her memory by cinemato- graphic claptrap, or merely break her coffin into sticks to beat the Germans with. There is a way in which we can pay our debt to her, and test the sincerity of her loudest champions. We cannot complain of the denial to her by military law of all the safeguards of human justice, because we have shot ten people ourselves without any of those safe- guards under the same law. We cannot plead her sex, because our own criminal law, civil and military, makes no distinction between men and women; and no woman asks that it should, any more than Edith Cavell did. We cannot vapour about chivalry, because if she had come back alive to demand the political rights granted to the meanest of men, and had broken a shop window to compel attention to her claim, she would have been mobbed, insulted, and subjected to gross physical violence with the full approval of many of the writers who are now canonising her. What we can do is very simple. We can enfranchise her sex in recognition of her proof of its valour. . . . If this proposal is received in dead silence, I shall know that Edith Cavell's sacrifice has been rejected by her country.[47]

»   »   »   »   »   »   »   »   »

In November Skeffington took the train to Worcester, Massachusetts, for his first speaking engagement outside the New York City area. The countryside he traveled through impressed him — Connecticut's "broad and stately river," and the "abundant woods and moors" of Massachusetts. He found that he enjoyed American trains and travel seemed not at all expensive considering the vast distances covered.[48]

His speech before the Emmet Association in Worcester — a *Clan na Gael* group (Irish nationalists affiliated with Irish Republican Brotherhood) — was received with great enthusiasm. At its conclusion, a collection was taken up for the Irish Volunteers and a copy of Skeffington's "Speech from the Dock" (see the Appendix) was auctioned off. "It fetched 12 dollars!" he reported to Hanna. He was treated royally by the local committee — put up in a "first-class hotel," given a tour of the city and the surrounding country- side, which he found very beautiful, and interviewed by the local press. He sent Hanna clippings from the Worcester *Sunday Telegram* and the *Daily Telegram*, reporting the meeting. The Worcester newspaper accounts, which Skeffington said were done in "the usual American slapdash style," made amusing reading. Skeffington was described as "former" editor of the *Irish Citizen*, a paper that had been "suppressed by the English government." As for his appearance, one account read: "Mr. Skeffington was an interesting figure in Worcester, unaccustomed as it is to the attire worn by many of the parliamentarian and professional men of Dublin, tweeds and knickerbockers or shorts as they are known in the old country."[49]

Skeffington's next stop, after fulfilling a speaking engagement in North Attleboro, Mass., a small city not too far from Worcester, was Boston, though he had no speaking engagements there. He thought it a charming city, more European than American. Although he realized that its culture was "intensely English in tone," Boston was a relief after New York. "New York is a chaos, but Boston is really a city," he wrote Hanna. He liked Cambridge, too, and the atmosphere surrounding Harvard University. "The students dominate the landscape — with their books slung over their shoulders in big loose green bags, with a string mouth; like a sort of return to the medieval hood!"[50]

Both the *Boston Globe* and the *Boston Traveler* interviewed Skeffington. The *Traveler* carried a lengthy story in mid-November. "We don't care who licks England," he had told their reporter. He was "seeing America," he said, and having a respite under the Cat and Mouse Act. Referring to a recent incident in which English officials had prevented Irishmen from leaving Ireland for the United States, he said:

«   «   «   «   «   «   «   «   «

It is conscription — the meanest kind of conscription. Most of those who wished to sail for America were men from the west of Ireland who had been forced to leave because of economic conditions. They were men who earned their living by going to Scotland and England each year for the harvest. This year they could not go because of registration, so they were forced to look toward America to get a living.

»   »   »   »   »   »   »   »   »

Pointing out that, during the preceding seventy years, England had allowed Ireland's population to dwindle from 8 million to 4.5 million, he said, "The best men left Ireland, and England was glad because she thought it was a way out of her difficulties." Now they were needed to fight England's battles. There could be only one result of Britain's action, he said: "Those Irishmen must starve or enlist in the British army." Once more Skeffington felt it necessary to make the so-called pro-German stand clear.

«   «   «   «   «   «   «   «   «

The majority of the people in Ireland do not want to fight for England because they know that England is still their enemy despite all the promises of home rule, etc. Whenever England has triumphed Ireland has suffered and vice versa. That's the only sense in which we are pro-German. . . . I think the war will result in a deadlock with Germany triumphant on land and England on sea. It is my opinion that they will have to sit around a table and settle it as they could have done in the beginning. War never settles anything.

» » » » » » » » »

Speaking of George Bernard Shaw, Skeffington said, "I hear that there is a boycott in London against Shaw because of his recent utterances, which have irritated the English. I saw a weekly paper, *New Days*, published in London . . . which stated in its columns that it had refused advertisements of Shaw's books. For my part I wish he were boycotted in London and driven back to Dublin. I wish Shaw would live there. He's perhaps the most distinguished living Irishman."[51]

Skeffington sent clippings from the Boston papers home, saying that these accounts were "fairly accurate." His two evenings in Boston were devoted to the theater, where he saw a "characteristic American farce, and an equally characteristic American 'revue' — both would, I fear, come under the ban of the Dublin Vigilance Committee." He spent his first day in Boston phoning people for appointments. He found the telephone invaluable and wrote Hanna that he thought he would have to get one at once upon his return, for "I'll never be able to dispense with it after my constant use of it here."

From Boston, Skeffington returned to New York City and began arrangements for the remainder of his tour. He also booked passage on the *St. Louis*, sailing 11 December and due to arrive at Liverpool on 19 December. Hanna had suggested that a reception-meeting might be held on his return and he told her to go ahead with scheduling. The possibility of arrest was, however, in his mind, and he added: "I am prepared for all contingencies, and I want my arrival to be made public in advance as much as possible."[52]

Skeffington had anticipated that his last three weeks in the United States would be crowded and he was not disappointed. He attended a Cooper Union meeting of the Women's Peace Party at which Max Eastman had spoken on "What Shall We Do with Patriotism," and afterward had "joined with the Eastman crowd, who are very interesting, for supper." He went to Philadelphia where he spoke at several meetings successfully, and where he was taken in charge by "McGarrity, one of the most remarkable personalities I have met in America. He is the wholesale liquor dealer who got the Abbey Players arrested when in Philadelphia, and whom Shaw flayed at the time!"[53] (This incident occurred early in 1912 when the Players were performing *Playboy of the Western World*. In fact, Lady Gregory had forestalled their actual arrest by issuing bail bonds, but technically they were under arrest on a charge of indecency.)

In Philadelphia he also saw Michael J. Ryan, president of the United Irish League of America, "now strongly pro-German though not working in harmony with the Gaelic American crowd." He found Philadelphia more attractive than New York — "that would be easy!" — but not as attractive as Boston. "Colum calls Boston 'a prosperous Dublin,' and that is about right." Just before leaving Philadelphia, he wrote Hanna that he was "in the full American rush now." Every minute would be occupied until he sailed. He assured her that he was "not a bit frightened about what steps the government might take on his return. "Don't be anxious — everything will be all right whatever happens," he added. [54]

Skeffington was beginning to feel pressed for time. He was booked for Chicago on 2 December, St. Louis — his farthest point both west and south — on 5 December, and then he would have just a few days in New York before sailing home. In late November, the possibility of sailing on Ford's peace ship arose once more. It would mean revising his entire schedule but he was prepared to do anything necessary, including sacrificing his trip to the Midwest, for the opportunity of joining the peace party. But a few days later he knew there was no chance that he would be allowed to go. He wrote Hanna, "The trip is managed jointly by Ford (Irish-American millionaire, automobile manufacturer, and philanthropist) and the Women's Peace Party; and a rule has been made that no *man* is to be included who is not an American citizen. . . . I am sorry to have missed this, as it would have suited me in many ways, and been of public value." [55]

It was characteristic of Skeffington that he never wasted time brooding over the inevitable. Once he had expressed his disappointment to Hanna, he went on to say "there are compensations in getting to the Middle West." He urged her to give space to the peace ship venture in the *Irish Citizen*. [56]

An editorial on Henry Ford and the peace ship was carried in the *Irish Citizen*, but much later. Written very much in Skeffington's style, Ford's virtues were extolled and he was contrasted with his "close friend, Thomas Edison." According to the editorial, Ford had, "throughout his career, displayed a social vision and a sense of community that Edison never showed. Perhaps the difference is due to race; for Henry Ford's father was born in Cork, and we may pardonably take pride in him as imbued with something of the Irish spirit." Ford was praised for his generosity toward his employees and his progressive wage policy (a five-dollar minimum for an eight-hour day). And now he was turning his attention to the cause of peace, heading a peace movement in the form of a peace ship. The editorial concluded:

«   «   «   «   «   «   «   «   «

It must be said, in justice both to Mr. Ford and the Women's Peace Movement, that the idea of the Peace Ship did not originate with Mr. Ford, but with the women pacifists. . . . We of the *Irish Citizen* will follow its fortunes with a special interest, for a double reason; because it is a product of the Women's Peace Movement originating in the brain of a suffrage leader, and because the means to carry it out came from the insight and sympathetic imagination of one whom we are proud to claim as a product of the Irish race. [57]

»   »   »   »   »   »   »   »   »

Skeffington did not live to learn that, after the United States entered the war in 1917, Henry Ford was a leading producer of ambulances, airplanes, munitions, tanks, and submarine chasers, or to read the anti-Semitic articles published in Ford's *Dearborn Independent*, which were so virulent that he was forced to apologize publicly.

On 1 December, Skeffington boarded the train to Chicago. It was a twenty-hour trip and he planned to relax and enjoy the luxuries. On board there were a library, a drawing room, a club car with writing desks, and even the free services of a stenographer and a manicurist. As the train neared Chicago, he wrote Hanna a description of the countryside: "a great plain, growing Indian corn, and with dotted towns all wearing the unfinished and juvenile air that is characteristic of American civilisation." In the night, he told her, he had awakened to look out on a snow-clad landscape which, under the moon, was "beautiful and brilliant." [58]

One of the people Skeffington wanted very much to meet with in Chicago was Jane Addams, president of the Women's Peace Party. He wanted particularly, he wrote her, to put before her the reasons why the Irish Section of the Women's International Peace Congress wanted separate representation for Ireland, as a nation, at all future congresses and on all committees of the congress, especially the permanent Executive Committee. The claims of the Irish delegates had not received an adequate hearing at the past congress, he said, because the English government had not permitted the Irish delegates — of whom his wife was one — to attend. He continued:

«   «   «   «   «   «   «   «   «

It is essential, both in principle and as a practical issue, that Ireland should be accorded separate representation, and not be treated as a province of England. As a matter of principle, to refuse it would be to stultify the Congress programme in one of its most important sections. In practice, denial of separate Irish representation would destroy all hope of successful peace propaganda in Ireland. At present, those who advocate an Irish rising and hope for a German landing in Ireland have the logic of facts on their side; for *that* would *compel* the Powers to recognise Ireland as a separate nation. Every denial of separate recognition to Ireland, just because Irishmen have not sprung to arms, is putting a premium on armed insurrection, and giving Irish Nationalists a reason for desiring the prolongation of the war until England is well beaten. If, on the other hand, the Women's Peace Movement recognises Ireland's national rights, — just as much as those of Belgium or Poland or Serbia, — and promises to open a peaceful road towards their attainment, then the Peace Movement will go ahead in Ireland. [59]

»   »   »   »   »   »   »   »   »

In Chicago, however, Skeffington found that Jane Addams was in the hospital. Not only would she be unable to see him, but she also had missed the opportunity to travel on the Ford peace ship.

Skeffington's first Chicago meeting was well attended and his speech was well received. He liked the city much better than New York. As a matter of fact, he felt that if he were staying longer in the United States he would make it his headquarters. "The Irish here seem a very good type, less tied up with the liquor trade and more progressive in their ideas than in the East," he wrote Hanna. "My chairman of last night had not only read my *Davitt* but made Christmas presents of it to his friends!" [60] Although there was no doubt in Skeffington's mind as to his own ability, he was not egotistical — he knew his capabilities as he knew his limitations. But he seemed always to be astonished, as well as pleased, when he won recognition.

Winter had set in at last and Skeffington, like most people, was bothered by the bitter wind off Lake Michigan — "that great inland sea which you couldn't distinguish from the ocean but for the absence of tides, sand, and salt. It's as wide as the Irish sea," he wrote. Padraic Colum had given Skeffington introductions to many of his Chicago friends, so he was being entertained for tea, lunch, and dinner by Irish-Americans among others. He enjoyed them all. One woman had been in Ireland in 1912 — in fact, in court at Hanna's trial. He met "Theosophists and Christian Scientists who revere AE and admire Cousins. I have formed important links in Chicago and am very glad I did not miss it." With one of James Larkin's friends, he saw Shaw's *Androcles and the Lion*, which he found "exceedingly funny." He did, however, feel that the American audience lost many of the allusions to suffrage. To Skeffington, the Chicago suffragists seemed much more "free-minded" than those on the east coast; as a matter of fact a Political Equality League meeting he attended reminded him very much of an I.W.F.L. meeting. James Larkin, who had set up permanent headquarters in Chicago, had been invited to speak but had declined. However, the fact that the fiery Jim had been invited at all, Skeffington felt, spoke well for this group, "for the New York suffragists would be afraid of their lives to touch Larkin!" [61]

En route to New York, Skeffington wrote Hanna, "I am very glad to have had this trip west, to see the Great Lakes and the Mississippi, and to have spoken in the four biggest cities in the States — New York, Chicago, Philadelphia, and St. Louis." This was to be his last letter from the States. [62] Once more he assured his wife that he was not worried about what might happen when he landed in Liverpool. From the USMS *St. Louis*, he sent a brief note, "just as a precaution. If it reaches you *before* you hear from me otherwise, you will know something has happened — though of course I'll do my best to let you know exactly *what*." He repeated that he was ready for "any contingency." [63] And the fates smiled.

NOTES TO CHAPTER 12

1. *Boston Traveler*, 18 November 1915.
2. F. Sheehy-Skeffington, "Woman's Sphere and Man's Chivalry," *Irish Citizen*, 4 September 1915.
3. F. Sheehy-Skeffington, "Suffrage in America," *Irish Citizen*, 11 September 1915.
4. *Irish Citizen*, 4 September 1915.
5. F. Sheehy-Skeffington, "Suffrage in the Air," *Irish Citizen*, 28 August 1915.
6. F. Sheehy-Skeffington to H. Sheehy-Skeffington, 23 October 1915.
7. *Irish Citizen*, 11 September 1915.
8. Ibid.
9. Ibid., 18 September 1915.
10. F. Sheehy-Skeffington to H. Sheehy-Skeffington, 23 October 1915.
11. *New York Times*, 5 October 1915.
12. Ibid.
13. Ibid.
14. F. Sheehy-Skeffington to H. Sheehy-Skeffington, 23 October 1915.
15. *Nationality*, 18 September 1915, p. 96.
16. F. Sheehy-Skeffington to H. Sheehy-Skeffington, 23 October 1915.
17. Byrne, *Silent Years*, p. 98.
18. F. Sheehy-Skeffington to H. Sheehy-Skeffington, 23 October 1915.
19. F. Sheehy-Skeffington to H. Sheehy-Skeffington, 15 October 1915.
20. F. Sheehy-Skeffington to H. Sheehy-Skeffington, 15 October 1915.
21. F. Sheehy-Skeffington to H. Sheehy-Skeffington, 26 October 1915.
22. F. Sheehy-Skeffington to H. Sheehy-Skeffington, 16 October 1915.
23. F. Sheehy-Skeffington to H. Sheehy-Skeffington, 15 October 1915.
24. F. Sheehy-Skeffington to H. Sheehy-Skeffington, 29 October 1915.
25. F. Sheehy-Skeffington to H. Sheehy-Skeffington, 16 October 1915.
26. F. Sheehy-Skeffington to H. Sheehy-Skeffington, 16 October 1915.
27. F. Sheehy-Skeffington to H. Sheehy-Skeffington, 30 October 1915.
28. F. Sheehy-Skeffington, "The Hearst Newspapers and The Women's Movement," *Irish Citizen*, 9 October 1915.
29. Ibid.
30. Ibid.
31. Ibid.
32. F. Sheehy-Skeffington to H. Sheehy-Skeffington, 30 October 1915.
33. *Irish Citizen*, 20 November 1915.
34. Ibid.
35. Ibid., 27 November 1915.
36. Byrne, *Silent Years*, p. 99.
37. F. Sheehy-Skeffington to H. Sheehy-Skeffington, 8 November 1915.
38. F. Sheehy-Skeffington's letter to President Wilson did appear in the *Workers' Republic*, 20 November 1915.
39. Ibid.
40. F. Sheehy-Skeffington to H. Sheehy-Skeffington, 12 November 1915.
41. Under Secretary Matthew Nathan to David Sheehy, 14 November 1915.

42. J. B. Skeffington to H. Sheehy-Skeffington, 26 November 1915.

43. F. Sheehy-Skeffington to H. Sheehy-Skeffington, 8 November 1915.

44. The movie, *Twilight Sleep*, must have been a discussion of a drug of that name which was administered to women in labor. It is not difficult to guess what the all-male audience's reaction, which distressed Sheehy-Skeffington, would have been.

45. F. Sheehy-Skeffington to H. Sheehy-Skeffington, 12 November 1915.

46. Ibid.

47. *Irish Citizen,* 13 November 1915.

48. F. Sheehy-Skeffington to H. Sheehy-Skeffington, 15 November 1915.

49. *Worcester Daily Telegram,* 16 November 1915 and, *Worcester Sunday Telegram,* 14 November and 21 November 1915.

50. F. Sheehy-Skeffington to H. Sheehy-Skeffington, 19 November 1915.

51. *Boston Traveler,* 18 November 1915.

52. F. Sheehy-Skeffington to H. Sheehy-Skeffington, 21 November 1915.

53. F. Sheehy-Skeffington to H. Sheehy-Skeffington, 25 November 1915.

54. F. Sheehy-Skeffington to H. Sheehy-Skeffington, 25 November 1915.

55. F. Sheehy-Skeffington to H. Sheehy-Skeffington, 30 November 1915.

56. F. Sheehy-Skeffington to H. Sheehy-Skeffington, 30 November 1915.

57. *Irish Citizen,* 25 December 1915.

58. F. Sheehy-Skeffington to H. Sheehy-Skeffington, 1 December 1915.

59. F. Sheehy-Skeffington to Jane Addams, President, Women's Peace Party, 7 October 1915.

60. F. Sheehy-Skeffington to H. Sheehy-Skeffington, 3 December 1915.

61. F. Sheehy-Skeffington to H. Sheehy-Skeffington, 6 December 1915.

62. F. Sheehy-Skeffington to H. Sheehy-Skeffington, 6 December 1915.

63. F. Sheehy-Skeffington to H. Sheehy-Skeffington, 16 December 1915.

Our readers will be glad to learn that Mr. Sheehy Skeffington
has arrived safely in Dublin. He was taken to the Bridewell in
Liverpool and his effects searched. After four hours' detention
he was released, but all his correspondence was retained for
examination. He is in first class form, and got a warm
welcome from all who saw him when he called at Liberty Hall.
— Workers' Republic, 25 December 1915

13

Steps Toward Martyrdom

Skeffington had arrived in Liverpool on 18 December. When, finally, in February, his baggage was forwarded to him from there, he discovered that many of his books and papers had been confiscated. Immediately he wrote to the Secretary of State for War, listing those items that had not been returned. Copies of five New York weeklies — the *Irish World, Gaelic American, Fatherland, Vital Issue,* and *Issues and Events* — had been held. All these papers had, Skeffington wrote, been circulated in Ireland and freely quoted by loyalist newspapers in that country. The authorities had also failed to return a number of copies of German dailies published in New York — *Staats Zeitung,* the *German Herald,* and *Deutsche Volkszeitung.* Since these were both for and against the German government's view of the war, Skeffington had come to the conclusion that "no logical method was followed in the seizure."[1]

As for books and pamphlets, they had not returned *The German American Plot* by F. W. Wile, nor several copies of Skeffington's pamphlet "War and Feminism." The former had been published in England and was strongly anti-German in tone. Of his pamphlet, Skeffington said, "I have no desire to prevent the military authorities from keeping and studying the pamphlet, but I object to their doing so without paying for it." A cartoon depicting John Redmond as a donkey before whom Prime Minister Asquith was dangling a carrot labeled "Home Rule" was also missing. "I am not aware," Skeffington wrote, "of any regulation under the Defence of the Realm Act which renders it unlawful (as yet) to caricature Mr. Redmond; and accordingly there exists no ground for detaining this cartoon."

Skeffington then made what the *Workers' Republic* called "A Kindly Offer." Either the books and pamphlets could be returned forthwith or he should receive full compensation for them. He would, however, be willing to waive both claims "on one condition."

«   «   «   «   «   «   «   «   «

I note that the Irish soldiers at the front are in need of reading matter,
and that the Lord Lieutenant is exerting himself to supply them with
literature. If you will undertake to see that they are duly forwarded, I
will gladly make a present of all these books and papers to the Irish
soldiers, and will waive all claim to compensation for the inconveni-
ence which has been caused me by their detention.[2]

»   »   »   »   »   »   »   »   »

The only record of a reply is a note from the War Office at Whitehall,
saying that the Secretary "presents his compliments to Mr. F. Sheehy
Skeffington and begs to acknowledge the receipt of his letter of February 8th
referring to the detention of certain documents and books on his arrival at
Liverpool."[3]

Skeffington's first scheduled lecture was some two weeks after his
reunion with Hanna and Owen. On 4 January 1916, under the auspices of
the Irish Women's Franchise League, he spoke on his experiences in the
United States; his hour-long speech covered the essential points made in his
letters to Hanna and in his *Irish Citizen* contributions. He made no secret of
his dislike for the "mammonised condition" of the United States, of what he
saw as its subordination of everything to the power of wealth. Finally, he paid
tribute to the Ford Peace Mission, which, he said, was being attacked
because it was to the advantage of the munitions makers to prolong the
profitable war. These remarks having been greeted with applause, Skeffington announced that he would cable an expression of the meeting's sympathy
to the Ford Mission; this suggestion was endorsed by further applause.[4]

Constance Markievicz took exception, however. In a brief speech, she
praised Skeffington for his courage in facing death by starvation but disagreed
strongly with his stand on peace. It was her feeling that there should be no
peace until the British Empire was smashed.[5] Skeffington, noting that the
applause seemed to be as great for her stand as his, sent a letter to the *Workers'
Republic* indicating that there seemed to be a "certain vagueness in the
public mind as to what they really want which it is desirable to clear up.
. . . I desire hereby, through your columns, to challenge Madame Markievicz to a public debate on the question — 'Do We Want Peace Now?' — in
which I would maintain the affirmative and she the negative side."[6] Without
hesitation, Mme. Markievicz accepted the challenge, adding, "unless the
Defenders of a certain tottering Realm intervene, I am prepared to meet him
when and where he pleases and prove to him — what I believe that he in his
heart believes — and what many a person worthier than I has suffered and
even died to prove, that now as ever 'England's difficulty is Ireland's opportunity.'"[7]

Jacqueline Van Voris, in her biography of Constance Markievicz,
states that there were two conflicting reports of the meeting. Louie Bennett, a
friend of the Skeffingtons, termed the countess a poor debater, the meeting

anti-Skeffington (his suppoarters numbered only twenty-six according to her), and the tone "bitter and sinister." [8] The other report was Hanna's — and it was mild. She merely said that Skeffington advocated peace while the countess wanted the war prolonged since she already saw Britain going down to defeat. "After a warmly contested word-duel, just before the vote was taken," Hanna's account read, "James Connolly, who had been a quiet on-looker, suddenly intervened, on Madame's side, swinging the meeting round. When Skeffington laughingly reproved him for throwing in his weight at the end, he replied, with twinkling eyes, 'I was afraid you might get the better of it, Skeffington. That would never do.' " [9] The tone of Hanna's report is not surprising. Both Skeffingtons were aware of Mme. Markievicz's sincerity and respected it; in addition, they were fond of her. Her home was always open to nationalists — no matter how diverse their opinions — and the Skeffingtons had spent many evenings at her fireside.

Skeffington had returned to a genuine crisis in the *Irish Citizen* office. The first year of the paper's existence had been a great struggle financially, but the second year — the year that preceded the outbreak of war — had shown income and expenditure almost completely balanced. The war, however, had changed the picture dramatically. While circulation improved, advertising dropped precipitously. All firms were curtailing their advertising and Skeffington's refusal, at all times, to accept ads for drink or tobacco or from advertisers in whom he did not believe did not help the situation. The paper was now in debt, and it was agreed that the debt must not be allowed to grow any larger. How desperately Skeffington was trying to obtain even small sums of money has already been shown. As his son wrote later, "It was then that, characteristically, to ensure the continuance of the paper if anything happened to him, he insured his life for £500." [10]

It was obvious that it would be necessary to limit production. The 8 January issue of the *Citizen* informed its readers regretfully that it would now be a monthly; the next issue would appear mid-February. At the same time a general appeal for financial assistance was made for the first time since the paper's founding. Even here Skeffington would not compromise. The final paragraph of the appeal read, "One final word. No one need trouble to send money accompanied by any conditions. The *Irish Citizen* must be assisted on its merits and on its record, or not at all. Whether its life be long or short, its policy will be exactly what it has been in the past. If it must go down, it will go down with all flags flying." [11]

All those who wished to aid the women's movement were urged to send in contributions, no matter how small. In fact, a Shilling Fund was set up, payable on St. Patrick's Day. The paper was still to be only four pages but the hope was that enough money would be raised to increase the size to eight pages. According to the mid-February issue, the response to the appeal was good, although it was pointed out that most of those who contributed had done so previously without solicitation. In another attempt at fund-raising, a

"Grand Concert and Dramatic Performance" was held in February in Foresters' Hall. Skeffington's *Prodigal Daughter* was performed by what *Nationality* called "a first-class cast, including members of both the Abbey and the Hardwicke St. Players." [12]

With the *Irish Citizen* now a monthly and the *Daily Herald* a weekly since the outbreak of war, Skeffington was able to devote more time to lecturing. In February, he spoke not only at meetings of the Irish Women's Franchise League but also at a meeting of the Irish Financial Relations Committee (of which he was a founder) on the overtaxation of Ireland, and at a Sinn Fein meeting on "Internationalism and World Politics." That month, too, an article of his, "Ireland and the War," which appeared in *Century Magazine,* caused consternation at Dublin Castle. It attempted to give a comprehensive account of conditions in Ireland as it pertained to the war, conscription, and Ireland's fight for independence, and its success can be measured by the fact that Under Secretary Nathan suggested to his colleagues that they read it to understand how the situation in Dublin was deteriorating. It read in part:

«   «   «   «   «   «   «   «   «

> Despite the subsidizing of the daily and the suppression of the weekly press; despite the pressure exerted by all the political machines and all the influence of social and economic resources; despite the prosecution, under the Defense of the Realm Act, of any who venture to advise an opposite course; despite military law, suspension of trial by jury, arbitrary imprisonment, and deportation, the Irish people have stood fast. Four hundred thousand Irishmen of military age have stood their ground quietly and tenaciously, and have refused to be stampeded into a war in which they have no concern. . . .
>
> Ireland is the most depopulated and impoverished country in Europe, thanks to the beneficent English rule of the last century, and has no blood or money to spare; and if Holland and Denmark and Sweden and Switzerland, all richer and more densely populated than Ireland, still feel that it is their duty to keep out of the war, *a fortiori* it is the duty of Irish statesmen to use every effort to keep their people out of it. Ireland's highest need is peace and the peaceful development of her resources; not a man can be spared for any chivalric adventure. . . .

»   »   »   »   »   »   »   »   »

Skeffington's article went on to list some, though, as he said, not all, of "an extraordinary series of inconsistent and muddle-headed actions" taken by the English government "to suppress Irish discontent and at the same time to convince the world that no Irish discontent existed." He then concluded:

«   «   «   «   «   «   «   «   «

> Meantime, O'Donovan Rossa, the old Fenian, has been buried in Dublin with a great display of military force by the Irish Volunteers. The funeral oration, pronounced by Mr. Pearse, was a defiant assertion

of Ireland's unconquerable resolution to achieve independence. Recruiting for the English army, despite all kinds of pressure and advertising, languishes, while the recruiting for the Irish Volunteers is so brisk that the headquarters of that body cannot keep pace with it.

And when peace comes, Ireland, with the other small nations, will stand at the door of the Hague Conference, and will claim the rights from the community of nations. Shall peace bring freedom to Belgium and Poland, perhaps to Finland and Bohemia, and not to Ireland? Must Irish freedom be gained in blood, or will the comity of nations, led by the United States, shame a weakened England into putting into practice at home the principles which are so loudly trumpeted for the benefit of Germany?[13]

»   »   »   »   »   »   »   »   »

Conscription had become legal in Great Britain in January 1916, but the British government realized that any attempt to enforce it in Ireland would be not only dangerous but futile. Feeling was running too high against it, and the government placed much of the blame for this on anti-recruiting literature. The police and the military felt it was time to act. On 24 March, they raided the offices of the Gaelic Press, which handled the printing of *The Spark, Honesty, The Gael,* and the *Gaelic Athlete.* Paper, office furniture, and printing materials were confiscated and the machinery dismantled. The *Irish Independent,* the following day, reported that "Mr. Sheehy-Skeffington" was "amongst the crowd of onlookers, and in the afternoon addressed the loiterers." [14] The premises of the Irish Workers Co-operative Society, which adjoined Liberty Hall, were also raided. James Connolly, hastily summoned, went through the connecting door and, seeing policemen rummaging through papers, demanded a search warrant — even though he knew that under wartime regulations this was unnecessary. When the police were unable to produce one, Connolly pulled out a revolver and said, "Then drop those papers or I'll drop you." [15] This was the type of action that Skeffington, as much as he admired and respected Connolly, found it impossible to condone. Connolly's justification, however, was his legitimate fear that the police would seize the press in Liberty Hall that printed the *Workers' Republic.* Since the outbreak of the war, the government had suppressed *Sinn Fein, Irish Freedom, Ireland, Scissors and Paste,* and the *Irish Worker.* The last had been succeeded by the *Workers' Republic.* [16]

From the time of the Gaelic Press raid until the Rising in April, Connolly saw to it that Liberty Hall was guarded by members of the Citizen Army. A few months earlier he had become a member of the Military Council of the Irish Republican Brotherhood, and, although Skeffington did not know it, Connolly had already set the date for the Rising. Proof exists that he did not approve of the Rising. Years later, the Belfast novelist St. John Ervine wrote Owen Sheehy-Skeffington that Skeffington had told him of his disapproval. [17] Further proof of Skeffington's opposition is given by

J. F. Byrne, who, just a few days before Skeffington's death, heard him say what he had said many times before — that he would rather be shot than shoot at anyone.[18]

In March, a copy of what became known as the Castle Document was given to Skeffington by F. J. Little, editor of *New Ireland*. Allegedly issued by the British in code, this document contained plans for seizing the headquarters of the Volunteers, the Citizen Army, Sinn Fein, and other buildings. It also authorized the arrest of the disloyal — such as members of Sinn Fein and the Volunteers. The government immediately disclaimed any connection with the document and labeled it a forgery. The editor of *New Ireland* had obtained the Castle Document in very dramatic fashion: it was presented to him in sections as, ostensibly, "a friendly official in Dublin Castle" managed to get hold of them. *New Ireland* had agreed to publish the document and Connolly, knowing it would carry more weight there than in the *Workers' Republic*, agreed not to carry it. It seemed imperative to give the contents of the Castle Document as much publicity as possible in order to defeat its stated purpose; a committee formed with that goal in mind counted Skeffington as one of its members. According to Desmond Ryan, all wanted to prevent bloodshed and all were opposed to any attempt at insurrection.[19]

J. F. Byrne had returned to Dublin and, early in April, Skeffington took him to meet Connolly at Liberty Hall. They had the Castle Document with them. Two other men were with Connolly, and all agreed that it might be wise to get the document into the hands of two members of Parliament, John Dillon and Lawrence Ginnell. Byrne, who was going to London in a few weeks, offered to act as messenger. He wrote later that he hid the copies between the pages of his *Daily Mail*. If he were searched, he speculated, no one would think to look through the pages of a Tory paper.[20]

As it developed, Byrne did not give a copy to Dillon. He said later that he thought Dillon was out of touch with the Irish situation and that there would be no advantage in doing so. He did, however, deliver a copy to Ginnell, and it seemed to him not entirely coincidental that on the day after his visit to Ginnell, Alderman T. Kelly read the cipher document at a meeting of Dublin's governing body, the Dublin Corporation, giving it its first public airing and causing a sensation in Dublin.[21] Authentic or not, the psychological effect of the Castle Document on the nationalists was exactly what Connolly and those who were plotting the Rising with him desired. Fuel had been added earlier by Skeffington, who, without mentioning the document, had inserted an item in the May issue of the *Irish Citizen* under the title "War in Ireland":

«   «   «   «   «   «   «   «   «

There is much reason to believe that the military authorities in Ireland are planning a pogrom of those who are opposed to them — are deliberately meditating such action as they know, in the present state of the popular temper, must provoke resistance and lead to bloodshed. To avert this militarist plot, which would deliver Ireland up to a regime of unchecked and undisguised martial law, is the duty of all Irish pacifists.[22]

»   »   »   »   »   »   »   »   »

Connolly and Skeffington were seeing a great deal of each other during this period, for they attended the same socialist, feminist, and anti-war meetings. Although Skeffington disagreed strongly with him on the question of an armed uprising, Connolly valued Skeffington's opinions and respected his honesty and integrity. When, on 26 March, the Workers' Dramatic Company produced a play by Connolly called *Under Which Flag?* it was Skeffington whom Connolly chose to review it for the *Workers' Republic*. The review was glowing. The play "breathes the true spirit of patriotism; and at the present time nothing could be healthier for the young of Ireland than the lesson it teaches," he wrote. He described the three-act play, set in rural surroundings at the time of the Fenian Rising of 1867, as a pleasing blend of Irish song and dance in which there was imbedded a serious story about the decision of a farmer's son to join the fighting forces of the Irish Republican Brotherhood instead of the English army. In a tribute to Connolly's writing ability, he called the dialogue excellent — "entirely unforced, and in harmony with the characters depicted." He found fault only with the soliloquy in the second act which he condemned as "dramatically inartistic."[23] Owen Dudley Edwards, in *The Mind of An Activist: James Connolly*, speculates:

«   «   «   «   «   «   «   «   «

One can imagine, I think with fidelity to the realities, Skeffington taking up the point further with Connolly, and holding forth on what Ibsen would have said, and what Shaw had taught us, and how Connolly must think of this point in his next play, and Connolly listening quietly, knowing that before a month was past he would have ended forever any prospect of his writing another play, and knowing, too, that Skeffington would never agree with what he was going to do. But the Easter Rising would not divide them, any more than their views of the soliloquy did, or indeed their earlier differences had done.[24]

»   »   »   »   »   »   »   »   »

Skeffington's highest praise went to Sean Connolly, who acted the part of an old, blind veteran of the 1848 struggle. Within a few weeks, Sean Connolly would be dead — the first rebel to be killed during the Easter Rising.[25]

Plans for the Rising were a well-kept, carefully guarded secret. But Skeffington must have realized that the time for some sort of armed insurrection was drawing near. Every sign pointed to it. For one reason or another, he often had occasion to visit Liberty Hall during that period. Here, on the ground floor, trade-union business was proceeding as usual, but great quantities of arms, ammunition, and medical supplies were being stored in the basement, which no one was allowed to enter. Another source of suspicion was an editorial that appeared in the *Workers' Republic:*

«   «   «   «   «   «   «   «   «

> The issue is clear, and we have done our part to clear it. Nothing we can say now can add point to the argument we have put before our readers in the past few months; nor shall we continue to labor the point. In solemn acceptance of our duty and the great responsibilities attached thereto, we have planted the seed in the hope that ere many of us are much older, it will ripen into action. For the moment and hour of that ripening, that fruitful blessed day of days, we are ready. Will it find you ready too?[26]

»   »   »   »   »   »   »   »   »

Hanna, too, must have been aware of what was taking place. In fact, Connolly had hinted at the imminence of the insurrection. She told Owen, years later, that, as Connolly talked, she speculated on his bravery in the face of possible death and whether his Catholicism was a source of comfort to him. "Tell me, Jim," she said, "have you ever any hope of anything on the other side." "The British Labour Party?" Connolly asked. "Oh, no, they won't lift a finger to help us." When Hanna laughed and explained that she meant a belief in an afterlife, Connolly replied, "Oh, no, I'm afraid I haven't time to be thinking about all that kind of thing just now."[27]

In addition, a few weeks prior to Easter, Connolly informed William O'Brien that plans were being made to form a Civil Provisional Government to look after food supplies and transport. He had been authorized, he said, to ask O'Brien to act as a member of this provisional government. One of the other members, according to O'Brien, was to be Hanna Sheehy-Skeffington. O'Brien says that only Connolly and two other people — in addition to himself — "were aware of the complete military plans," but it is difficult to imagine what Hanna thought the Civil Provisional Government was for if not for a possible insurrection.[28]

The militaristic atmosphere must have distressed Skeffington. From every platform he was urging peace and preaching pacifism. And, when friends pointed out to him that pacifism was an unpopular stand with the Nationalists, he replied, "If I thought I was in danger of becoming popular, I would examine my conscience."[29] There is a vague possibility that he believed that the conversion of Liberty Hall into a military base was a precaution against the attack promised in the Castle Document, but the strength of the statements in his Open Letter to the *New Statesman* makes that seem highly unlikely. The letter was uncannily prophetic. "The situation in Ireland is extremely grave," he began, and continued:

«   «   «   «   «   «   «   «   «

> Thanks to the silence of the daily Press, the military authorities are parading their Prussian plans in Ireland unobserved by the British

public; and, when the explosion which they have provoked occurs, they will endeavour to delude the British public as to where the responsibility lies. I write in the hope that, despite war-fever, there may be enough sanity and common-sense left to restrain the militarists while there is yet time.

»   »   »   »   »   »   »   »   »

Skeffington then outlined briefly the events leading up to the "state of extreme exasperation" in which the Irish nationalists and labor supporters presently found themselves — the systematic persecution of the Irish Volunteers from the time of their formation, months before the war began; the provocations of the military; the raids on printing offices; the arbitrary deportations; and the "savage sentences" in Redmond's recruiting appeals during the preceding eighteen months. There were two danger points in the position of the British military, he said. First, the Irish Volunteers were ready, if any attempt was made to disarm them, to "defend their rifles with their lives." Second, the Citizen Army — Skeffington called them "the Labour Volunteers" — would offer similar resistance, not only to any attempt to disarm them but also to any attack on their press. "There is no bluff in either case." He went on:

«   «   «   «   «   «   «   «   «

The British military authorities in Ireland know perfectly well that the members of both these organisations are earnest, determined men. If, knowing this, General Friend [commander of the British forces in Ireland] and his subordinate militarists proceed either to disarm the Volunteers or to raid the Labour press, it can only be because they want bloodshed — because they *want* to provoke another '98, and to get an excuse for a machine-gun massacre.

Irish pacifists who have watched the situation closely are convinced that this is precisely what the militarists do want. The younger English officers in Dublin make no secret of their eagerness "to have a whack at the Sinn Feiners"; they would much rather fight them than the Germans.

»   »   »   »   »   »   »   »   »

Twice already, Skeffington wrote, General Friend had "been on the point of setting Ireland in a blaze" — when he had issued a warrant for the arrest of Bishop O'Dwyer of Limerick and when he had held a detachment of soldiers with machine guns in readiness to raid Liberty Hall. And he cautioned the military authorities: "Once bloodshed is started in Ireland, who can say where or how it will end?"[30]

Understanding well the temper of the times, Skeffington did not expect his letter to the *New Statesman* to see the light of day. On the same day that he wrote it, he sent a copy to George Bernard Shaw with an accompanying letter saying that he had sent it to several London newspapers. "I think it is quite likely that none of them will publish it; so I am sending you a copy for your personal information, that you may understand how critical the position is here. It will require all the efforts of all men of goodwill to avert bloodshed in Ireland; and perhaps you, having the ear of the press, may be able to intervene effectively."[31] It was not Shaw's intervention but Skeffington's murder that finally brought about the publication of his letter in the *New Statesman*, a fortnight after his death.

If Skeffington was shocked when plans for the insurrection were finally revealed, he was not alone. The week preceding the Rising was one of complete confusion. Eoin MacNeill, Chief of Staff of the Irish Volunteers, had not been kept informed by Connolly and the handful of Irish Republican Brotherhood members plotting with him. When on Thursday, 20 April, he learned, purely by chance, that orders had gone out to the various commands to prepare for an insurrection on Easter Sunday, he was stunned. It was his carefully considered position that armed insurrection should take place only if the government suppressed the Volunteers or imposed conscription on Ireland, or if the Germans landed in Ireland. Furthermore, they had no arms. Immediately he made plans to countermand the orders sent out by Connolly and Padraic Pearse. The next day, Good Friday, a deputation led by Pearse called on him, pleading with him not to do so. The only result, they told him, would be confusion. Only when they informed him that a German ship, the *Aud*, was on its way with arms and ammunition did MacNeill agree.[32]

Less than twenty-four hours later, two Volunteer officers came to MacNeill with the news that the *Aud* had been sunk. They also gave him what he considered positive proof that the Castle Document was a forgery. Convinced now that he had been deceived on all sides and that the British were not planning to strike, MacNeill had a bitter confrontation with Pearse. MacNeill then met with some of his followers, afterwards sending the following order to his Volunteers: "Volunteers completely deceived. All orders for special action are hereby cancelled, and on no account will action be taken." This order went out very early Sunday morning. Since the Rising was planned for late Sunday afternoon, there was time to reach most of those involved. He also gave a cancellation notice to the *Sunday Independent*.[33]

In *Ireland Since the Famine*, F. S. L. Lyons sums up the situation:

«   «   «   «   «   «   «   «   «

The conspirators recognised that MacNeill, in trying to stop the rising, was acting consistently and courageously along the lines he had publicly and repeatedly laid down. And so, although his countermanding orders of Easter Sunday struck a fearful blow at their plans, Pearse, MacDermott and MacDonagh all in their last hours were careful to exonerate him from any charge of disloyalty or lack of patriotism. And MacNeill for his part, deeply injured though he was at the moment

when he faced his crisis of confidence, steadfastly defended the honour
of his former comrades at his own court-martial and in later life.[34]

»   »   »   »   »   »   »   »   »

Skeffington read the notice in the *Irish Independent* Easter Sunday
morning, and this may have been the first intimation he had of the exact
time planned for the insurrection. He decided to go down to Liberty Hall to
see if he could learn anything further. William O'Brien had the same idea.
In *Forth the Banners Go*, O'Brien says that Connolly had confided all the
details of the Rising to him, and that therefore the *Independent*'s notice had
come as a complete surprise to him. The previous evening he had been with
Connolly until 11:30. At that time Connolly had said to him, "I will have a
good sleep tonight. I don't know when I'll have another one." He had also
said that everything was going very well indeed and that there had been no
important hitches in their arrangements. When Skeffington and O'Brien
reached Liberty Hall they found that Connolly was in a meeting and
unavailable. Neither could enlighten the other.[35]

The meeting — taking place in Connolly's bedroom, which was also
his office — had been called to try to restore order out of the chaos resulting
from the sinking of the *Aud* and from MacNeill's countermanding order.
Present were Sean MacDermott, Tom Clarke, Padraic Pearse, and Connolly. Clarke wanted to carry out the original plan with the hope that the
Irish Volunteers would respond spontaneously. The others preached cau-
tion. None hoped for any great success. By noon they had come to a
decision; the Rising would take place, but it would be postponed until noon
the following day. A few remarks made by Connolly during the meeting
probably reflected the general mood: "If we don't fight now, all that we have
to hope and pray for is that an earthquake will come and swallow Ireland
up." Later, when one of the group talked of the responsibility connected with
allowing people to go to their death when they were sure of defeat, Connolly
said, "There is only one responsibility I am afraid of and that is preventing
the men and women of Ireland fighting and dying for Ireland if they are so
minded."[36] The following morning he made his feelings equally clear to
O'Brien. "We are going to be slaughtered," he said. When O'Brien asked,
"Is there no chance of success?" he replied, "None whatever."[37]

As soon as the decision was made to begin operations the following
noon, Thomas MacDonagh, who had directed the training of the Volunteers, was dispatched to alert the Dublin members. Only about thirteen
hundred of that group took his message seriously and, of the Citizen Army,
he was able to reach only about two hundred. Originally a march had been
scheduled for Sunday afternoon, preceding the outbreak of hostilities, and it
seemed advisable to carry that through. It was led by Connolly — from City
Hall to Dublin Castle to the Four Courts. Constance Markievicz drew the
most attention in her green woolen blouse with brass buttons, green tweed

knee-breeches, black stockings, heavy boots, and cartridge belt. On one side of the belt hung an automatic pistol, on the other a convertible Mauser rifle. Across her shoulders she had slung a ceremonial strap and a knapsack.[38] The effect was extremely dashing.

Skeffington's reactions to all of this were mixed. Intellectually he agreed with a statement made by Eoin MacNeill, who had said months earlier, "I do not know at this moment whether the time and the circumstances will yet justify distinct revolutionary action, but of this I am certain, that the only possible basis for successful revolutionary action is deep and widespread popular discontent. We have only to look around us in the streets to realize that no such condition exists in Ireland."[39] But Skeffington also understood that conditions were changing and that there was ample reason for the revolt. Although he considered it illtimed, as did MacNeill, and although he firmly believed that the world's problems should be solved by reason and not by bloodshed, his sympathies were clearly with Connolly and his men.

The Rising can be described in many ways — as foolhardy, premature, desperate, among other things — but one cannot doubt the courage nor the love of country of its leaders. The poet and novelist James Stephens, who was an eyewitness to the Rising, says "She [Ireland] was not with the revolution, but in a few months she will be, and her heart which was withering will be warmed by the knowledge that men have thought her worth dying for. She will prepare to make herself worthy of devotion, and that devotion will never fail her."[40] Since the leaders realized that their forces would be smaller than they had originally hoped, they modified their plans somewhat. The best thing to do seemed to be to seize certain buildings and attempt to hold them as long as possible. They hoped that when the rest of their countrymen saw what was taking place, their forces might be greatly augmented. Failing that, there was the possibility that if they could hold out long enough they might be given a seat at the peace table at the end of the war — something that they, as well as Skeffington, ardently desired. Headquarters were to be set up in the General Post Office with garrisons throughout the city.

Promptly at noon on Easter Monday, a contingent of sixteen men, led by Sean Connolly, was sent to seal off Dublin Castle by seizing the guardroom, and to occupy City Hall, the *Evening Mail* offices, and other adjacent buildings. This was easily done. Actually, they could have taken the castle just as easily, for it was sparsely manned because of the holiday. Also because it was a holiday, crowds were milling about outside the castle gates; Skeffington was among them. It was at these gates, and by one of Sean Connolly's men, that the first shot of the insurrection was fired. In the flurry of shooting that followed, Sean was killed — the first Irishman in generations to die under the Irish flag — and a British officer wounded. He lay bleeding to death and, because of the cross-fire, no one was going to his aid. Realizing this, Skeffington ran for a pharmacist, and both of them dashed through a hail of bullets to the gates of the castle. When they got there, however, they found only a pool of blood; British soldiers had succeeded in dragging the wounded man inside. When Hanna later remonstrated with him for risking his life, he said, "I could not let anyone bleed to death while I could help."[41]

Leaving the Dublin Castle area, Skeffington decided to go to the General Post Office, where he hoped to find James Connolly. He could scarcely believe what he saw as he approached it. From the tenements in the area surrounding O'Connell Street, hundreds had descended on Clery's Department Store (Dublin's most popular emporium, owned by the villain of the 1913 lockout, William Martin Murphy), Noblett's confectionery store, Dunn the hatter, Saxone Shoe Shop, and many other establishments. Full-scale looting was taking place. After the shooting of a British officer at the castle and another at St. Stephen's Green, the uniformed police had been recalled, so the looters had a free field. It was understandable, he thought, but inexcusable. It had to be stopped. Feeling helpless, Skeffington entered the Post Office to talk with the insurgent commanders about the problem, but he found them already well aware of it and powerless to stop it. Sean MacDermott had addressed the crowd in his best oratorical manner without success. Sean O'Kelly, an officer of the Neutrality League who was assisting Connolly, had then been assigned a dozen men, armed with rifles and police sticks, to drive the looters out of Clery's. This they did but, just as soon as they went on to the next store, the looters swarmed back. O'Kelly reported to Connolly that he had never seen such industrious Irishmen in his life.[42]

At home that evening, Skeffington discussed with Hanna the possibility of holding a meeting at the I.W.F.L. headquarters the following day to take up the problem. Perhaps they could organize a Citizen's Defence Force to police the downtown area, he said. He also prepared a notice signed "F. Sheehy-Skeffington," that read:

«   «   «   «   «   «   «   «   «

When there are no regular police on the streets, it becomes the duty of citizens to police the streets themselves and to prevent such spasmodic looting as has taken place in a few streets. Civilians (men and women) who are willing to cooperate to this end are asked to attend at Westmoreland Chambers (over Eden Bros.) at five o'clock this [Tues.] afternoon.[43]

»   »   »   »   »   »   »   »   »

Owen Sheehy-Skeffington described his father's efforts:

«   «   «   «   «   «   «   «   «

Some of the press was smearing the insurgents as a rabble mob, and he felt he *had* to try to organize a group of peaceful citizens to combat chaos and expose false reports. The late "Alfie" Byrne [ten times Lord Mayor of Dublin] told me not long before his own death some years ago: "Your father was a terrible man, God rest him. You couldn't say no to him. He had about thirty of us with armbands patrolling the streets near the Pillar. But it got too hot for *me*. When he went up the street, I went home!"[44]

»   »   »   »   »   »   »   »   »

The next day, Tuesday, 25 April, was a sultry, cloudy day. Skeffington went into town to tack up notices and attempt to mobilize as many people as possible for the defense force. Hanna, meanwhile, went to the General Post Office to see if there was any assistance — such as carrying messages — she might offer. At noon William O'Brien saw Skeffington and they talked about the looting and the meeting planned to control it. O'Brien had talked with Connolly about it earlier but had been brushed aside with the comment, "That will be one more problem for the British." Skeffington had learned that two gunboats were landing British troops in Kingstown and he asked that O'Brien pass that information on to Connolly. The two men then went down to Mrs. Wyse-Power's shop where she, even though she had closed her shop, gave them some tea and an egg. Characteristically, Skeffington then took time to go to O'Connell Street to obtain medicine for Mrs. Wyse-Power's eldest daughter. This was the last time O'Brien ever saw him.[45]

At 5:30 that afternoon, as previously arranged, the Skeffingtons met for tea at the I.W.F.L. headquarters. He was tired and disappointed, he told Hanna, even though he had managed to enlist the aid of a few civilians, including some priests, and had made a few speeches. He attributed his lack of success to the fear of anyone but looters to venture out into the streets but, in actuality, the apathy with which Dublin's citizenry had greeted the Rising was its main cause. Before 7 P.M., Hanna left her husband, since she was eager to get home to Owen and the trams were not running. They urged each other to be careful because of the shooting; the sound of the guns could be heard as she walked away. Hanna never saw her husband again.

When, by the following morning — Wednesday — Skeffington had not returned home, Hanna was more puzzled than apprehensive. Something had gone wrong, she was sure, but with the Rising in full swing she was not too surprised. Perhaps he had been detained by the police and word would reach her momentarily. Finally, toward noon, she went into town. The fighting was heavy that day but, according to the *Irish Times*, which had resumed publication after a two-day hiatus, the country was peaceful. Martial law had been declared and everyone was warned to remain indoors from seven at night until five in the morning. It was a beautiful day, and people on the street were smiling and talkative and almost in a holiday mood. James Stephens analyzes this reaction in *Insurrection in Dublin*:

«   «   «   «   «   «   «   «   «

In the last two years of world war our ideas on death have undergone a change. It is not now the furtive thing that crawled into your bed and which you fought with pill-boxes and medicine bottles. It has become again a rider of the wind whom you may go coursing with through the fields and open places. All the morbidity is gone, and the sickness, and what remains to Death is now health and excitement. So Dublin laughed at the noise of its own bombardment, and made no moan about its dead — in the sunlight. . . . It is possible that in the night Dublin did not laugh, and that she was gay in the sunlight for no other reason than that the night was past. [46]

» » » » » » » » »

So Hanna walked about, making inquiries and listening to conflicting rumors. Skeffington was lying in hospital, wounded; a looter had shot him dead; the military were holding him at Portobello Barracks. She also heard that he had been executed, but she was sure that could not be true. Even if he had been condemned to die, there would have to be a semblance of a trial. Liam O'Broin, in an article in the 1916 *Capuchin Annual*, said that he saw her at about 5 P.M. on Wednesday. He was in a house on York Street overlooking the Green, which had been occupied by the Citizen Army, and Hanna had stopped by. When he asked her how Skeffington was, she said that she did not know; he had not been home the night before, but she wasn't worried. [47]

By Thursday morning, however, Hanna was sick with fear and foreboding. It was not conceivable that Skeffington could be all right and not get some word to her after two nights. She went into town once more and was greeted with the sound of heavy gunfire and with more rumors. One seemed to her authentic — that Skeffington had been arrested. This was the fourth day of the Rising and it was going badly. About ten o'clock that morning a shell had struck the reserve print shop of the *Irish Times*, fire had broken out, and it was now spreading. It was becoming increasingly difficult, thanks to the fires, for the insurgents to hold confiscated buildings and, although Hanna was of course unaware of it, James Connolly had already been badly wounded. Finally, with flames all about and unable to get any definite word of her husband, Hanna returned home.

Friday morning came and still no word. Now Hanna was ready to believe anything. In an attempt to reassure her, her sisters Mary Kettle and Margaret Culhane went to Portobello Barracks. There they saw Captain J. C. Bowen-Colthurst, who told them flatly that he knew nothing of Skeffington. He refused to say anything further and ordered them to leave; according to Hanna's account, they were "marched off under armed guard and forbidden to speak till they left the premises." [48] That afternoon Hanna obtained a reliable report that her husband's body had been seen in the Portobello Barracks mortuary. It was then that Hanna forced herself to accept, as far as she was able, the reality of Skeffington's death. [49]

The day was not yet over for Hanna, however. At about seven o'clock, when she was getting Owen ready for bed, a party of some forty soldiers, including Captain Colthurst, broke in and for almost three hours ransacked the house. Colthurst had Skeffington's keys, which enabled him to plunder the study — always kept locked. "All my private letters, letters from my husband to me before our marriage, his articles, a manuscript play, the labour of a lifetime, were taken. After endless application I received back a small part of these, but most of my most cherished possessions have never been returned, nor was any attempt made to find them," Hanna said. Owen also remembered it clearly: "A volley fired in the air, the ground floor windows smashed, British soldiers pouring in from the front and from the back."[50] Hanna, Owen, and a maid were ordered to stay in the front room under armed guard. At least one soldier showed some pity, for Hanna heard him say — and she recognized a Belfast accent — "I didn't enlist for this. They are taking the whole bloomin' house with them."[51]

It would be a long time before Hanna would know the full story of her husband's death. Many years later she wrote that, as she looked back, what shocked her most was "not the brutality of the British Army in action against a people in revolt (we learned to take this for granted, and indeed it is part of war everywhere), but the automatic and tireless efforts on the part of the entire official machinery, both military and political, to prevent the truth being made public."[52] But when Hanna saw her husband's keys in Colthurst's hands, the full extent of her tragedy came home to her. Her shock and disbelief were mixed with rage.

NOTES TO CHAPTER 13

1. *Workers' Republic*, 26 February 1916.
2. Ibid.
3. Secretary, War Office, Whitehall, to F. Sheehy-Skeffington, 22 February 1916.
4. *Irish Citizen*, 8 January 1916.
5. Ibid.
6. *Workers' Republic*, 5 January 1915.
7. Van Voris, *Constance de Markievicz*, p. 159.
8. Ibid.
9. Ibid., p. 160.
10. O. Sheehy-Skeffington, "Francis Sheehy-Skeffington," p. 144.
11. *Irish Citizen*, 8 January 1916.
12. *Nationality*, 12 February 1916.
13. *Century Magazine*, February 1916.
14. *Irish Independent*, 25 March 1916.
15. R. M. Fox, *James Connolly: The Forerunner* (Tralee: The Kerryman Limited, 1946), p. 182.
16. Dorothy Macardle, *The Irish Republic* (New York: Farrar, Straus and Giroux, 1965), pp. 125–126. Also Robert Kee, *The Green Flag* (London: Weidenfeld & Nicholson, 1972), p. 533.
17. St. John Ervine to O. Sheehy-Skeffington, 18 November 1955, in the possession of Andrée Sheehy-Skeffington, Dublin. St. John Ervine recalled that

he had talked with Skeffington just an hour before the latter's execution. Skeffington told him then that he was opposed to the Rising. Ervine was in the British army during World War I and must have been stationed at Portobello Barracks where Skeffington was held prisoner.

18. Byrne, *Silent Years*, p. 122.

19. Desmond Ryan, *The Rising: The Complete Story of Easter Week*, 4th ed. (Dublin: Golden Eagle Books, 1966), p. 70.

20. Byrne, *Silent Years*, pp. 134–137.

21. Ibid.

22. *Irish Citizen*, cover page, May 1916.

23. *Workers' Republic*, 8 April 1916.

24. Owen Dudley Edwards, *The Mind of An Activist: James Connolly* (Dublin: Gill and Macmillan, 1971), p. 89.

25. Samuel Levenson, *James Connolly* (London: Martin Brian and O'Keeffe, 1973), p. 304.

26. *Workers' Republic*, 29 January 1916.

27. Levenson, *James Connolly*, p. 291.

28. O'Brien, *Forth the Banners Go*, p. 278.

29. *Irish Citizen*, September 1919.

30. *New Statesman*, 6 May 1916.

31. George Bernard Shaw, *The Matter with Ireland* (New York: Hill and Wang, 1961), p. 110n.

32. Lyons, *Ireland Since the Famine*, pp. 356–358.

33. Ibid.

34. Ibid., p. 357.

35. O'Brien, *Forth the Banners Go*, pp. 286–288.

36. Levenson, *James Connolly*, p. 295.

37. Ibid., p. 297.

38. Ibid., p. 295.

39. F. X. Martin, O.S.A., "Select Documents: XX Eoin MacNeill on the 1916 Rising," *Irish Historical Studies*, Vol. XII (1961), p. 240.

40. James Stephens, *The Insurrection in Dublin* (Chicago: Scepter Books, 1966), p. 8.

41. Hanna Sheehy-Skeffington, "A Pacifist Dies," in Roger McHugh (ed.), *Dublin 1916* (New York: Hawthorn Books, 1966), p. 276.

42. Levenson, *James Connolly*, p. 302.

43. "John Dillon's Speech in the House of Commons on 11 May 1916," in Edwards and Pyle (eds.), *1916: The Easter Rising*, p. 77.

44. O. Sheehy-Skeffington, "Francis Sheehy-Skeffington," p. 145.

45. William O'Brien Papers, Ms 13,962, National Library of Ireland.

46. Stephens, *Insurrection in Dublin*, pp. 38–39.

47. Liam O'Broin, "Portobello Bridge," in *Capuchin Annual 1916*, p. 229.

48. H. Sheehy-Skeffington, "A Pacifist Dies," p. 282.

49. Ibid.

50. O. Sheehy-Skeffington, "Francis Sheehy-Skeffington," p. 146.

51. H. Sheehy-Skeffington, "A Pacifist Dies," p. 283.

52. O. Sheehy-Skeffington, "Francis Sheehy-Skeffington," p. 148.

14

Murder Most Foul

The events that transpired after the Sheehy-Skeffingtons parted on Tuesday evening had all the qualities of a nightmare. Sometime between seven and eight o'clock, Skeffington decided to start for home. It was dusk, the fighting had now been going on for some thirty hours, and the gathered crowds were visible as he walked along Rathmines Road nearing Portobello Bridge. Since he was such a well-known figure, various people called out to him by name. As though that were the signal, within minutes Lieutenant M. C. Morris, who was in charge of about thirty men guarding the bridge, placed Skeffington under arrest and assigned two of his soldiers to escort him to Portobello Barracks, situated about 350 yards beyond the bridge. Skeffington, unarmed and carrying a walking stick, did not resist. The lieutenant said later that he had thought it advisable to arrest pedestrians who seemed to be attracting attention rather than risk possible altercations and blocking of the roadway.

At Portobello Barracks, he was searched and then questioned by the adjutant of the 3rd Royal Irish Rifles, Lieutenant Samuel Valentine Morgan. No papers of an incriminating nature were found on him. When Lieutenant Morgan asked him if he were a Sinn Feiner, Skeffington replied truthfully that he was in sympathy with the Sinn Fein movement but opposed to militarism and in favor of passive resistance. The adjutant duly reported his arrest to headquarters and, since there was no charge against him, asked if he should be released with others whose cases were similar. He was told to release the others but to detain Skeffington.

About ten-thirty that evening, Captain J. C. Bowen-Colthurst, one of the officers of the Royal Irish Rifles, formed a raiding party of about forty soldiers and, for reasons incomprehensible, took Skeffington with them as a hostage. He was taken from his cell, his hands were tied behind his back, and, as they left the barracks, Colthurst told him to kneel and say his prayers. When he refused, the officer ordered his men to take off their hats and, standing over Skeffington, he said, "O Lord God, if it shall please Thee to take this man's life, forgive him, for Christ's sake." [1]

Who was this man who, contrary to army regulations, took Skeffington from his cell and from the barracks? Colthurst was a member of the Anglo-

Irish ascendancy (his family owned Blarney Castle, and his cousin, Elizabeth Bowen, won fame as a writer). He had fought in the Boer War and for a dozen years watched with dismay the growth of Home Rule sentiment. After participating in the bloody retreat from Mons during World War I, he suffered a mental breakdown that caused him to be temporarily suspended from duty. Some weeks later he was wounded at the battle of the Aisne River and sent back to Ireland. He was well known in Dublin Castle circles, since he had acted as an aide-de-camp to the former viceroy.[2] (It was alleged, incidentally, that he had a hatred of all Sinn Feiners that dated from the time of that assignment.) His record of instability and his religious fanaticism were also well known.

Exceptionally tall, Colthurst walked with a slight stoop. Now, wearing his usual grave expression, he marched his little band out of Portobello Barracks by way of the Rathmines Gate and down Rathmines Road, a street lined with rather unimposing red brick post-Georgian villas. It had been raining but by then it had ceased, the sky was starlit, and a gusty wind was blowing. As they approached Rathmines Catholic Church, two teen-aged boys were coming out of church. Colthurst rushed over to them, asked if they did not realize that martial law had been declared, and shouted that he could shoot them like dogs. When one of the boys turned away to light a cigarette, Colthurst was so infuriated that he ordered one of his men to "bash" him. It was proved later that the officer who followed that command broke the boy's jaw with his rifle butt. As the lad fell, Colthurst, by now in a frenzy, whipped out his revolver and shot him. The boy was taken by ambulance to the barracks, where he died that night without regaining consciousness. When Skeffington protested against this horrible murder, Colthurst told him to say his prayers since he probably would be next.[3]

At Portobello Bridge twenty men and Skeffington were left behind under the command of Second Lieutenant Leslie Wilson. Colthurst instructed Wilson to shoot Skeffington if any of the soldiers were fired upon; Wilson testified later that he saw nothing strange in the order and would certainly have carried it out. Colthurst then marched off with the remainder of his men and, a few hundred yards along, began firing his rifle in the air. He also fired at heads in windows whenever they appeared. According to Lieutenant Wilson, this was to make sure people stayed indoors. The raiding party's target was Alderman James Kelly's tobacco shop. Kelly was a justice of the peace, had been High Sheriff of Dublin, and had recruited for the British army. There was never any question of his loyalty. But the men mistakenly believed that the shop was owned by Alderman Tom Kelly, who was active in many nationalist causes. (It was Tom Kelly whom James Connolly, along with Hanna and others, had named to set up a Civil Provisional Government.) Bowen-Colthurst's party threw a bomb into James Kelly's shop, riddled the place with bullets, and arrested five men. They later released three of them, but they kept Thomas Dickson, a deformed Scotsman who edited a

Loyalist paper called the *Eye-Opener,* and Patrick MacIntyre, who edited
another paper called the *Searchlight.* Undoubtedly the soldiers had confused
the *Searchlight* with the notorious rebel paper, the *Spark.* Neither Dickson
nor MacIntyre had any connection whatsoever with the Sinn Fein
movement.[4]

Rejoining the group left behind at Portobello Bridge, the patrol and
their three prisoners returned to the barracks about 11:20 P.M. Dickson and
MacIntyre were held in the detention room and Skeffington was returned to
his cell, still bound. (According to a Royal Commission Report some
months later, "Mr. Sheehy Skeffington, as being of a superior social position, was put into a separate cell and was made as comfortable as possible.")
Colthurst spent the rest of the night reading and praying. One passage in the
Bible, from St. Luke, he interpreted as a direct order: "But those mine
enemies, which would not that I should reign over them, bring hither, and
slay them before me."[5] For Colthurst this was an injunction to slay those
who refused to accept His Majesty's rule.

The previous day, Easter Monday, a nineteen-year-old Dublin-born
and Oxford-educated officer named Monk Gibbon, on leave from his
regiment in England, had reported to Portobello Barracks. He was following
army regulations that prescribed this action in case of any civil disturbance or
upheaval. Sixty-five years later, in April 1981, Gibbon, well into his eighties,
recalled the events surrounding Skeffington's imprisonment and murder on
a telecast called "The Crime of Captain Colthurst." His orders were to report
to the nearest barracks, Gibbon said, and "tragically enough the nearest
barracks was Portobello Barracks where I was to see a good many things and
hear a good many things which I would sooner not." Describing the
atmosphere there, he said that "fifty different things were happening at the
same time. Nobody knew anyone else. The ranking adjutant told us a little
about each other but otherwise we were a complete miscellaneous hodge-
podge of the services. Nobody knew what was happening or where it was
happening."[6]

Wednesday morning Monk Gibbon got some of the details when he
talked with a soldier who had been out with Colthurst on his evening raid.
Speaking of Skeffington, the man was lost in admiration. "He was just
wonderful, sir," he said to Gibbon. "I never heard a man talk like that before.
And he showed no fear, no fear at all." Such praise made Gibbon eager to
meet Skeffington, and when, at about 9:30 A.M., the quartermaster went to
inspect the prisoners' breakfasts, Gibbon accompanied him. Describing his
meeting with Skeffington that morning, Monk Gibbon said:

«   «   «   «   «   «   «   «   «

You don't often meet people in life who impress you by their innate
greatness and goodness. At first when I saw Francis Sheehy-Skeffington,
in his knickerbockers, very much the tweedy male suffragette, I had
thought he was a figure of fun. But then his greatness impressed me

and I asked him was there anything I could do for him. He said "send my wife a message and say I am in safekeeping" and, of course, in retrospect those are some of the most tragic words I have ever heard spoken to me. He was in safekeeping but within, I trust, twenty minutes — perhaps half an hour — that man was going to be, in my opinion, foully and unjustifiably murdered.

»   »   »   »   »   »   »   »   »

At the end of that brief period, Gibbon returned to the courtyard and was met with the sight of Skeffington's body being carried out. "The hands were hanging down either side," he said, "absolutely dripping blood, and that is the memory that has stuck with me right down the years." [7]

Gibbon's impression of his brief visit with Skeffington never left him either. In his memoirs, *Inglorious Soldier*, he wrote, "Second impressions efface the earliest ones and I see only his dignity, the quiet dignity of a man in a terrible position meeting it quietly. He has a wonderful smile and there is a gentleness about the whole man, in every move, in every word he says. He has a slight stoop and dark brown earnest-looking eyes. Was this gentle creature, almost comical in his tweed cycling breeches à la Bernard Shaw, who could speak so eloquently that even the bomber corporal in charge of him had been impressed, really a dangerous revolutionary whose escape must be prevented at all costs? I did not believe it for one instant." [8]

Obviously Colthurst did believe it. Shortly after 10 A.M., he came into the guardroom, approached the sergeant of the guard, John William Aldridge, and asked that Skeffington, MacIntyre, and Dickson be taken to the yard so that he might speak with them. This yard, within the same block of buildings, could be reached by a short passage from the guardroom. It was less than forty feet in length, approximately fifteen feet wide, and surrounded by a twelve-foot-high wall. While Aldridge carried out his order, Colthurst, restless, walked outside to talk with the lieutenant on guard duty there, William Price Dobbyn, only eighteen years old and newly commissioned. He informed Dobbyn, as he had not Aldridge, that he intended to take the three men out to be shot, for he believed it was the best course and the right thing to do.

Skeffington, meanwhile, was taken from his cell and, with MacIntyre and Dickson, marched into the yard. Colthurst followed with seven soldiers, apparently chosen simply because they had been near the yard passage. He then ordered the three prisoners to stand against the back wall. While they were doing this, the soldiers fell into line against the opposite wall and were immediately given the order to fire. Some accounts say that Skeffington refused to have his eyes blindfolded, that he smiled and said, "You have made a terrible mistake." Others say that it all happened so fast that none of the three victims realized that they were about to meet their deaths. The former account seems romanticized; the latter is undoubtedly closer to the truth. Aside from the rapidity of the act, the sheer madness would have made it impossible to grasp. James Stephens may have portrayed Skeffington's thoughts the most accurately:

«   «   «   «   «   «   «   «   «

Other men have been shot, but they faced the guns knowing that they faced justice, however stern and oppressive; and that what they had engaged to confront was before them. He had no such thought to soothe from his mind anger or unforgiveness. He who was a pacifist was compelled to revolt to his last breath, and on the instruments of his end he must have looked as on murderers. I am sure that to the end he railed against oppression, and that he fell marvelling that the world can truly be as it is. [10]

»   »   »   »   »   »   »   »   »

As soon as the men fell, Colthurst went to the orderly room to report to the adjutant what he had done. He had been afraid, he said, that they might try to escape or that an attempt might be made to rescue them by armed force. Somewhat disjointedly, Colthurst went on to say that he had lost a brother in the war and that he was just as good an Irishman as the men he had shot. Monk Gibbon, who was an eyewitness, said, "I don't remember the exact words in which Colthurst made his statement. If it was that Skeffington was in a position to escape under the conditions in which I saw him, it is a lie and it is a damned lie. His wrists were handcuffed behind his back. He was completely helpless — but I mean it's laughable!" According to the narrator of the telecast, "Evidence of the difficulty of escape still survives. The cell at Portobello still exists. It is small, the door is strong, the only window is high and barred. The adjoining exercise yard [where the executions took place] has just one entrance from the cells and has walls 12 feet high." [11]

While Colthurst was reporting to the adjutant, Lieutenant Dobbyn heard the volley being fired and went into the yard to investigate. He saw the three men lying in blood on the ground, and he recognized Skeffington. To his horror, he saw movement in one of his legs. He immediately sent an officer back to the orderly room to ascertain what should be done. The order, issued by Colthurst, was "Shoot him again." Dobbyn, this "gentlest and quietest of subalterns," as Gibbon described him, then stood by while four men fired once more into Skeffington's body. Near the end of that catastrophic Wednesday, sometime around 11 P.M., the three bodies were removed from the mortuary, sewn into sacks, and buried in quicklime in the barracks yard. Now the military authorities could attempt to deny that they had ever arrested, executed, or even seen the three Dublin citizens. Had one of them not been Francis Sheehy-Skeffington, they might have succeeded.

As the news of Skeffington's murder reached Dubliners, Hanna's grief and rage were echoed throughout the city. To the average citizen, Skeffington was perhaps better known than any of the leaders of the Rising. There was for him a kind of affection that his mild manner and wit inspired. That this very gentle man should have met his death before a firing squad was beyond belief. His friend, Louie Bennett, herself a suffragist, pacifist, and trade union leader, summed it up this way: "For us in Ireland the typical example of pacific heroism must always be Sheehy Skeffington going forth to quell looting with a cane in his hand whilst a rebellion was in full swing!" [12] Skeffington — this man who had wanted to help the wounded and to maintain a semblance of order and sanity — had become the first martyr of the 1916 Rebellion.

During the Rising, the sympathies of the Irish people were, for the most part, with the British soldiers. It was understandable. For one thing, many Dublin sons had enlisted in the British army, and Irish regiments were fighting in France and other parts of Europe. In addition, large portions of the population, particularly those in the slums, were apathetic to the Rising for they were busy with their own worries. In the period following the Rising, however, the mood of the people began to shift to one of bitterness. Public sentiment had been aroused not only in Ireland but in the United States and Great Britain as well. The leaders of the Rising were becoming martyrs and, as James Stephens wrote, Ireland would never be satisfied with Home Rule "as a peaceful present such as is sometimes given away with a pound of tea." [13] The events that followed rapidly assured that the developing bitterness would increase from day to day.

On Saturday, 29 April, the insurrection came to an end when Padraic Pearse and James Connolly surrendered unconditionally. Connolly, very badly wounded and in a great deal of pain, was taken to the Castle infirmary. On 9 May he was tried and sentenced to death. Two days before his execution, pale and feverish, he asked his wife, Lillie, to gather his writings and give them to Skeffington, whom he wanted to be his literary executor. Lillie, well aware of Skeffington's fate, could not bring herself to tell Connolly that he was dead. The next night he talked once more of turning his writings over to Skeffington with the hope that they might be sold to augment his family's income. His daughter, Nora, finally told him the truth. [14] The irony of his pacifist friend's murder must have been obvious to Connolly.

James Connolly, so wounded that he was unable to stand, was strapped to a chair and executed in the early hours of 12 May. His execution had been preceded by those of Padraic Pearse, Thomas MacDonagh, and Tom Clarke on 3 May; Joseph Plunkett, Edward Daly, Michael O'Hanrahan, and William Pearse, Padraic's younger brother, on 4 May; John MacBride, Maud Gonne's former husband, on 5 May; Cornelius Colbert, Eamonn Kent, Michael Mallin, and Sean Heuston on 8 May; and Thomas Kent on 9 May. Sean MacDermott was executed the same morning as Connolly. Ireland had fifteen more martyrs.

John Dillon, leader of the Irish Parliamentary Party, had predicted what the outcome of the executions would be. On 30 April he had written to John Redmond advising him to "urge the government" to avoid any executions, any mass shooting of prisoners. "If there were shootings of prisoners on any large scale the effect on public opinion might be disastrous in the extreme," he had cautioned. [15] Obviously the government paid no heed, and an infuriated Dillon would not only attack them for their errors but would also make the Sheehy-Skeffington case his cause.

In doing so, Dillon joined Hanna Sheehy-Skeffington, who saw as her salvation and her mission an attempt to lend meaning to the deaths of her husband and of those who had been executed for fighting for Irish freedom. She wasted no time in mourning. As the *Irish Citizen* put it, "Her conduct throughout her terrible experiences . . . give her a place in the nation's gallery of remarkable Irish women. We are deeply indebted to her for the strength of mind and character which enabled her to rise above mere grief and set herself to make out of her husband's death a torch for the pioneers of liberty." [16] Without her goal, however, Hanna believed she could not have survived her "terrible experiences." Her first task was to bring to trial her husband's murderer — to see that all the facts became known. In this she was aided by the one man who, according to Monk Gibbon, could and would have prevented the murder of Skeffington — Sir Francis Fletcher Vane, then in charge of Portobello Barracks' defenses.

Gibbon was on guard duty early Tuesday morning, 25 April, relieving Lieutenant Dobbyn, when he saw Vane for the first time. He described him as about fifty-five, with a flushed face, "a rather dogged, buccaneering expression. He walked with a slight poke of the head forward, had a habit of linking his hands together behind his back, and carried a . . . swagger stick under his arm." [17] Vane had served in South Africa during the Boer War, and had made himself unpopular with the authorities by complaining publicly about the conditions under which women and children were interned in different areas. A known advocate of Home Rule for Ireland, he was promptly retired when the war was over; his response was to repeat his anti-imperialist views in a book, *Pax Britannica in South Africa*. When World War I broke out, he immediately offered his services to the army and was recommissioned as a major.

On the morning that Skeffington was murdered, Sir Francis Vane was not at the barracks but was supervising the placing of an observation post on the tower of the Rathmines Town Hall. It was not until he returned to the Portobello Barracks that morning that he learned of Colthurst's actions. He knew little of Colthurst other than a few facts about his military career. He had, however, seen him in the mess hall the previous day, sitting alone with his elbows on the table and his head between his hands. When Vane walked into the room, Colthurst had looked up and asked, "Is it not dreadful, Sir Francis, to have to shoot Irishmen?" Vane had agreed heartily. [18]

Immediately upon hearing of the executions, Major Vane went to see Major Rossborough, who was temporarily in command, and asked that Colthurst be confined to barracks. He could not, otherwise, be responsible for its defense, he said. "If these proceedings continue," he told his superior officer, "instead of having the rebels against us we shall have all of Ireland."

Rossborough promised to take immediate action. Although he did, in fact, communicate with the headquarters of the Irish Command and give directions that Colthurst was not to be detailed for duty outside the barracks, within hours Colthurst was out on another raid. This time he captured Councillor Richard O'Carroll, one of the members of the Dublin City Council, at an evacuated Irish Volunteer post. When Colthurst asked O'Carroll whether he was a Sinn Feiner, the reply was "From the backbone out!" Colthurst promptly marched O'Carroll into a back yard and shot him. [19] And, of course, later that same week Colthurst participated in the raid on Skeffington's home.

Five days after Francis's murder, the Skeffington home was again raided. On that same day Major Vane was informed that he would be relieved of his duties as officer in charge of defenses and that Captain Colthurst would replace him. Astonished at the army's choice of a replacement and livid with rage, Vane invaded Dublin Castle. He talked with some of the officers in charge, including the head of the intelligence service, but all refused to take any action. "Some of us think it was a good thing Sheehy-Skeffington was put out of the way, anyhow," Major Price said. "Thank you," replied Major Vane, "then my line of action is clear." [20]

Taking an eight-day leave, Vane went to London, saw Lord Kitchener, Minister of War, and heard him dictate a telegram ordering Colthurst to be put under arrest pending trial by courtmartial. The telegram was completely disregarded. Colthurst was not arrested, nor did his activities outside the barracks cease. So effectively was Vane's wrath dissipated, however, that he returned to Dublin satisfied with his efforts and sure that the government was not at fault. When, shortly thereafter, he was deprived of his rank and dismissed from the service, he still did not blame the government — merely the military. As he wrote Hanna more than four years later:

«   «   «   «   «   «   «   «   «

The murders in Portobello Barracks — in which you sustained — and Ireland sustained — so great a loss, were certainly not connived at by the then Government. I happen to know and can prove that neither [Under Secretary for War] Tennant, nor Asquith, nor Kitchener, knew anything about these horrible things when I reported them in London on the 2nd May 1916. On the other hand, I have clear proof that the Army Council knew all about them and had concealed the facts from the Civil Authorities who were, in ordinary course, their superiors. Remember that Kitchener was then a Civil Authority as Secretary of State for War.

The action they took when they learnt from me — except K's [Kitchener's] — was I admit putrid. Instead of getting up and saying a crime has been committed by the military — they shuffled and shuffled until we shuffled them into doing something. Of course directly Ld. K. had sent off the telegram ordering the arrest of B. Colthurst, which he did in my presence a Court Martial was inevitable. [21]

»   »   »   »   »   »   »   »   »

Vane's first task, when he returned to Dublin, was to call on Hanna, for he felt he must apologize to her in the name of the army. By his own admission, the task was a frightening one. He was delighted when he met Owen outside the house, made friends with him, and could face Hanna with Owen's hand in his. The atmosphere was chilly at first, but when he finished his story Hanna shook his hand and assured him that she believed he would have prevented the murder if he had been able to do so. From that time on they were friends and, throughout her fight to expose the crimes of Easter Week, he was by her side. He wrote to Hanna in November 1916 thanking her for sending him an inscribed copy of *In Dark and Evil Days*, and said, in part, "Believe me I value it very highly as a memento of dark and evil days which had at least one gleam of light in causing me to become acquainted with you and Owen. . . . You may be certain that I will not rest until the whole truth is known about Portobello Barracks." [22]

On 8 May, Skeffington's body was exhumed and reburied in Glasnevin Cemetery. This was without Hanna's knowledge; apparently it was under J. B.'s direction, for the Simon Commission reported later that he "was present at the exhumation of his son's body." [23] On that same day Hanna went to see John Dillon with a prepared statement giving the details of Skeffington's murder. Never had she seen a man more moved, she said later. [24] Dillon took action almost immediately. On 11 May he read Hanna's statement in the House of Commons as part of a burning attack on the events transpiring in Dublin. "But it is not murderers who are being executed," he said. "It is insurgents who have fought a clean fight, a brave fight, however misguided, and it would be a damned good thing for you if your soldiers were able to put up as good a fight as did these men in Dublin — three thousand men against twenty thousand with machine-guns and artillery." As he concluded reading Hanna's statement, he added:

«   «   «   «   «   «   «   «   «

I think the Prime Minister will readily admit that nothing but a public inquiry is demanded as a matter of elementary justice to this unhappy lady for this cruel injury which has been inflicted upon her. To tell us that there will be a court-martial, which, of course, will be secret, and that we may be sure justice will be done, is really an outrage upon every principle of fair play. [25]

»   »   »   »   »   »   »   »   »

Before the day ended Colthurst had been placed under arrest and Prime Minister Asquith had arranged to visit Dublin. Soon a courtmartial was ordered.

The courtmartial took place in Richmond Barracks, Dublin, on 6 and 7 June 1916; the verdict was made known on Saturday, 10 June. The presiding officer was Lord Cheylesmore. Both J. B. and Hanna were present. Neither was asked to testify, nor was Major Vane. During the trial Colthurst was under no restraint; he and his family stayed, in splendor, at the Hibern-

ian Hotel in Dawson Street. The court found Colthurst guilty but insane at
the time of the murders. He was to be "detained in a criminal lunatic asylum
during his Majesty's pleasure," and Tim Healy declared that there had never
been a greater travesty of justice since the trial of Christ. Monk Gibbon
agreed. In the 1981 telecast, he said, "I have always regarded this as the act of
a sadistic monster, he was a political bigot mixed up with religion."[26]

After many months, this is the way Hanna began to perceive her
husband's reaction to his murder. "My husband would have gone to his
death with a smile on his lips, knowing that by his murder he had struck a
heavier blow for his ideals than by any act in his life. His death will speak
trumpet-tongued against the system that slew him."[27] But would Francis
Sheehy-Skeffington have desired his death to speak out "against the system
that slew him"? Would he have felt that it was indeed the system that had
caused Colthurst to commit his insane act? Or would he have felt it was the
brutalization of men by the military and the misteaching of his religion —
the failure of the organized church to make clear its message of love? Would
he have seen that there was in the Protestant Anglo-Irish Colthurst a fear that
a Catholic Ireland might emerge? Would he have wanted the people of Ireland to react as they did both to his murder and to the executions of the
leaders of the Easter Rising? The answers to these questions lie not only in
this study of Skeffington's life — the life of a man who lived only thirty-
seven years — but in the concluding chapter of his biography of Michael
Davitt, "Davitt as Prophet of the Future Ireland." The ideas expressed in it
can stand as Skeffington's creed; they embodied his hopes for the country he
loved.

Michael Davitt's outlook on the world was free from the spirit of hate,
Skeffington declared, though he hated injustice and tyranny with a passion-
ate hatred. For persons and peoples, however, he felt no hate; not even for
England. In Skeffington's words:

«   «   «   «   «   «   «   «   «

Firm as a rock in the manly self-respect of his attitude towards England,
— scouting as unworthy the weak attempts of latter-day conciliators to
lower the national flag, — he nevertheless was prepared at any moment
to grasp the hand of friendship should the English people once extend it;
the only condition being that he would first ascertain beyond all
possibility of doubt that the offer was sincere. For, though he had a
fellow-feeling for the masses of the English people, for the statesmen
through whom their offers come he entertained a profound mistrust."[28]

»   »   »   »   »   »   »   »   »

If the Irish people were to gain self-respect and self-confidence, however,
there would be no need for fear or hatred.

Skeffington defined democracy for Ireland, in its ultimate aspect, as
"the fairer distribution of the goods of this earth among the dwellers thereon
— the elimination of the very rich and the very poor." Because individual

liberty was so important to him and because he, like Davitt, shared "the apprehensions of Herbert Spencer (a philosopher for whose social theories [Davitt] had the greatest admiration) as to possible restrictions of human liberty under a Socialist regime," he could not consider himself a socialist with a capital S. The "semi-militarist, semi-imperialist Socialism of the Fabian school" repelled him. But he could support the practical goals of the various Socialist parties. What he desired for Ireland, really, was "a humanized Socialist party, which should concentrate its immediate efforts upon practical reforms instead of upon the propagation of a creed."[29]

He tempered his own nationalism in this fashion. "National parties," he said, "are too often led by men representative of petty privileged classes, who desire to be free from any controlling power, that they may be able to give the freer scope to their own will." To his mind, nationalism of that kind could not survive; an awakened social conscience would not permit it to exist. He maintained that "a nationalism which, like that of the Magyar nobles, aims mainly at the prevention of the spread of democratic ideas among the people, stinks in the nostrils of Europe." A free Ireland, which he so desperately desired, would not be truly free if it represented the interests of a privileged class only.[30]

Sincerity and honesty were so deeply ingrained in Skeffington that opportunism of any kind was abhorrent to him. In Ireland, he saw the political opportunist as an ever-present threat. Because Ireland was a weak nation contending against a much stronger one, such an opportunist found a congenial atmosphere for the unfolding of his general principles. At times he would urge that democratic ideas be kept in the background or abandoned entirely in order to obtain the clergy's support for the nationalist cause. At times he would excuse irresponsible acts on the part of those who governed Ireland because they were, at the moment, perpetrated in the name of so-called liberalism. At times he would sing the praises of German militarism with the excuse that it opposed British power. Skeffington wrote:

«   «   «   «   «   «   «   «   «

There are degrees of obnoxiousness in these various forms of an obnoxious theory; but in their essence all are alike unworthy. Perhaps the average politician will never wholly be cured of them save by the conviction that they do not pay; that in politics, as elsewhere, honesty is the best policy in the long-run — nay, in politics more than elsewhere, inasmuch as results cannot be measured by the observation of a single generation.[31]

»   »   »   »   »   »   »   »   »

The Irish nationalism that Skeffington wanted to see emerge was necessarily anticlerical. Concerning the church and education, he believed that "owing to the absence of any popularly controlled system of education in Ireland, young Irish men and women in each generation have to grow up ignorant of the true state of affairs in Ireland, in particular of the hostility of the clerical power to their National aspirations." He felt that no true progress — intellectual, industrial, or social — would be possible in Ireland until the education system was completely reformed, controlled by the people rather than the clergy. And beyond that, "Just as the Land League had substituted for spasmodic attacks upon individual landlords a general attack upon landlordism, so now must an assault in force be made upon the whole fortress of clericalism." [32]

It was obvious to Skeffington that different peoples have different needs. Consequently, the existence of independent nations can be beneficial. But those nations cannot be hostile to each other, for that threatens their very existence and precludes healthy growth. And their basic aims must be similar. If coercion were to be opposed in Ireland, it could not be countenanced in Wales. If a party were nonsectarian in Ireland, it could not defend Catholic interests in England. "These things have been done," Skeffington wrote, "but, representing a state of moral impossibility, they can only be the fleeting symbols of a transitory reality. The party which is reactionary in its foreign relationships will inevitably find itself drawn into the maintenance of reaction at home." [33]

Cautioning his readers not to become followers — even of someone as worthy of following as Davitt — Skeffington concluded with words of warning:

«   «   «   «   «   «   «   «   «

The Irish tendency to hero-worship stands particularly in need of a corrective on this point. . . . Movements which associate themselves too closely with the name of a departed hero are apt to grow conservative by dint of too close an adherence to the principles which once were regarded as the limit of progress; and thus it has more than once been the lamentable posthumous fate of a great reformer to become the eponymous hero of a reactionary party. . . . But his influence must be constantly regarded as a living force. It is only the commonplace man who grows cold and conservative with age; the rare spirits who have made the world worth living in widen their outlook and strengthen their faith in progress year by year.

»   »   »   »   »   »   »   »   »

Remain faithful, he urged, to the spirit of liberty, of truth, and of justice. [34]

These were the sentiments of Francis Sheehy-Skeffington when he was only in his late twenties. There is no reason to believe that they would have changed had he lived beyond his thirty-seventh year.

NOTES TO CHAPTER 14

1. Proceedings of Courts-Martial at Richmond Barracks," *Sinn Fein Rebellion Handbook, Easter 1916* (Dublin: Irish Times, 1916), p. 87.

2. Ibid. Also "Report of the Royal Commission on the Arrest and Subse-

quent Treatment of Mr. Francis Sheehy-Skeffington, Mr. Thomas Dickson and Mr. Patrick James McIntyre," *Sinn Fein Rebellion Handbook*. Proceedings were held at the Four Courts, Dublin, beginning 23 August 1916. This report is also known as the Simon Commission Report.

3. Ibid.

4. "Report of the Royal Commission."

5. Ibid.

6. "The Crime of Captain Colthurst," British Broadcasting Company 2 Telecast, 8 April 1981. This drama-documentary was the first in a series of eight programs called *Chronicle*. The part of Captain Colthurst was played by Philip Bowen, Sir Francis Vane by Jeffrey Wickham, Francis Sheehy-Skeffington by Tony Robinson, and Hanna Sheehy-Skeffington by Angela Harding. Monk Gibbon, at this time in his eighties, assisted in the preparation of the telecast and did part of the narrating.

7. Ibid.

8. Monk Gibbon, *Inglorious Soldier* (London: Hutchinson, 1968), pp. 29–81.

9. Ibid.

10. Stephens, *Insurrection in Dublin*, pp. 48–49.

11. "Crime of Captain Colthurst." See note 4.

12. *Irish Citizen*, December 1918.

13. Stephens, *Insurrection in Dublin*, p. 11.

14. Levenson, *James Connolly*, pp. 324–325.

15. Kee, *The Green Flag*, p. 573.

16. *Irish Citizen*, November 1916.

17. Gibbon, "Murder in Portobello Barracks," p. 12.

18. Sir Francis Fletcher Vane, *Agin the Governments: Memories and Adventures* (London: Sampson Low, 1929), pp. 262–266.

19. Gibbon, "Murder in Portobello Barracks," p. 20.

20. Vane, *Agin the Governments*, p. 266.

21. Sir Francis Vane to H. Sheehy-Skeffington, 23 December 1920.

22. Ibid., 17 November 1916.

23. "Report of the Royal Commission."

24. H. Sheehy-Skeffington, "A Pacifist Dies," p. 285.

25. "John Dillon's Speech in the House of Commons on 11 May 1916," in Edwards and Pyle (eds.), *1916: The Easter Rising*, pp. 77–78.

26. "Crime of Captain Colthurst."

27. H. Sheehy-Skeffington, "A Pacifist Dies," p. 288.

28. F. Sheehy-Skeffington, *Michael Davitt*, p. 216.

29. Ibid., p. 218.

30. Ibid., p. 217.

31. Ibid., pp. 219–220.

32. Ibid., p. 221.

33. Ibid., p. 220.

34. Ibid., p. 223.

Epilogue

Following his conviction, Captain J. C. Bowen-Colthurst was confined to Broadmoor, an asylum for the criminally insane. He was released after twenty months and emigrated to Vancouver, British Columbia, where, according to fragmentary reports, he worked in a bank and prospered until his death in 1965.

Hanna Sheehy-Skeffington, never convinced of Bowen-Colthurst's insanity, considered the courtmartial only a first step in her attempt to have the true facts of her husband's murder and the atrocities of the military revealed. By 1 July 1916 she was in London, badgering members of Parliament and the press in an effort to obtain a full and formal inquiry. By 19 July she was meeting with Prime Minister Asquith. He could not, he told her, promise a full inquiry at that time — the House of Commons would not allow it; the military would not approve it — but he could offer her "adequate and even generous compensation."[1] Hanna's refusal was unequivocal. She did not want "hush money." She would accept only a full inquiry. (According to her son Owen, the compensation offered by the Prime Minister was ten thousand pounds.)[2]

Barely one month later, on 17 August, a Royal Commission was convened with Sir John Simon as its chairman and its findings were made known late the next month. Uncovered by the Royal Commission were the following facts: The execution of the three civilians — Francis Sheehy-Skeffington, Thomas Dickson, and Patrick James MacIntyre — was reported by telephone to Garrison Headquarters and to the H.Q. Irish Command an hour or so after it occurred; the military had failed to take disciplinary steps against any of the guilty officers and, as a matter of fact, had promoted Bowen-Colthurst; the dismissal of Sir Francis Vane was unwarranted; and the Skeffington home was raided twice within days after the murders.

The Royal Commission also exposed Bowen-Colthurst's attempt to shield himself by producing a copy of "Secret Orders to the Military" (the Castle Document), which he claimed was found on Skeffington when he was searched at the time of his arrest. This document, the commission concluded, must have been taken from Skeffington's home during one of the raids and added to the only document he was carrying: his appeal for volunteers to stop the looting. The commission's report called this "a further instance of the endeavors made by Captain Bowen-Colthurst, after the event, to excuse his action."[3]

Once again, Hanna Sheehy-Skeffington was not satisfied. She felt that both the government and the military were using every possible means "to defeat the ends of justice." But she did admit that despite its limitations, such as failing to call Bowen-Colthurst as a witness, the commission did do much to expose the "unrelieved brutality" of the military.[4] There is no doubt that their findings did much to arouse the ire of Dublin's citizenry to a fever pitch.

Without delay, Hanna prepared, though not in good health, to go the United States to tell her story. Denied a passport by the British government, she nevertheless managed to elude the authorities by traveling disguised and under an assumed name. Only her family and a few close friends were told the name of her ship. By late December 1916, she and Owen were in New York City. In the States, she captivated audience after audience, speaking in twenty-one states and in most of the large cities such as San Francisco, New York, and Boston. She also spoke in Washington, D. C. and had a private interview with President Wilson. She returned to Ireland in August 1918.

For the thirty years after his death, until her own in 1946, Hanna Sheehy-Skeffington lived as her husband had lived: as a nonconformist, as an untiring rebel against the existing economic and political order, and as one not afraid to oppose the mightiest powers of his time — the British Empire, the Catholic hierarchy, and the cruder aspects of capitalism. What she accomplished is the subject of another study.

How Francis Sheehy-Skeffington would have reacted to the events that took place in Ireland after his death must, of course, be pure speculation. It is almost certain, however, that he would have wanted the words spoken by his brother-in-law, Thomas Kettle, to stand as a warning to future generations. Just one day before Kettle was killed in the battle of the Somme, September 1916, he wrote: "If I live, I mean to spend the rest of my life working for perpetual peace. I have seen war and faced artillery and know what an outrage it is against simple men."[5] That Skeffington would be sickened by the bloodshed in Northern Ireland today must be accepted as a foregone conclusion. It is only necessary to read once more these lines from his now-famous letter to Thomas MacDonagh, written in May 1915:

«   «   «   «   «   «   «   «   «

European militarism has drenched Europe in blood; Irish militarism may only crimson the fields of Ireland. For us that would be disaster enough. You fervently hope never to employ armed force against a fellow Irishman. But a few weeks ago I heard a friend . . . speaking from the same platform with me, win plaudits by saying that the hills of Ireland would be crimsoned with blood rather than that the partition of Ireland should be allowed. That is the spirit that I dread. I am opposed to partition; but partition could be defeated at too dear a price. I advocate no mere servile lazy acquiescence in injustice. I am, and always will be, a fighter. But I want to see the age-long fight against injustice clothe itself in new forms suited to a new age. I want to see the manhood of Ireland no longer hypnotised by the glamour of "the glory of arms", no longer blind to the horrors of organised murder.[6]

»　　　»　　　»　　　»　　　»　　　»　　　»　　　»　　　»

NOTES TO THE EPILOGUE

1. Hanna Sheehy-Skeffington, "A Pacifist Dies," in *Dublin 1916*, p. 286.

2. Owen Sheehy-Skeffington, "Francis Sheehy-Skeffington," in *1916: The Easter Rising*, p. 147.

3. Royal Commission Report.

4. Hanna Sheehy-Skeffington, "A Pacifist Dies," p. 288.

5. Roger McHugh, "Kettle and Sheehy-Skeffington," in *The Shaping of Modern Ireland*, p. 139. At the time of the Rising, Tom Kettle had been a recruiting officer in the British Army for two years. When the news of Skeffington's murder reached him, he first thought that he would resign. Instead, he decided to give up recruiting and ask for active duty. Roger McHugh believes that Kettle was swayed by the realization that a great many men were fighting and dying as a result of his recruiting speeches and that to risk his own life was the only course open to him. His request was granted within weeks; three months later he was killed in action.

6. *Irish Citizen*, 22 May 1915.

APPENDIX

"War and Feminism" appeared in the 12 September 1914
issue of the Irish Citizen. *It illustrates perfectly the depth of*
Skeffington's dedication to two of his causes, the emancipa-
tion of women and the abolition of war.

War and Feminism

By F. Sheehy Skeffington

That the logical and necessary antithesis between War and the Woman's Movement is not clearly recognised is due to a want of consistent and penetrative thought as to the bases of these two antipodal factors in human affairs.

I propose to demonstrate, first, that war is necessarily bound up with the destruction of Feminism; secondly, that Feminism is necessarily bound up with the abolition of war.

I.

In the course of the evolution of Life on this planet, we observe a steady replacement of the ideal of quantity of life by that of quality.

The lowest forms of life spawn freely, produce an enormous number of seeds or eggs. Concurrently with this stage, we find that the progeny thus prolifically produced are subject to wholesale destruction from co-existing natural causes. The individual life has very small chances of survival; it is only by producing it in overwhelming quantities that the low-grade animal or plant can hope to escape the entire destruction of the species.

As we proceed up the line of evolution, we find this prolific spawning and wholesale destruction gradually giving way to a life-cycle in which less fertility, with increased chance of survival, is the rule. It is generally true that, the higher an organism is in the evolutionary scale, the fewer individuals of the species are born, and the greater proportion of these survive to complete the full life-cycle.

Mankind, at the top of the scale relatively to other living forms, repeats within its own evolutionary ascent the features of biological evolution in general. Lower races of mankind — and lower types among the higher races — are very prolific; but only a small proportion of the progeny survives. The others are weeded out by the natural forces co-existent with a low state of civilisation; by famine, by pestilence, and above all by war.

Following the analogy of other forms of life, we might expect two related phenomena to present themselves in the evolution of human society — a greatly reduced fertility, and a greatly increased chance of survival.

The diseased state of modern civilisation arises mainly from the fact that the latter phenomenon has presented itself without the former. Pestilence and famine are of increasingly rare occurrence; the progress of science makes life day by day easier, lessens hardship, lengthens the average duration of the individual life. The result is that the world is "filling up." Mankind, having become the dominant form of life on the earth, finds itself confronted with a condition of affairs — not too remote for the earth as a whole, and immediately pressing for certain portions of its surface — in which the resources of the planet may prove insufficient to nourish its human colony. It is this fact, the despair of believers in human perfectibility, which has hitherto proved an insuperable stumbling block in the way of the creators of utopias.

They, and other philosophic and scientific minds, have wrestled with this problem and attempted its solution along many different lines. Crude theorists have advocated infanticide as a solution — only a few months ago a bulky volume, seriously propounding this "solution," appeared from the London press. Devotees of science, agriculture and land reform point with enthusiasm to the as yet unexhausted possibilities of the earth. But to these there must be some limit; postponement, not solution, is the most that is to be looked for in that direction. Certain misusers of the name of Malthus advocate artificial restrictions on population. But the instinctive aesthetic repugnance which these evoke in normal minds is shown by experience to be justified by the grave physical and moral evils which they bring in their train. No healthy solution can be found in that direction.

There are two methods, and two only, of solving the difficulty. One is War; the other is the Emancipation of Women.

                                                    II.

The systematic upholders of war as a beneficent factor in human affairs (and they are not by any means confined to Germany) declare that not only is war a tonic to prevent mankind from growing torpid and slothful, not only is it valuable as a "shaker-up," but that it presents the only practicable solution of the population question. Like the older school of surgeons, they think occasional blood-letting, as a matter of deliberate policy, is the proper cure for the congested social system. Whenever the pressure of excessive population becomes too great, war will automatically reduce the numbers of mankind, and at the same time — so say the war-mongers — provide for the survival and dominance of the "fittest" race.

This is a simple, blunt, and logical theory. But it is based on the logic of barbarism. It implies that war is to be retained as a permanent factor while its old co-partners, pestilence and famine, have been weeded out by science — except in so far as they are again and inevitably brought back in the train of war itself. It implies that the qualities which lead to success in war are those which ought to be perpetuated in the race. With the present revelation of what success in war means before our eyes, the falsity of this theory needs no demonstration.

This theory implies that, ever and anon, the fabric of civilisation, so painfully built up by generations, is to be overturned in catastrophe, and a fresh start made. It condemns mankind, at best, to a wearisome treadmill; at worst, to the total decay and disappearance of civilisation and human society. For in every such outbreak of barbarism something is lost; mankind is left several steps nearer to the primeval beast at its conclusion than at its commencement.

This theory renders impossible the emancipation of women. By the war-maker, woman is, and must be, regarded merely as a breeding machine. No escape is possible along the line of "quality rather than quantity"; in war it is the quantity that counts, the overwhelming numbers of human beings wantonly flung to slaughter. Moreover, the increasing destructiveness of modern weapons renders this slaughter greater in every war than in the preceding one.

Men, and more men, is the cry of the war-lords. Women count only as producers of men. Woman must remain, as one writer of this school has coarsely put it, "an appendage of the uterus." We should be thankful to him for his bluntness. Woman as a human being disappears; she is of value but to reproduce "food for powder."

III.

Start now from the other theory — the antipodes of the war-theory of society; start by assuming the emancipation of women. This, in its broadest aspect, means that woman must cease to be "an appendage of the uterus." Woman must count in and for herself, as a human being, with the human rights of an individual. Woman's vital energy, hitherto dammed up into one channel — that of reproduction — will be spread over all the fields of constructive human thought and action. And automatically, by the quiet action of the conservative processes of nature, the amount of woman's vital energy available for reproduction will diminish. The ideal of "quality, not quantity," will prevail; the nightmare of over-population will disappear. Humanity — man and woman — can proceed to construct its Utopias, to organise a social system based on peace and co-operation, without being haunted by the dread of an overcrowded and starving world. War, which is in ultimate analysis the expression of the savage competition of the hungry for food — "commercial competition" is the polite term — will be gen-erally recognised as the crime and madness it always is, and will cease to trouble the earth.

This is the line of true human progress — the only possible line of human progress. The Emancipation of Woman is the essential condition of progress in that direction. That is why the Emancipation of Woman is incomparably the greatest World-Question for Humanity.

IV.

So much for general principles. In the application of them to contemporary circumstances, one runs some risk of provoking disagreement among those who have followed the argument thus far. Nevertheless, I shall proceed to show how, in my opinion, these principles ought to be applied at the present moment by those who accept them.

If we want to stop war, we must begin **now**. This war is the product of a system — a system for which every statesman in Europe must bear his share of the blame. All deliberately accepted war as a permanent factor in the adjustment of international relations. All prepared to be as strong as possible against the day of the "inevitable" war. None took any sincere or effective steps to make **Peace** inevitable.

Pacifists were fooled by the pretence that great armaments would maintain the peace. We now know the folly, or the hypocrisy, or both, of that pretence. But we are insensibly yielding to a new cant, preached by Mr. H. G. Wells and others of his school — that this war will make an end of war. It is false. War can breed nothing but a fresh crop of wars.

By accepting this war, in any degree whatever, we are helping to perpetuate war. If we want to stop war, we must begin by stopping this war. The only way we can do that is to hamper as far as possible the conduct of it. The best way to do that is to **stop recruiting**.

We shall be told, of course, that "the country is in danger." What is in danger is the governing bureaucracy, which tries to identify itself with the nation. **No conquest could possibly be so disastrous as the continuance of war.** We cannot admit that "now we are in it, we must go through with it." That is the argument of all tyrants and evil-doers. We must simply say to the governing bureaucracy, "You have brought on this war. If you say you could not have prevented it, you stand condemned as incompetent. It was your business to prevent it. We cannot allow you to use the weapon of war, any more than we could allow you to use the weapon of forcible feeding, under plea of necessity. Stand aside, and let us start afresh on a better path."

Nothing that has been alleged of "German atrocities" in the hot blood of war exceeds in horror the callous brutality of forcible feeding, in cold blood. And the man that is guilty of that crime is on a recruiting mission — to get more men to strengthen his hold on power.

The woman who does not, in the measure of her opportunities, discourage recruiting, has an imperfect understanding of the basis of the feminist movement. The woman who deliberately encourages recruiting is betraying that movement — though her name be Christabel Pankhurst.

Francis Sheehy-Skeffington's Speech from the Dock, *which follows, was made at his June 1915 trial. It was issued as a pamphlet — together with a letter from George Bernard Shaw to Hanna Sheehy-Skeffington — by the Irish Workers' Cooperative Society.*

Mr. Sheehy-Skeffington: I do not think it will be necessary for me to detain you very long in my defence. I do not propose to call any witnesses, for, though there are certain textual errors that do not materially affect the case, the police report is a very fair one of what I said, apart from some small details. I shall not have to detain you very long and I am sure you will understand that I do not intend any personal discourtesy if I begin by complaining against the form of this trial — of having been deprived of the right to appear before a jury. I perfectly understand why the military authorities, who, in pursuance of their war against German militarism are exercising an absolute military despotism in this country, did not choose to bring a case of this kind before a jury. They have recognised that it is not possible to get a jury, in Dublin at all events, to make themselves the amenable instruments for the enforcement of this most iniquitous of the Coercion Acts — the Act known as the Defence of the Realm Act — and they have decided, perhaps mistakenly, that they will have a better chance before a tribunal less amenable and responsible to public opinion. That action of theirs is a confession of defeat. It is an admission that they have not got the popular sentiment behind them in this country.

    Whatever may be said with regard to the motives actuating me — I do not expect you will look on them favourably — but, whether you agree or not with the views I put forward, I claim *as an elementary right of a citizen in a free state* the right to put forward those opinions. It is clearly a matter of constitutional right to tell the people of Ireland that they had a right to take no part in a war as to which they were not consulted. When I say the people of Ireland were not consulted, I do not wish to imply that the peoples of other countries under the same rulers were consulted. It is notorious they were not. To take that portion of the population which suffers most in war time — the women — no pretence ever was made of consulting them. As regards the men who do the actual fighting, there is a pretence that they were consulted; but that it is merely a pretence is proved by the action of the Government. They found themselves quite unable to face an election in their own constituencies and, have passed a special Indemnity Bill absolving Members of Parliament who have been appointed to the Cabinet from facing their electors. So evident is it that the war was brought on by oligarchs that even in Great Britain the cry has gone out for the impeachment of Mr. Asquith and Sir Edward Grey. In England a "Stop-the-War Society" has been formed for the purpose of getting the people of England to bring pressure to bear on the oligarchs to stop the War. If I lived in England I should still deem it my duty to join such a society and to insist on the propaganda to stop the war in the only way in which the people can stop the war, namely by stopping recruiting, by ceasing to provide the food for powder. It is true that some friends of mine, both in England and in Ireland, say that while opposed to enlistment in the Army, they prefer to leave it to the free decision of individuals whether they should join or not. I should agree, if it were really left to the free decision of individuals; but in a time like this, when every force and influence both in the Press and on the platform, and every kind of social and economic pressure is being brought to bear upon men of military age to join the Army, it is the right and duty of every person of articulate speech to do what he can to produce the contrary pressure so as to give real freedom of decision to the people on the question. So much is true even of England, and of Ireland it is strengthened and intensified. Whatever may be said of the English people, the Irish people never at any time gave the slightest mandate of authority to their leaders, or representatives to commit them to a European war. No leader has any right to pledge the Irish people without such a mandate.

Everything I have said at these meetings fits in with what I consider my constitutional right and moral duty. It was necessary. In order to prevent the pressure being brought to bear on the weaker and more cowardly section and individuals being coerced, it was necessary to go into such questions as the origin of the war. Here I have based myself largely upon the literature published by the Independent Labour Party in England. I have shown, by quoting from a pamphlet entitled "How the War Came About," how the war was forced on by Russia against the wishes of Germany. I have also had to go into the causes of the war (going further back than the immediate year) and have based myself here largely on a book published in England "Ten Years of Secret Diplomacy" by E. D. Morel, in which the whole of the plot by which the war was brought about is laid bare — the plot for the encirclement and final crushing of Germany. It was necessary for me to go into the question of the progress and conduct of the war for the benefit of those weak individuals who are liable to be attracted by success, and to show that there was no prospect, no probability — one might even say, possibility — of England winning a decisive victory. It was necessary to expose (as was done by *Forward* in Glasgow) the infamous cascade of lies poured forth in the papers of so-called German atrocities in Belgium and elsewhere. It was also necessary for me to expose the humbug of the saying that Ireland had a special right to fight for Catholic Belgium. If it is true that Ireland had a right to fight for Catholic Belgium then it is true that Ireland had a right to fight for Catholic Galicia against the Russians —

Mr. Reardon: I am most unwilling to interfere, having regard to the fact that Mr. Sheehy-Skeffigton is defending himself, but I think a great many things he is referring to are irrelevant.

Mr. Mahoney: I think it is better not to intervene. [*Inaudible.*]

Mr. Sheehy-Skeffington: I have lastly dealt with the special Irish case: that Ireland has no direct quarrel with Germany. Ireland, from its depopulation, from its impoverishment, requires peace more than any other nation in Europe. That is one of the strongest points in the case I present. On the basis of that claim for "small nationalities," which is assumedly the basis of this war, it is now taken for granted that it is right and rational for the people of Bohemia and Transylvania to rejoice in the defeats and break-up of the Austrian Empire; that it is right and rational for the people of Alsace-Lorraine and of Posen to rejoice in the break-up of the German Empire. It used to be taken for granted that the people of Poland had a right to rejoice in the break-up of the Russian Empire, but that opinion is no longer —

Mr. Mahoney: You are wandering very far away. You must be brief. The only point I have to consider is whether you spoke against recruiting in His Majesty's Army, and I know nothing about Irish politics, or Austrian politics, or Transylvanian politics.

Mr. Sheehy-Skeffington: I claim that to put this argument before the Irish people in the form which I have shown, and to tell them that it was just as right and natural for them to rejoice in the danger of the British Empire was a constitutional right.

Mr. Mahoney: I cannot allow you to go on in this way.

Mr. Sheehy-Skeffington: You will say that is a breach of the law. What of it? We have had distinguished law-breakers before in Ireland. I am sure you will not prevent me referring to them, as you allowed Mr. Healy to do in a previous case.

Mr. Mahoney: I did not wish him to do so.

Mr. Sheehy-Skeffington: It is not necessary for me to refer to the cases of passive resisters in England, who refused to obey the law at the dictates of their consciences. It is not necessary for me to refer to the imprisonment of Mr. Redmond and Mr. Dillon on behalf of the welfare of the people. It is only necessary for me to refer to Sir Edward Carson —

Mr. Mahoney: It will do you no good to talk about that. It will not affect your position.

Mr. Sheehy-Skeffington: It may not affect my position as regards Your Worship, but it may have a great effect on my position as regards the people. If Sir Edward Carson, as a reward for saying that he would break every law possible, gets a Cabinet appointment, what is the logical position as regards myself? [*Laughter and applause in Court.*] Your Worship cannot make me Attorney-General for England, nor even Lord Chancellor for Ireland, and it may even happen that Your Worship may think it necessary to send me to prison for a small breach of an infamous law —

Mr. Mahoney: Strike out the word "infamous" and I accept your description as accurate.

Mr. Sheehy-Skeffington: I think the word "infamous" adds to the accuracy of the description. You may think it necessary to add to the eleven days I have spent in prison a few days more. If so I will serve them, provided I can do so under conditions suitable to political offenders, but I wish it clearly understood that I will serve no long sentence under any conditions, and I will serve no sentence whatever which does not recognise my rights as a political prisoner.

I am prosecuted, not for the attacks on recruiting, on voluntary enlistment in the Army — but for my attacks on Conscription. In attacking Conscription not only were my moral duty and my constitutional right equally strong, but here there was no breach of law whatever. To say that "if Conscription comes we will not have it" is no more a breach of law than it was treason for Sir Edward Carson to say that "if Home rule comes we will not have it." In England an anti-Conscription League has been formed whose members declare their intention to resist to the death. In this case you will not find it possible to condemn me for breaking the law. I have only advocated passive resistance, because I believe that that form of resistance is sufficient to smash any Compulsory Military Service Act that may be put in force. It is because I have advocated passive resistance and because as Conscription came nearer, I have pledged an increasing number every Sunday to resist Conscription, it is because of this that this prosecution is brought against me, after holding similar meetings for forty weeks. For twenty or thirty weeks I have pledged audiences of from 500 to 1,000 that they would passively resist Conscription. That does not mean that 30,000 were pledged. No doubt many of them were the same each Sunday; but take it at the lowest figure, suppose it was 500, suppose there were only 100 who will keep the pledge to resist Conscription to the death, that 100 is enough to kill Conscription in Ireland. Whatever happens to me to-day, the work is done. If those men keep their pledges the enforcement of Conscription becomes impossible in Ireland.

In doing this, I have done what I regarded both as a duty and a right, both in opposing recruiting and conscription, and in the latter case I have broken no law. This prosecution would be intelligible in a country ruled by an autocrat, in a country under the iron heel of military despotism, in a country ruled by a narrow oligarchy fearing the smallest breath of criticism. It would be intelligible above all in a country held by force by another country, the rulers of which would fear to allow any expression of opinion amongst the subject people. If you condemn me, you condemn the system you represent as being some or all of these things. Any sentence you may pass on me is a sentence upon British rule in Ireland.

Mr. Mahoney: Mr. Skeffington admits the offence and glories in it. The chances are that he will repeat the offence when he gets his liberty. I know nothing of political offences. I am a long time here, but I do not know what a political offence is. The only offence I know is an offence against the law, and this is a grave offence. I will sentence him to six months' imprisonment with hard labour; and, at the expiration of that period, he will have to find bail in £50 or, in default, go to prison for another period of six months.

Mr. Sheehy-Skeffington: I will serve no such sentence. I will eat no food from this moment, and long before the expiration of the sentence I shall be out of prison, alive or dead! [*Loud cheering in Court.*]

Bibliography

Beckett, J. C. *A Short History of Ireland*. London: Hutchinson, 1973.

————. *The Making of Modern Ireland, 1603–1923*. New York: Alfred A. Knopf, 1977.

Brennan, John. *The Years Flew By — Recollections of Sydney Gifford Czira*. Dublin: Gifford & Craven, 1974.

Brown, Malcolm. *The Politics of Irish Literature: From Thomas Davis to W. B. Yeats*. Seattle: University of Washington Press, 1972.

Burke's Irish Family Records. London: Burke's Peerage Ltd., 1976.

Byrne, J. F. *Silent Years: An Autobiography*. New York: Farrar, Straus and Young, 1953.

Cahalan, James M. "Michael Davitt: The Preacher of Ideas, 1881–1906," *Eire-Ireland* (Spring 1976), pp. 13–33.

Carty, James, ed. *Ireland: From the Great Famine to the Treaty of 1921. A Documentary Record*. Dublin: C. J. Fallon, 1966.

Caulfield, Max. *The Easter Rebellion*. London: Four Square Books, 1965.

Coffey, Thomas M. *Agony at Easter: The 1916 Irish Uprising*. New York: Macmillan, 1969.

Colum, Mary. *Life and the Dream*. New York: Doubleday, 1947.

Colum, Mary, and Padraic Colum. *Our Friend James Joyce*. London: Gollancz, 1959.

Colum, Padraic. "Francis Sheehy-Skeffington," in Maurice Joy, ed., *The Irish Rebellion of 1916 and Its Tragic Martyrs*. New York: Devin-Adair, 1916, pp. 380–392.

"Courts-Martial at Richmond Barracks," in *Sinn Fein Rebellion Handbook, Easter 1916*. Compiled by *Weekly Irish Times*. Dublin, 1916, pp. 84–90.

Cousins, James H., and Margaret E. Cousins. *We Two Together*. London: Luzac, 1951.

Curran, C. P. *James Joyce Remembered*. London: Oxford University Press, 1968.

————. *Under the Receding Wave*. Dublin: Gill & Macmillan, 1970.

Dangerfield, George. *The Damnable Question — A Study in Anglo-Irish Relations*. Boston: Little, Brown, 1976.

———. *The Strange Death of Liberal England*. New York: Harrison Smith & Robert Haas, 1935.

Davis, Richard P. *Arthur Griffith and Non-Violent Sinn Fein*. Dublin: Anvil Books, 1974.

Davitt, Michael. *Within the Pale: The True Story of Anti-Semitic Persecutions in Russia*. New York: Barnes, 1903.

Denson, Alan, ed. *Letters from AE*. London: Abelard Schuman, 1961.

Devoy, John. *Recollections of an Irish Rebel*. New York: Chas. P. Young, 1929.

Donoghue, Denis, ed. and transcriber. *W. B. Yeats Memoirs: Autobiography — First Draft Journal*. London: Macmillan, 1972.

Duff, Charles. *Six Days to Shake an Empire*. London: J. M. Dent & Sons, 1966.

Edwards, Owen Dudley. *The Mind of an Activist — James Connolly*. Dublin: Gill & Macmillan, 1971.

Edwards, Owen Dudley, G. Evans, and H. MacDairmid. *Celtic Nationalism*. New York: Barnes & Noble, 1968.

Edwards, Owen Dudley, and Bernard Ransom, eds. *James Connolly: Selected Political Writings*. London: Jonathan Cape, 1973.

Edwards, Ruth Dudley. *Patrick Pearse: The Triumph of Failure*. New York: Taplinger, 1978.

Ellmann, Richard. *James Joyce*. New York: Oxford University Press, 1959.

———. *James Joyce*, new and rev. ed. New York: Oxford University Press, 1982.

———, ed. *Selected Joyce Letters*. New York: Viking Press, 1975.

Fox, R. M. *James Connolly: The Forerunner*. Tralee, Ireland: The Kerryman Limited, 1946.

———. *Jim Larkin: Irish Labor Leader*. New York: International Publishers, 1957.

———. *Louie Bennett — Her Life and Times*. Dublin: Talbot Press Limited, 1958.

———. *Rebel Irishwomen*. Dublin: Progress House Ltd., 1935 (reprinted 1967).

Gibbon, Monk. *Inglorious Soldier*. London: Hutchinson, 1968.

Glendinning, Victoria. *Elizabeth Bowen — Portrait of a Writer*. London: Weidenfeld and Nicolson, 1977.

Gorman, Herbert. *James Joyce*. New York: Rinehart, 1948.

Greaves, C. Desmond. *The Life and Times of James Connolly*. London: Lawrence & Wishart, 1961.

————. *Sean O'Casey — Politics and Art*. London: Lawrence & Wishart, 1979.

Gwynn, Stephen Lucius. *John Redmond's Last Years*. London: E. Arnold, 1919.

Hahn, Emily. *Fractured Emerald: Ireland*. New York: Weathervane Books, 1971.

Hannigan, Ken. *Francis Sheehy-Skeffington*. Dissertation, University College Dublin, 1975.

Healy, T. M. *Letters and Leaders of My Day*, Vol. II. London: Thornton Butterworth, 1928.

Hogan, Robert, ed. *Feathers from the Green Crow — Sean O'Casey, 1905–1925*. London: Macmillan, 1963.

Hutchins, Patricia. *James Joyce's Dublin*. London: Grey Walls Press, 1950.

————. *James Joyce's World*. London: Methuen, 1957.

Hyman, Louis. *The Jews of Ireland: From Earliest Times to the Year 1910*. Shannon: Irish University Press, 1972.

Jeffares, A. Norman, and K. G. W. Cross. *In Excited Reverie: A Centenary Tribute*. New York: St. Martin's Press, 1965.

Joyce, James. *A Portrait of the Artist as a Young Man*. New York: Modern Library, 1928.

————. *Stephen Hero*. New York: New Directions, 1963.

Joyce, Stanislaus. *My Brother's Keeper*. New York: Viking Press, 1969.

Kee, Robert. *The Green Flag*. London: Weidenfeld and Nicolson, 1972.

Keogh, Dermot. "William Martin Murphy and the Origins of the 1913 Lockout," in Father Henry, O.F.M. Cap., ed. *Capuchin Annual*. Dublin, 1977, pp. 130–158.

Kettle, Thomas M. *The Day's Burden: Studies, Literary and Political and Miscellaneous Essays*. Dublin: Browne & Nolan, 1937.

————. *The Ways of War*. Dublin: Talbot Press Limited, 1917.

King, Clifford. *The Orange and the Green*. London: Macdonald, 1965.

Kilroy, James. *The Playboy Riots*. Dublin: The Dolman Press, 1971.

Larkin, Emmet. *James Larkin, 1876–1947: Irish Labour Leader*. London: Routledge & Kegan Paul, 1965.

Lee, Joseph. *The Modernisation of Irish Society, 1848–1918*. Dublin: Gill & Macmillan, 1973.

Levenson, Samuel. *James Connolly*. London: Martin Brian & O'Keeffe, 1973.

————. *Maud Gonne*. New York: Reader's Digest Press, 1976.

Linklater, Andro. *An Unhusbanded Life: Charlotte Despard — Suffragette, Socialist & Sinn Feiner*. London: Hutchinson, 1980.

Lynd, Robert. *If the Germans Conquered England and Other Essays.* Dublin: Maunsel, 1917.

Lyons, F. S. L. "Dillon, Redmond and the Irish Home Rulers," in F. X. Martin, ed., *Leaders and Men of the Easter Rising: Dublin, 1916.* Ithaca, N.Y.: Cornell University Press, 1967. pp. 29–41.

———. "Introduction" to *Michael Davitt* by Francis Sheehy-Skeffington. London: MacGibbon and Kee, 1967.

———. *John Dillon — A Biography.* Chicago: Chicago University Press, 1968.

———. *Ireland Since the Famine.* London: Collins/Fontana, 1973.

———. *Charles Stewart Parnell.* New York: Oxford University Press, 1977.

Macardle, Dorothy. *The Irish Republic.* New York: Farrar, Straus & Giroux, 1965.

MacCurtain, Margaret, and Donncha O'Corrain, eds. *Women in Irish Society: The Historical Dimension.* Dublin: Arlen House, 1978.

McHugh, Roger. "Thomas Kettle and Francis Sheehy-Skeffington," in Conor Cruise O'Brien, ed., *The Shaping of Modern Ireland.* London: Routledge & Kegan Paul, 1960.

———, ed. *Dublin 1916.* New York: Hawthorn Books, 1966.

MacKenna, Stephen. *Memories of the Dead.* Dublin: Powell Press, 1916.

Mackenzie, Midge. *Shoulder to Shoulder — A Documentary.* New York: Alfred A. Knopf, 1975.

MacManus, Seumas. *The Rocky Road to Dublin.* New York: Devin-Adair, 1938.

Manganiello, Dominic. *Joyce's Politics.* London, Boston, and Henley: Routledge & Kegan Paul, 1980.

Mannin, Ethel. *Privileged Spectator.* London: Jacobs, 1939.

Marreco, Anne. *The Rebel Countess: The Life and Times of Constance Markievicz.* Philadelphia: Chilton Books, 1967.

Martin, F. X. "1916 — Myth, Fact, and Mystery," *Studia Hibernica,* No. 7 (1967), pp. 7–126.

———, ed. *Leaders and Men of the Easter Rising: Dublin 1916.* Ithaca, New York: Cornell University Press, 1967.

———. "Select Documents, XX. MacNeill on the 1916 Rising," *Irish Historical Studies* 12 (March 1961), pp. 226–227.

Martin, F. X., and F. J. Byrne. *The Scholar Revolutionary: Eoin MacNeill, 1867–1945.* Shannon: Irish University Press, 1973.

Mason, Ellsworth, and Richard Ellmann, eds. *James Joyce: The Critical Writings.* New York: Viking Press, 1964.

Meenan, James, ed. *Centenary History of the Literary and Historical Society of University College, Dublin, 1855–1955.* Tralee, Ireland: The Kerryman Limited, 1957.

Milroy, Sean. *Memories of Mountjoy*. Pamphlet. Dublin: Maunsel, 1917.

Mitchell, Arthur. "William O'Brien, 1881–1968, and the Irish Labour Movement," *Studies* (Autumn–Winter 1917), pp. 311–331.

Mitchell, David. *Women on the Warpath: The Story of the Women of the First World War*. London: Jonathan Cape, 1966.

———. *The Fighting Pankhursts: A Study in Tenacity*. New York: Macmillan, 1967.

Moody, T. W., and F. X. Martin, eds. *The Course of Irish History*. New York: Weybright and Talley, 1967.

Moya, Carmela. "The Mirror and the Plough," *The Sean O'Casey Review* 2, No. 2 (Spring 1976), pp. 141–153.

Nevinson, Henry W. *Changes and Chances*. London: Nisbet, 1923.

Nic Shiublaigh, Maire. *Story of the Irish National Theatre*. Dublin: James Duffy, 1955.

O'Brien, Conor Cruise. *Parnell and His Party, 1880–1890*. New York: Oxford University Press, 1957.

———, ed. *The Shaping of Modern Ireland*. London: Routledge & Kegan Paul, 1960.

———. *States of Ireland*. London. Hutchinson, 1972.

O'Brien, Joseph V. *William O'Brien and the Course of Irish Politics, 1881–1918*. Berkeley: University of California Press, 1976.

O'Brien, William (as told to Edward MacLysaght). *Forth the Banners Go*. Dublin: The Three Candles Ltd., 1969.

O'Brien, William, and Desmond Ryan, eds. *John Devoy's Post Bag*, 2 vols. Dublin: C. J. Fallon, 1948.

O'Broin, Leon. *Dublin Castle and the 1916 Rising*. Dublin: Helicon, 1965.

———. *Revolutionary Underground: The Story of the Irish Republican Brotherhood, 1858–1924*. Dublin: Gill & Macmillan, 1976.

O'Casey, Sean. *The Story of the Irish Citizen Army*. Dublin: Maunsel, 1919.

O'Connor, Ulick, ed. *The Joyce We Knew*. Cork, Ireland: The Mercier Press, 1967.

O'Donnell, (Commandant) P. D. "The Barracks and Posts of Ireland," *An Consantoir* (February 1969), pp. 37–39.

O'Heideain, Eustas. *National School Inspection in Ireland: The Beginnings*. Dublin: Scepter Books, 1967.

Pankhurst, Dame Christabel. *Unshackled, or How We Won the Vote*. London: Hutchinson, 1959.

Pankhurst, Emmeline. *My Own Story*. London: Eveleigh Nash, 1914.

Pankhurst, E. Sylvia. *The Suffragette Movement*. London: Longmans Green & Co., 1931.

———. *The Suffragette*. London: Gay and Hancock, 1911.

Pearson, Hesketh. *GBS: A Full-Length Portrait*. New York: Harper & Bros., 1950.

Pethick-Lawrence, Emmeline. *My Part in a Changing World*. London: Gollancz, 1938.

Porter, Raymond J. "O'Casey and Pearse," *The Sean O'Casey Review* 2, No. 2 (Spring 1976), pp. 104–114.

Redmond-Howard, L. G. *John Redmond: The Man and the Demand*. New York: John Lane, 1911.

Rose, Catherine. *The Female Experience*. Galway, Ireland: Arlen House, 1976.

Rosset, B. C. *Shaw of Dublin: The Formative Years*. University Park: The Pennsylvania State University Press, 1964.

Ryan, Desmond. *Remembering Sion*. London: Arthur Barker, 1934.

———. *The Phoenix Flame: A Study of Fenianism and John Devoy*. London: Arthur Barker, 1937.

———. *The Rising*. Dublin: Golden Eagle Books, 1949.

Ryan, W. P. *The Pope's Green Island*. London: James Nisbet & Co., 1912.

Schneir, Miriam, ed. *Feminism: The Essential Historical Writings*. New York: Vintage Books, 1972.

Sheehy, Eugene. *May It Please the Court*. Dublin: C. J. Fallon, 1951.

Sheehy, Michael. *Is Ireland Dying? Culture and the Church in Modern Ireland*. New York: Taplinger, 1969.

Sheehy-Skeffington, Francis. *In Dark and Evil Days*. Dublin: James Duffy, 1916.

———. *Michael Davitt: Revolutionary Agitator and Labour Leader*. London: MacGibbon and Kee, 1967. Reprint.

———. *Speech from the Dock*. Pamphlet. Dublin: Liberty Hall, 1915.

———. *The Prodigal Daughter: A Play*. Dublin, 1915.

———. *War and Feminism*. Pamphlet. Dublin, 1914.

———. *A Forgotten Small Nationality*. Pamphlet. New York, 1917.

Sheehy-Skeffington, Francis, and James A. Joyce. *Two Essays*. Pamphlet. Dublin: Gerrard Bros., 1901.

Sheehy-Skeffington, Hanna. "Biographical Notice," in *Dark and Evil Days* by Francis Sheehy-Skeffington. Dublin: James Duffy, 1916, pp. xi–xviii.

———. "An Irish Pacifist," in Julian Bell, ed., *We Did Not Fight*. London: Cobden-Sanderson, 1935, pp. 339–353.

———. "A Pacifist Dies," in Roger McHugh, ed., *Dublin 1916*. New York: Hawthorn Books, 1966, pp. 276–288.

Sheehy-Skeffington, Owen. "Francis Sheehy-Skeffington," in Owen Dudley Edwards and Fergus Pyle, eds., *1916: The Easter Rising*. London: MacGibbon and Kee, 1968, pp. 135–148.

Shoemaker, Michael Myers. *Wanderings in Ireland.* New York: G. P. Putnam's Sons, 1908.

Simon, John. "Report of the Inquiry into the Skeffington Murder," *Irish Times Handbook.* Dublin: The *Irish Times,* 1916.

Society of Jesus, Fathers of the. *A Page of Irish History: Story of University College, Dublin, 1883–1909.* Dublin: Talbot Press Limited, 1930.

Somerville-Large, Peter. *Irish Eccentrics.* New York: Harper & Row, 1975.

Stephens, James. *The Insurrection in Dublin.* Dublin: Maunsel, 1916.

Strachey, Ray. *The Cause: A Short History of the Women's Movement in Great Britain.* Port Washington, N.Y.: Kennikat Press, 1969 (first publication 1925).

Strauss, Emil. *Irish Nationalism and British Democracy.* London: Methuen, 1951.

Sullivan, Kevin. *Joyce Among the Jesuits.* New York: Columbia University Press, 1967.

Tierney, Michael, ed. *Struggle with Fortune: A Miscellany for the Centenary of the Catholic University of Ireland, 1854–1954.* Dublin: Browne & Nolan, 1954.

Tuohy, Frank. *Yeats.* New York: Macmillan, 1976.

Vane, Sir Francis Fletcher. *Agin the Governments: Memories and Adventures.* London: Sampson Low, 1929.

Van Voris, Jacqueline. *Constance de Markievicz: In the Cause of Ireland.* Amherst: University of Massachusetts Press, 1967.

Wade, Allan, ed. *The Letters of W. B. Yeats.* London: Rupert Hart-Davis, 1954.

Index